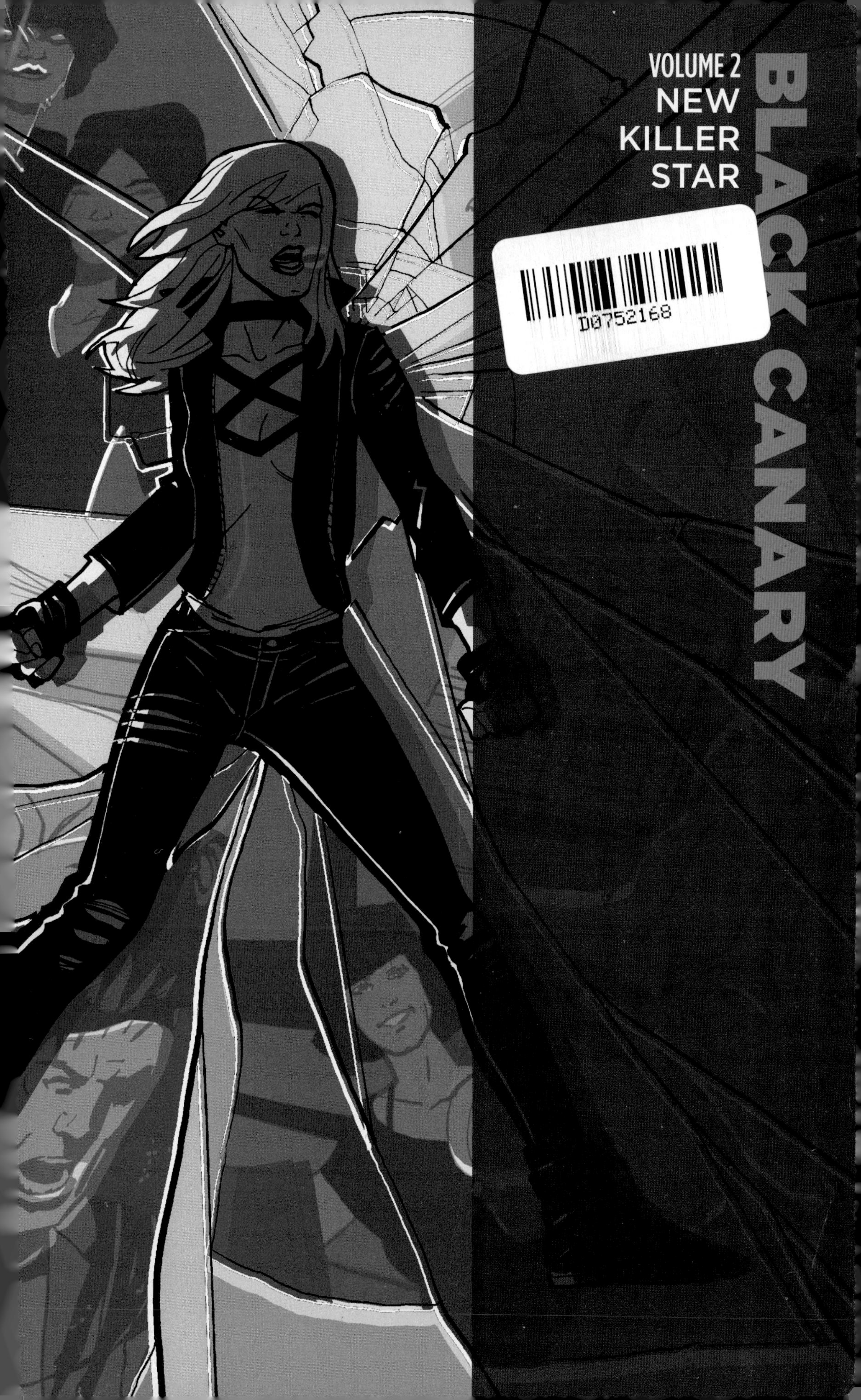
VOLUME 2
NEW
KILLER
STAR
BLACK CANARY
D0752168

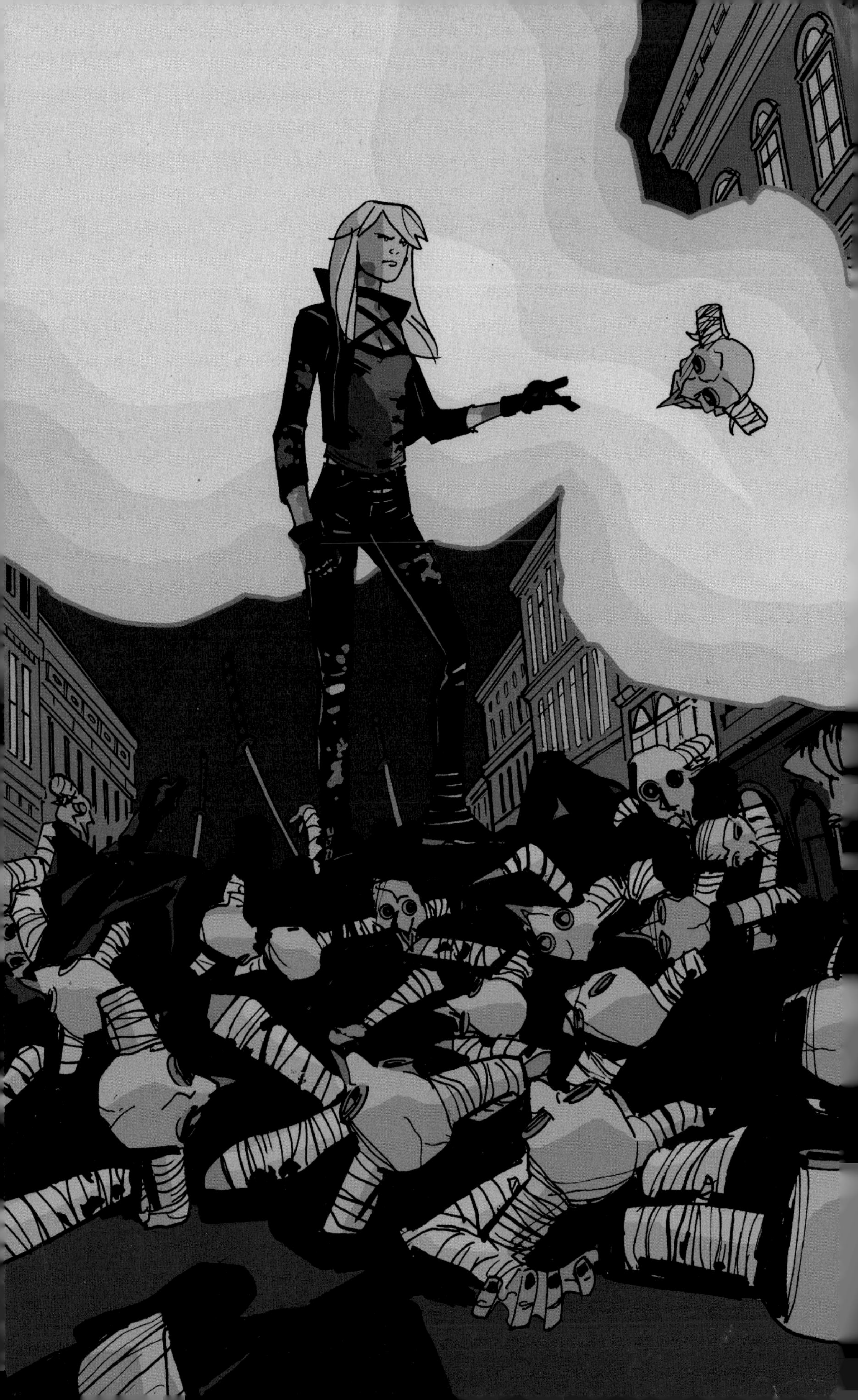

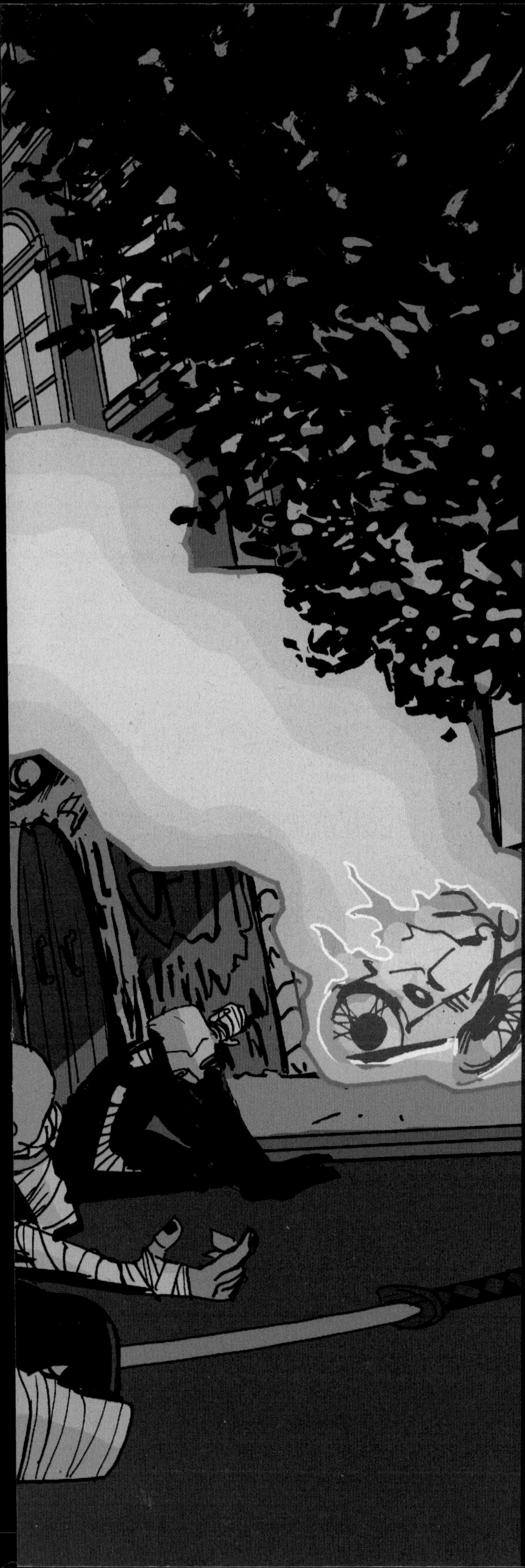

BLACK CANARY

VOLUME 2
NEW KILLER STAR

WRITTEN BY
BRENDEN FLETCHER
MATTHEW ROSENBERG

ART BY
SANDY JARRELL
MORITAT
ANNIE WU
WAYNE FAUCHER

COLOR BY
LEE LOUGHRIDGE
SERGE LaPOINTE

LETTERS BY
STEVE WANDS
MARILYN PATRIZIO

COLLECTION COVER ART BY
ANNIE WU

BATMAN CREATED BY
BOB KANE
WITH **BILL FINGER**

CHRIS CONROY Editor – Original Series
DAVE WIELGOSZ Assistant Editor – Original Series
JEB WOODARD Group Editor – Collected Editions
ROBIN WILDMAN Editor – Collected Edition
STEVE COOK Design Director – Books
DAMIAN RYLAND Publication Design

BOB HARRAS Senior VP – Editor-in-Chief, DC Comics

DIANE NELSON President
DAN DiDIO Publisher
JIM LEE Publisher
GEOFF JOHNS President & Chief Creative Officer
AMIT DESAI Executive VP – Business & Marketing Strategy,
Direct to Consumer & Global Franchise Management
SAM ADES Senior VP – Direct to Consumer
BOBBIE CHASE VP – Talent Development
MARK CHIARELLO Senior VP – Art, Design & Collected Editions
JOHN CUNNINGHAM Senior VP – Sales & Trade Marketing
ANNE DePIES Senior VP – Business Strategy, Finance & Administration
DON FALLETTI VP – Manufacturing Operations
LAWRENCE GANEM VP – Editorial Administration & Talent Relations
ALISON GILL Senior VP – Manufacturing & Operations
HANK KANALZ Senior VP – Editorial Strategy & Administration
JAY KOGAN VP – Legal Affairs
THOMAS LOFTUS VP – Business Affairs
JACK MAHAN VP – Business Affairs
NICK J. NAPOLITANO VP – Manufacturing Administration
EDDIE SCANNELL VP – Consumer Marketing
COURTNEY SIMMONS Senior VP – Publicity & Communications
JIM (SKI) SOKOLOWSKI VP – Comic Book Specialty Sales & Trade Marketing
NANCY SPEARS VP – Mass, Book, Digital Sales & Trade Marketing

BLACK CANARY VOLUME 2: NEW KILLER STAR

DC Comics, 2900 West Alameda Avenue, Burbank, CA 91505
Printed by Solisco Printers, Scott, QC, Canada. 10/21/16. First Printing.
ISBN: 978-1-4012-6527-4

Library of Congress Cataloging-in-Publication Data is available.

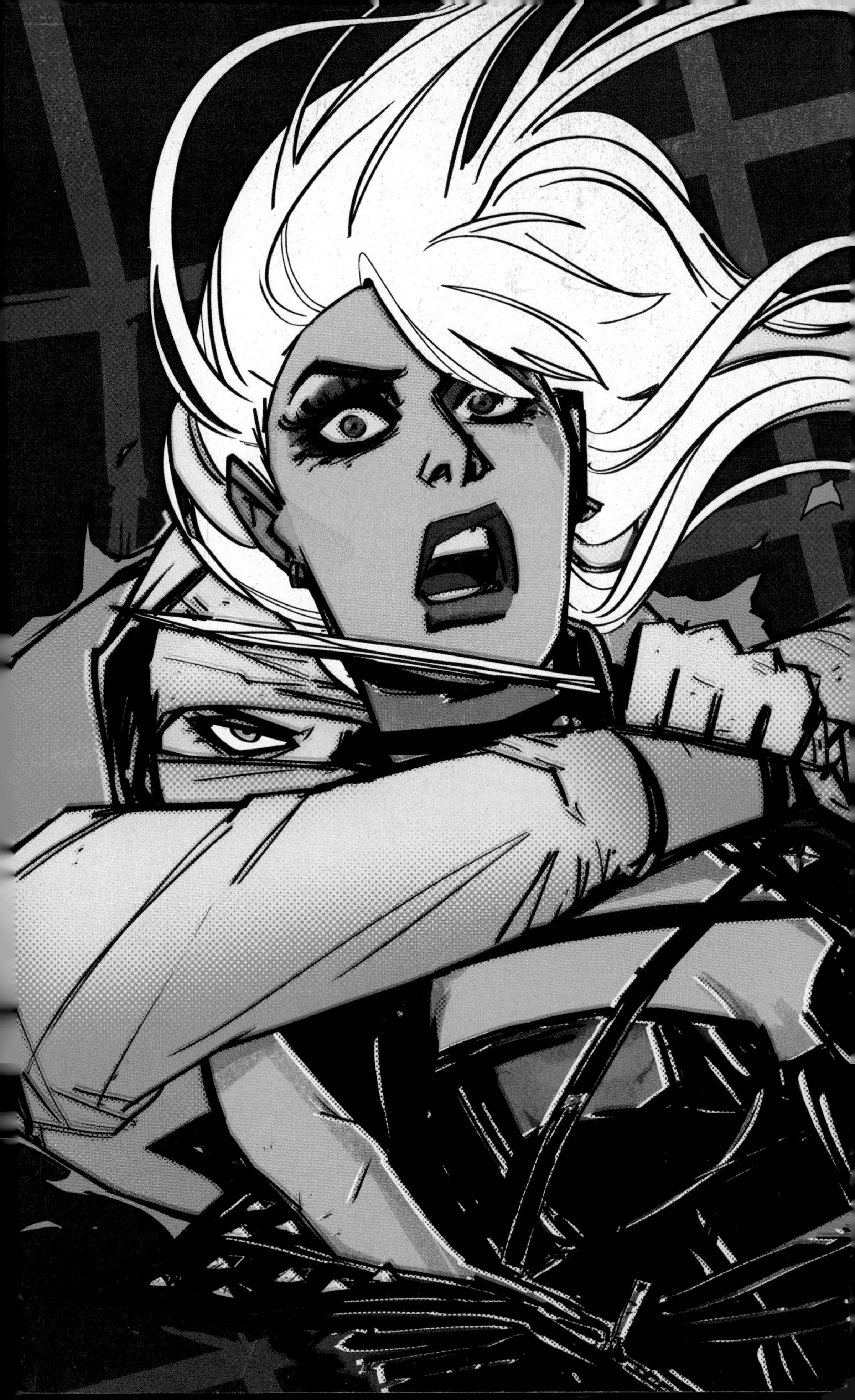

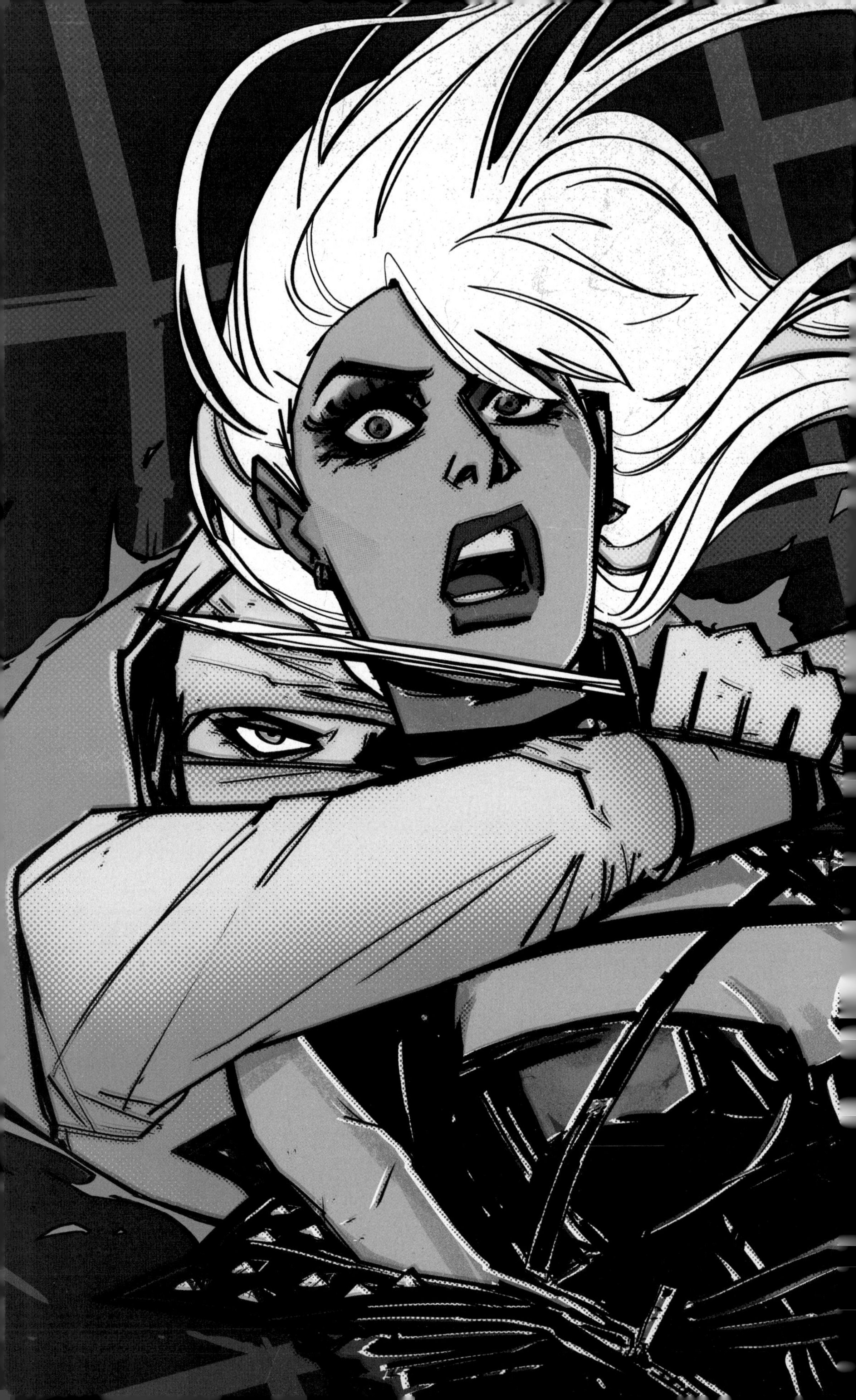

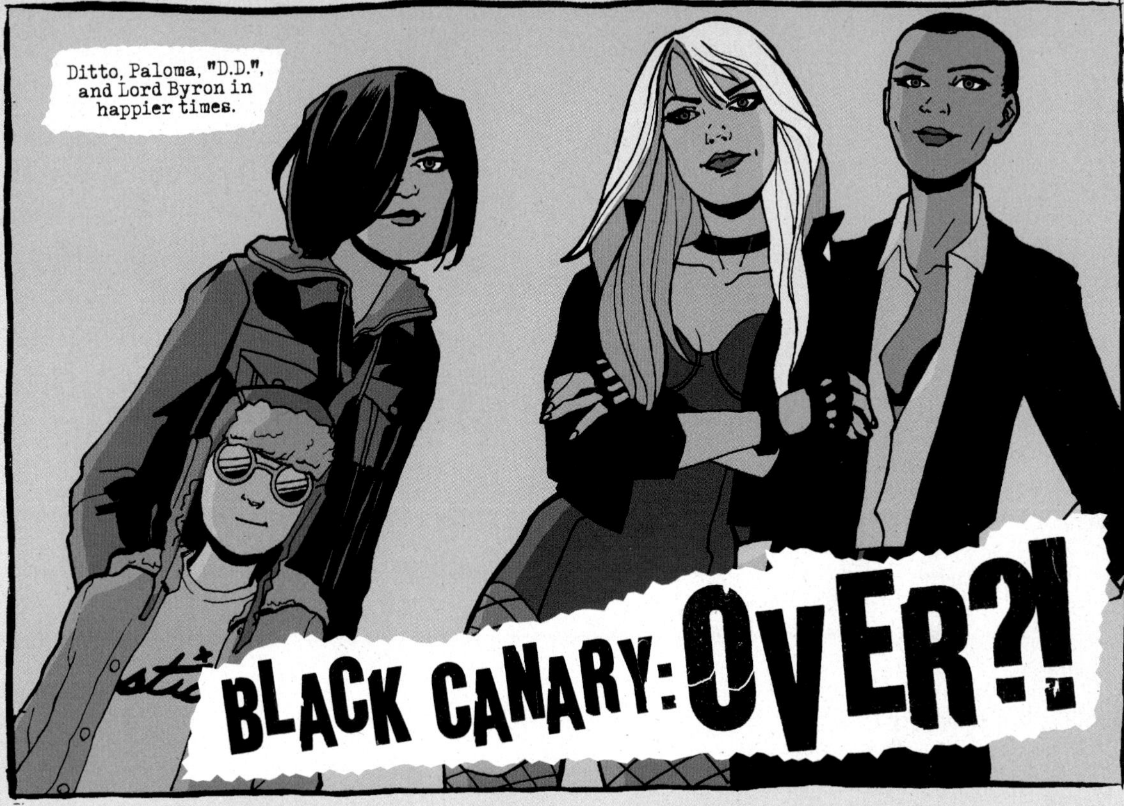
Ditto, Paloma, "D.D.", and Lord Byron in happier times.
BLACK CANARY: OVER?!

TWO MISSING SINCE ONSTAGE ACCIDENT DURING TRAGIC BATTLE OF THE BANDS, INCLUDING CANARY GUITARIST—A BURNSIDE TOFU EXCLUSIVE BY TANTOO LA BICHE

Some might call it fate. Some might say it was an act of God. But for those, like us, who watched Black Canary's meteoric rise to stardom amongst the spilled blood and broken bones of each and every one of their debut tour gigs, it seemed the band could have no other end but this, the saddest and most tragic of finales.

With their lead singer missing, their guitarist presumed dead, and authorities hunting for answers from remaining members of the band and their record label, it seems Black Canary is all but done.

"THIS IS ***RIDICULOUS.*** WE'VE BEEN INTERVIEWING YOU ALL FOR TWO WEEKS NOW AND YOU SAY YOU ***STILL*** HAVE NO IDEA WHAT HAPPENED TO YOUR LEAD SINGER? THIS, UH, ***"D.D."*** WOMAN?"

Full story on page 2

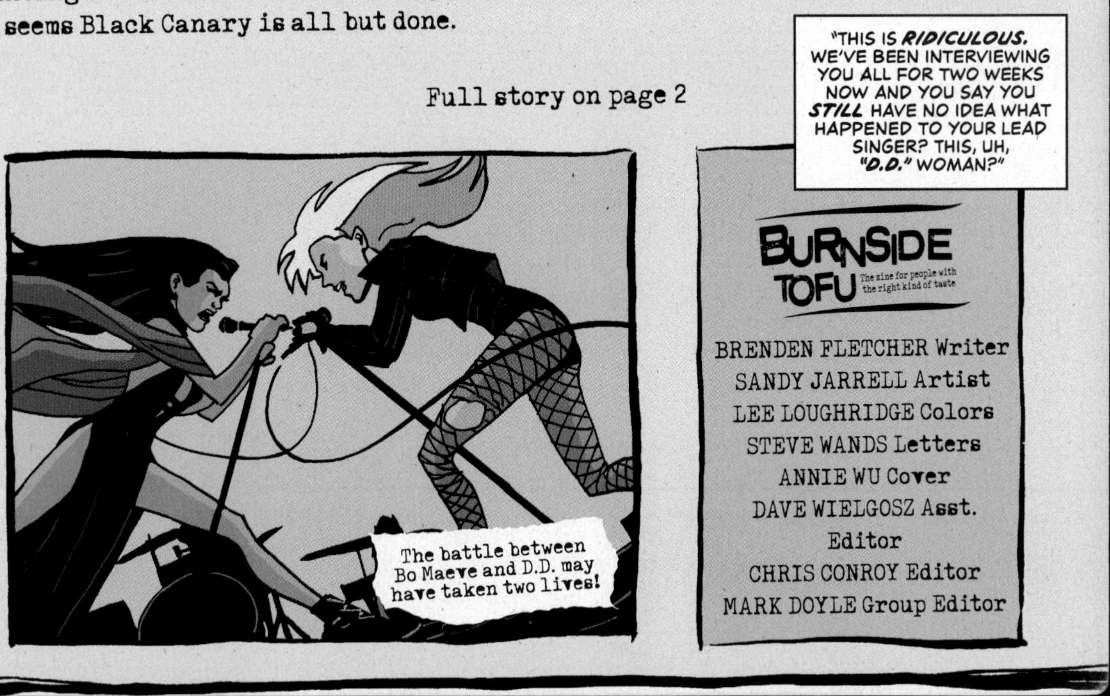
The battle between Bo Maeve and D.D. may have taken two lives!

BURNSIDE TOFU
The zine for people with the right kind of taste

BRENDEN FLETCHER Writer
SANDY JARRELL Artist
LEE LOUGHRIDGE Colors
STEVE WANDS Letters
ANNIE WU Cover
DAVE WIELGOSZ Asst. Editor
CHRIS CONROY Editor
MARK DOYLE Group Editor

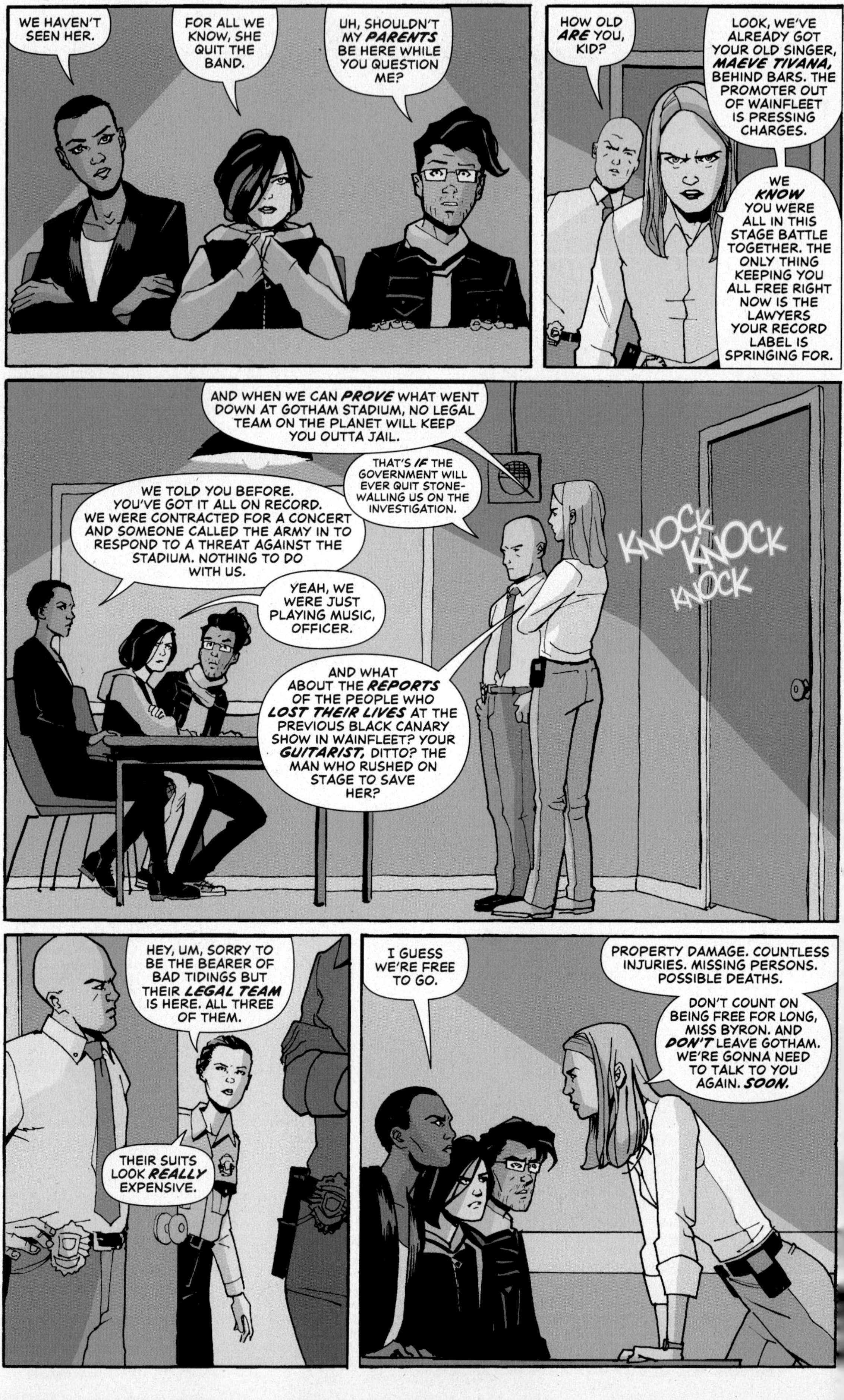
WE HAVEN'T SEEN HER.
FOR ALL WE KNOW, SHE QUIT THE BAND.
UH, SHOULDN'T MY PARENTS BE HERE WHILE YOU QUESTION ME?
HOW OLD ARE YOU, KID?
LOOK, WE'VE ALREADY GOT YOUR OLD SINGER, MAEVE TIVANA, BEHIND BARS. THE PROMOTER OUT OF WAINFLEET IS PRESSING CHARGES.
WE KNOW YOU WERE ALL IN THIS STAGE BATTLE TOGETHER. THE ONLY THING KEEPING YOU ALL FREE RIGHT NOW IS THE LAWYERS YOUR RECORD LABEL IS SPRINGING FOR.
AND WHEN WE CAN PROVE WHAT WENT DOWN AT GOTHAM STADIUM, NO LEGAL TEAM ON THE PLANET WILL KEEP YOU OUTTA JAIL.
THAT'S IF THE GOVERNMENT WILL EVER QUIT STONE-WALLING US ON THE INVESTIGATION.
WE TOLD YOU BEFORE. YOU'VE GOT IT ALL ON RECORD. WE WERE CONTRACTED FOR A CONCERT AND SOMEONE CALLED THE ARMY IN TO RESPOND TO A THREAT AGAINST THE STADIUM. NOTHING TO DO WITH US.
YEAH, WE WERE JUST PLAYING MUSIC, OFFICER.
AND WHAT ABOUT THE REPORTS OF THE PEOPLE WHO LOST THEIR LIVES AT THE PREVIOUS BLACK CANARY SHOW IN WAINFLEET? YOUR GUITARIST, DITTO? THE MAN WHO RUSHED ON STAGE TO SAVE HER?
KNOCK KNOCK KNOCK
HEY, UM, SORRY TO BE THE BEARER OF BAD TIDINGS BUT THEIR LEGAL TEAM IS HERE. ALL THREE OF THEM.
THEIR SUITS LOOK REALLY EXPENSIVE.
I GUESS WE'RE FREE TO GO.
PROPERTY DAMAGE. COUNTLESS INJURIES. MISSING PERSONS. POSSIBLE DEATHS.
DON'T COUNT ON BEING FREE FOR LONG, MISS BYRON. AND DON'T LEAVE GOTHAM. WE'RE GONNA NEED TO TALK TO YOU AGAIN. SOON.

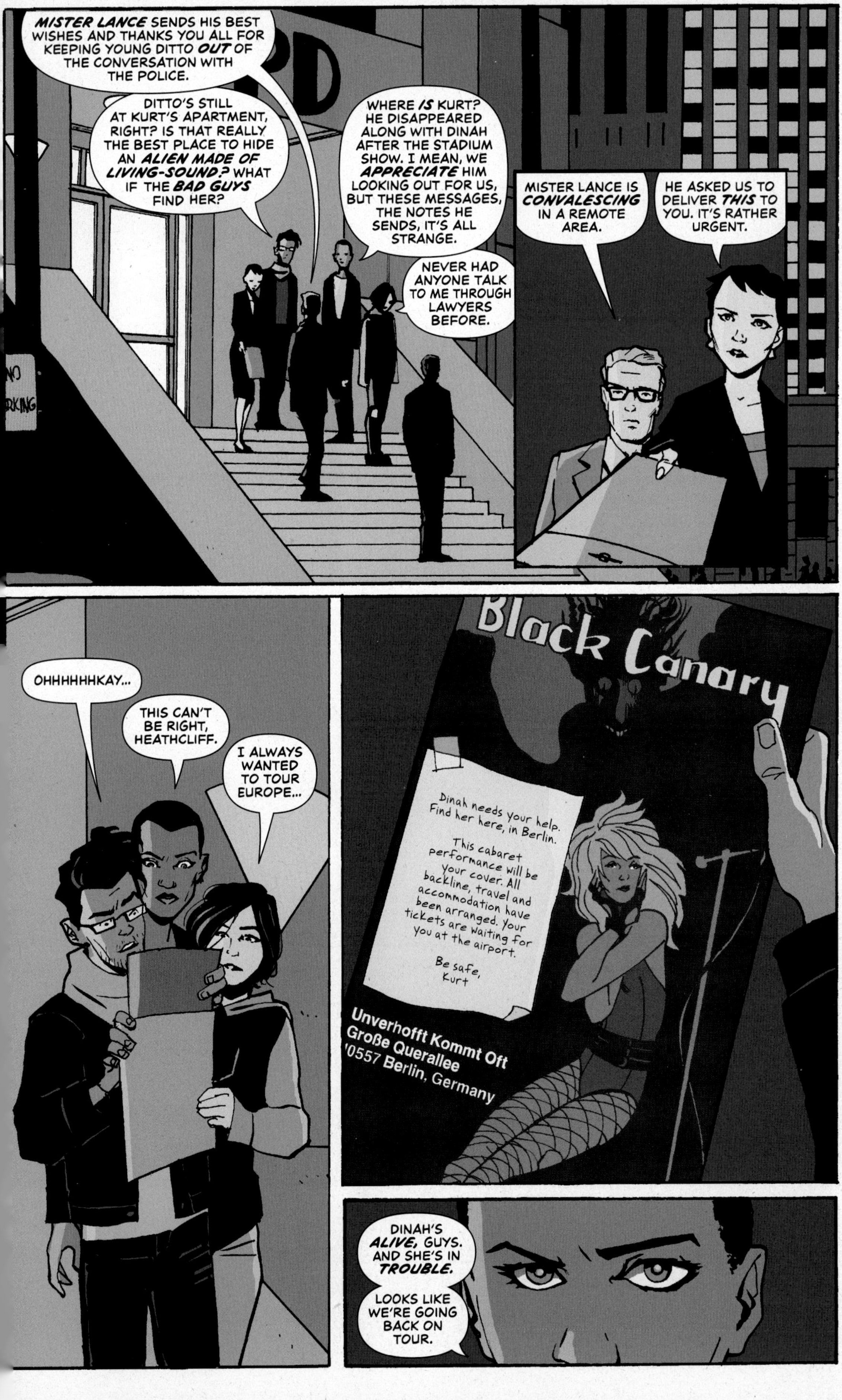

MISTER LANCE SENDS HIS BEST WISHES AND THANKS YOU ALL FOR KEEPING YOUNG DITTO OUT OF THE CONVERSATION WITH THE POLICE.
DITTO'S STILL AT KURT'S APARTMENT, RIGHT? IS THAT REALLY THE BEST PLACE TO HIDE AN ALIEN MADE OF LIVING-SOUND? WHAT IF THE BAD GUYS FIND HER?
WHERE IS KURT? HE DISAPPEARED ALONG WITH DINAH AFTER THE STADIUM SHOW. I MEAN, WE APPRECIATE HIM LOOKING OUT FOR US, BUT THESE MESSAGES, THE NOTES HE SENDS, IT'S ALL STRANGE.
NEVER HAD ANYONE TALK TO ME THROUGH LAWYERS BEFORE.
MISTER LANCE IS CONVALESCING IN A REMOTE AREA.
HE ASKED US TO DELIVER THIS TO YOU. IT'S RATHER URGENT.
OHHHHHHKAY...
THIS CAN'T BE RIGHT, HEATHCLIFF.
I ALWAYS WANTED TO TOUR EUROPE...
Black Canary
Dinah needs your help. Find her here, in Berlin.
This cabaret performance will be your cover. All backline, travel and accommodation have been arranged. Your tickets are waiting for you at the airport.
Be safe, Kurt
Unverhofft Kommt Oft
Große Querallee
10557 Berlin, Germany
DINAH'S ALIVE, GUYS. AND SHE'S IN TROUBLE.
LOOKS LIKE WE'RE GOING BACK ON TOUR.

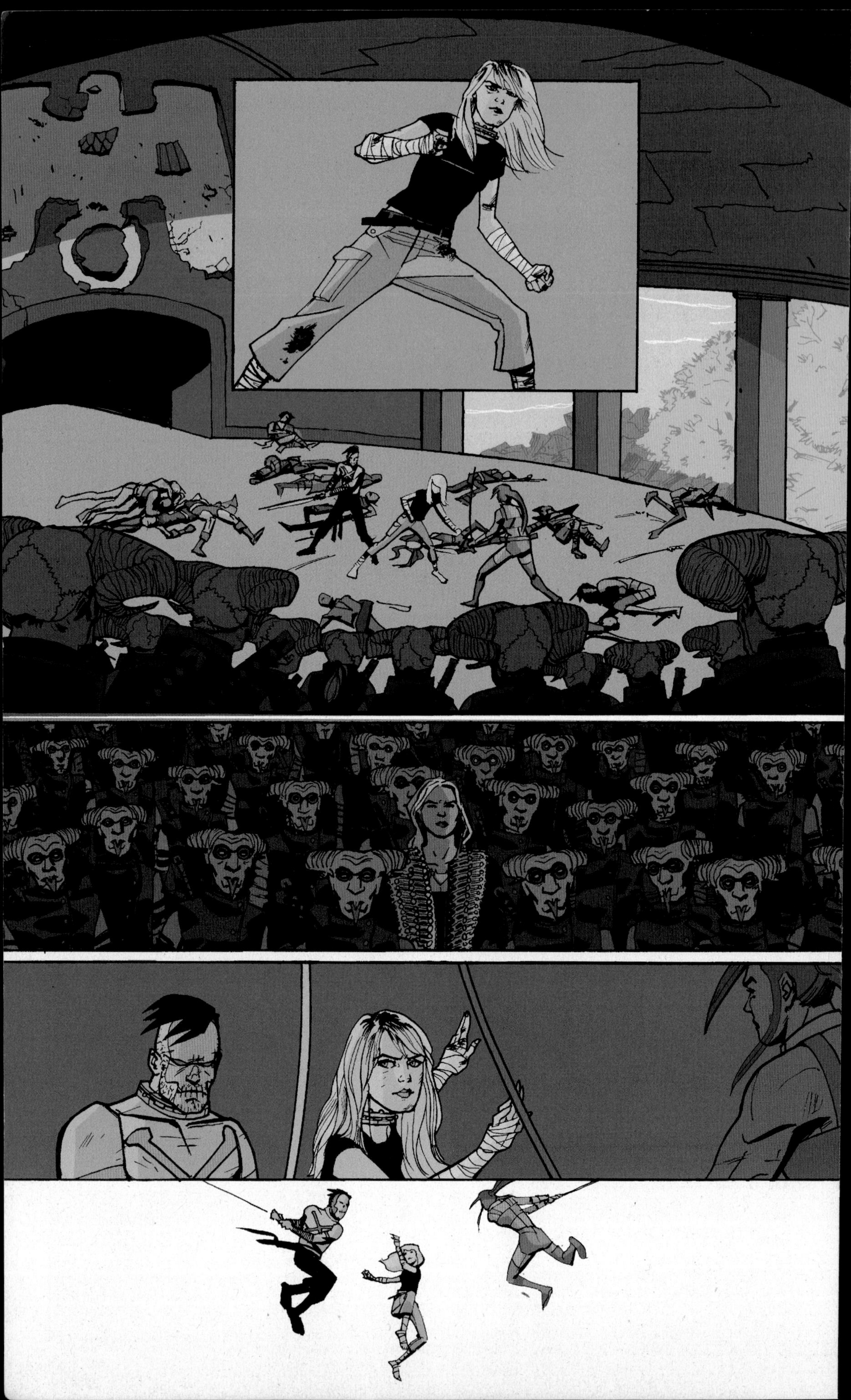

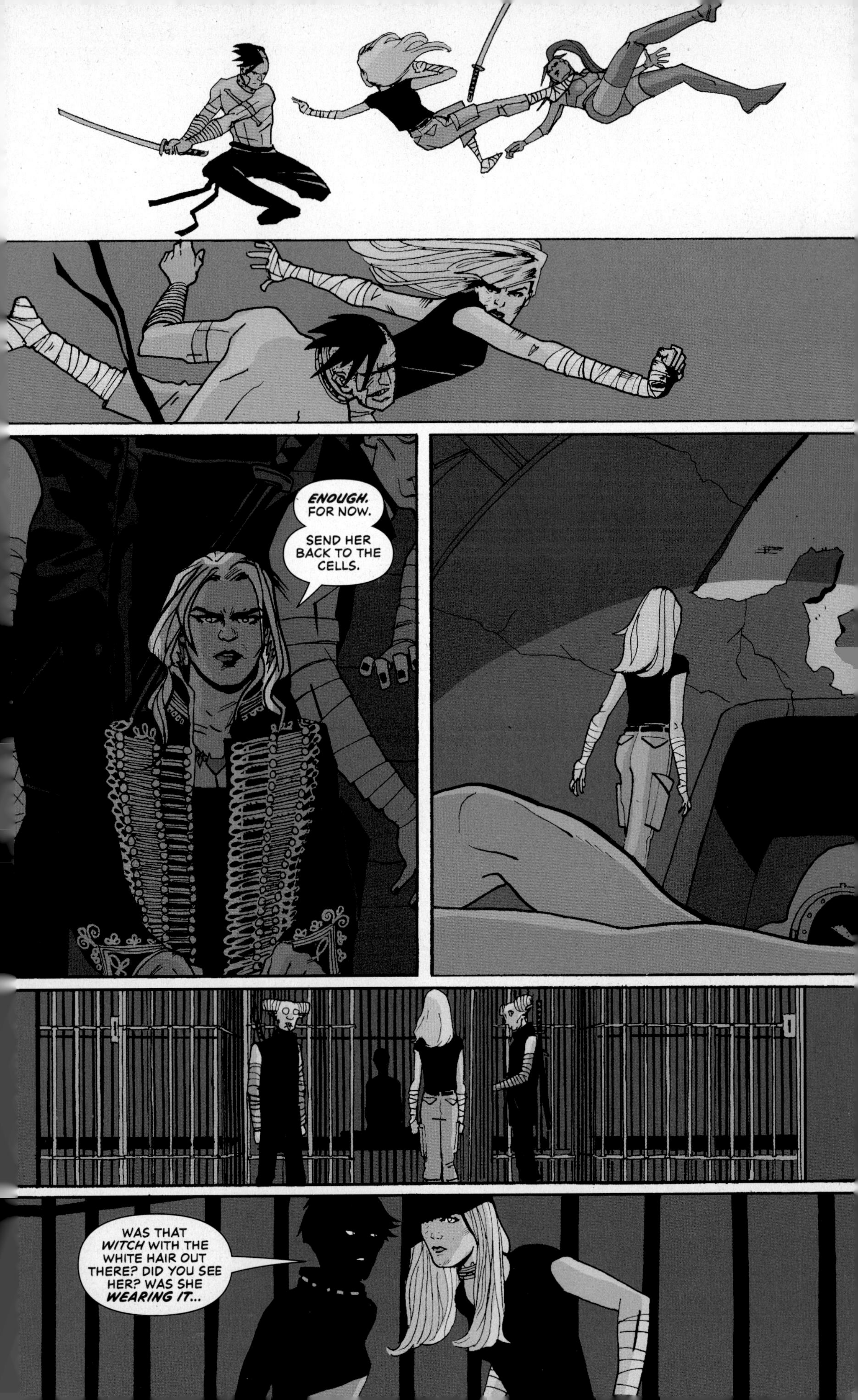
ENOUGH. FOR NOW.
SEND HER BACK TO THE CELLS.
WAS THAT WITCH WITH THE WHITE HAIR OUT THERE? DID YOU SEE HER? WAS SHE WEARING IT...

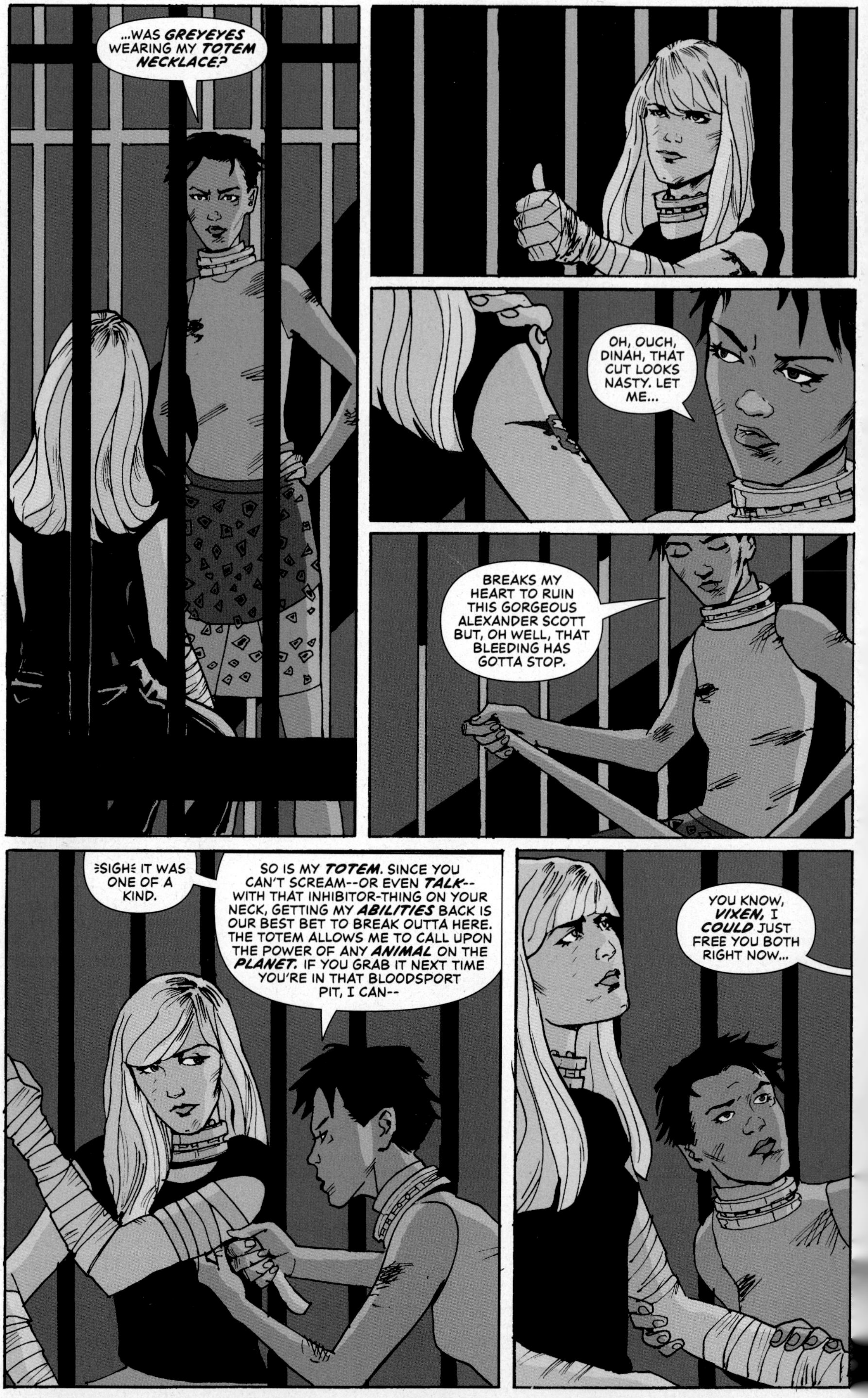
...WAS GREYEYES WEARING MY TOTEM NECKLACE?
OH, OUCH, DINAH, THAT CUT LOOKS NASTY. LET ME...
BREAKS MY HEART TO RUIN THIS GORGEOUS ALEXANDER SCOTT BUT, OH WELL, THAT BLEEDING HAS GOTTA STOP.
SIGH IT WAS ONE OF A KIND.
SO IS MY TOTEM. SINCE YOU CAN'T SCREAM--OR EVEN TALK--WITH THAT INHIBITOR-THING ON YOUR NECK, GETTING MY ABILITIES BACK IS OUR BEST BET TO BREAK OUTTA HERE. THE TOTEM ALLOWS ME TO CALL UPON THE POWER OF ANY ANIMAL ON THE PLANET. IF YOU GRAB IT NEXT TIME YOU'RE IN THAT BLOODSPORT PIT, I CAN--
YOU KNOW, VIXEN, I COULD JUST FREE YOU BOTH RIGHT NOW...

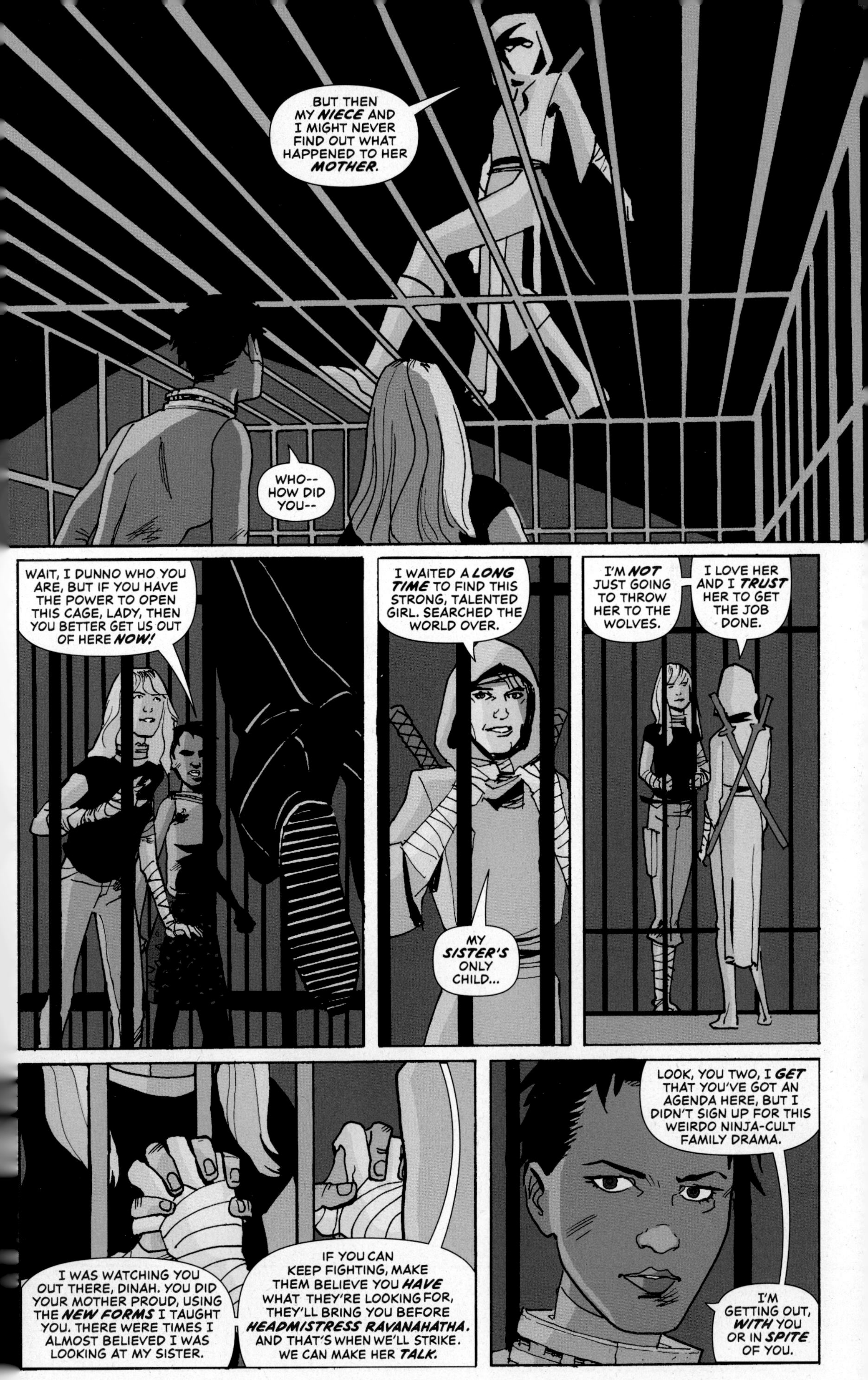
BUT THEN MY NIECE AND I MIGHT NEVER FIND OUT WHAT HAPPENED TO HER MOTHER.
WHO-- HOW DID YOU--
WAIT, I DUNNO WHO YOU ARE, BUT IF YOU HAVE THE POWER TO OPEN THIS CAGE, LADY, THEN YOU BETTER GET US OUT OF HERE NOW!
I WAITED A LONG TIME TO FIND THIS STRONG, TALENTED GIRL. SEARCHED THE WORLD OVER.
MY SISTER'S ONLY CHILD...
I'M NOT JUST GOING TO THROW HER TO THE WOLVES.
I LOVE HER AND I TRUST HER TO GET THE JOB DONE.
I WAS WATCHING YOU OUT THERE, DINAH. YOU DID YOUR MOTHER PROUD, USING THE NEW FORMS I TAUGHT YOU. THERE WERE TIMES I ALMOST BELIEVED I WAS LOOKING AT MY SISTER.
IF YOU CAN KEEP FIGHTING, MAKE THEM BELIEVE YOU HAVE WHAT THEY'RE LOOKING FOR, THEY'LL BRING YOU BEFORE HEADMISTRESS RAVANAHATHA. AND THAT'S WHEN WE'LL STRIKE. WE CAN MAKE HER TALK.
LOOK, YOU TWO, I GET THAT YOU'VE GOT AN AGENDA HERE, BUT I DIDN'T SIGN UP FOR THIS WEIRDO NINJA-CULT FAMILY DRAMA.
I'M GETTING OUT, WITH YOU OR IN SPITE OF YOU.

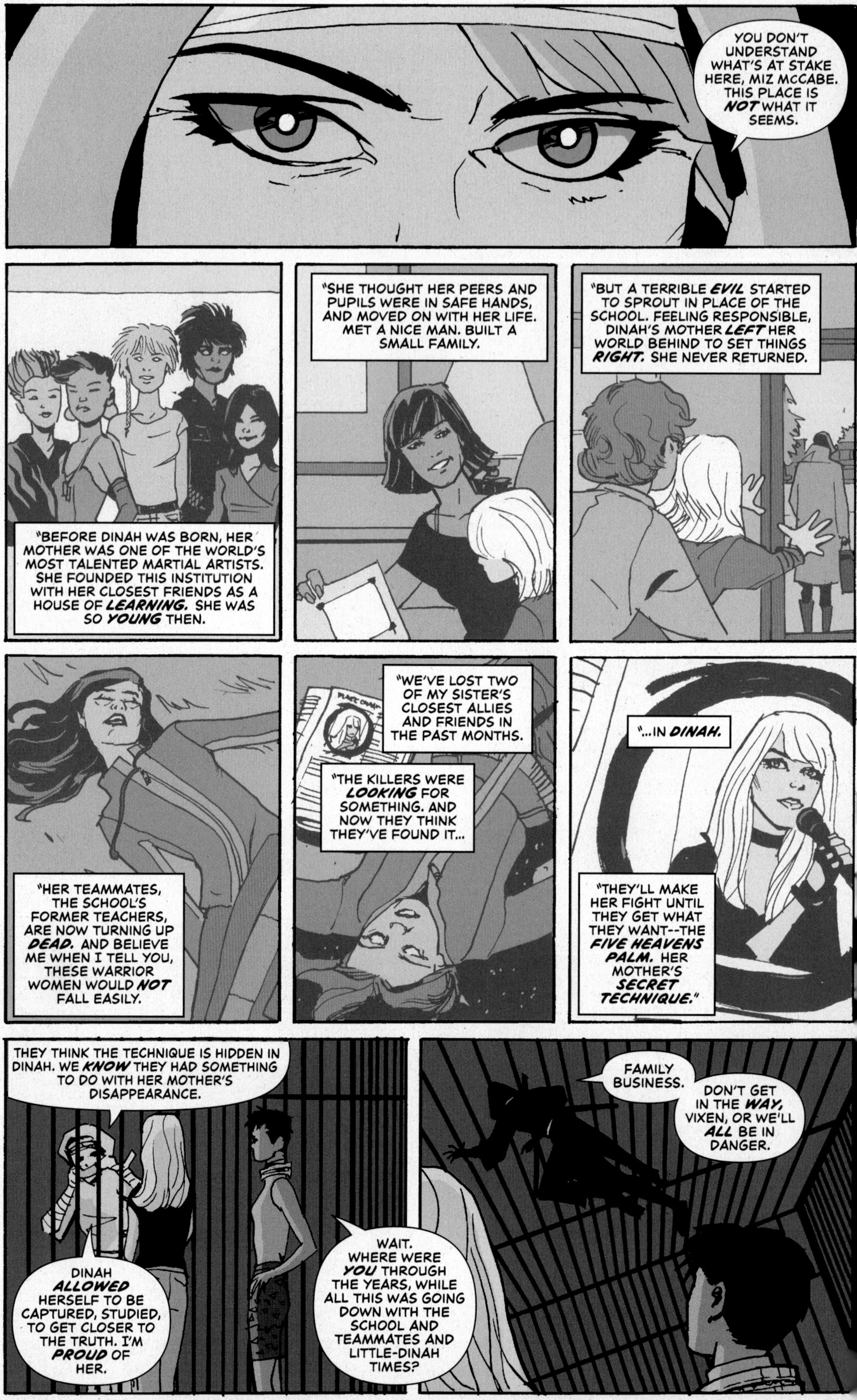
YOU DON'T UNDERSTAND WHAT'S AT STAKE HERE, MIZ McCABE. THIS PLACE IS NOT WHAT IT SEEMS.
"BEFORE DINAH WAS BORN, HER MOTHER WAS ONE OF THE WORLD'S MOST TALENTED MARTIAL ARTISTS. SHE FOUNDED THIS INSTITUTION WITH HER CLOSEST FRIENDS AS A HOUSE OF LEARNING. SHE WAS SO YOUNG THEN.
"SHE THOUGHT HER PEERS AND PUPILS WERE IN SAFE HANDS, AND MOVED ON WITH HER LIFE. MET A NICE MAN. BUILT A SMALL FAMILY.
"BUT A TERRIBLE EVIL STARTED TO SPROUT IN PLACE OF THE SCHOOL. FEELING RESPONSIBLE, DINAH'S MOTHER LEFT HER WORLD BEHIND TO SET THINGS RIGHT. SHE NEVER RETURNED.
"HER TEAMMATES, THE SCHOOL'S FORMER TEACHERS, ARE NOW TURNING UP DEAD. AND BELIEVE ME WHEN I TELL YOU, THESE WARRIOR WOMEN WOULD NOT FALL EASILY.
"WE'VE LOST TWO OF MY SISTER'S CLOSEST ALLIES AND FRIENDS IN THE PAST MONTHS.
"THE KILLERS WERE LOOKING FOR SOMETHING. AND NOW THEY THINK THEY'VE FOUND IT...
"...IN DINAH.
"THEY'LL MAKE HER FIGHT UNTIL THEY GET WHAT THEY WANT--THE FIVE HEAVENS PALM. HER MOTHER'S SECRET TECHNIQUE."
THEY THINK THE TECHNIQUE IS HIDDEN IN DINAH. WE KNOW THEY HAD SOMETHING TO DO WITH HER MOTHER'S DISAPPEARANCE.
DINAH ALLOWED HERSELF TO BE CAPTURED, STUDIED, TO GET CLOSER TO THE TRUTH. I'M PROUD OF HER.
WAIT. WHERE WERE YOU THROUGH THE YEARS, WHILE ALL THIS WAS GOING DOWN WITH THE SCHOOL AND TEAMMATES AND LITTLE-DINAH TIMES?
FAMILY BUSINESS.
DON'T GET IN THE WAY, VIXEN, OR WE'LL ALL BE IN DANGER.

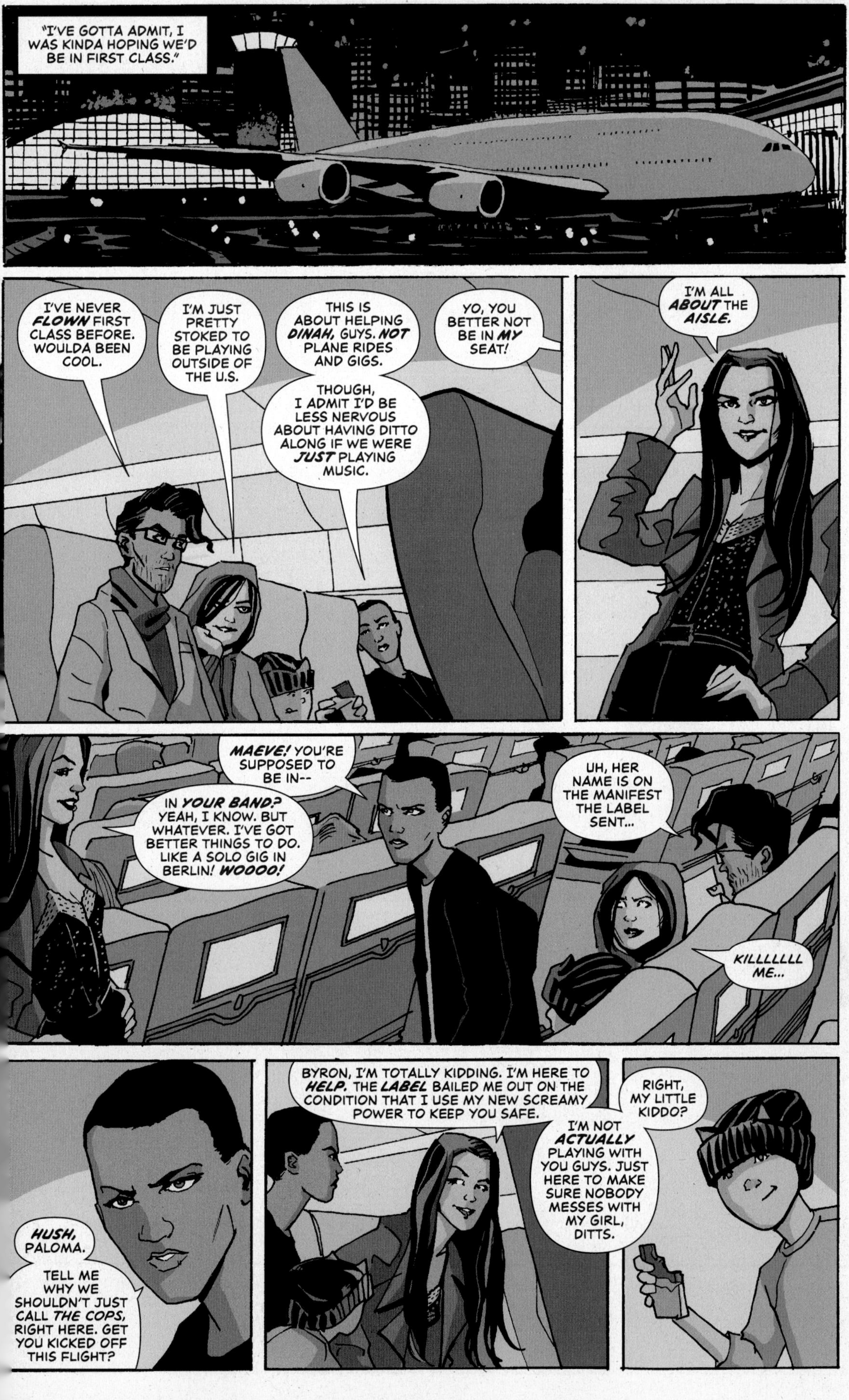
"I'VE GOTTA ADMIT, I WAS KINDA HOPING WE'D BE IN FIRST CLASS."
I'VE NEVER FLOWN FIRST CLASS BEFORE. WOULDA BEEN COOL.
I'M JUST PRETTY STOKED TO BE PLAYING OUTSIDE OF THE U.S.
THIS IS ABOUT HELPING DINAH, GUYS. NOT PLANE RIDES AND GIGS.
THOUGH, I ADMIT I'D BE LESS NERVOUS ABOUT HAVING DITTO ALONG IF WE WERE JUST PLAYING MUSIC.
YO, YOU BETTER NOT BE IN MY SEAT!
I'M ALL ABOUT THE AISLE.
MAEVE! YOU'RE SUPPOSED TO BE IN--
IN YOUR BAND? YEAH, I KNOW. BUT WHATEVER. I'VE GOT BETTER THINGS TO DO. LIKE A SOLO GIG IN BERLIN! WOOOO!
UH, HER NAME IS ON THE MANIFEST THE LABEL SENT...
KILLLLLLL ME...
HUSH, PALOMA.
TELL ME WHY WE SHOULDN'T JUST CALL THE COPS, RIGHT HERE. GET YOU KICKED OFF THIS FLIGHT?
BYRON, I'M TOTALLY KIDDING. I'M HERE TO HELP. THE LABEL BAILED ME OUT ON THE CONDITION THAT I USE MY NEW SCREAMY POWER TO KEEP YOU SAFE.
I'M NOT ACTUALLY PLAYING WITH YOU GUYS. JUST HERE TO MAKE SURE NOBODY MESSES WITH MY GIRL, DITTS.
RIGHT, MY LITTLE KIDDO?

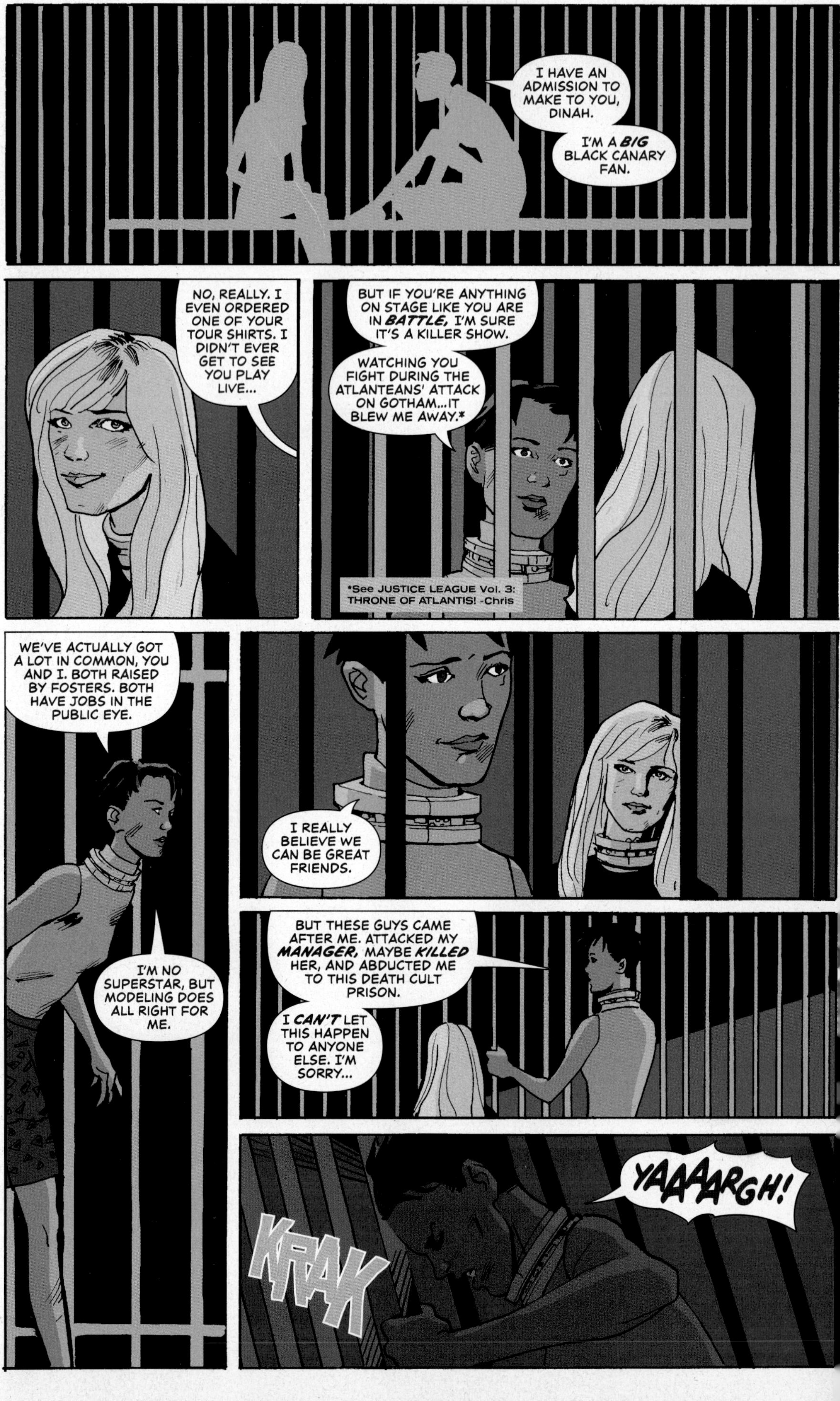

I HAVE AN ADMISSION TO MAKE TO YOU, DINAH.
I'M A BIG BLACK CANARY FAN.
NO, REALLY. I EVEN ORDERED ONE OF YOUR TOUR SHIRTS. I DIDN'T EVER GET TO SEE YOU PLAY LIVE...
BUT IF YOU'RE ANYTHING ON STAGE LIKE YOU ARE IN BATTLE, I'M SURE IT'S A KILLER SHOW.
WATCHING YOU FIGHT DURING THE ATLANTEANS' ATTACK ON GOTHAM...IT BLEW ME AWAY.*
*See JUSTICE LEAGUE Vol. 3: THRONE OF ATLANTIS! -Chris
WE'VE ACTUALLY GOT A LOT IN COMMON, YOU AND I. BOTH RAISED BY FOSTERS. BOTH HAVE JOBS IN THE PUBLIC EYE.
I'M NO SUPERSTAR, BUT MODELING DOES ALL RIGHT FOR ME.
I REALLY BELIEVE WE CAN BE GREAT FRIENDS.
BUT THESE GUYS CAME AFTER ME. ATTACKED MY MANAGER, MAYBE KILLED HER, AND ABDUCTED ME TO THIS DEATH CULT PRISON.
I CAN'T LET THIS HAPPEN TO ANYONE ELSE. I'M SORRY...
YAAAAARGH!
KRAK

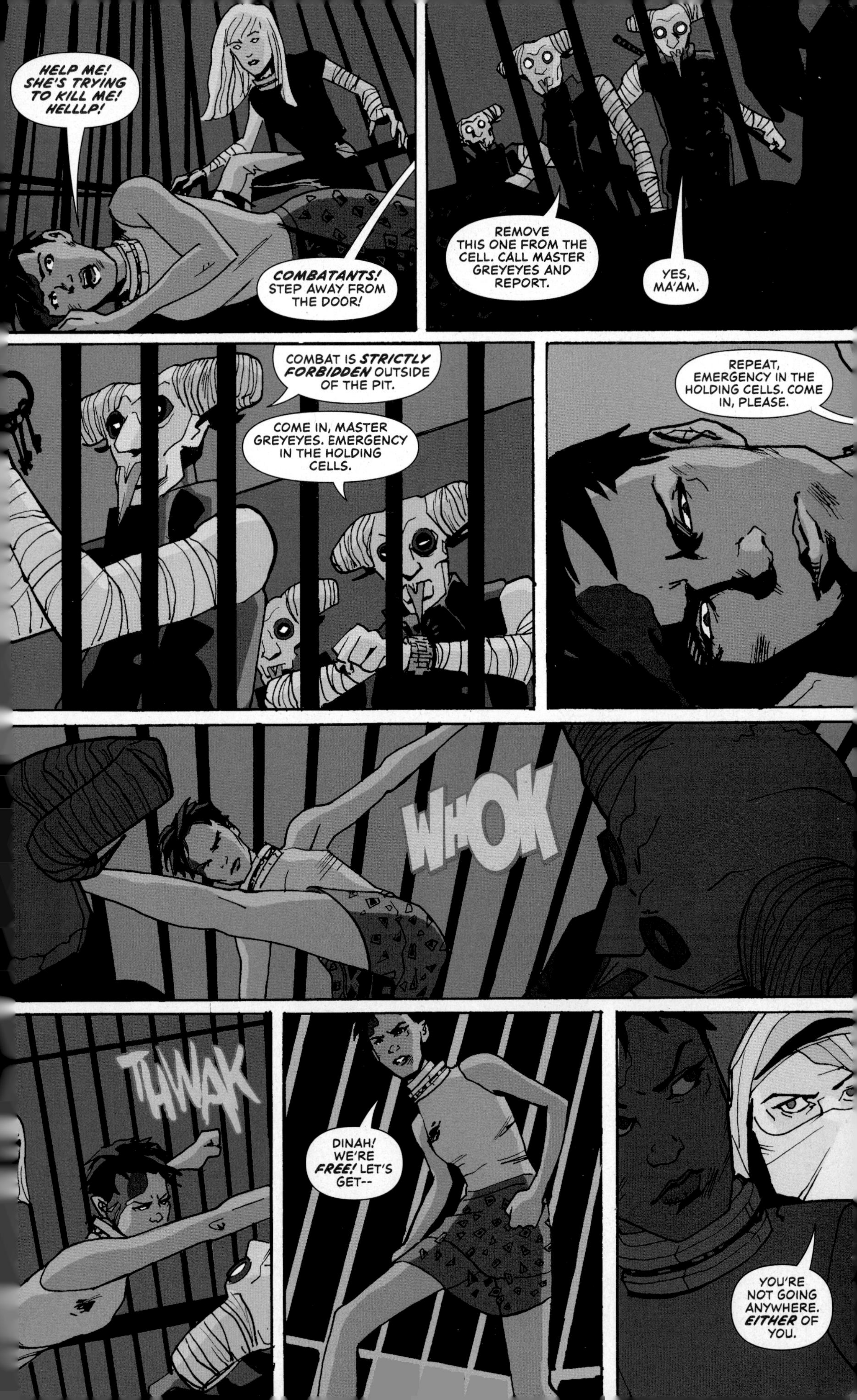
HELP ME! SHE'S TRYING TO KILL ME! HELLLP!
COMBATANTS! STEP AWAY FROM THE DOOR!
REMOVE THIS ONE FROM THE CELL. CALL MASTER GREYEYES AND REPORT.
YES, MA'AM.
COMBAT IS STRICTLY FORBIDDEN OUTSIDE OF THE PIT.
COME IN, MASTER GREYEYES. EMERGENCY IN THE HOLDING CELLS.
REPEAT, EMERGENCY IN THE HOLDING CELLS. COME IN, PLEASE.
WHOK
THWAK
DINAH! WE'RE FREE! LET'S GET--
YOU'RE NOT GOING ANYWHERE. EITHER OF YOU.

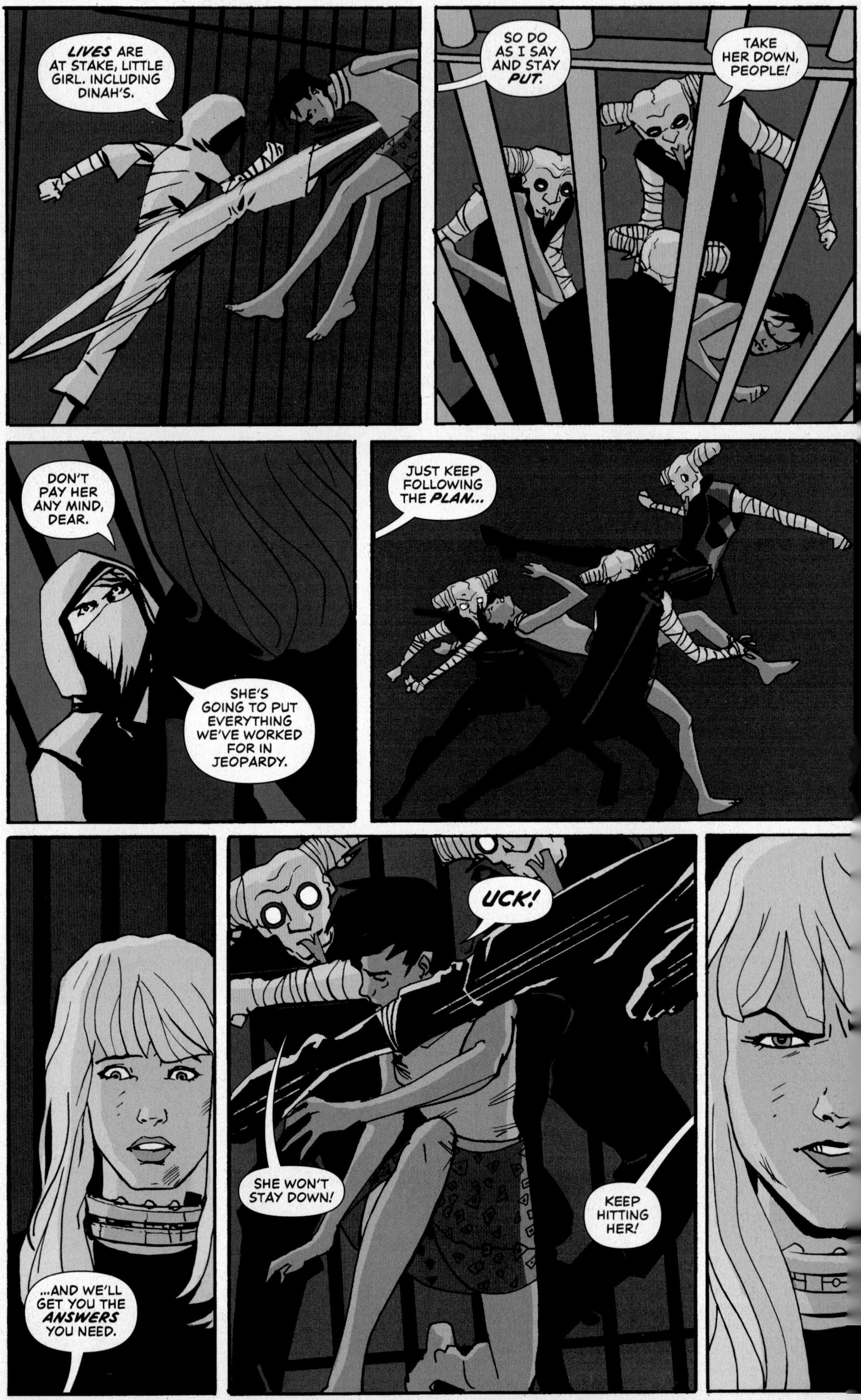
LIVES ARE AT STAKE, LITTLE GIRL. INCLUDING DINAH'S.
SO DO AS I SAY AND STAY PUT.
TAKE HER DOWN, PEOPLE!
DON'T PAY HER ANY MIND, DEAR.
SHE'S GOING TO PUT EVERYTHING WE'VE WORKED FOR IN JEOPARDY.
JUST KEEP FOLLOWING THE PLAN...
...AND WE'LL GET YOU THE ANSWERS YOU NEED.
UCK!
SHE WON'T STAY DOWN!
KEEP HITTING HER!

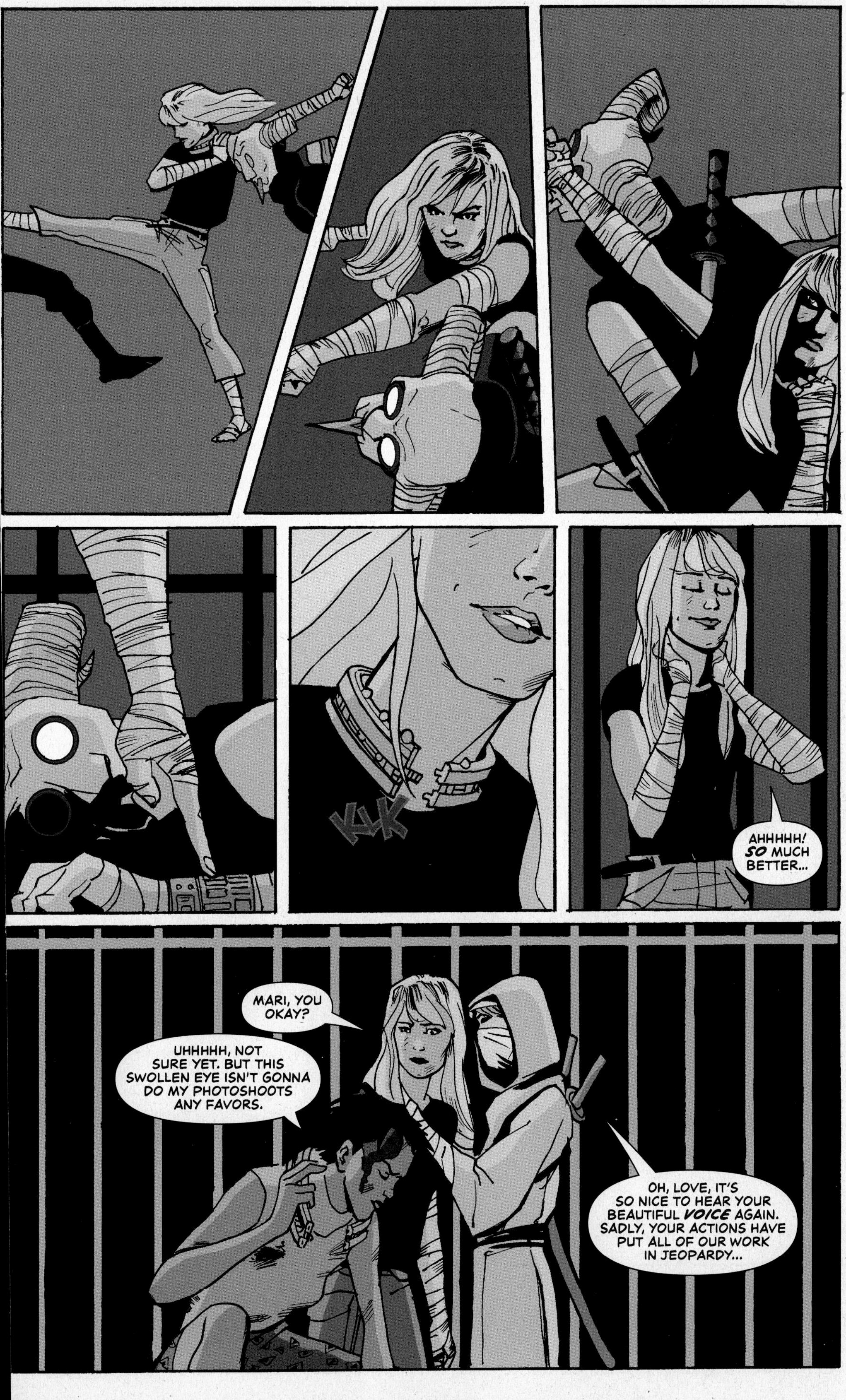
KLIK
AHHHHH! SO MUCH BETTER...
MARI, YOU OKAY?
UHHHHH, NOT SURE YET. BUT THIS SWOLLEN EYE ISN'T GONNA DO MY PHOTOSHOOTS ANY FAVORS.
OH, LOVE, IT'S SO NICE TO HEAR YOUR BEAUTIFUL VOICE AGAIN. SADLY, YOUR ACTIONS HAVE PUT ALL OF OUR WORK IN JEOPARDY...

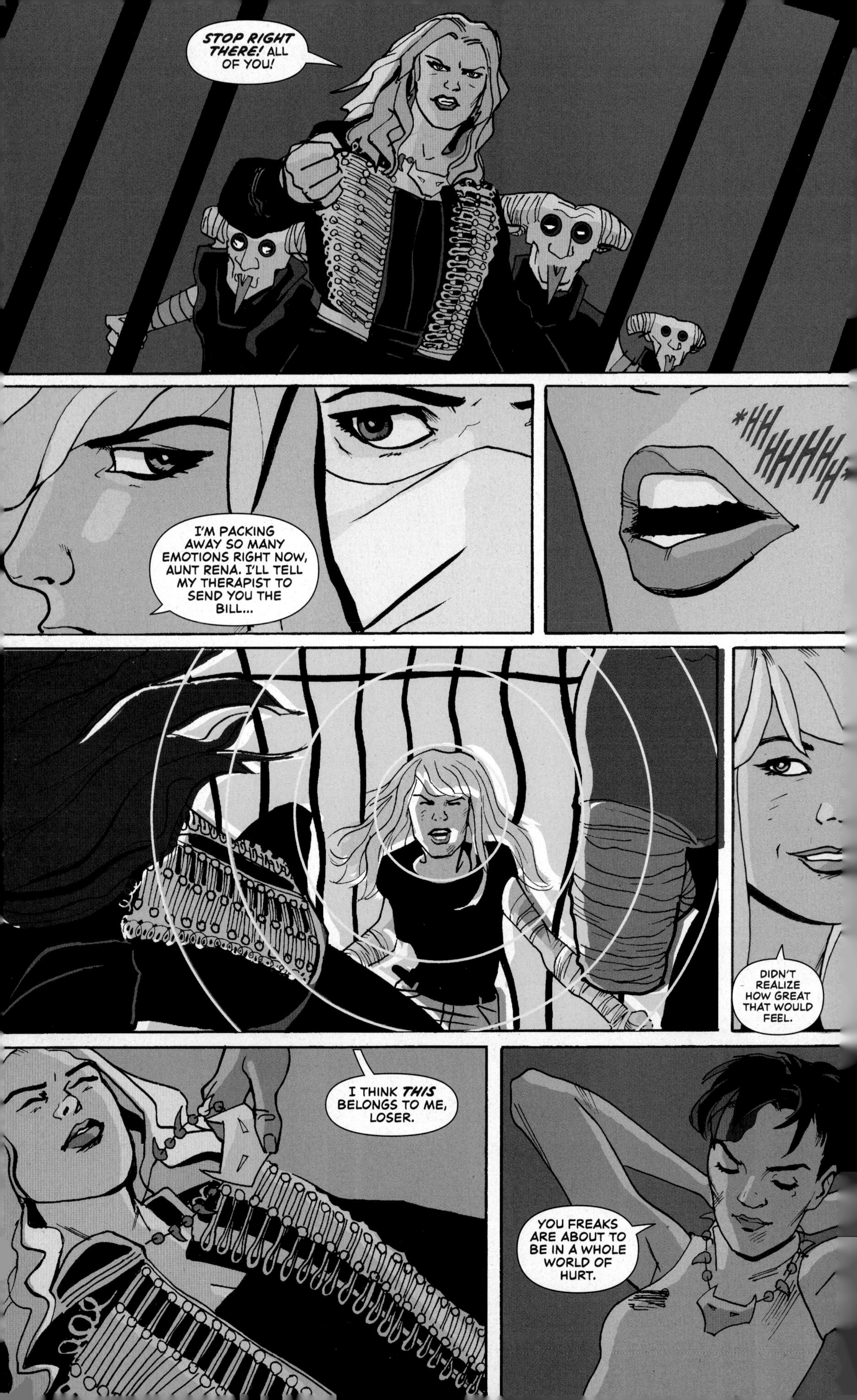
STOP RIGHT THERE! ALL OF YOU!
I'M PACKING AWAY SO MANY EMOTIONS RIGHT NOW, AUNT RENA. I'LL TELL MY THERAPIST TO SEND YOU THE BILL...
HHHHHHH
DIDN'T REALIZE HOW GREAT THAT WOULD FEEL.
I THINK THIS BELONGS TO ME, LOSER.
YOU FREAKS ARE ABOUT TO BE IN A WHOLE WORLD OF HURT.

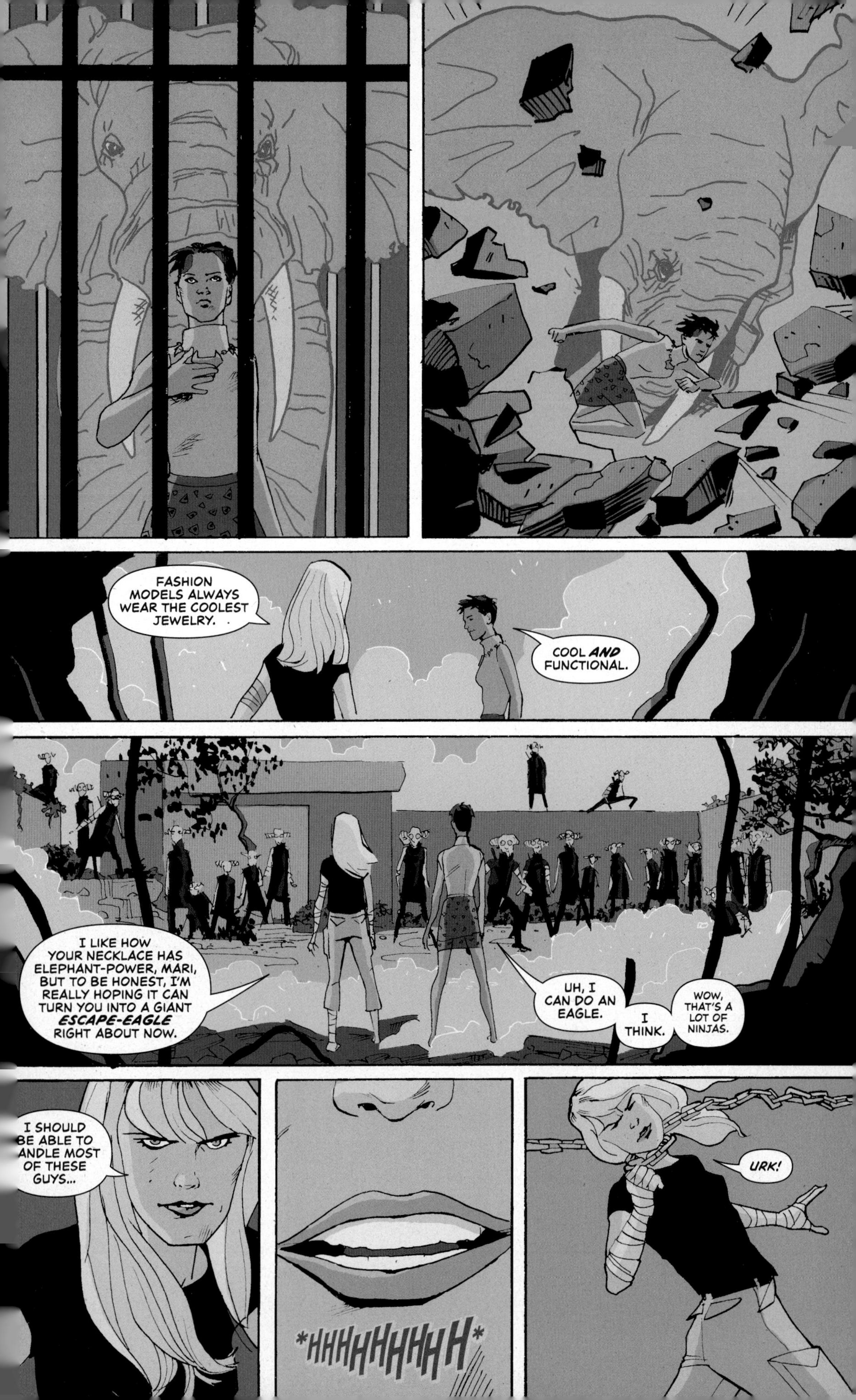
FASHION MODELS ALWAYS WEAR THE COOLEST JEWELRY.
COOL AND FUNCTIONAL.
I LIKE HOW YOUR NECKLACE HAS ELEPHANT-POWER, MARI, BUT TO BE HONEST, I'M REALLY HOPING IT CAN TURN YOU INTO A GIANT ESCAPE-EAGLE RIGHT ABOUT NOW.
UH, I CAN DO AN EAGLE.
I THINK.
WOW, THAT'S A LOT OF NINJAS.
I SHOULD BE ABLE TO ANDLE MOST OF THESE GUYS...
HHHHHHHHH
URK!

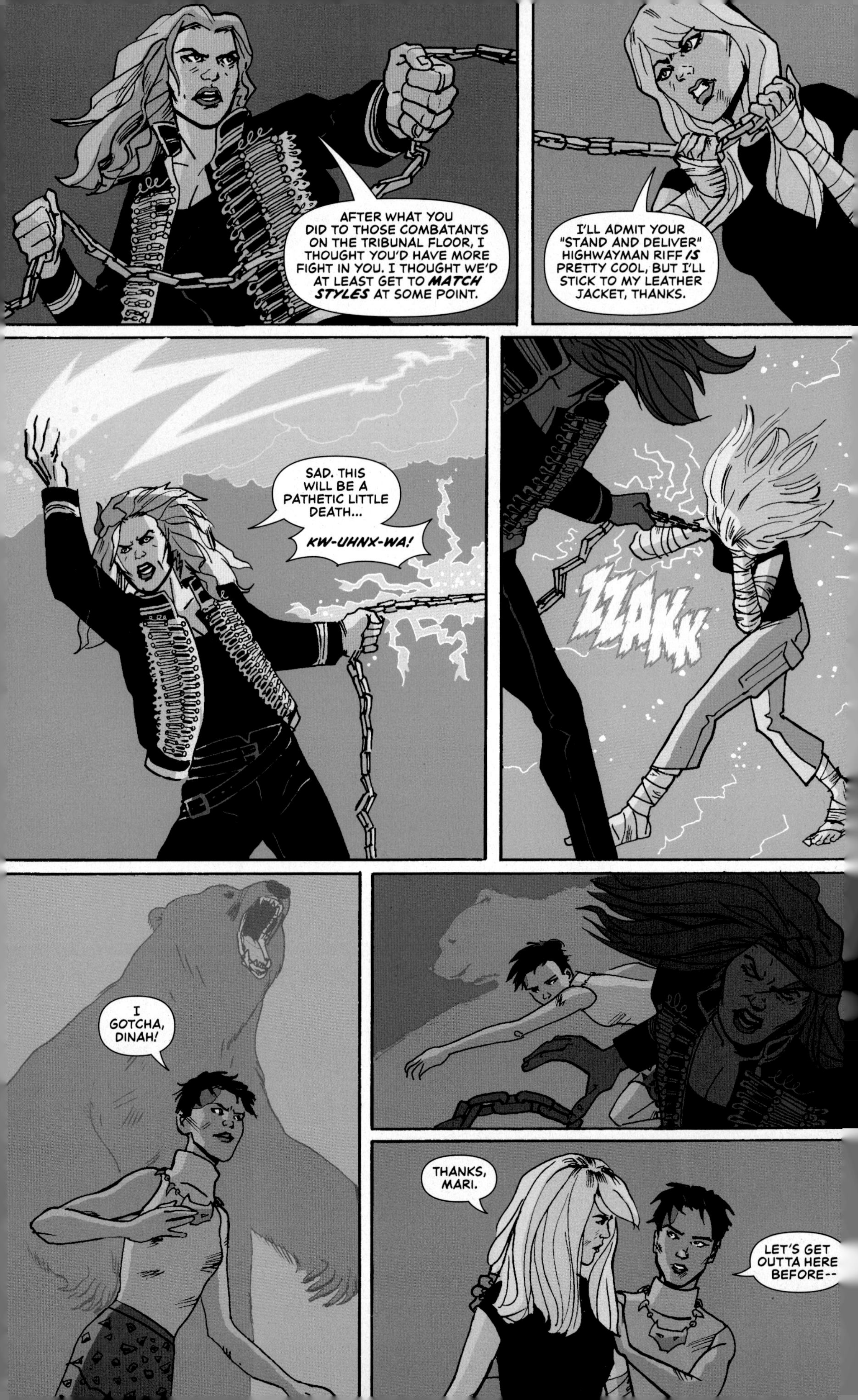
AFTER WHAT YOU DID TO THOSE COMBATANTS ON THE TRIBUNAL FLOOR, I THOUGHT YOU'D HAVE MORE FIGHT IN YOU. I THOUGHT WE'D AT LEAST GET TO MATCH STYLES AT SOME POINT.
I'LL ADMIT YOUR "STAND AND DELIVER" HIGHWAYMAN RIFF IS PRETTY COOL, BUT I'LL STICK TO MY LEATHER JACKET, THANKS.
SAD. THIS WILL BE A PATHETIC LITTLE DEATH...
KW-UHNX-WA!
ZZAKK
I GOTCHA, DINAH!
THANKS, MARI.
LET'S GET OUTTA HERE BEFORE--

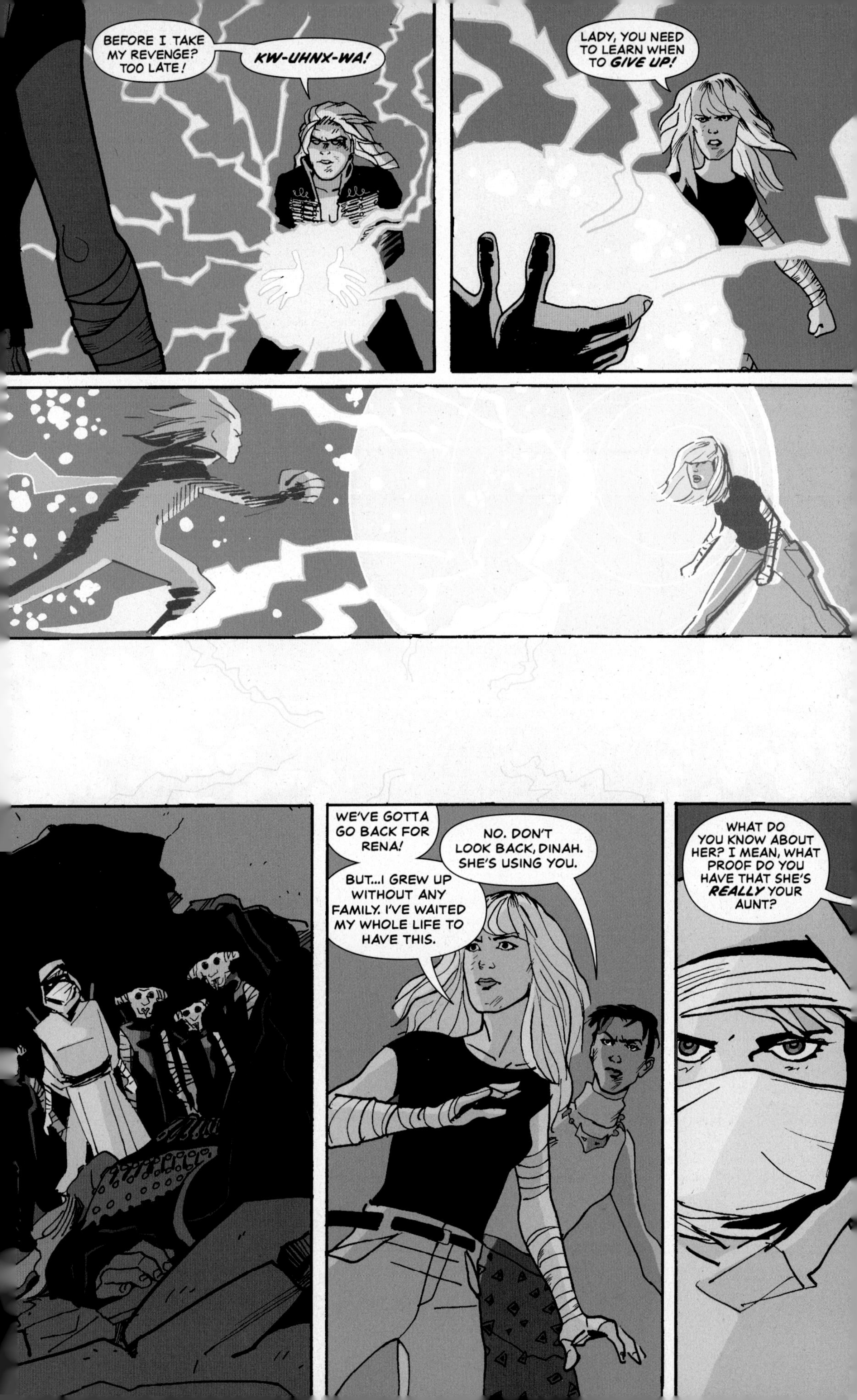
BEFORE I TAKE MY REVENGE? TOO LATE!
KW-UHNX-WA!
LADY, YOU NEED TO LEARN WHEN TO GIVE UP!
WE'VE GOTTA GO BACK FOR RENA!
NO. DON'T LOOK BACK, DINAH. SHE'S USING YOU.
BUT...I GREW UP WITHOUT ANY FAMILY. I'VE WAITED MY WHOLE LIFE TO HAVE THIS.
WHAT DO YOU KNOW ABOUT HER? I MEAN, WHAT PROOF DO YOU HAVE THAT SHE'S REALLY YOUR AUNT?

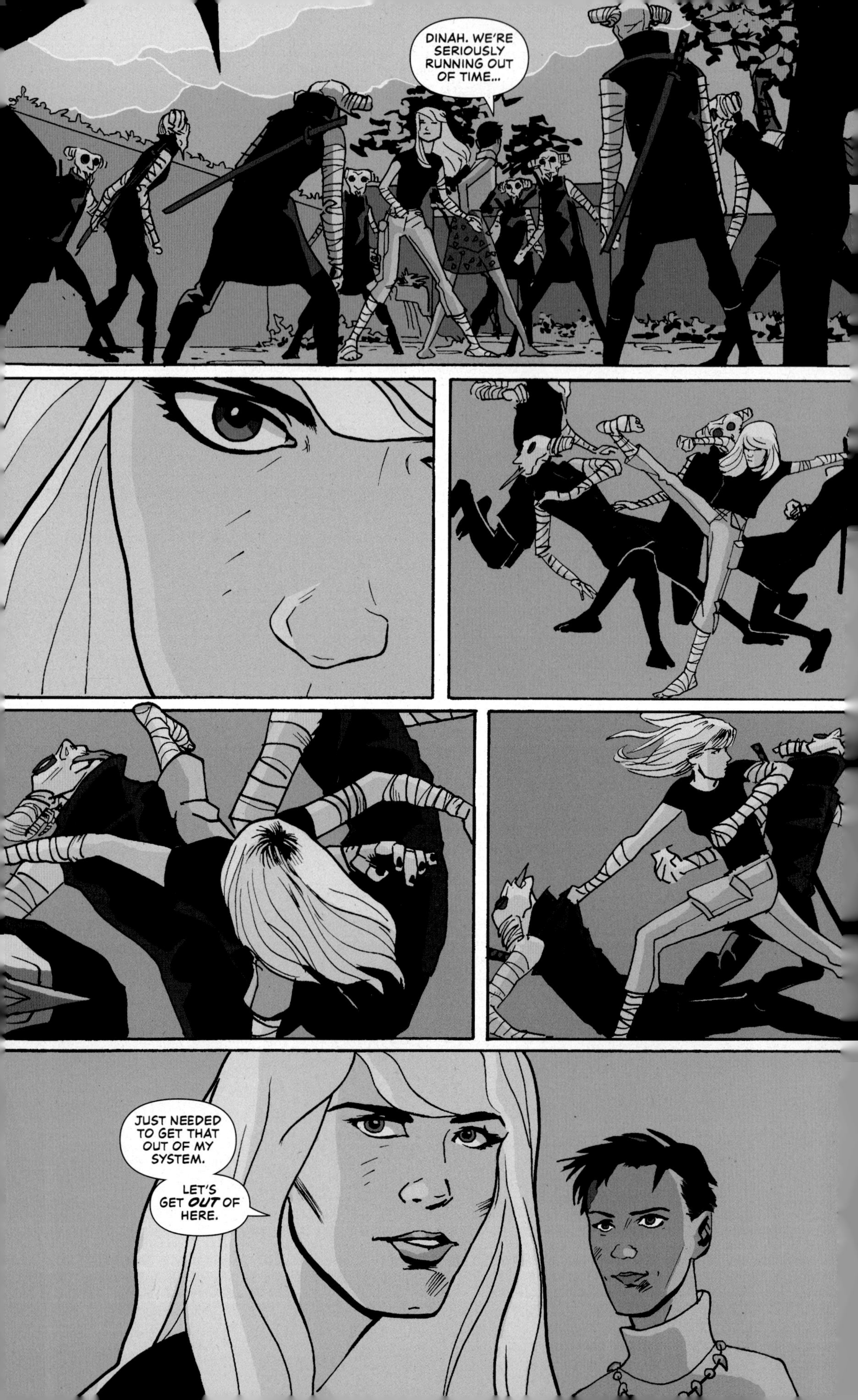
DINAH. WE'RE SERIOUSLY RUNNING OUT OF TIME...
JUST NEEDED TO GET THAT OUT OF MY SYSTEM.
LET'S GET *OUT* OF HERE.

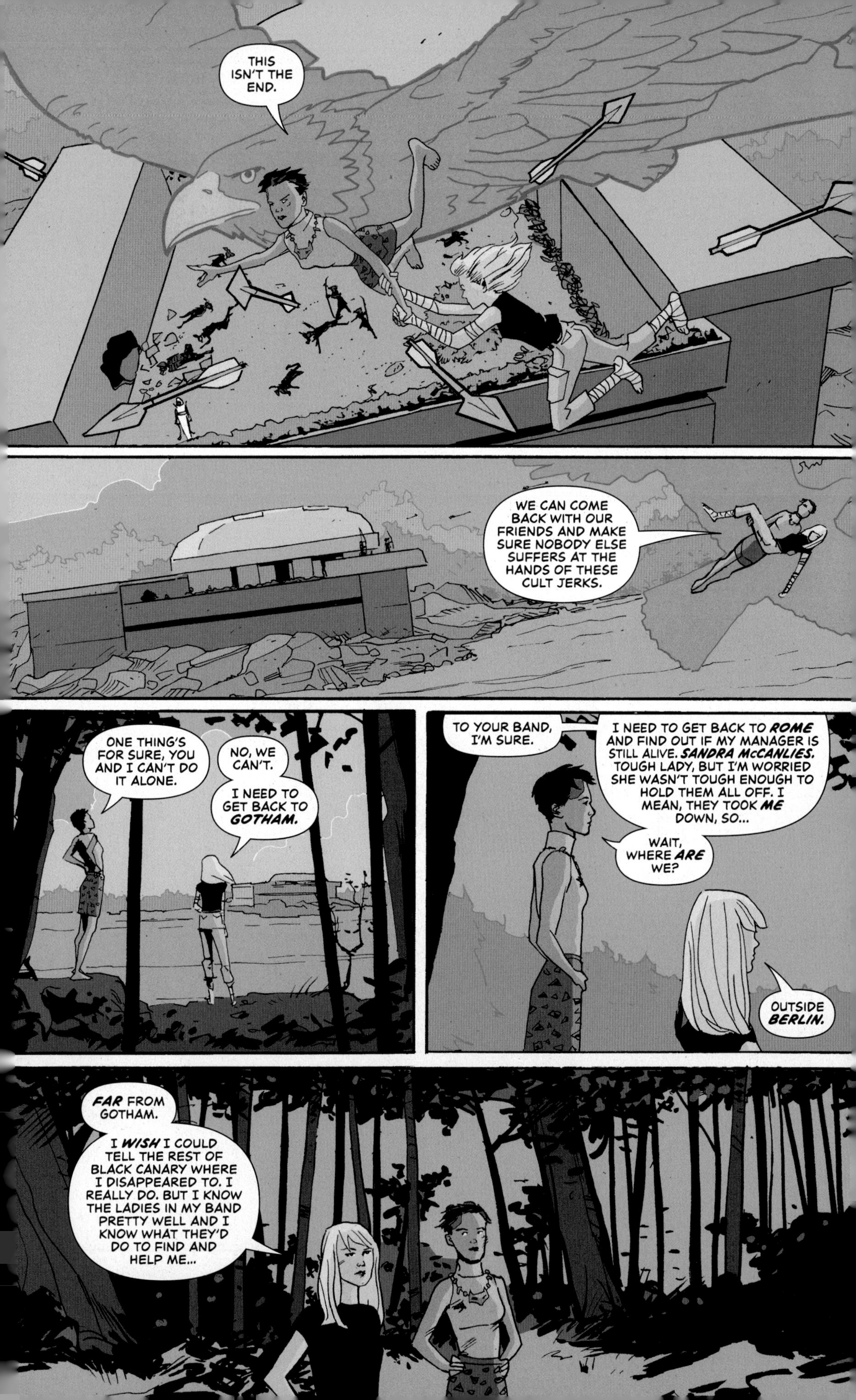
THIS ISN'T THE END.
WE CAN COME BACK WITH OUR FRIENDS AND MAKE SURE NOBODY ELSE SUFFERS AT THE HANDS OF THESE CULT JERKS.
ONE THING'S FOR SURE, YOU AND I CAN'T DO IT ALONE.
NO, WE CAN'T.
I NEED TO GET BACK TO GOTHAM.
TO YOUR BAND, I'M SURE.
I NEED TO GET BACK TO ROME AND FIND OUT IF MY MANAGER IS STILL ALIVE. SANDRA McCANLIES. TOUGH LADY, BUT I'M WORRIED SHE WASN'T TOUGH ENOUGH TO HOLD THEM ALL OFF. I MEAN, THEY TOOK ME DOWN, SO...
WAIT, WHERE ARE WE?
OUTSIDE BERLIN.
FAR FROM GOTHAM.
I WISH I COULD TELL THE REST OF BLACK CANARY WHERE I DISAPPEARED TO. I REALLY DO. BUT I KNOW THE LADIES IN MY BAND PRETTY WELL AND I KNOW WHAT THEY'D DO TO FIND AND HELP ME...

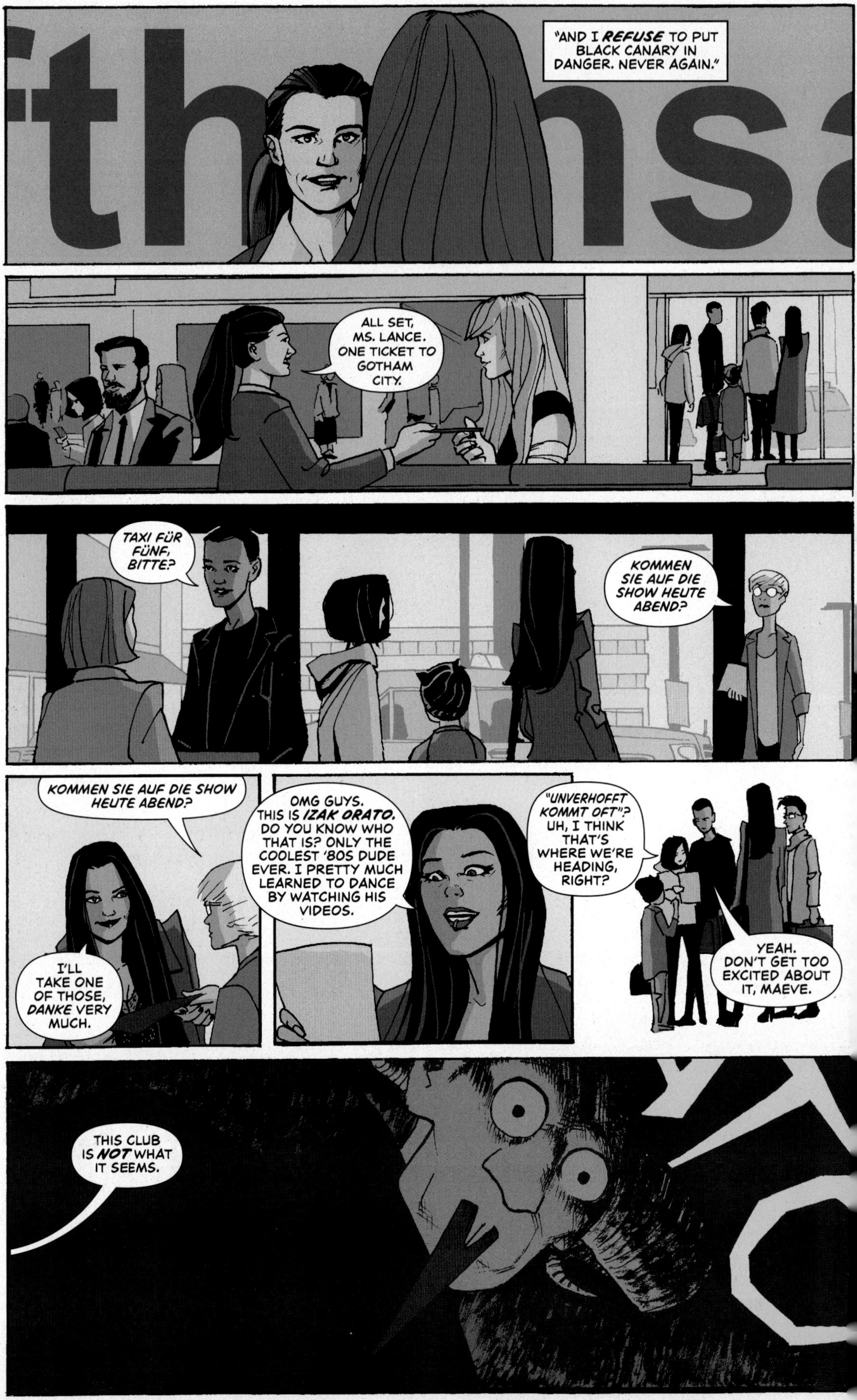
"AND I REFUSE TO PUT BLACK CANARY IN DANGER. NEVER AGAIN."
ALL SET, MS. LANCE. ONE TICKET TO GOTHAM CITY.
TAXI FÜR FÜNF, BITTE?
KOMMEN SIE AUF DIE SHOW HEUTE ABEND?
KOMMEN SIE AUF DIE SHOW HEUTE ABEND?
I'LL TAKE ONE OF THOSE, DANKE VERY MUCH.
OMG GUYS. THIS IS IZAK ORATO. DO YOU KNOW WHO THAT IS? ONLY THE COOLEST '80S DUDE EVER. I PRETTY MUCH LEARNED TO DANCE BY WATCHING HIS VIDEOS.
"UNVERHOFFT KOMMT OFT"? UH, I THINK THAT'S WHERE WE'RE HEADING, RIGHT?
YEAH. DON'T GET TOO EXCITED ABOUT IT, MAEVE.
THIS CLUB IS NOT WHAT IT SEEMS.

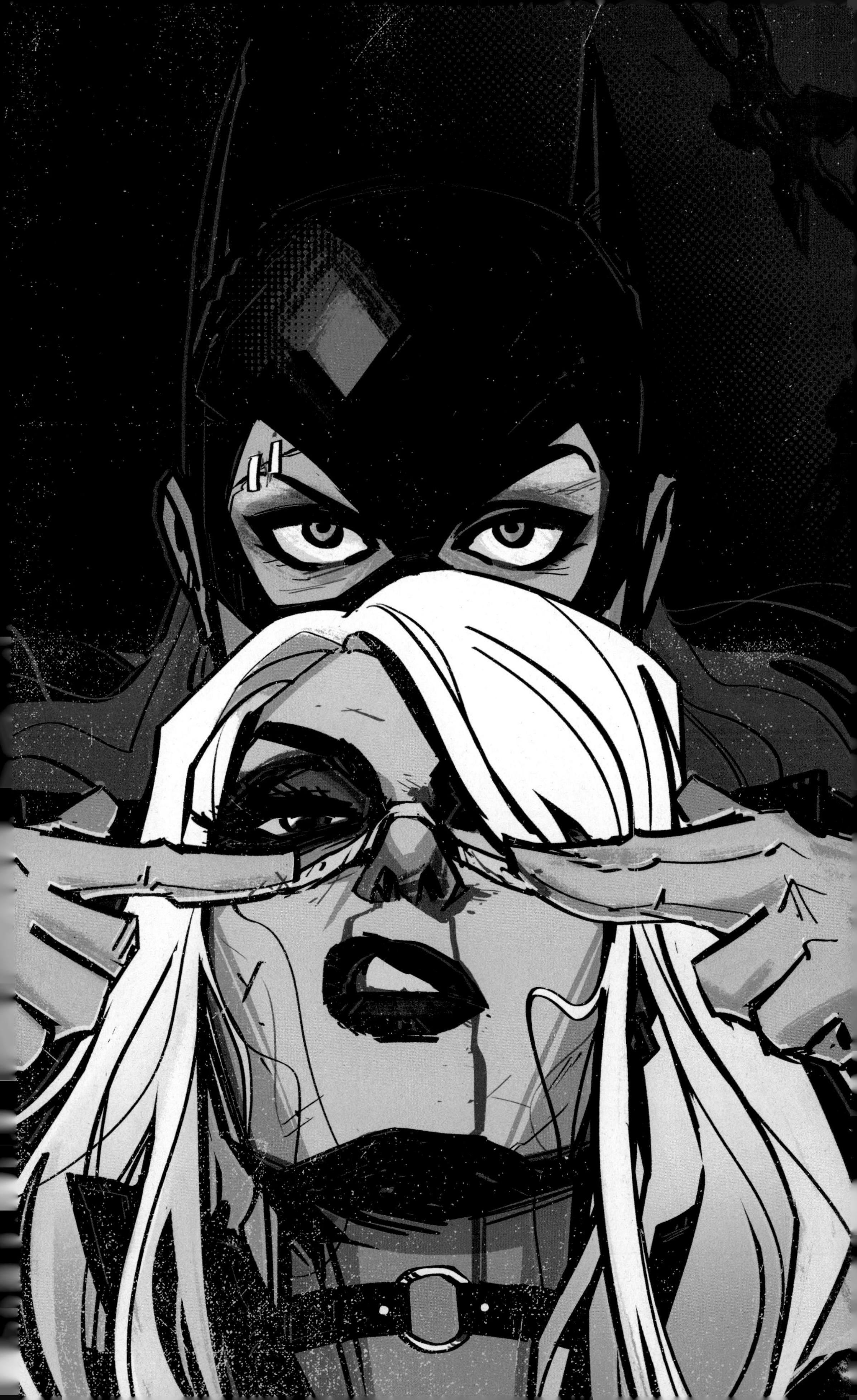

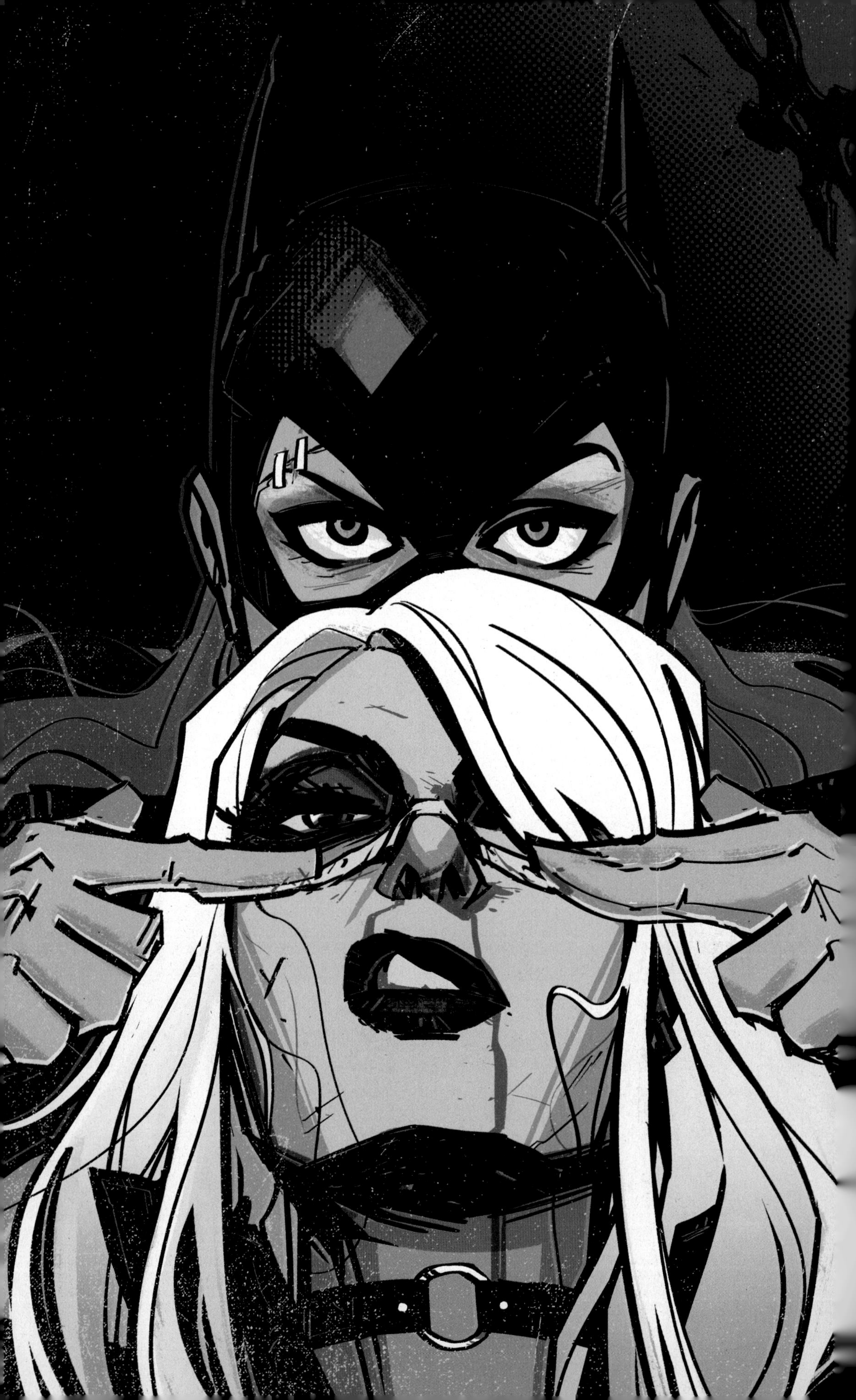

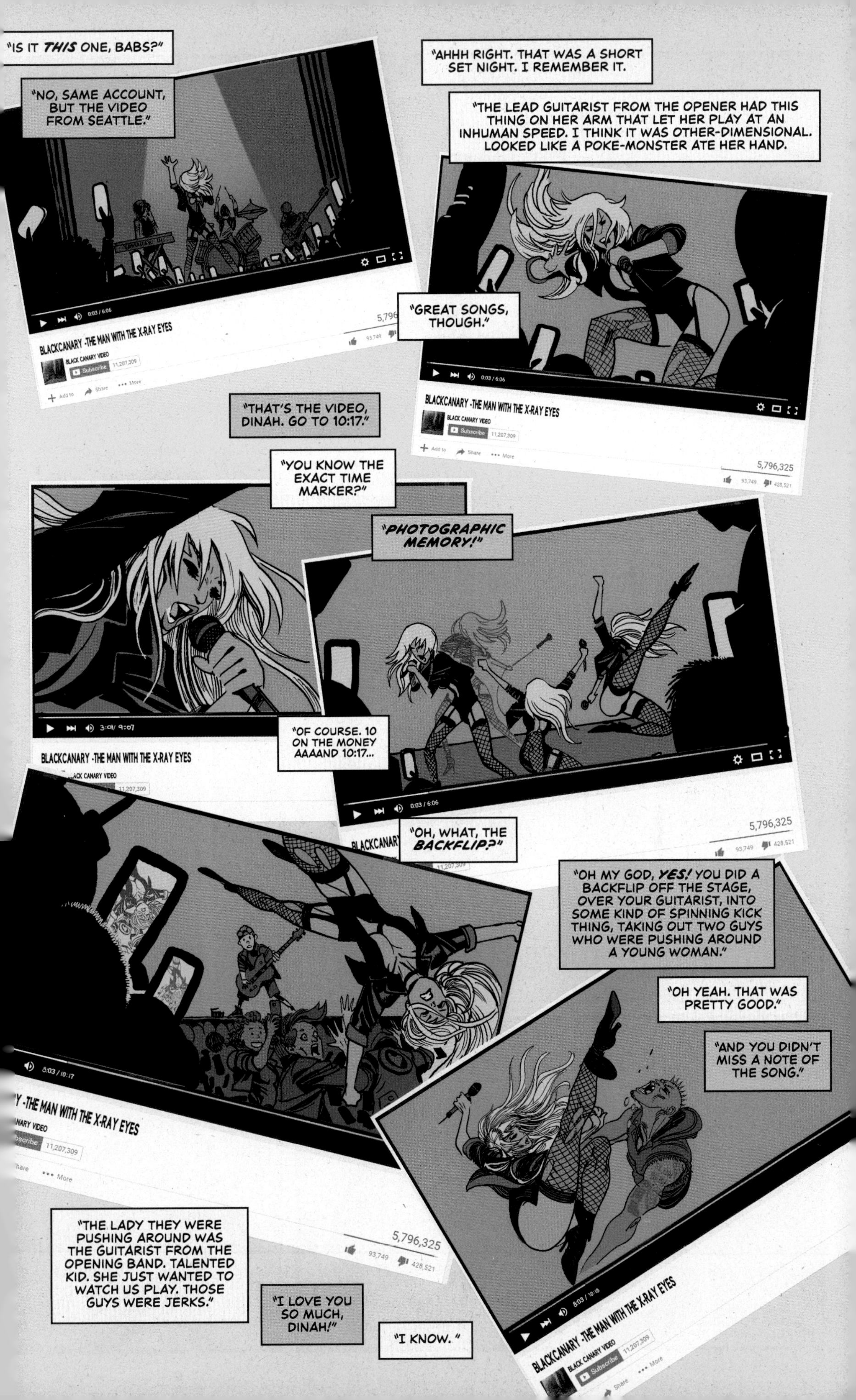
"IS IT *THIS* ONE, BABS?"
"NO, SAME ACCOUNT, BUT THE VIDEO FROM SEATTLE."
"AHHH RIGHT. THAT WAS A SHORT SET NIGHT. I REMEMBER IT.
"THE LEAD GUITARIST FROM THE OPENER HAD THIS THING ON HER ARM THAT LET HER PLAY AT AN INHUMAN SPEED. I THINK IT WAS OTHER-DIMENSIONAL. LOOKED LIKE A POKE-MONSTER ATE HER HAND.
BLACKCANARY -THE MAN WITH THE X-RAY EYES
"GREAT SONGS, THOUGH."
BLACKCANARY -THE MAN WITH THE X-RAY EYES
5,796,325
"THAT'S THE VIDEO, DINAH. GO TO 10:17."
"YOU KNOW THE EXACT TIME MARKER?"
"*PHOTOGRAPHIC MEMORY!*"
BLACKCANARY -THE MAN WITH THE X-RAY EYES
"OF COURSE. 10 ON THE MONEY AAAAND 10:17...
5,796,325
"OH, WHAT, THE *BACKFLIP?*"
"OH MY GOD, *YES!* YOU DID A BACKFLIP OFF THE STAGE, OVER YOUR GUITARIST, INTO SOME KIND OF SPINNING KICK THING, TAKING OUT TWO GUYS WHO WERE PUSHING AROUND A YOUNG WOMAN."
"OH YEAH. THAT WAS PRETTY GOOD."
"AND YOU DIDN'T MISS A NOTE OF THE SONG."
5,796,325
"THE LADY THEY WERE PUSHING AROUND WAS THE GUITARIST FROM THE OPENING BAND. TALENTED KID. SHE JUST WANTED TO WATCH US PLAY. THOSE GUYS WERE JERKS."
"I LOVE YOU SO MUCH, DINAH!"
"I KNOW."
BLACKCANARY -THE MAN WITH THE X-RAY EYES

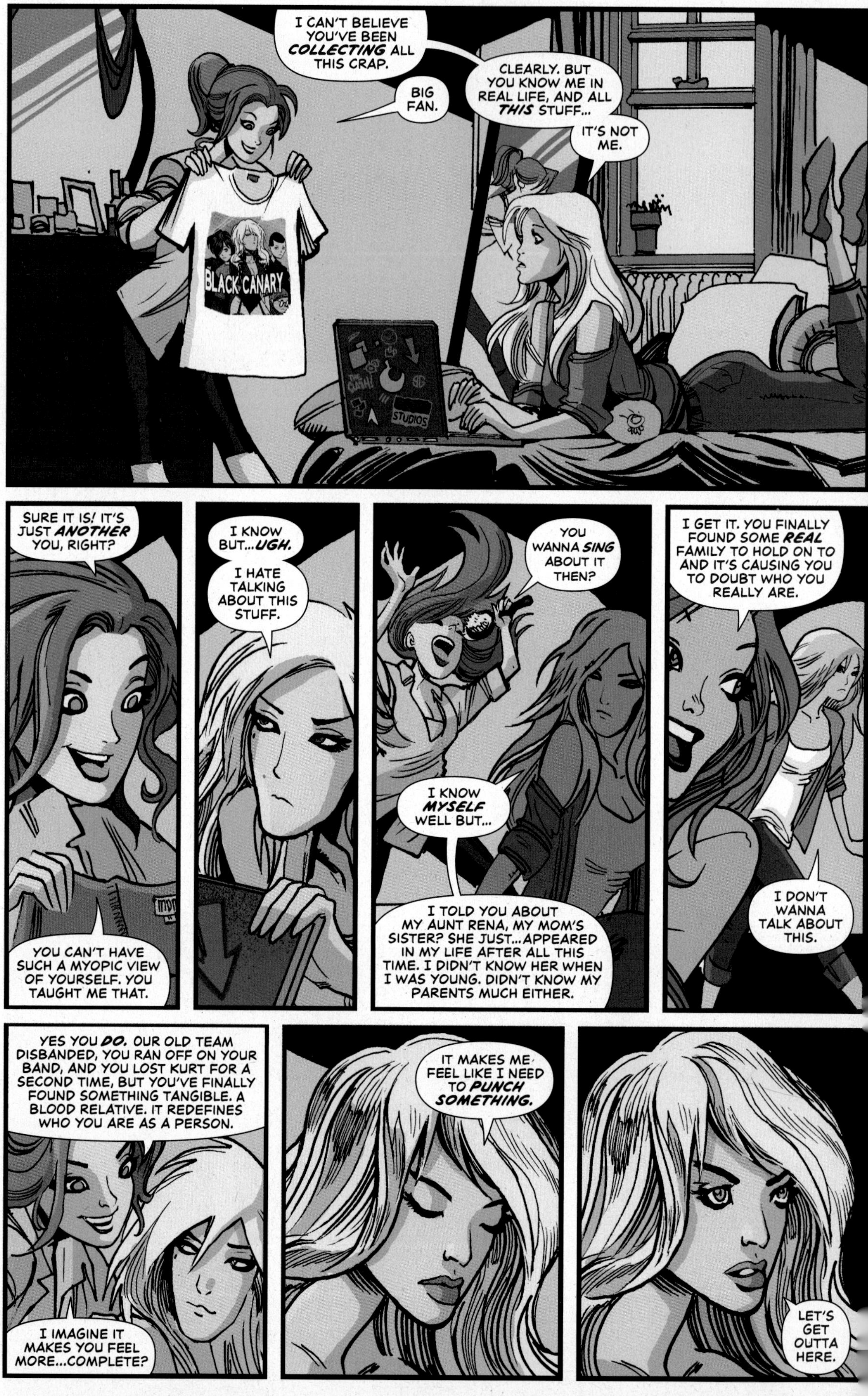

I CAN'T BELIEVE YOU'VE BEEN COLLECTING ALL THIS CRAP.
BIG FAN.
CLEARLY. BUT YOU KNOW ME IN REAL LIFE, AND ALL THIS STUFF...
IT'S NOT ME.
BLACK CANARY
STUDIOS
SURE IT IS! IT'S JUST ANOTHER YOU, RIGHT?
YOU CAN'T HAVE SUCH A MYOPIC VIEW OF YOURSELF. YOU TAUGHT ME THAT.
I KNOW BUT...UGH.
I HATE TALKING ABOUT THIS STUFF.
YOU WANNA SING ABOUT IT THEN?
I KNOW MYSELF WELL BUT...
I TOLD YOU ABOUT MY AUNT RENA, MY MOM'S SISTER? SHE JUST...APPEARED IN MY LIFE AFTER ALL THIS TIME. I DIDN'T KNOW HER WHEN I WAS YOUNG. DIDN'T KNOW MY PARENTS MUCH EITHER.
I GET IT. YOU FINALLY FOUND SOME REAL FAMILY TO HOLD ON TO AND IT'S CAUSING YOU TO DOUBT WHO YOU REALLY ARE.
I DON'T WANNA TALK ABOUT THIS.
YES YOU DO. OUR OLD TEAM DISBANDED, YOU RAN OFF ON YOUR BAND, AND YOU LOST KURT FOR A SECOND TIME, BUT YOU'VE FINALLY FOUND SOMETHING TANGIBLE. A BLOOD RELATIVE. IT REDEFINES WHO YOU ARE AS A PERSON.
I IMAGINE IT MAKES YOU FEEL MORE...COMPLETE?
IT MAKES ME FEEL LIKE I NEED TO PUNCH SOMETHING.
LET'S GET OUTTA HERE.

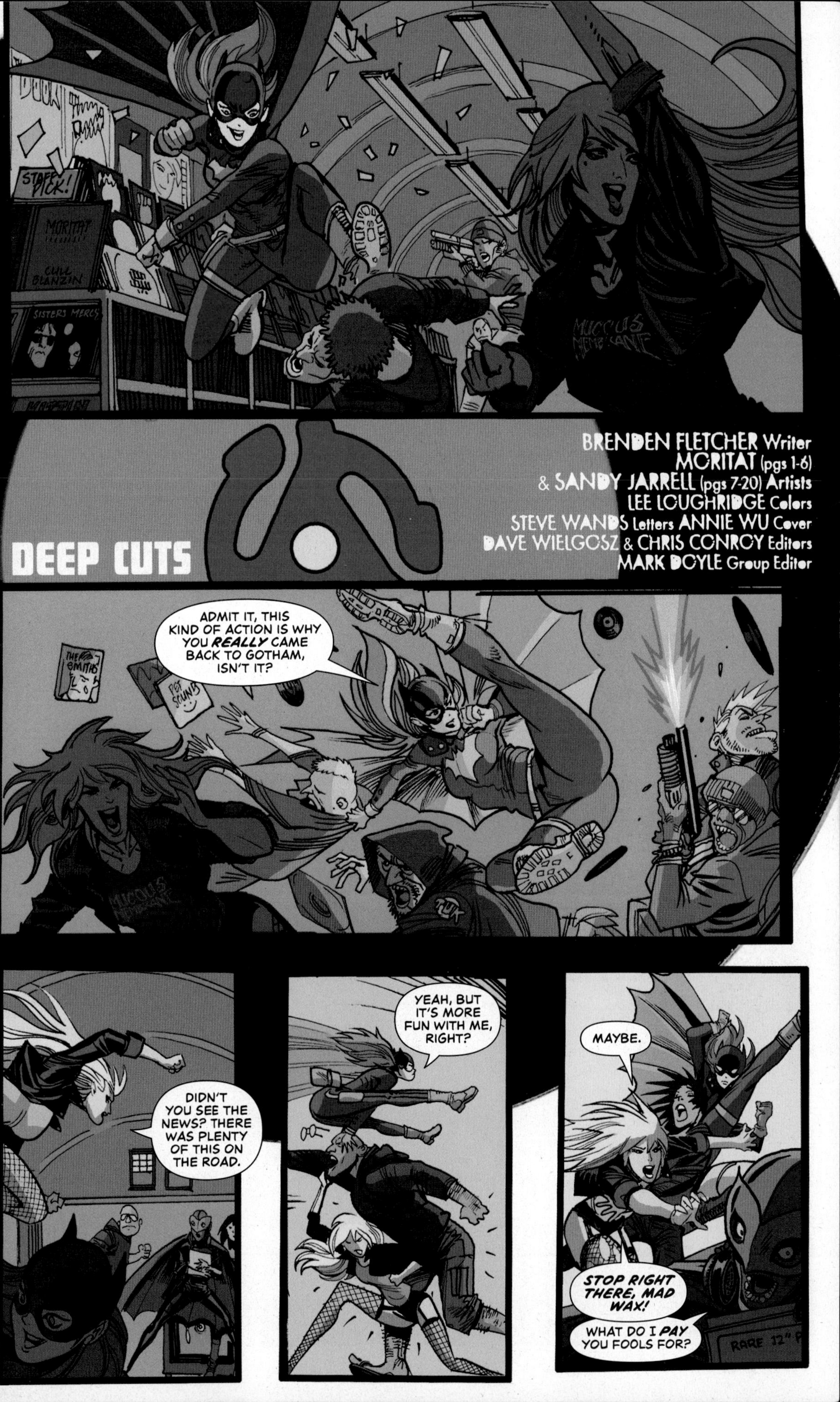
STAFF PICK!
MORITAT
SISTERS MERCY
DEEP CUTS
BRENDEN FLETCHER Writer
MORITAT (pgs 1-6)
& SANDY JARRELL (pgs 7-20) Artists
LEE LOUGHRIDGE Colors
STEVE WANDS Letters ANNIE WU Cover
DAVE WIELGOSZ & CHRIS CONROY Editors
MARK DOYLE Group Editor
ADMIT IT, THIS KIND OF ACTION IS WHY YOU *REALLY* CAME BACK TO GOTHAM, ISN'T IT?
THE SMITHS
PET SOUNDS
DIDN'T YOU SEE THE NEWS? THERE WAS PLENTY OF THIS ON THE ROAD.
YEAH, BUT IT'S MORE FUN WITH ME, RIGHT?
MAYBE.
STOP RIGHT THERE, MAD WAX!
WHAT DO I *PAY* YOU FOOLS FOR?

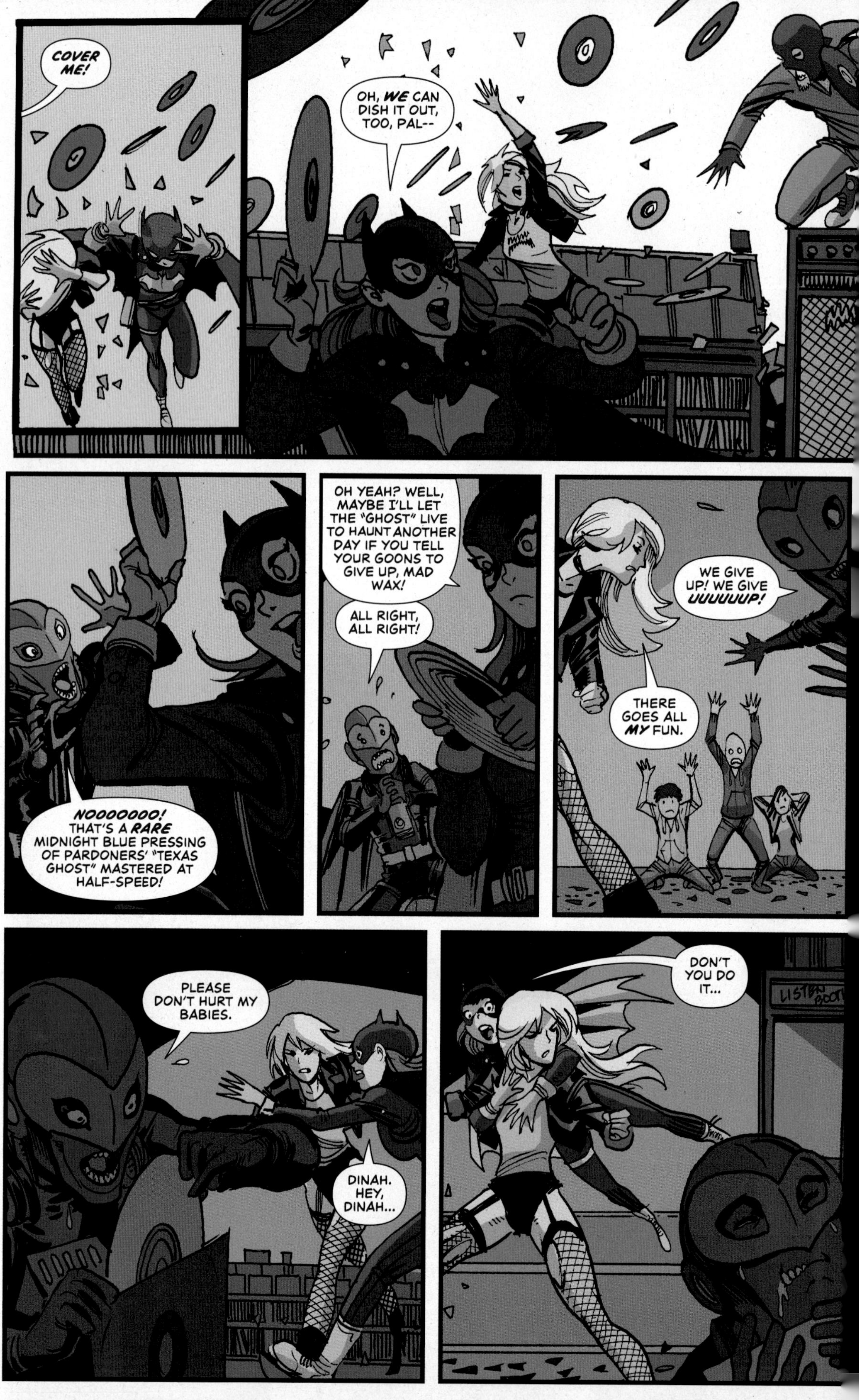
COVER ME!
OH, WE CAN DISH IT OUT, TOO, PAL--
NOOOOOOO! THAT'S A RARE MIDNIGHT BLUE PRESSING OF PARDONERS' "TEXAS GHOST" MASTERED AT HALF-SPEED!
OH YEAH? WELL, MAYBE I'LL LET THE "GHOST" LIVE TO HAUNT ANOTHER DAY IF YOU TELL YOUR GOONS TO GIVE UP, MAD WAX!
ALL RIGHT, ALL RIGHT!
WE GIVE UP! WE GIVE UUUUUUP!
THERE GOES ALL MY FUN.
PLEASE DON'T HURT MY BABIES.
DINAH. HEY, DINAH...
DON'T YOU DO IT...
LISTEN BOOTH

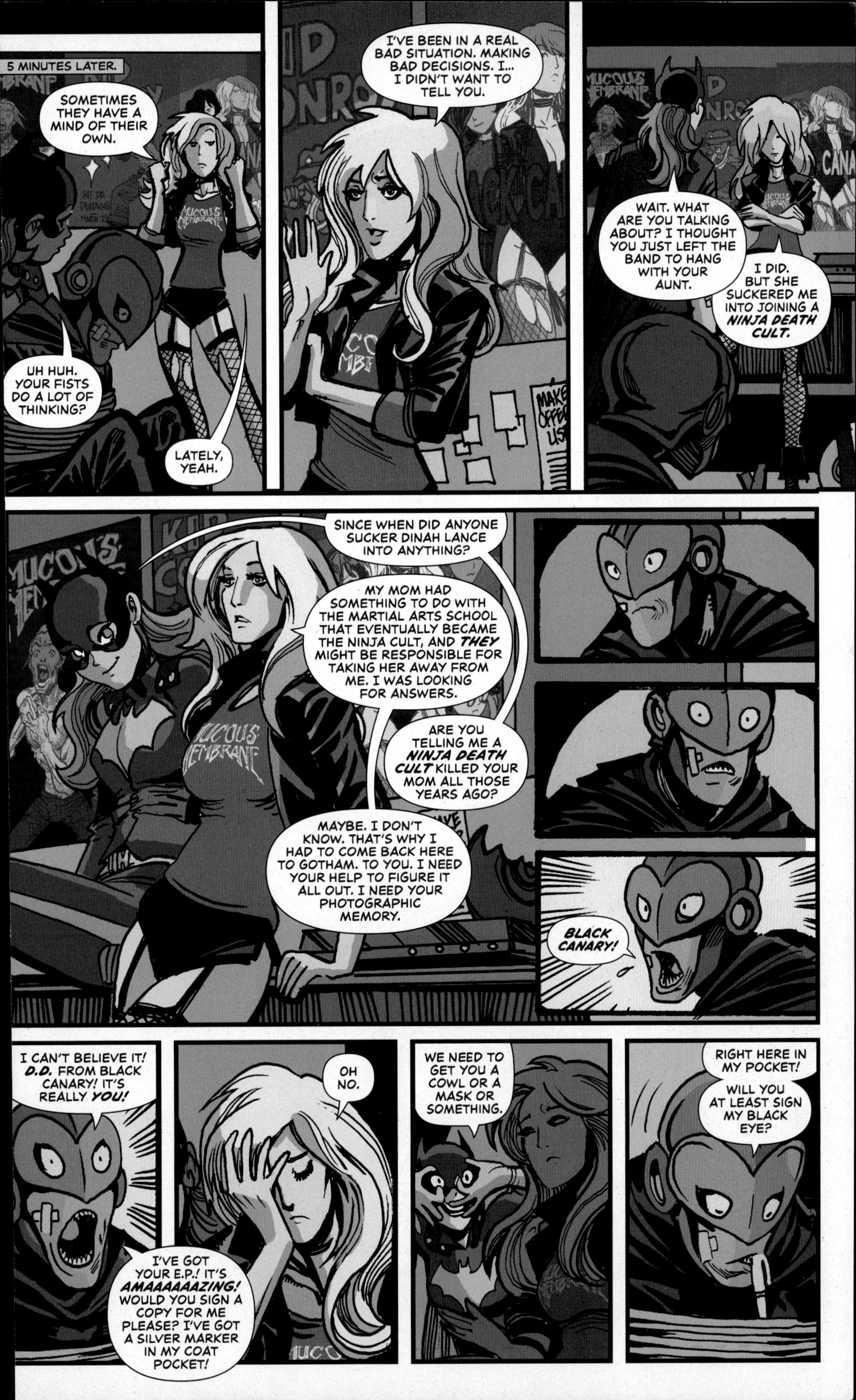
5 MINUTES LATER.
SOMETIMES THEY HAVE A MIND OF THEIR OWN.
UH HUH. YOUR FISTS DO A LOT OF THINKING?
LATELY, YEAH.
I'VE BEEN IN A REAL BAD SITUATION. MAKING BAD DECISIONS. I... I DIDN'T WANT TO TELL YOU.
WAIT. WHAT ARE YOU TALKING ABOUT? I THOUGHT YOU JUST LEFT THE BAND TO HANG WITH YOUR AUNT.
I DID. BUT SHE SUCKERED ME INTO JOINING A ***NINJA DEATH CULT.***
SINCE WHEN DID ANYONE SUCKER DINAH LANCE INTO ANYTHING?
MY MOM HAD SOMETHING TO DO WITH THE MARTIAL ARTS SCHOOL THAT EVENTUALLY BECAME THE NINJA CULT, AND ***THEY*** MIGHT BE RESPONSIBLE FOR TAKING HER AWAY FROM ME. I WAS LOOKING FOR ANSWERS.
ARE YOU TELLING ME A ***NINJA DEATH CULT*** KILLED YOUR MOM ALL THOSE YEARS AGO?
MAYBE. I DON'T KNOW. THAT'S WHY I HAD TO COME BACK HERE TO GOTHAM. TO YOU. I NEED YOUR HELP TO FIGURE IT ALL OUT. I NEED YOUR PHOTOGRAPHIC MEMORY.
BLACK CANARY!
I CAN'T BELIEVE IT! ***D.D.*** FROM BLACK CANARY! IT'S REALLY ***YOU!***
I'VE GOT YOUR E.P.! IT'S ***AMAAAAAAZING!*** WOULD YOU SIGN A COPY FOR ME PLEASE? I'VE GOT A SILVER MARKER IN MY COAT POCKET!
OH NO.
WE NEED TO GET YOU A COWL OR A MASK OR SOMETHING.
RIGHT HERE IN MY POCKET!
WILL YOU AT LEAST SIGN MY BLACK EYE?

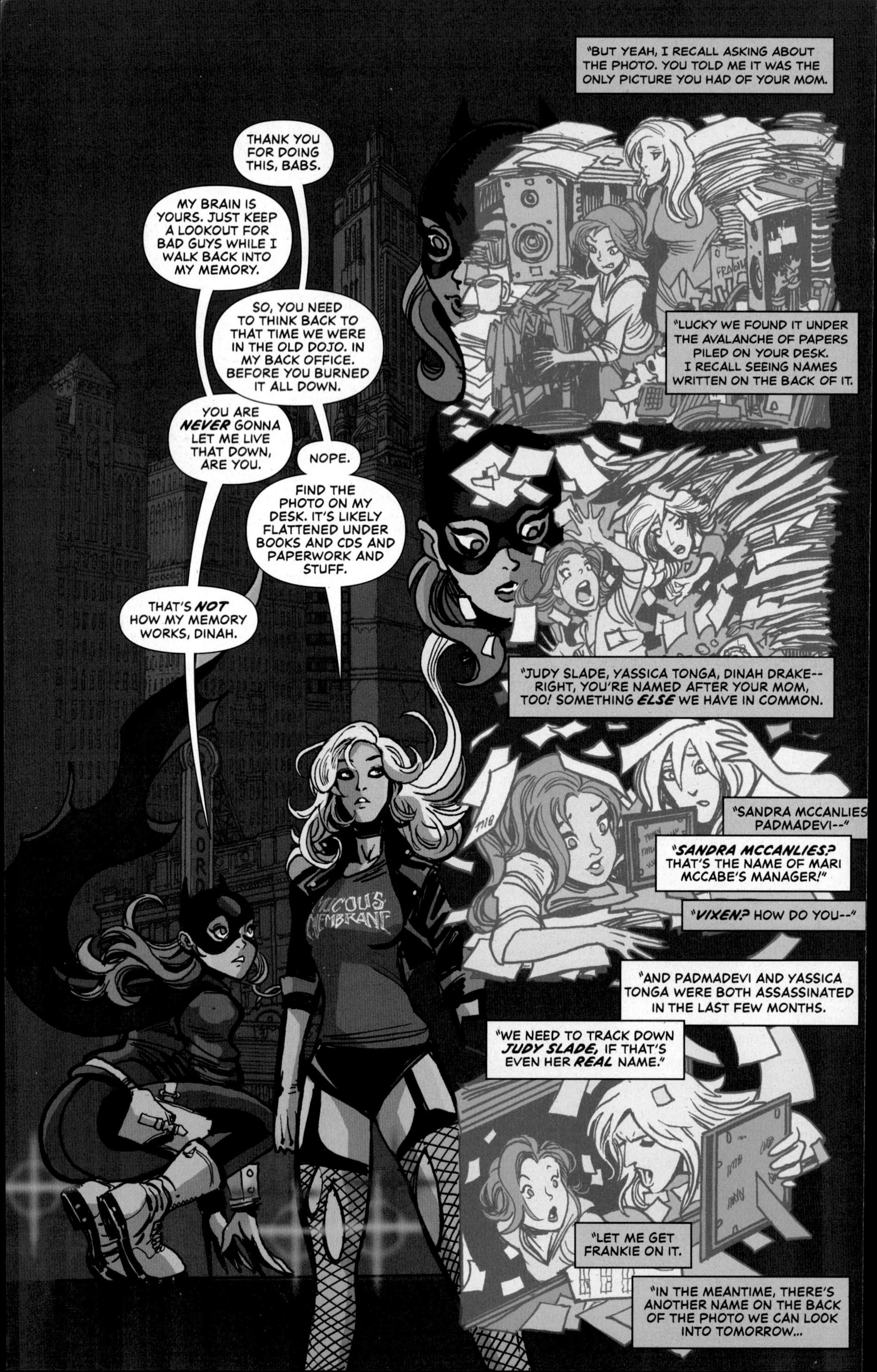
"BUT YEAH, I RECALL ASKING ABOUT THE PHOTO. YOU TOLD ME IT WAS THE ONLY PICTURE YOU HAD OF YOUR MOM.
THANK YOU FOR DOING THIS, BABS.
MY BRAIN IS YOURS. JUST KEEP A LOOKOUT FOR BAD GUYS WHILE I WALK BACK INTO MY MEMORY.
SO, YOU NEED TO THINK BACK TO THAT TIME WE WERE IN THE OLD DOJO. IN MY BACK OFFICE. BEFORE YOU BURNED IT ALL DOWN.
YOU ARE NEVER GONNA LET ME LIVE THAT DOWN, ARE YOU.
NOPE.
FIND THE PHOTO ON MY DESK. IT'S LIKELY FLATTENED UNDER BOOKS AND CDS AND PAPERWORK AND STUFF.
THAT'S NOT HOW MY MEMORY WORKS, DINAH.
"LUCKY WE FOUND IT UNDER THE AVALANCHE OF PAPERS PILED ON YOUR DESK. I RECALL SEEING NAMES WRITTEN ON THE BACK OF IT.
"JUDY SLADE, YASSICA TONGA, DINAH DRAKE--RIGHT, YOU'RE NAMED AFTER YOUR MOM, TOO! SOMETHING ELSE WE HAVE IN COMMON.
"SANDRA MCCANLIES, PADMADEVI--"
"SANDRA MCCANLIES? THAT'S THE NAME OF MARI MCCABE'S MANAGER!"
"VIXEN? HOW DO YOU--"
"AND PADMADEVI AND YASSICA TONGA WERE BOTH ASSASSINATED IN THE LAST FEW MONTHS.
"WE NEED TO TRACK DOWN JUDY SLADE, IF THAT'S EVEN HER REAL NAME."
"LET ME GET FRANKIE ON IT.
"IN THE MEANTIME, THERE'S ANOTHER NAME ON THE BACK OF THE PHOTO WE CAN LOOK INTO TOMORROW...

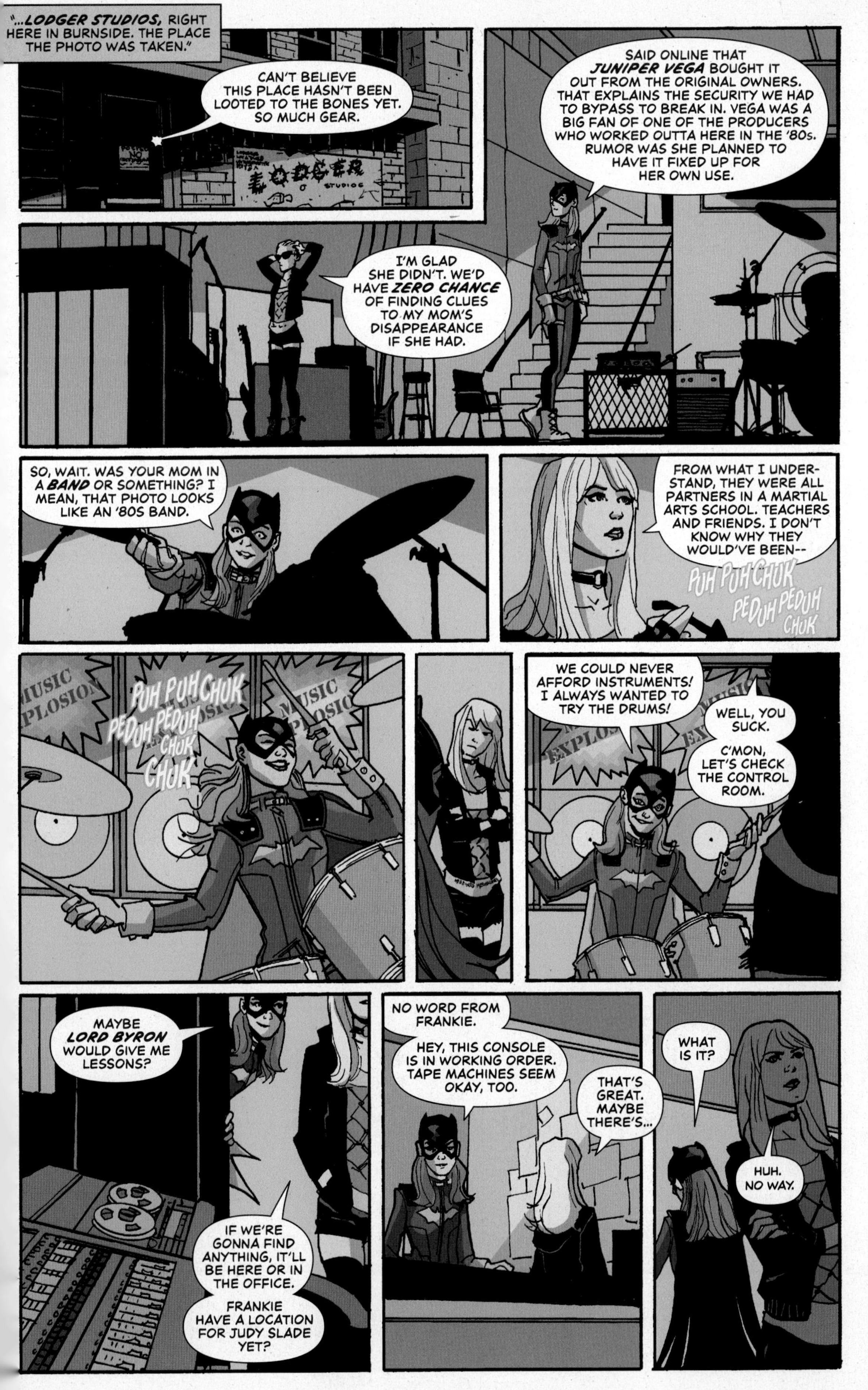
"...LODGER STUDIOS, RIGHT HERE IN BURNSIDE. THE PLACE THE PHOTO WAS TAKEN."
CAN'T BELIEVE THIS PLACE HASN'T BEEN LOOTED TO THE BONES YET. SO MUCH GEAR.
SAID ONLINE THAT JUNIPER VEGA BOUGHT IT OUT FROM THE ORIGINAL OWNERS. THAT EXPLAINS THE SECURITY WE HAD TO BYPASS TO BREAK IN. VEGA WAS A BIG FAN OF ONE OF THE PRODUCERS WHO WORKED OUTTA HERE IN THE '80s. RUMOR WAS SHE PLANNED TO HAVE IT FIXED UP FOR HER OWN USE.
I'M GLAD SHE DIDN'T. WE'D HAVE ZERO CHANCE OF FINDING CLUES TO MY MOM'S DISAPPEARANCE IF SHE HAD.
SO, WAIT. WAS YOUR MOM IN A BAND OR SOMETHING? I MEAN, THAT PHOTO LOOKS LIKE AN '80S BAND.
FROM WHAT I UNDERSTAND, THEY WERE ALL PARTNERS IN A MARTIAL ARTS SCHOOL. TEACHERS AND FRIENDS. I DON'T KNOW WHY THEY WOULD'VE BEEN--
PUH PUH CHUK PEDUH PEDUH CHUK
MUSIC EXPLOSION
PUH PUH CHUK PEDUH PEDUH CHUK CHUK
WE COULD NEVER AFFORD INSTRUMENTS! I ALWAYS WANTED TO TRY THE DRUMS!
WELL, YOU SUCK.
C'MON, LET'S CHECK THE CONTROL ROOM.
MAYBE LORD BYRON WOULD GIVE ME LESSONS?
IF WE'RE GONNA FIND ANYTHING, IT'LL BE HERE OR IN THE OFFICE.
FRANKIE HAVE A LOCATION FOR JUDY SLADE YET?
NO WORD FROM FRANKIE.
HEY, THIS CONSOLE IS IN WORKING ORDER. TAPE MACHINES SEEM OKAY, TOO.
THAT'S GREAT. MAYBE THERE'S...
WHAT IS IT?
HUH. NO WAY.

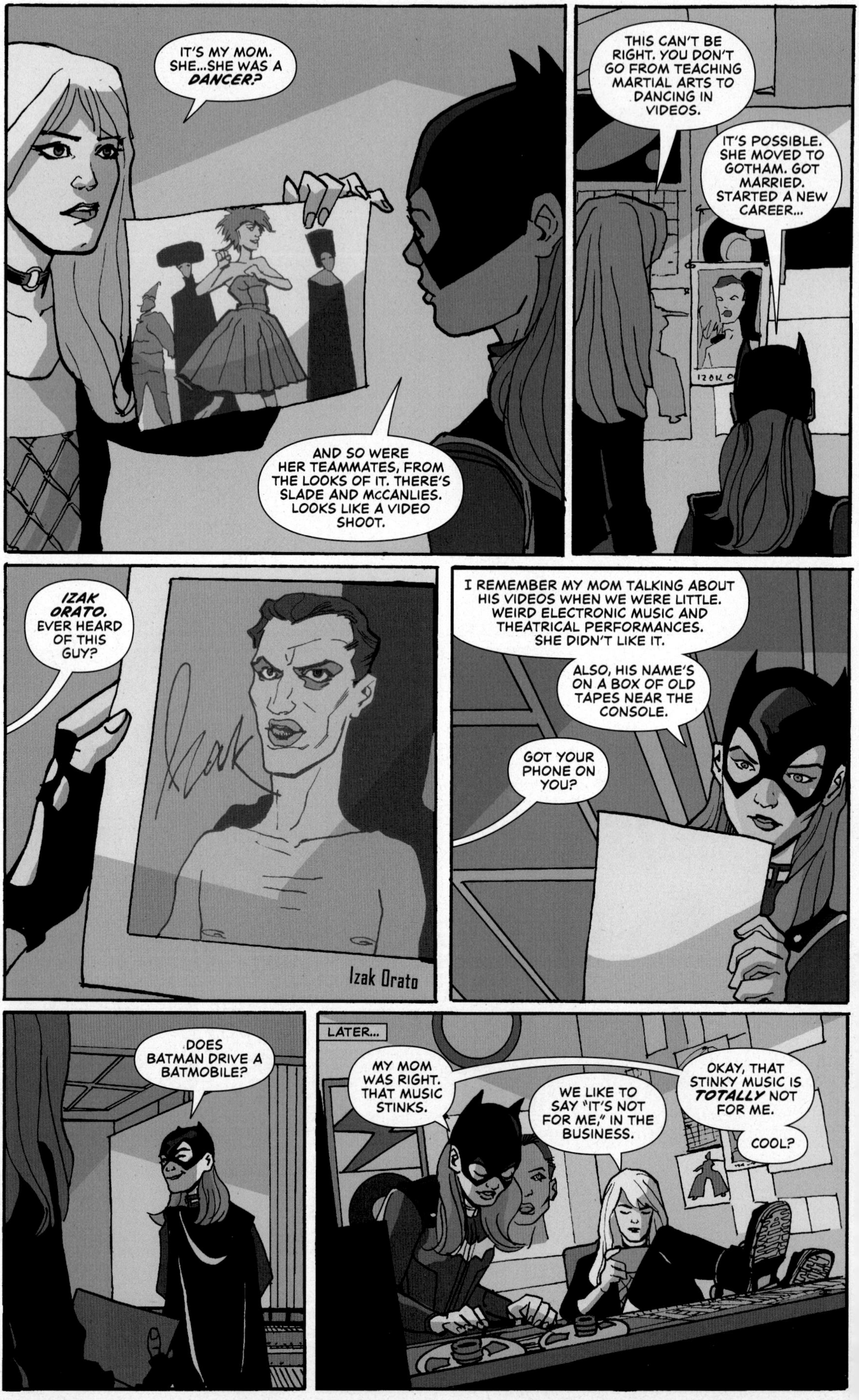
IT'S MY MOM. SHE...SHE WAS A DANCER?
AND SO WERE HER TEAMMATES, FROM THE LOOKS OF IT. THERE'S SLADE AND McCANLIES. LOOKS LIKE A VIDEO SHOOT.
THIS CAN'T BE RIGHT. YOU DON'T GO FROM TEACHING MARTIAL ARTS TO DANCING IN VIDEOS.
IT'S POSSIBLE. SHE MOVED TO GOTHAM. GOT MARRIED. STARTED A NEW CAREER...
IZAK ORATO. EVER HEARD OF THIS GUY?
Izak Orato
I REMEMBER MY MOM TALKING ABOUT HIS VIDEOS WHEN WE WERE LITTLE. WEIRD ELECTRONIC MUSIC AND THEATRICAL PERFORMANCES. SHE DIDN'T LIKE IT.
ALSO, HIS NAME'S ON A BOX OF OLD TAPES NEAR THE CONSOLE.
GOT YOUR PHONE ON YOU?
DOES BATMAN DRIVE A BATMOBILE?
LATER...
MY MOM WAS RIGHT. THAT MUSIC STINKS.
WE LIKE TO SAY "IT'S NOT FOR ME," IN THE BUSINESS.
OKAY, THAT STINKY MUSIC IS TOTALLY NOT FOR ME.
COOL?

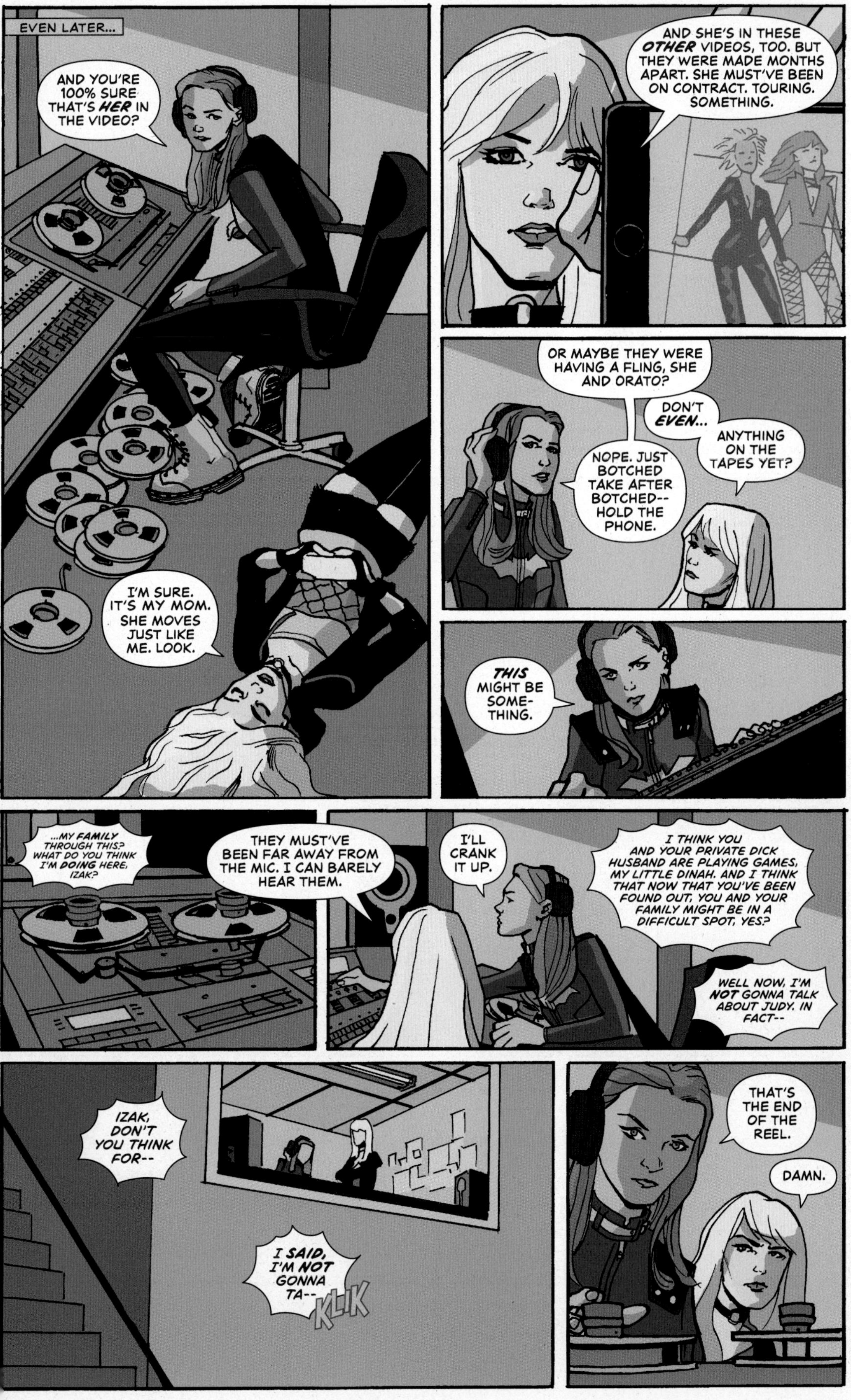

EVEN LATER...
AND YOU'RE 100% SURE THAT'S HER IN THE VIDEO?
I'M SURE. IT'S MY MOM. SHE MOVES JUST LIKE ME. LOOK.
AND SHE'S IN THESE OTHER VIDEOS, TOO. BUT THEY WERE MADE MONTHS APART. SHE MUST'VE BEEN ON CONTRACT. TOURING. SOMETHING.
OR MAYBE THEY WERE HAVING A FLING, SHE AND ORATO?
DON'T EVEN...
ANYTHING ON THE TAPES YET?
NOPE. JUST BOTCHED TAKE AFTER BOTCHED-- HOLD THE PHONE.
THIS MIGHT BE SOME-THING.
...MY FAMILY THROUGH THIS? WHAT DO YOU THINK I'M DOING HERE, IZAK?
THEY MUST'VE BEEN FAR AWAY FROM THE MIC. I CAN BARELY HEAR THEM.
I'LL CRANK IT UP.
I THINK YOU AND YOUR PRIVATE DICK HUSBAND ARE PLAYING GAMES, MY LITTLE DINAH. AND I THINK THAT NOW THAT YOU'VE BEEN FOUND OUT, YOU AND YOUR FAMILY MIGHT BE IN A DIFFICULT SPOT, YES?
WELL NOW, I'M NOT GONNA TALK ABOUT JUDY. IN FACT--
IZAK, DON'T YOU THINK FOR--
I SAID, I'M NOT GONNA TA--
KLIK
THAT'S THE END OF THE REEL.
DAMN.

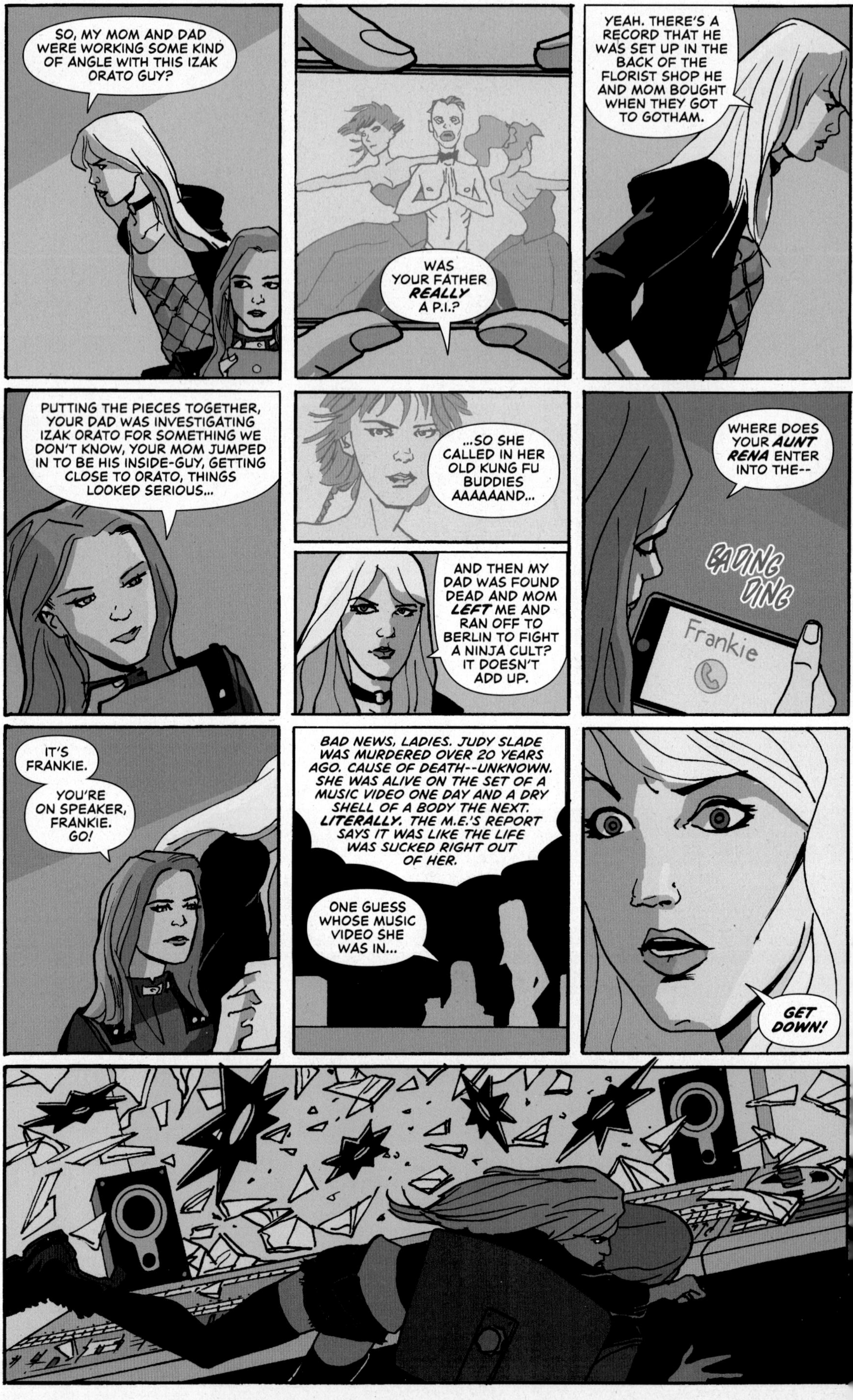

SO, MY MOM AND DAD WERE WORKING SOME KIND OF ANGLE WITH THIS IZAK ORATO GUY?
WAS YOUR FATHER REALLY A P.I.?
YEAH. THERE'S A RECORD THAT HE WAS SET UP IN THE BACK OF THE FLORIST SHOP HE AND MOM BOUGHT WHEN THEY GOT TO GOTHAM.
PUTTING THE PIECES TOGETHER, YOUR DAD WAS INVESTIGATING IZAK ORATO FOR SOMETHING WE DON'T KNOW, YOUR MOM JUMPED IN TO BE HIS INSIDE-GUY, GETTING CLOSE TO ORATO, THINGS LOOKED SERIOUS...
...SO SHE CALLED IN HER OLD KUNG FU BUDDIES AAAAAAND...
AND THEN MY DAD WAS FOUND DEAD AND MOM LEFT ME AND RAN OFF TO BERLIN TO FIGHT A NINJA CULT? IT DOESN'T ADD UP.
WHERE DOES YOUR AUNT RENA ENTER INTO THE--
BADING DING
Frankie
IT'S FRANKIE.
YOU'RE ON SPEAKER, FRANKIE. GO!
BAD NEWS, LADIES. JUDY SLADE WAS MURDERED OVER 20 YEARS AGO. CAUSE OF DEATH--UNKNOWN. SHE WAS ALIVE ON THE SET OF A MUSIC VIDEO ONE DAY AND A DRY SHELL OF A BODY THE NEXT. LITERALLY. THE M.E.'S REPORT SAYS IT WAS LIKE THE LIFE WAS SUCKED RIGHT OUT OF HER.
ONE GUESS WHOSE MUSIC VIDEO SHE WAS IN...
GET DOWN!

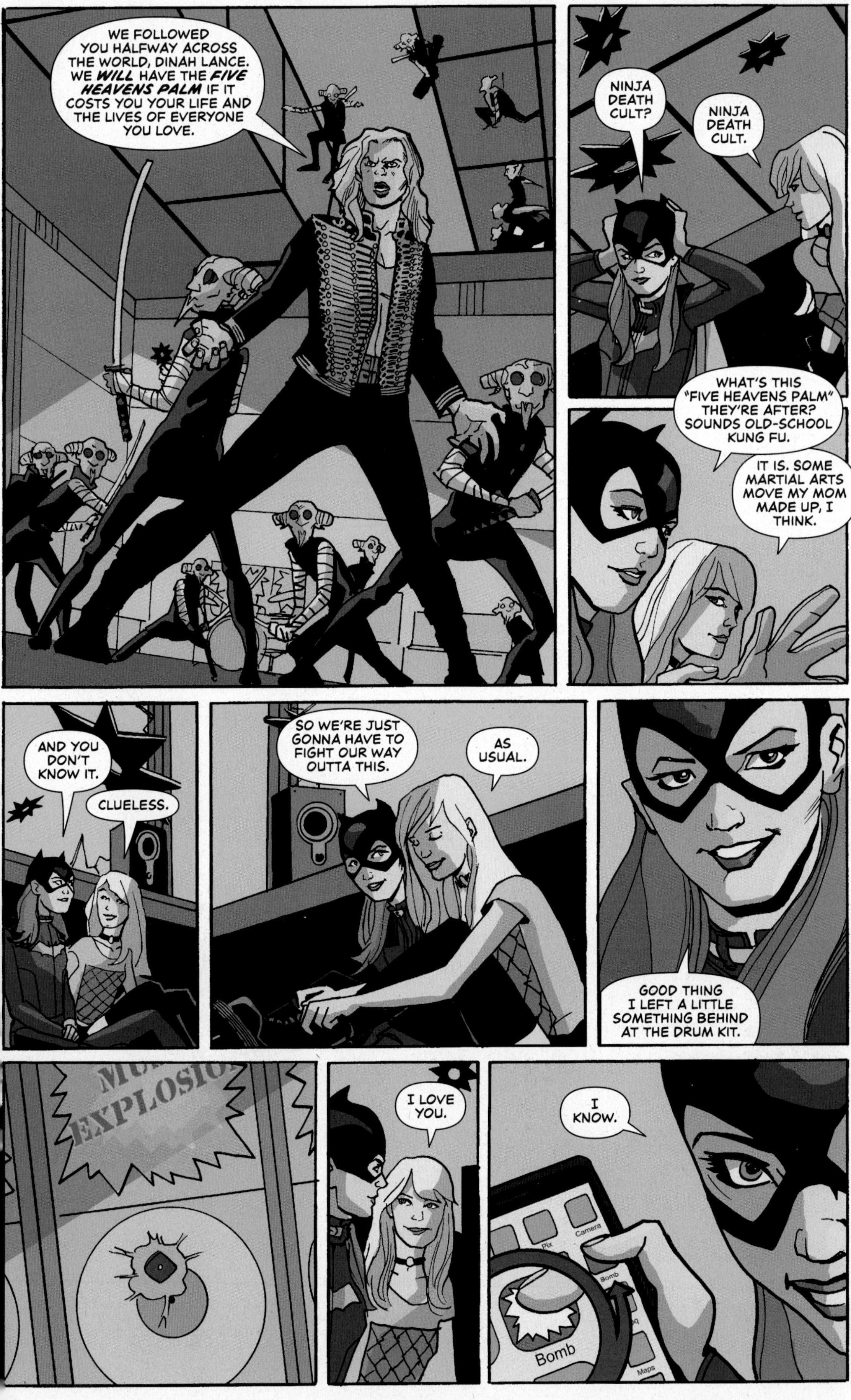
WE FOLLOWED YOU HALFWAY ACROSS THE WORLD, DINAH LANCE. WE *WILL* HAVE THE *FIVE HEAVENS PALM* IF IT COSTS YOU YOUR LIFE AND THE LIVES OF EVERYONE YOU LOVE.
NINJA DEATH CULT?
NINJA DEATH CULT.
WHAT'S THIS "FIVE HEAVENS PALM" THEY'RE AFTER? SOUNDS OLD-SCHOOL KUNG FU.
IT IS. SOME MARTIAL ARTS MOVE MY MOM MADE UP, I THINK.
AND YOU DON'T KNOW IT.
CLUELESS.
SO WE'RE JUST GONNA HAVE TO FIGHT OUR WAY OUTTA THIS.
AS USUAL.
GOOD THING I LEFT A LITTLE SOMETHING BEHIND AT THE DRUM KIT.
EXPLOSION
I LOVE YOU.
I KNOW.
Pix
Camera
Bomb
Bomb
Maps

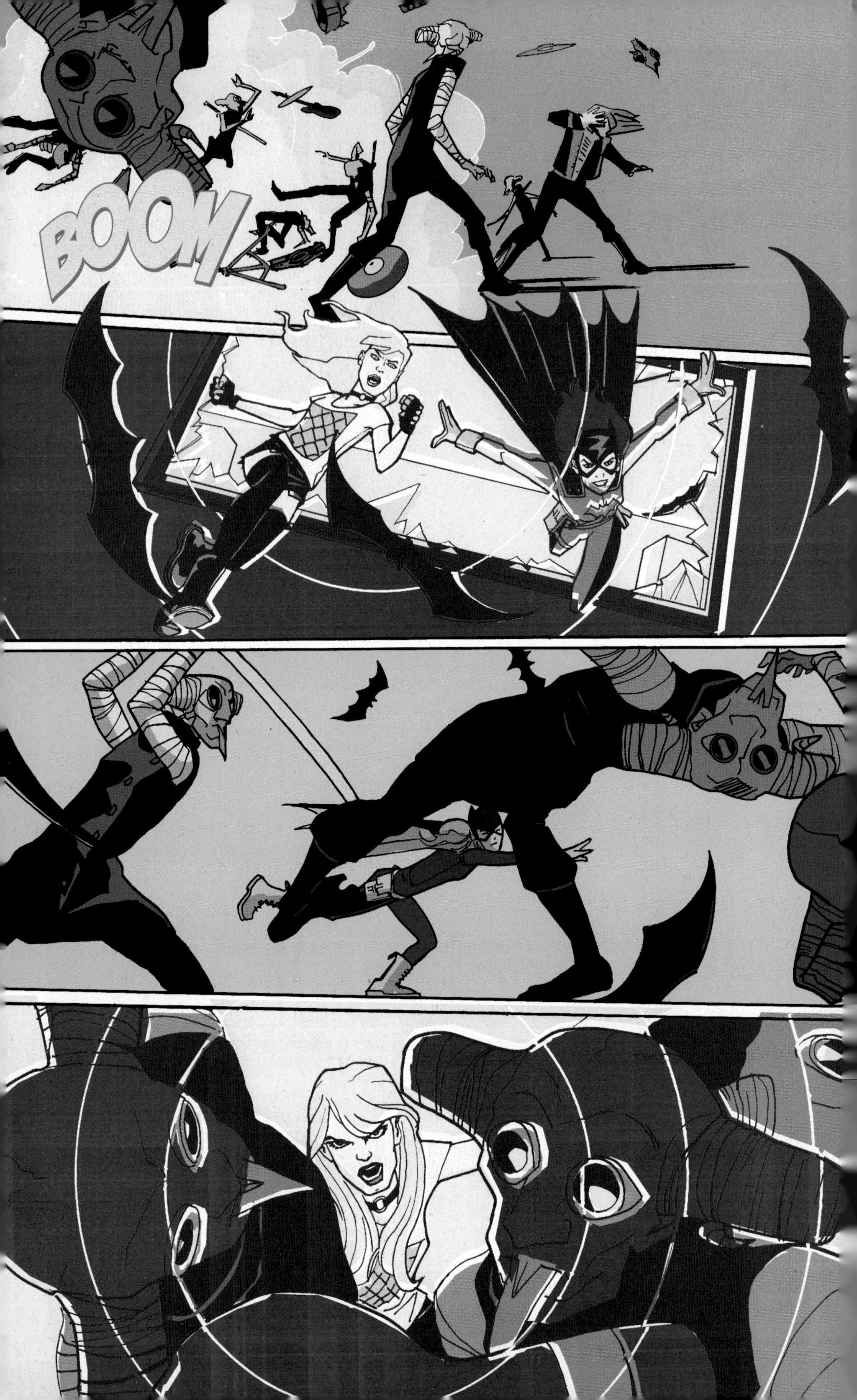
BOOM

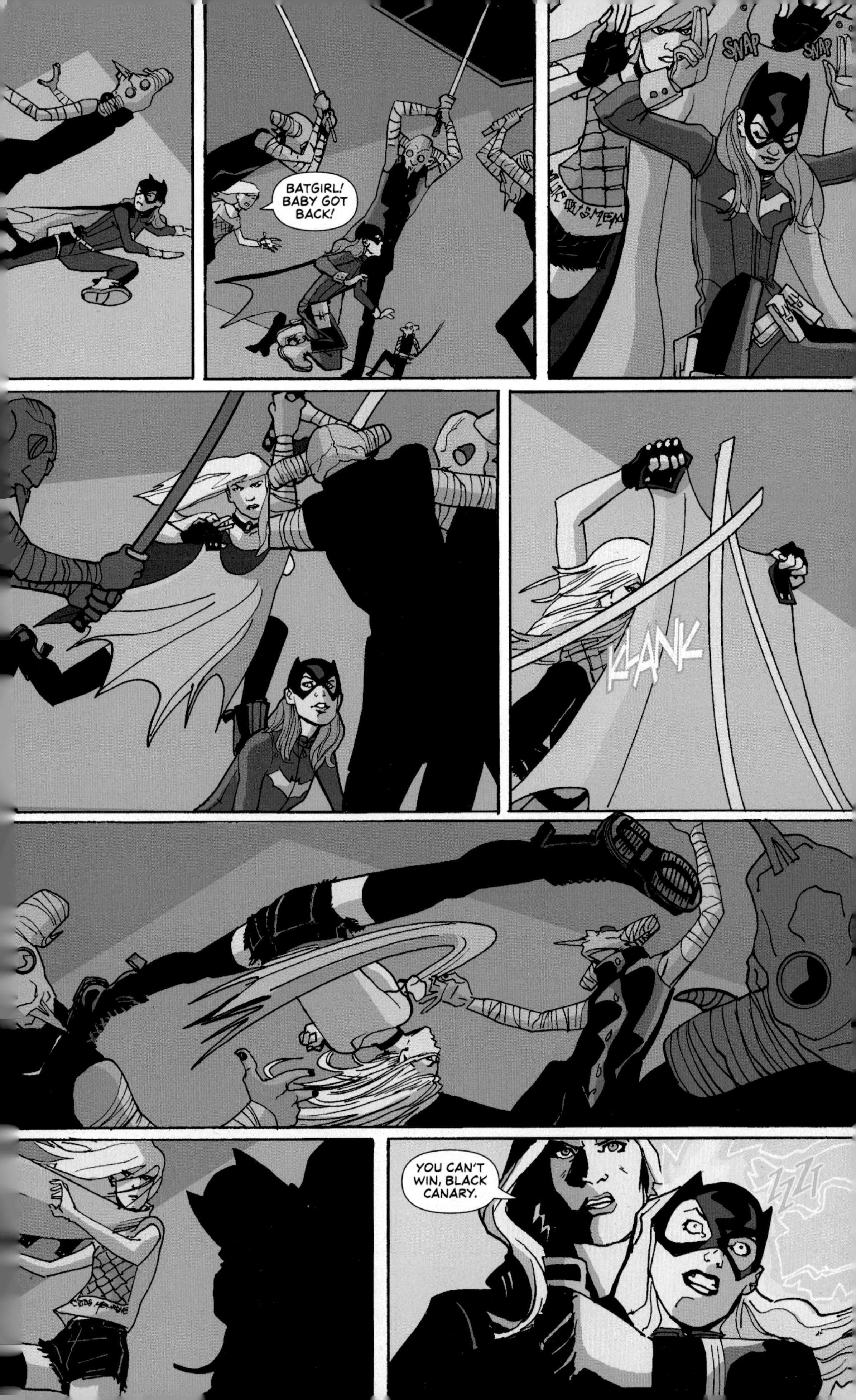
BATGIRL! BABY GOT BACK!
SNAP
SNAP
KLANK
YOU CAN'T WIN, BLACK CANARY.
ZZZT

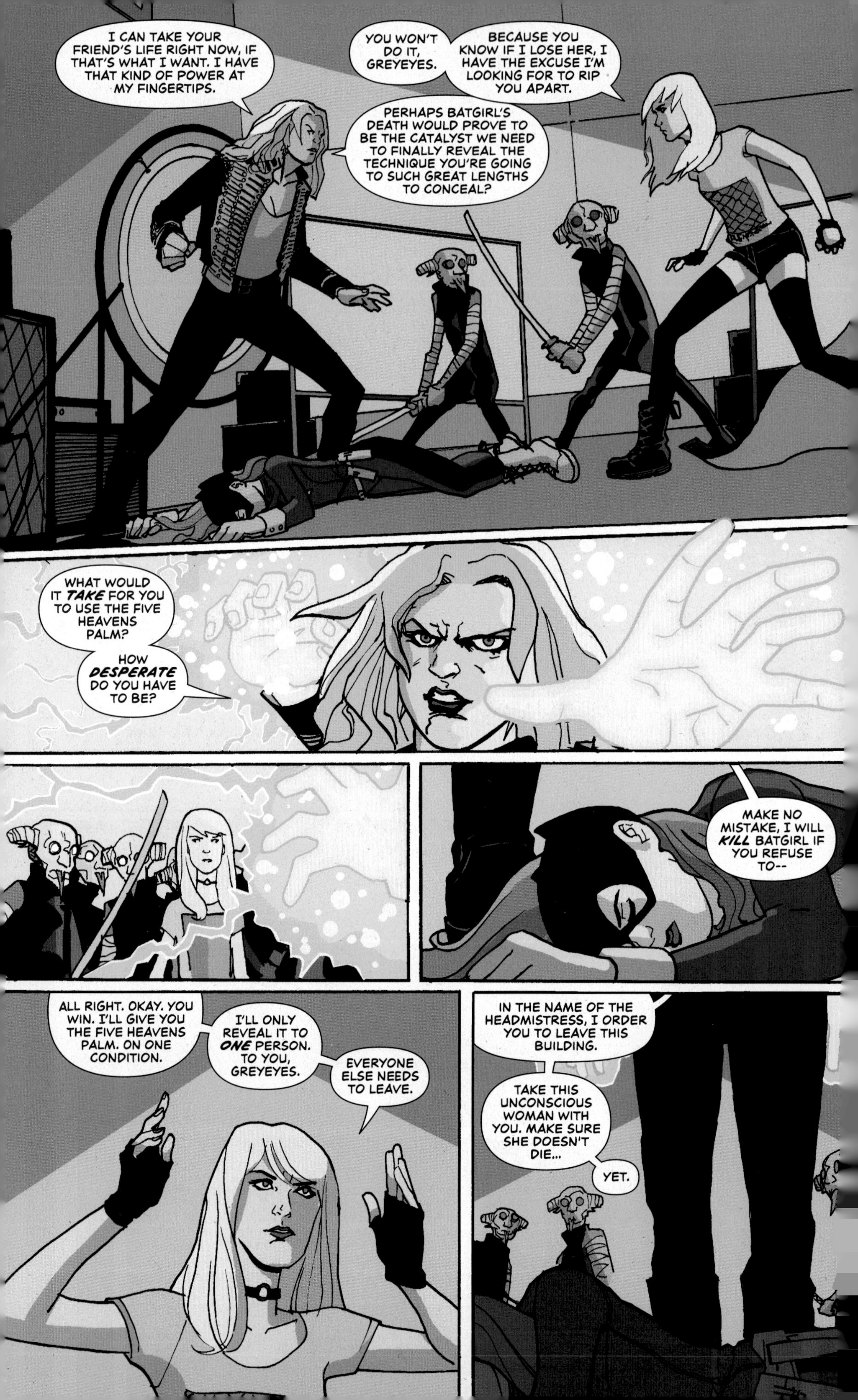
I CAN TAKE YOUR FRIEND'S LIFE RIGHT NOW, IF THAT'S WHAT I WANT. I HAVE THAT KIND OF POWER AT MY FINGERTIPS.
YOU WON'T DO IT, GREYEYES.
BECAUSE YOU KNOW IF I LOSE HER, I HAVE THE EXCUSE I'M LOOKING FOR TO RIP YOU APART.
PERHAPS BATGIRL'S DEATH WOULD PROVE TO BE THE CATALYST WE NEED TO FINALLY REVEAL THE TECHNIQUE YOU'RE GOING TO SUCH GREAT LENGTHS TO CONCEAL?
WHAT WOULD IT *TAKE* FOR YOU TO USE THE FIVE HEAVENS PALM?
HOW *DESPERATE* DO YOU HAVE TO BE?
MAKE NO MISTAKE, I WILL *KILL* BATGIRL IF YOU REFUSE TO--
ALL RIGHT. OKAY. YOU WIN. I'LL GIVE YOU THE FIVE HEAVENS PALM. ON ONE CONDITION.
I'LL ONLY REVEAL IT TO *ONE* PERSON. TO YOU, GREYEYES.
EVERYONE ELSE NEEDS TO LEAVE.
IN THE NAME OF THE HEADMISTRESS, I ORDER YOU TO LEAVE THIS BUILDING.
TAKE THIS UNCONSCIOUS WOMAN WITH YOU. MAKE SURE SHE DOESN'T DIE...
YET.

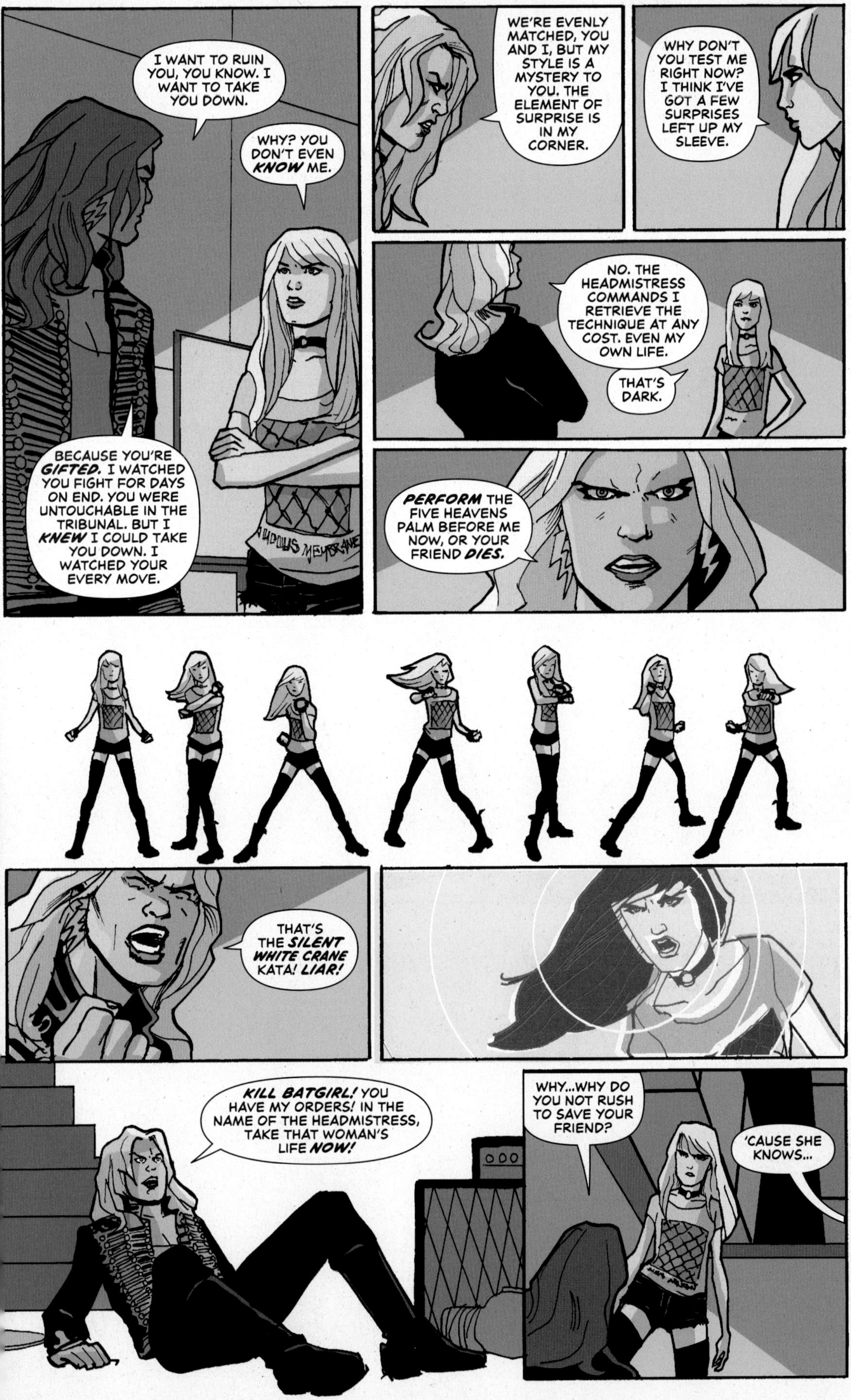
I WANT TO RUIN YOU, YOU KNOW. I WANT TO TAKE YOU DOWN.
WHY? YOU DON'T EVEN KNOW ME.
BECAUSE YOU'RE GIFTED. I WATCHED YOU FIGHT FOR DAYS ON END. YOU WERE UNTOUCHABLE IN THE TRIBUNAL. BUT I KNEW I COULD TAKE YOU DOWN. I WATCHED YOUR EVERY MOVE.
WE'RE EVENLY MATCHED, YOU AND I, BUT MY STYLE IS A MYSTERY TO YOU. THE ELEMENT OF SURPRISE IS IN MY CORNER.
WHY DON'T YOU TEST ME RIGHT NOW? I THINK I'VE GOT A FEW SURPRISES LEFT UP MY SLEEVE.
NO. THE HEADMISTRESS COMMANDS I RETRIEVE THE TECHNIQUE AT ANY COST. EVEN MY OWN LIFE.
THAT'S DARK.
PERFORM THE FIVE HEAVENS PALM BEFORE ME NOW, OR YOUR FRIEND DIES.
THAT'S THE SILENT WHITE CRANE KATA! LIAR!
KILL BATGIRL! YOU HAVE MY ORDERS! IN THE NAME OF THE HEADMISTRESS, TAKE THAT WOMAN'S LIFE NOW!
WHY...WHY DO YOU NOT RUSH TO SAVE YOUR FRIEND?
'CAUSE SHE KNOWS...

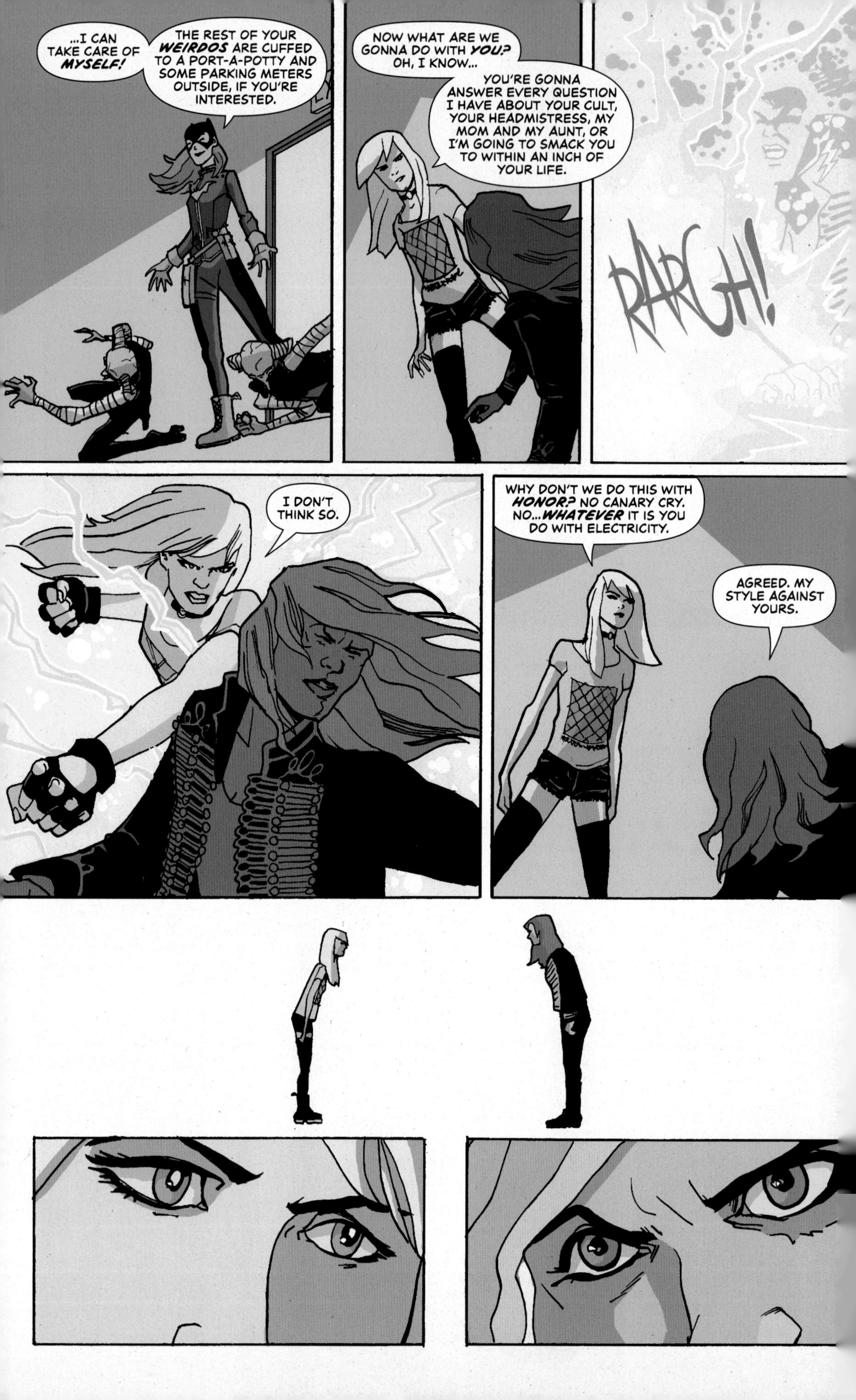
...I CAN TAKE CARE OF *MYSELF!*
THE REST OF YOUR *WEIRDOS* ARE CUFFED TO A PORT-A-POTTY AND SOME PARKING METERS OUTSIDE, IF YOU'RE INTERESTED.
NOW WHAT ARE WE GONNA DO WITH *YOU?* OH, I KNOW...
YOU'RE GONNA ANSWER EVERY QUESTION I HAVE ABOUT YOUR CULT, YOUR HEADMISTRESS, MY MOM AND MY AUNT, OR I'M GOING TO SMACK YOU TO WITHIN AN INCH OF YOUR LIFE.
RARGH!
I DON'T THINK SO.
WHY DON'T WE DO THIS WITH *HONOR?* NO CANARY CRY. NO...*WHATEVER* IT IS YOU DO WITH ELECTRICITY.
AGREED. MY STYLE AGAINST YOURS.

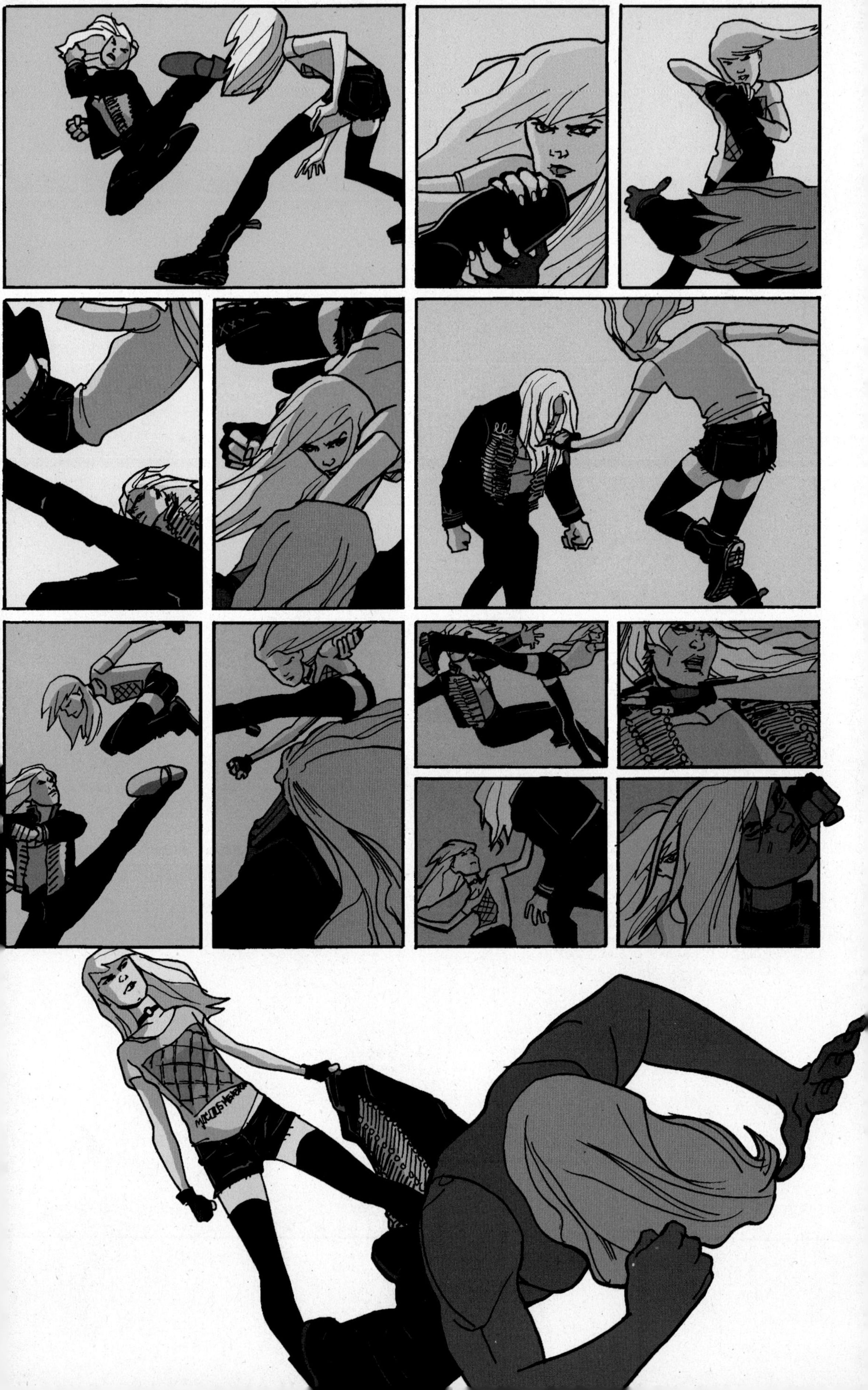

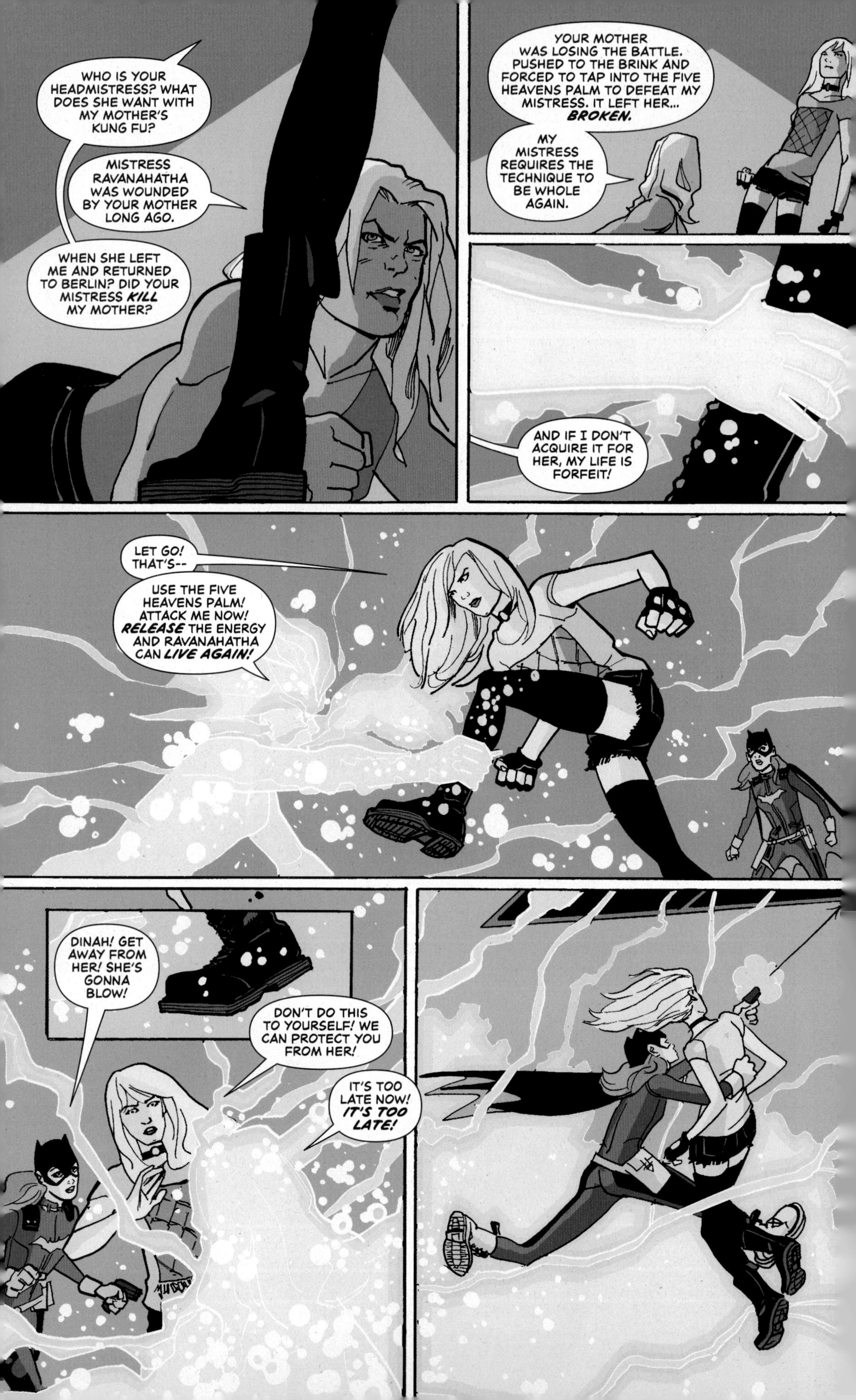
WHO IS YOUR HEADMISTRESS? WHAT DOES SHE WANT WITH MY MOTHER'S KUNG FU?
MISTRESS RAVANAHATHA WAS WOUNDED BY YOUR MOTHER LONG AGO.
WHEN SHE LEFT ME AND RETURNED TO BERLIN? DID YOUR MISTRESS *KILL* MY MOTHER?
YOUR MOTHER WAS LOSING THE BATTLE. PUSHED TO THE BRINK AND FORCED TO TAP INTO THE FIVE HEAVENS PALM TO DEFEAT MY MISTRESS. IT LEFT HER... ***BROKEN.***
MY MISTRESS REQUIRES THE TECHNIQUE TO BE WHOLE AGAIN.
AND IF I DON'T ACQUIRE IT FOR HER, MY LIFE IS FORFEIT!
LET GO! THAT'S--
USE THE FIVE HEAVENS PALM! ATTACK ME NOW! ***RELEASE*** THE ENERGY AND RAVANAHATHA CAN ***LIVE AGAIN!***
DINAH! GET AWAY FROM HER! SHE'S GONNA BLOW!
DON'T DO THIS TO YOURSELF! WE CAN PROTECT YOU FROM HER!
IT'S TOO LATE NOW! ***IT'S TOO LATE!***

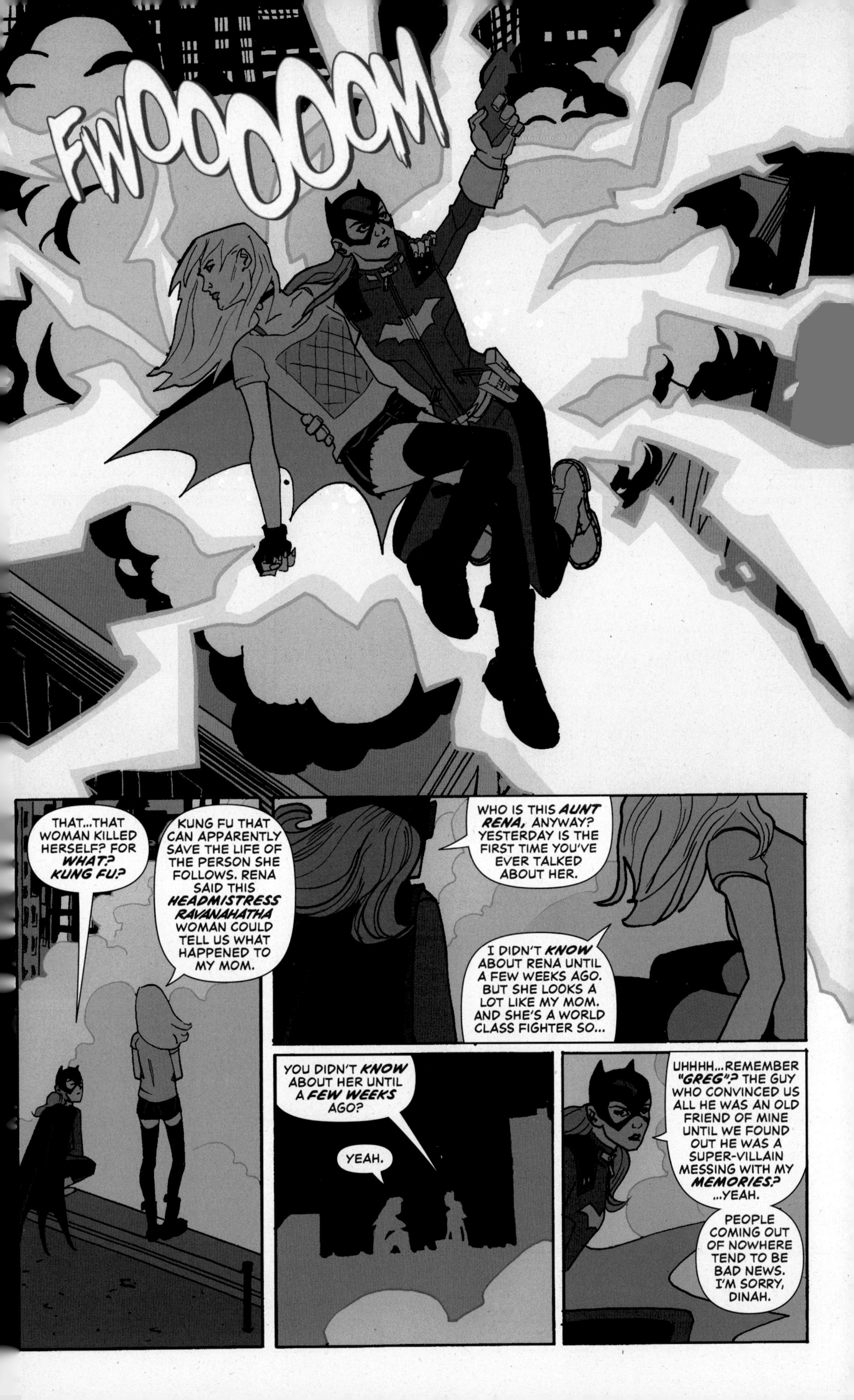
FWOOOOOM
THAT...THAT WOMAN KILLED HERSELF? FOR WHAT? KUNG FU?
KUNG FU THAT CAN APPARENTLY SAVE THE LIFE OF THE PERSON SHE FOLLOWS. RENA SAID THIS HEADMISTRESS RAVANAHATHA WOMAN COULD TELL US WHAT HAPPENED TO MY MOM.
WHO IS THIS AUNT RENA, ANYWAY? YESTERDAY IS THE FIRST TIME YOU'VE EVER TALKED ABOUT HER.
I DIDN'T KNOW ABOUT RENA UNTIL A FEW WEEKS AGO. BUT SHE LOOKS A LOT LIKE MY MOM. AND SHE'S A WORLD CLASS FIGHTER SO...
YOU DIDN'T KNOW ABOUT HER UNTIL A FEW WEEKS AGO?
YEAH.
UHHHH...REMEMBER "GREG"? THE GUY WHO CONVINCED US ALL HE WAS AN OLD FRIEND OF MINE UNTIL WE FOUND OUT HE WAS A SUPER-VILLAIN MESSING WITH MY MEMORIES? ...YEAH.
PEOPLE COMING OUT OF NOWHERE TEND TO BE BAD NEWS. I'M SORRY, DINAH.

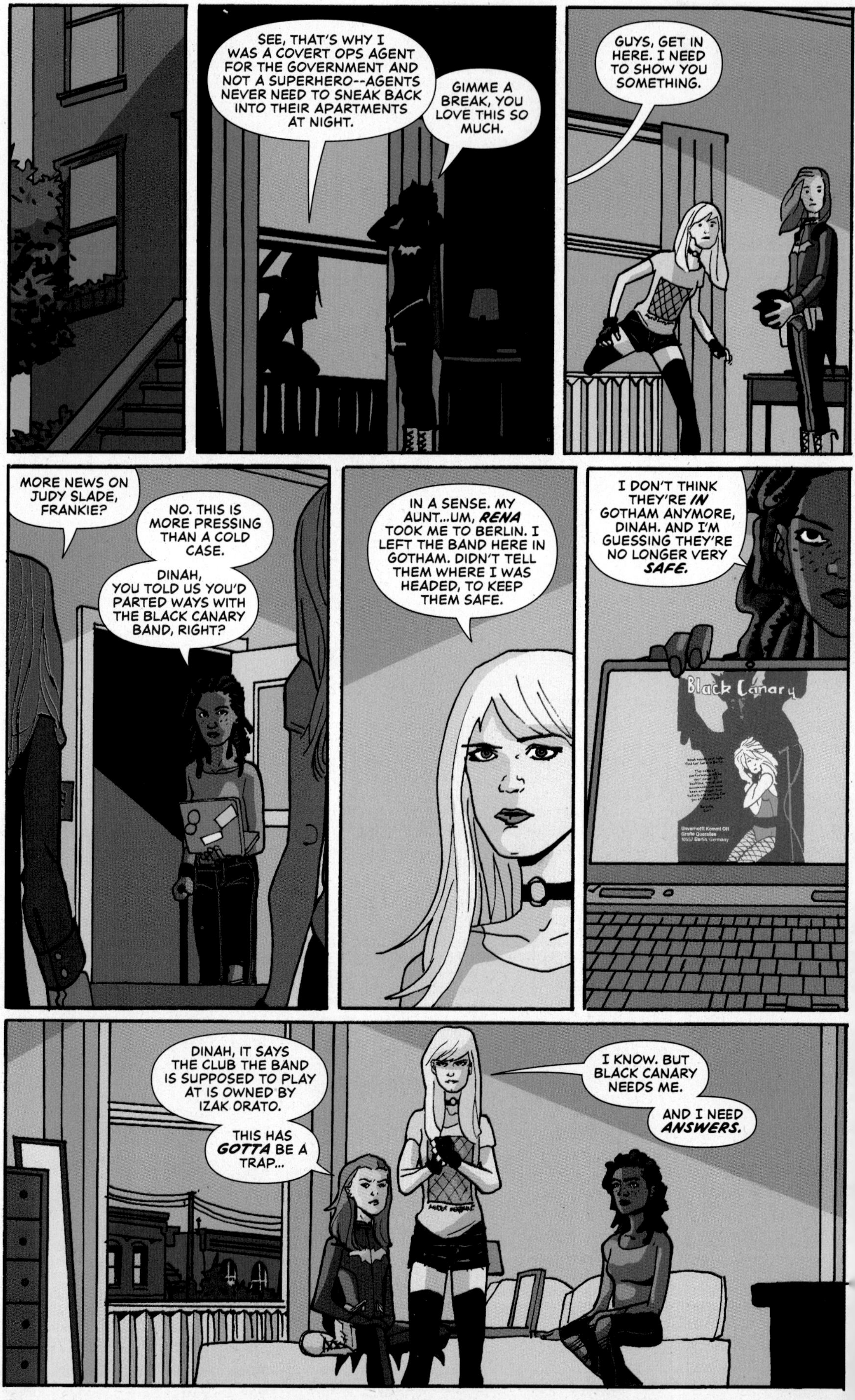
SEE, THAT'S WHY I WAS A COVERT OPS AGENT FOR THE GOVERNMENT AND NOT A SUPERHERO--AGENTS NEVER NEED TO SNEAK BACK INTO THEIR APARTMENTS AT NIGHT.
GIMME A BREAK, YOU LOVE THIS SO MUCH.
GUYS, GET IN HERE. I NEED TO SHOW YOU SOMETHING.
MORE NEWS ON JUDY SLADE, FRANKIE?
NO. THIS IS MORE PRESSING THAN A COLD CASE.
DINAH, YOU TOLD US YOU'D PARTED WAYS WITH THE BLACK CANARY BAND, RIGHT?
IN A SENSE. MY AUNT...UM, ***RENA*** TOOK ME TO BERLIN. I LEFT THE BAND HERE IN GOTHAM. DIDN'T TELL THEM WHERE I WAS HEADED, TO KEEP THEM SAFE.
I DON'T THINK THEY'RE ***IN*** GOTHAM ANYMORE, DINAH. AND I'M GUESSING THEY'RE NO LONGER VERY ***SAFE.***
Black Canary
Unverhofft Kommt Oft
Große Querallee
10557 Berlin, Germany
DINAH, IT SAYS THE CLUB THE BAND IS SUPPOSED TO PLAY AT IS OWNED BY IZAK ORATO.
THIS HAS ***GOTTA*** BE A TRAP...
I KNOW. BUT BLACK CANARY NEEDS ME.
AND I NEED ***ANSWERS.***

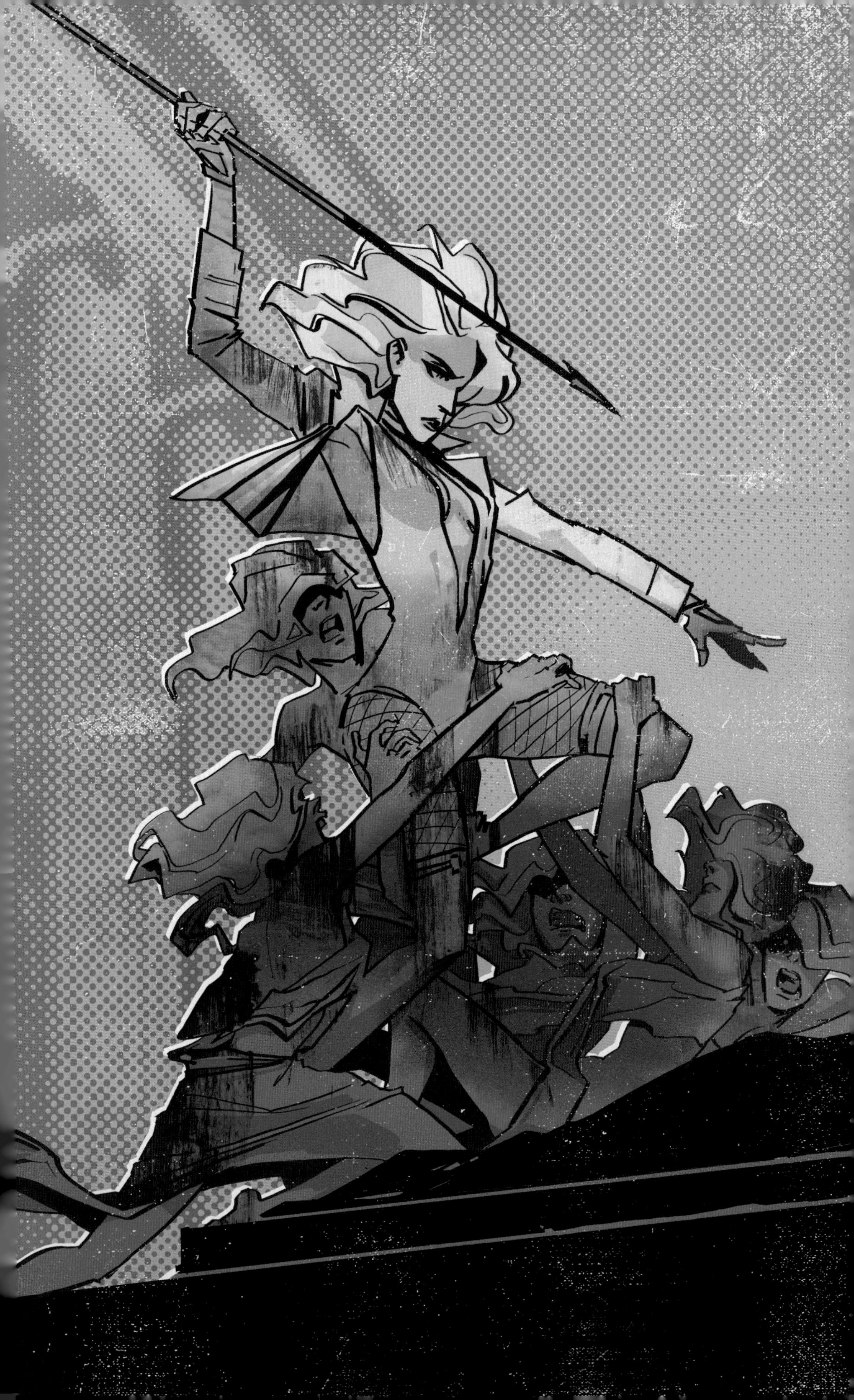

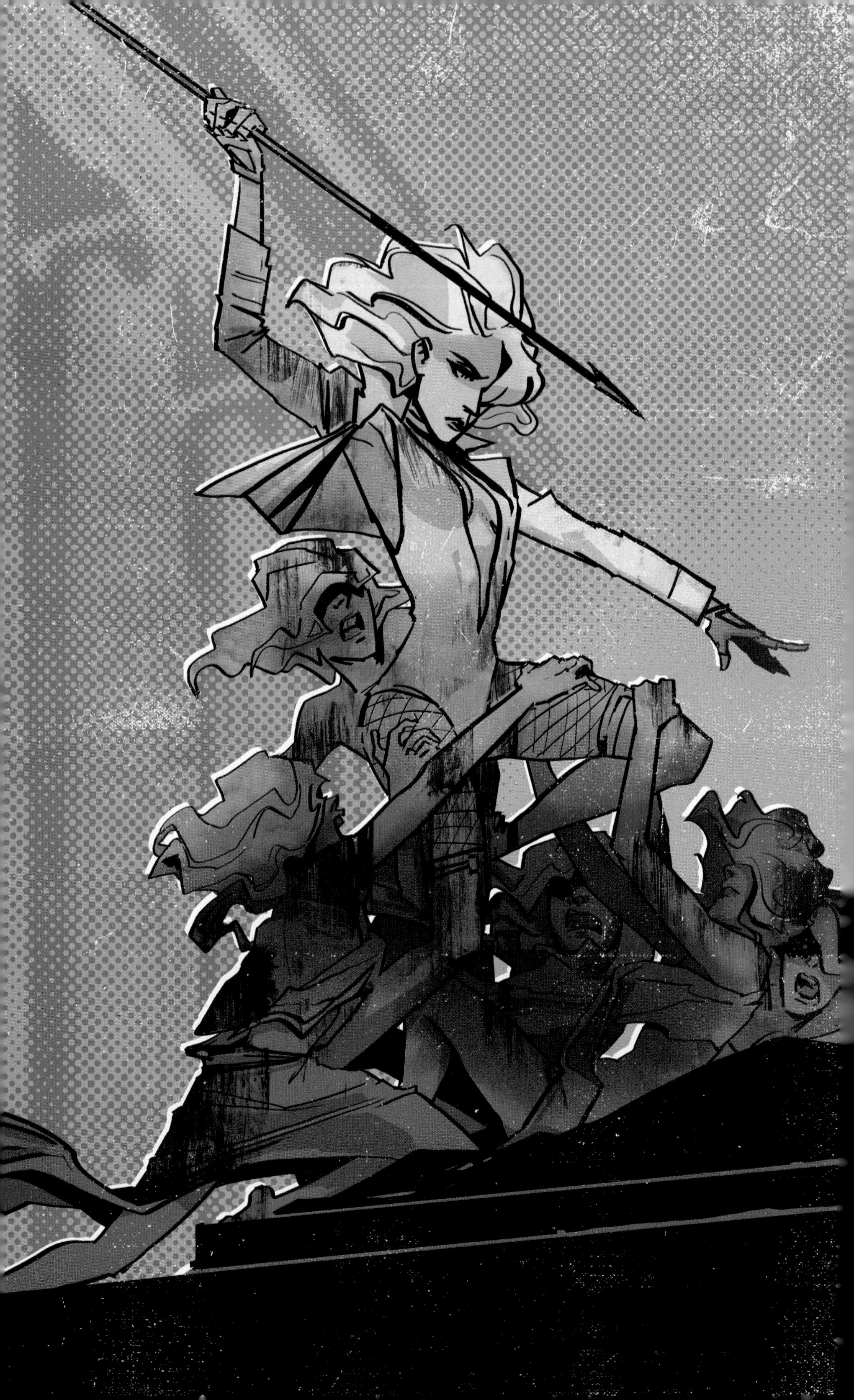

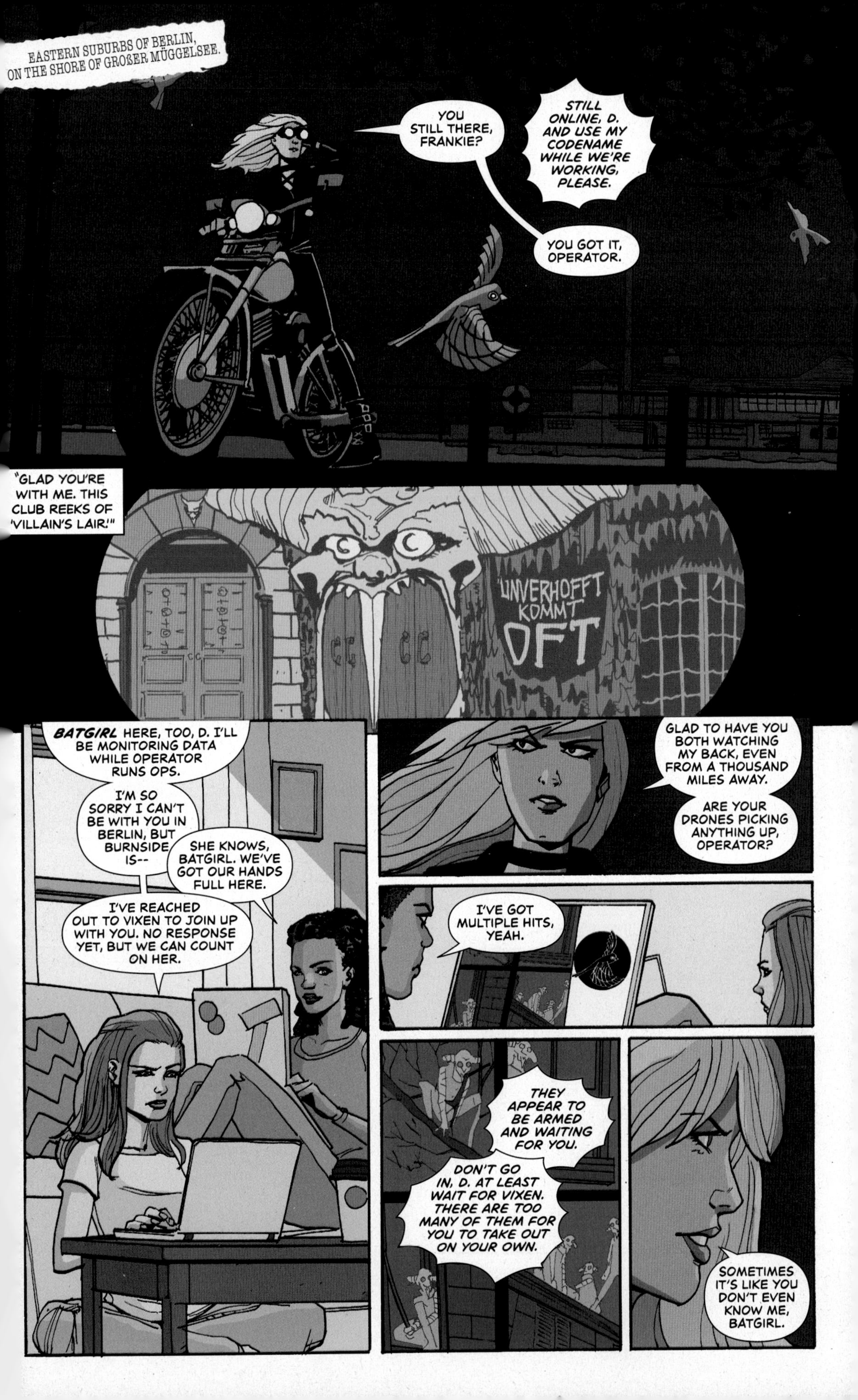
EASTERN SUBURBS OF BERLIN, ON THE SHORE OF GROßER MÜGGELSEE.
YOU STILL THERE, FRANKIE?
STILL ONLINE, D. AND USE MY CODENAME WHILE WE'RE WORKING, PLEASE.
YOU GOT IT, OPERATOR.
"GLAD YOU'RE WITH ME. THIS CLUB REEKS OF 'VILLAIN'S LAIR.'"
'UNVERHOFFT KOMMT OFT
BATGIRL HERE, TOO, D. I'LL BE MONITORING DATA WHILE OPERATOR RUNS OPS.
I'M SO SORRY I CAN'T BE WITH YOU IN BERLIN, BUT BURNSIDE IS--
SHE KNOWS, BATGIRL. WE'VE GOT OUR HANDS FULL HERE.
I'VE REACHED OUT TO VIXEN TO JOIN UP WITH YOU. NO RESPONSE YET, BUT WE CAN COUNT ON HER.
GLAD TO HAVE YOU BOTH WATCHING MY BACK, EVEN FROM A THOUSAND MILES AWAY.
ARE YOUR DRONES PICKING ANYTHING UP, OPERATOR?
I'VE GOT MULTIPLE HITS, YEAH.
THEY APPEAR TO BE ARMED AND WAITING FOR YOU.
DON'T GO IN, D. AT LEAST WAIT FOR VIXEN. THERE ARE TOO MANY OF THEM FOR YOU TO TAKE OUT ON YOUR OWN.
SOMETIMES IT'S LIKE YOU DON'T EVEN KNOW ME, BATGIRL.

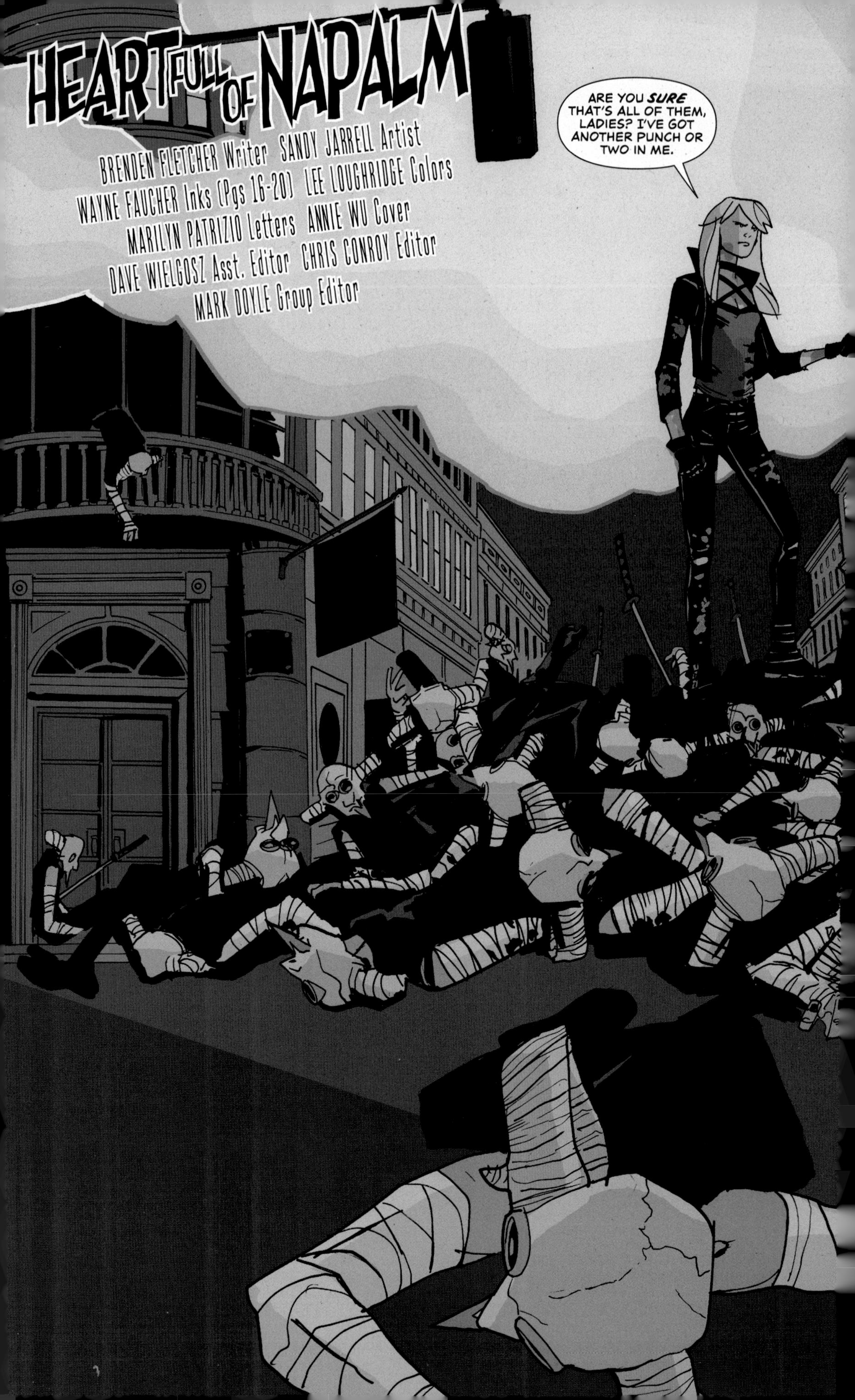
HEART FULL OF NAPALM
BRENDEN FLETCHER Writer SANDY JARRELL Artist
WAYNE FAUCHER Inks (Pgs 16-20) LEE LOUGHRIDGE Colors
MARILYN PATRIZIO Letters ANNIE WU Cover
DAVE WIELGOSZ Asst. Editor CHRIS CONROY Editor
MARK DOYLE Group Editor
ARE YOU SURE THAT'S ALL OF THEM, LADIES? I'VE GOT ANOTHER PUNCH OR TWO IN ME.

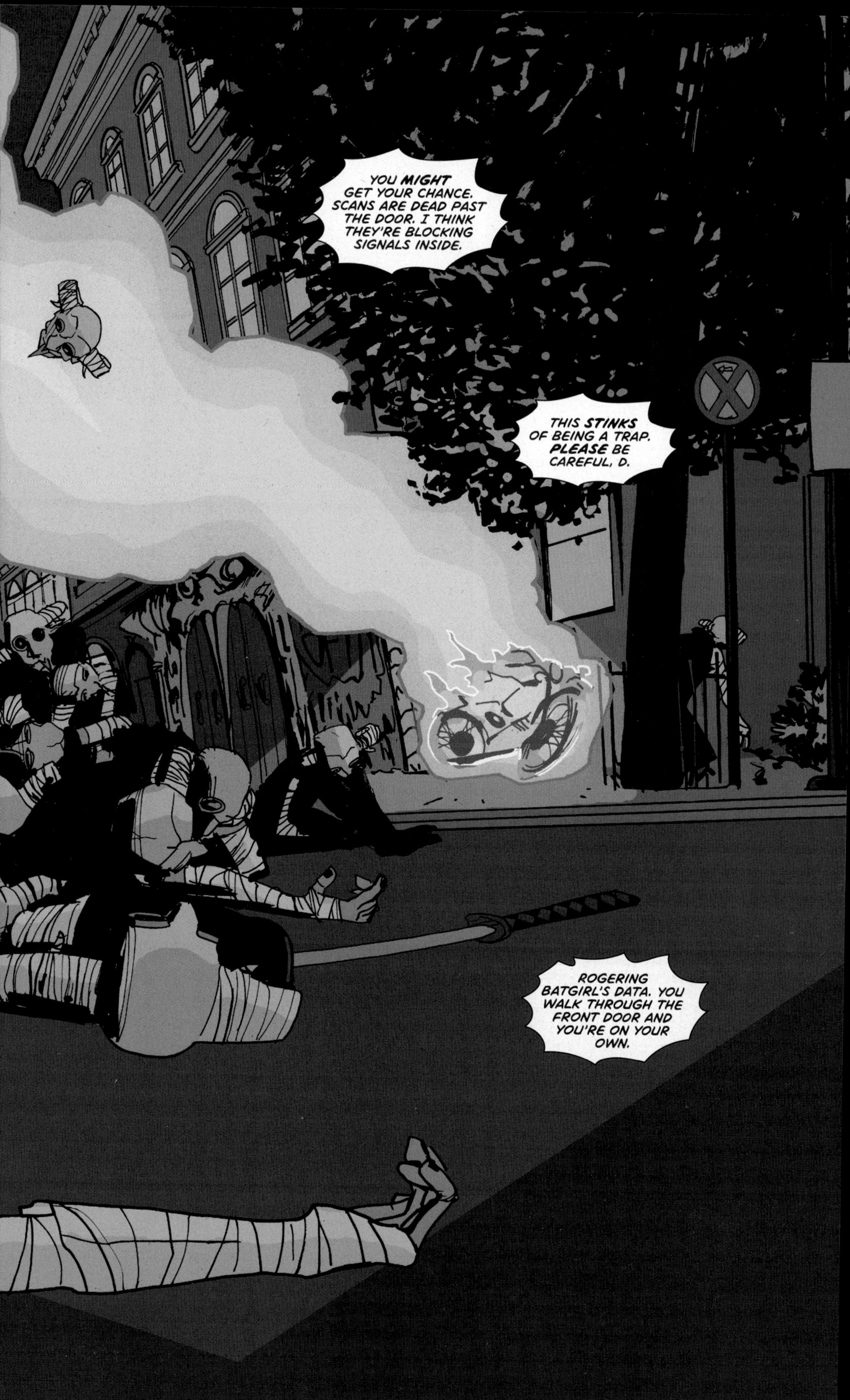
YOU MIGHT GET YOUR CHANCE. SCANS ARE DEAD PAST THE DOOR. I THINK THEY'RE BLOCKING SIGNALS INSIDE.
THIS STINKS OF BEING A TRAP. PLEASE BE CAREFUL, D.
ROGERING BATGIRL'S DATA. YOU WALK THROUGH THE FRONT DOOR AND YOU'RE ON YOUR OWN.

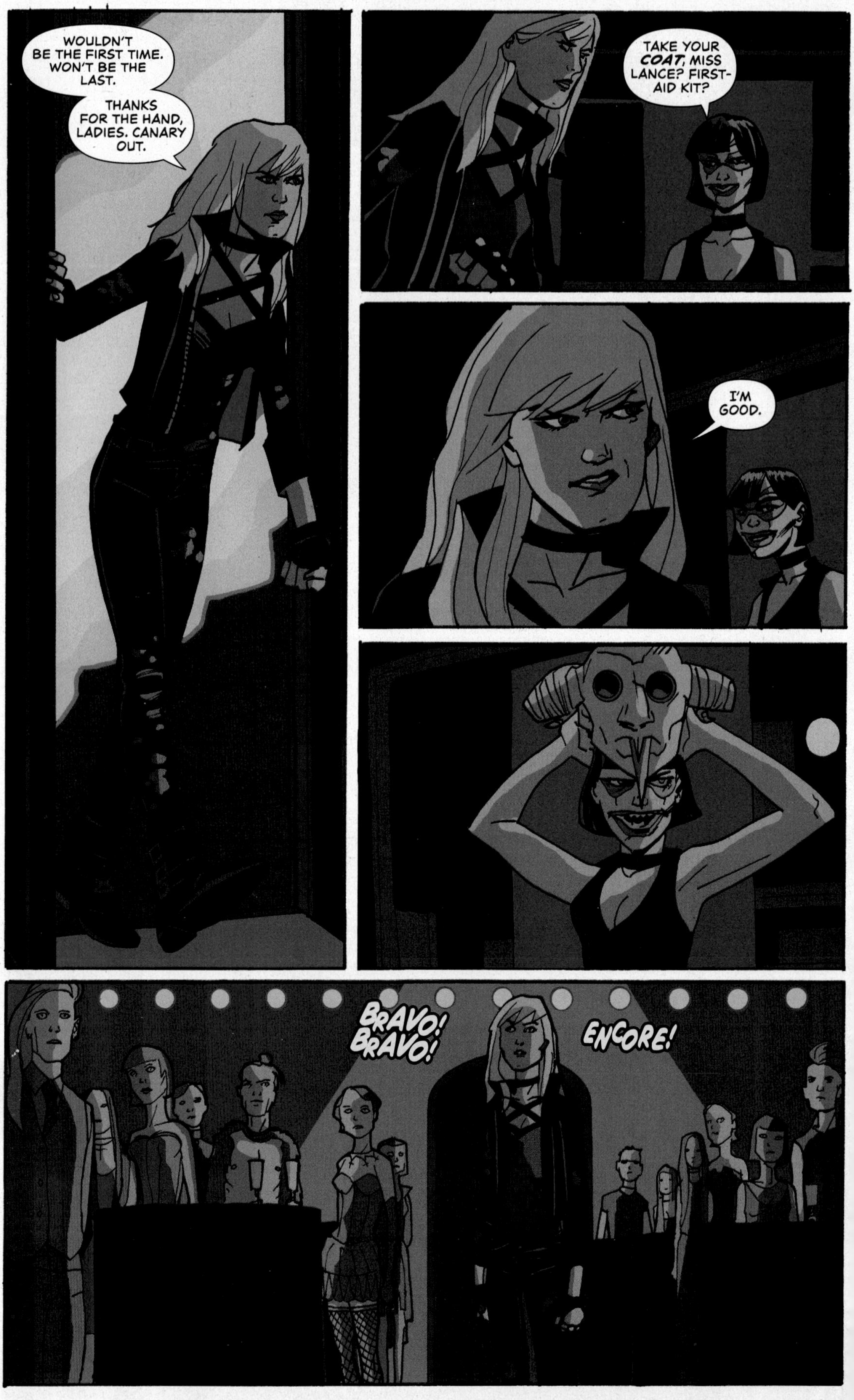
WOULDN'T BE THE FIRST TIME. WON'T BE THE LAST.
THANKS FOR THE HAND, LADIES. CANARY OUT.
TAKE YOUR COAT, MISS LANCE? FIRST-AID KIT?
I'M GOOD.
BRAVO! BRAVO!
ENCORE!

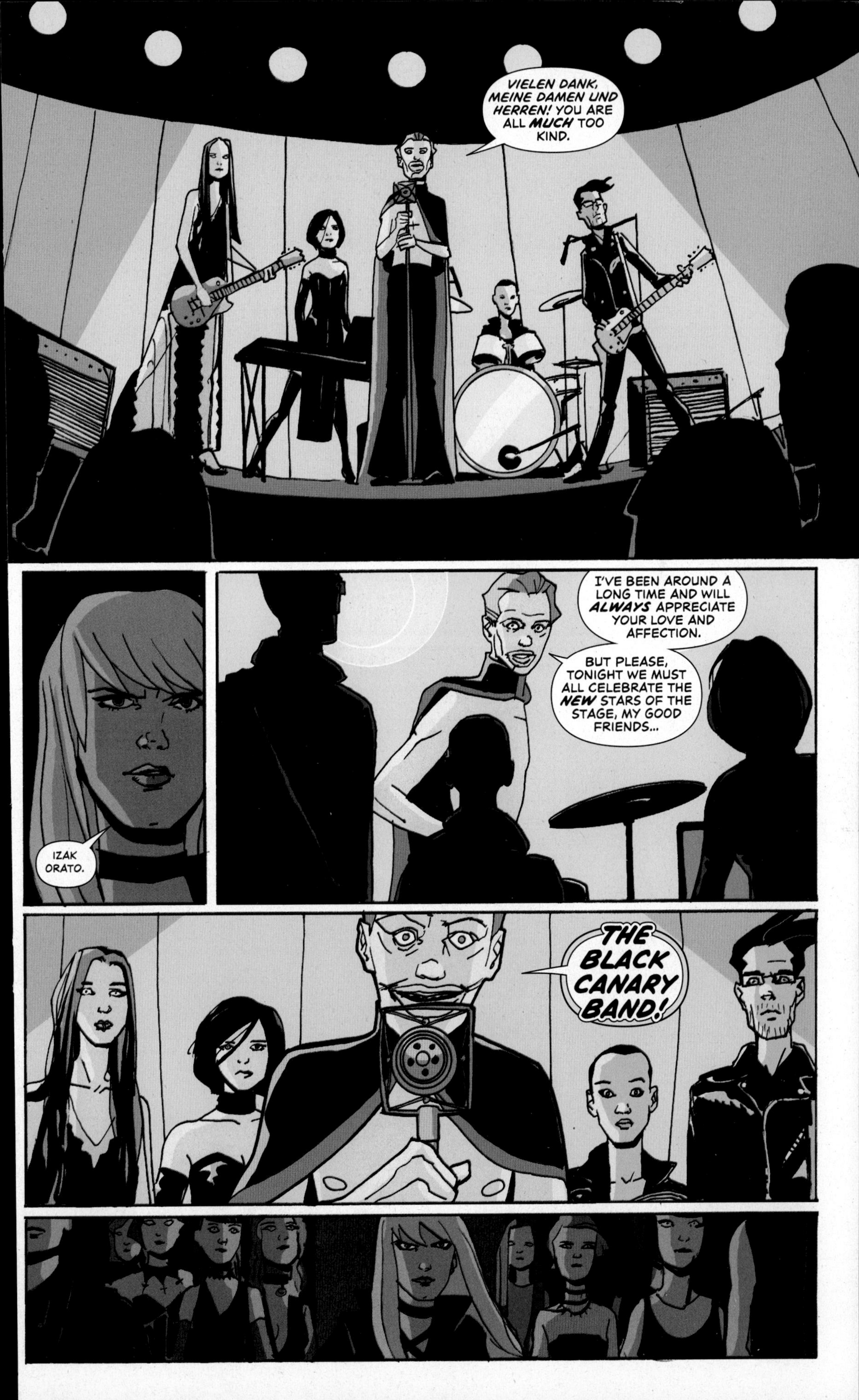
VIELEN DANK, MEINE DAMEN UND HERREN! YOU ARE ALL MUCH TOO KIND.
IZAK ORATO.
I'VE BEEN AROUND A LONG TIME AND WILL ALWAYS APPRECIATE YOUR LOVE AND AFFECTION.
BUT PLEASE, TONIGHT WE MUST ALL CELEBRATE THE NEW STARS OF THE STAGE, MY GOOD FRIENDS...
THE BLACK CANARY BAND!

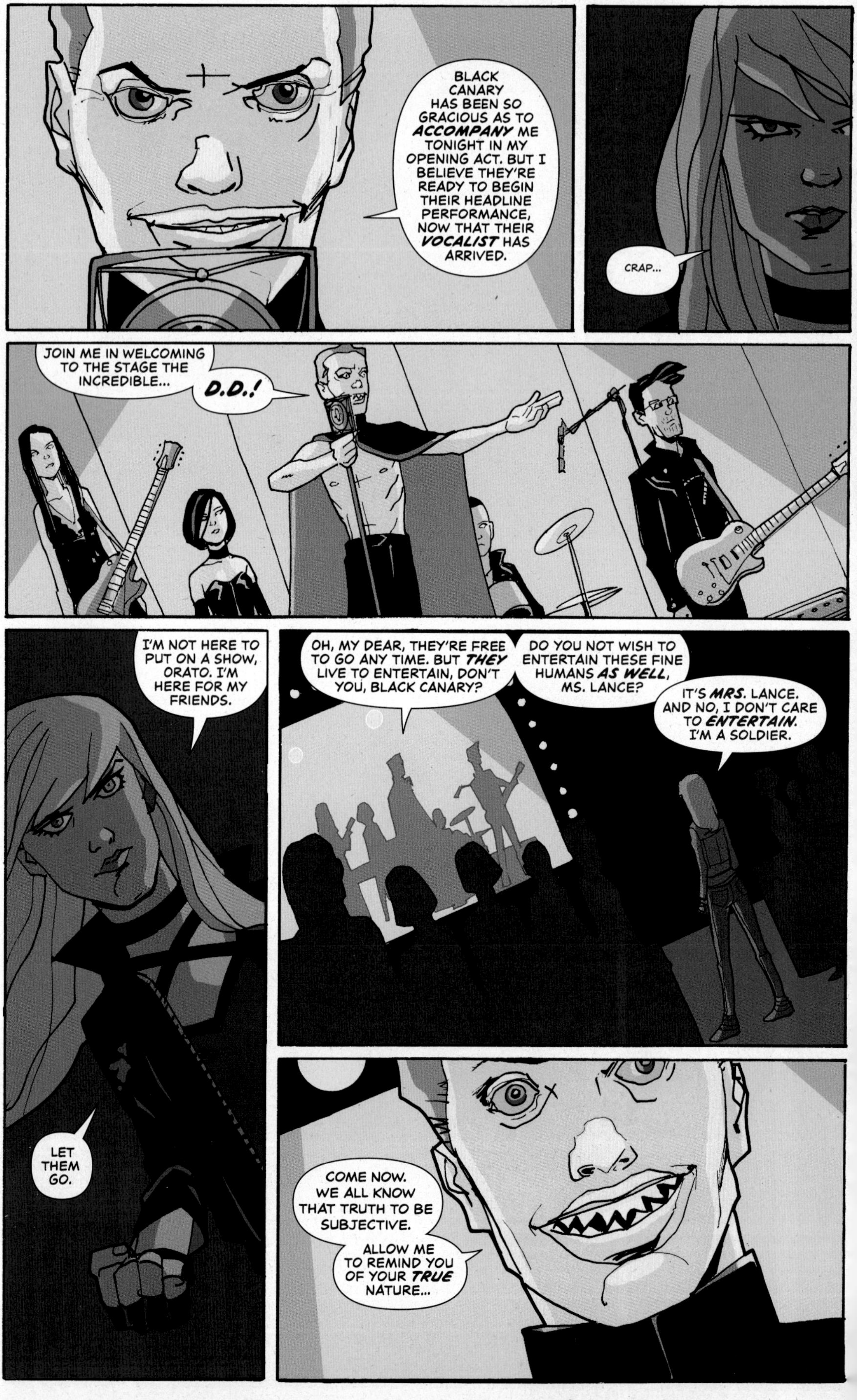
BLACK CANARY HAS BEEN SO GRACIOUS AS TO ACCOMPANY ME TONIGHT IN MY OPENING ACT. BUT I BELIEVE THEY'RE READY TO BEGIN THEIR HEADLINE PERFORMANCE, NOW THAT THEIR VOCALIST HAS ARRIVED.
CRAP...
JOIN ME IN WELCOMING TO THE STAGE THE INCREDIBLE...
D.D.!
I'M NOT HERE TO PUT ON A SHOW, ORATO. I'M HERE FOR MY FRIENDS.
LET THEM GO.
OH, MY DEAR, THEY'RE FREE TO GO ANY TIME. BUT THEY LIVE TO ENTERTAIN, DON'T YOU, BLACK CANARY?
DO YOU NOT WISH TO ENTERTAIN THESE FINE HUMANS AS WELL, MS. LANCE?
IT'S MRS. LANCE. AND NO, I DON'T CARE TO ENTERTAIN. I'M A SOLDIER.
COME NOW. WE ALL KNOW THAT TRUTH TO BE SUBJECTIVE.
ALLOW ME TO REMIND YOU OF YOUR TRUE NATURE...

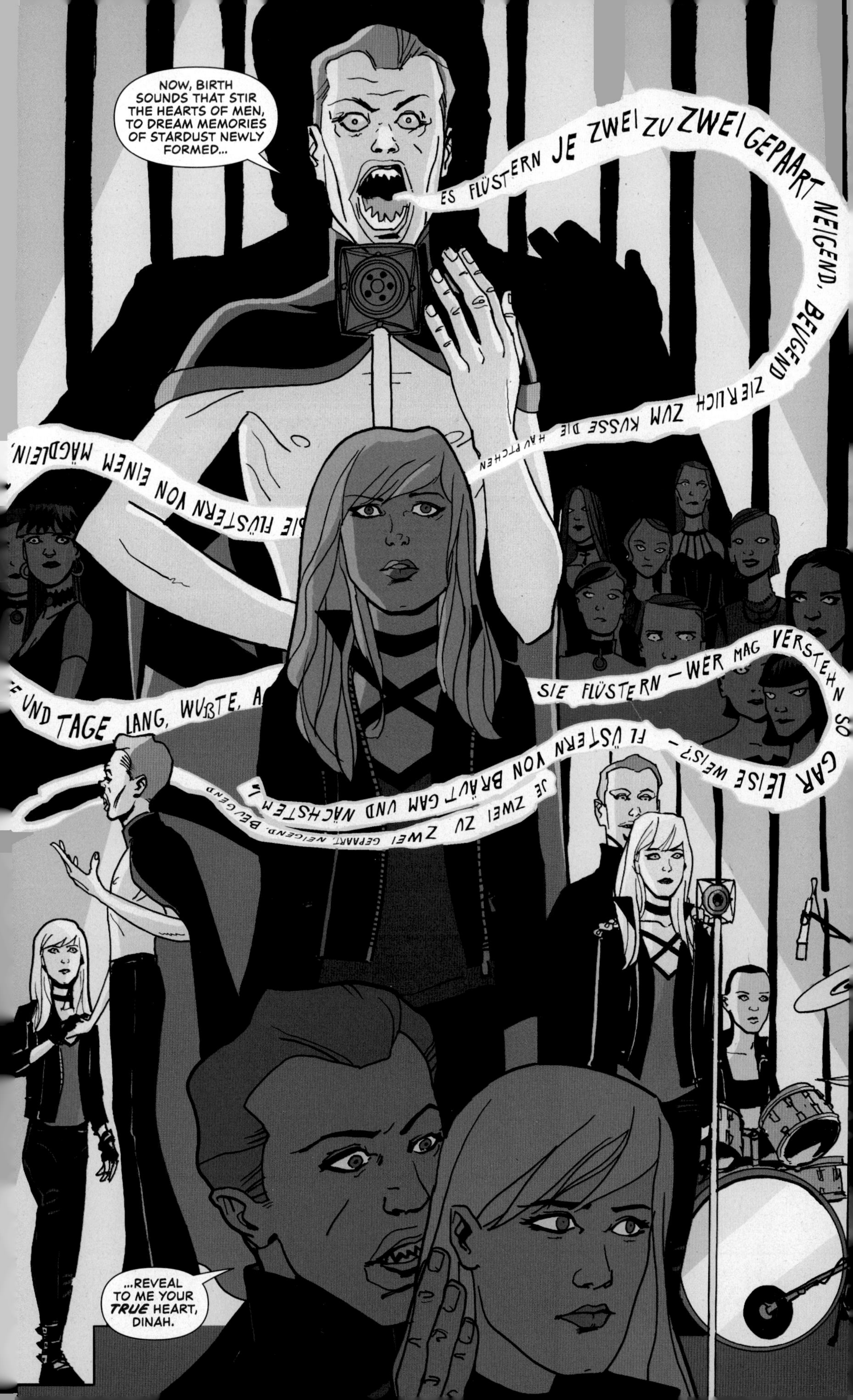
NOW, BIRTH SOUNDS THAT STIR THE HEARTS OF MEN, TO DREAM MEMORIES OF STARDUST NEWLY FORMED...
ES FLÜSTERN JE ZWEI ZU ZWEI GEPAART NEIGEND, BEUGEND ZIERLICH ZUM KUSSE DIE HÄUPTCHEN
SIE FLÜSTERN VON EINEM MÄGDLEIN,
UND TAGE LANG, WUßTE,
SIE FLÜSTERN — WER MAG VERSTEHN SO GAR LEISE WEIS'? — FLÜSTERN VON BRÄUTGAM UND NÄCHSTEM
JE ZWEI ZU ZWEI GEPAART, NEIGEND, BEUGEND
...REVEAL TO ME YOUR *TRUE* HEART, DINAH.

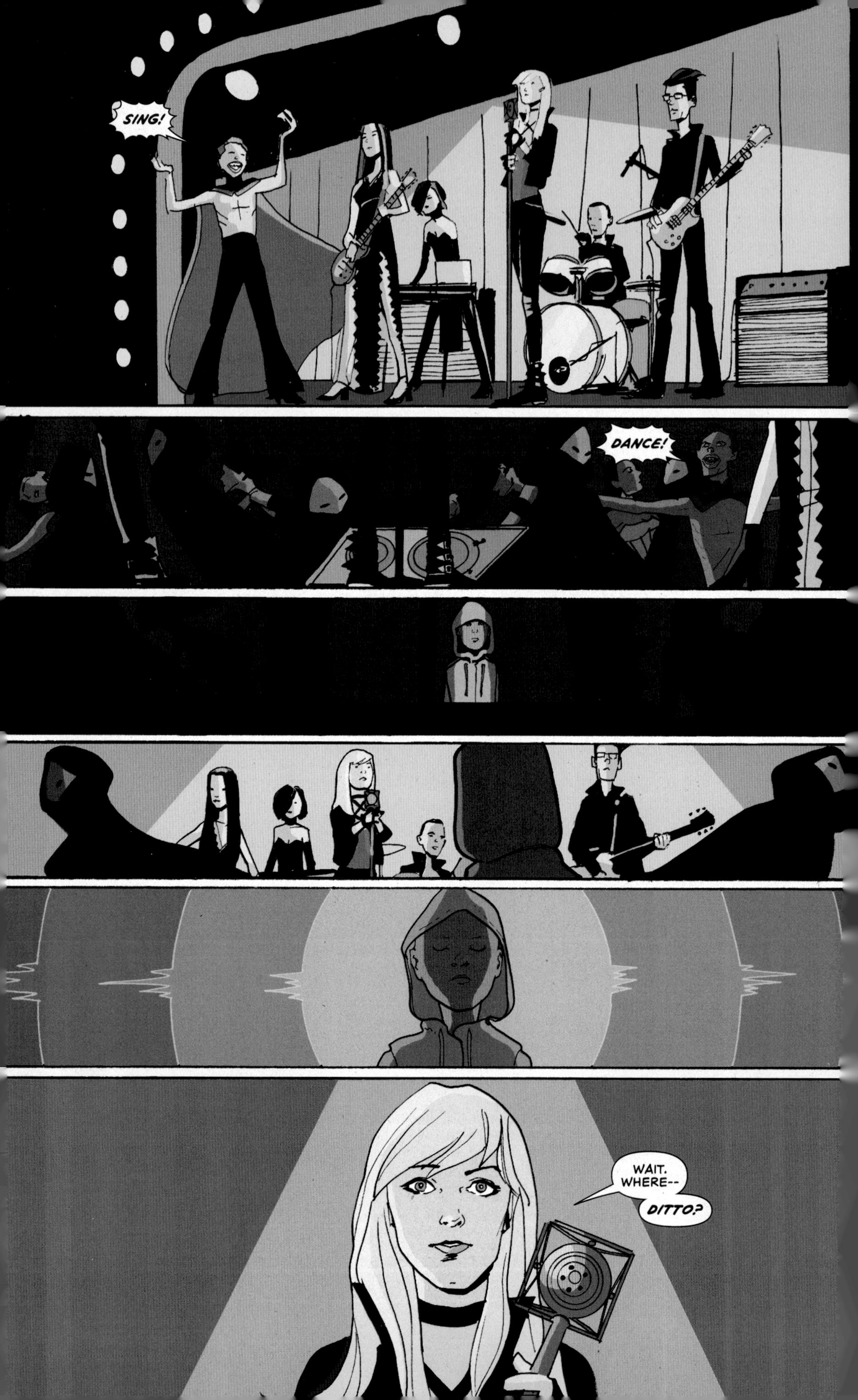
SING!
DANCE!
WAIT. WHERE--
DITTO?

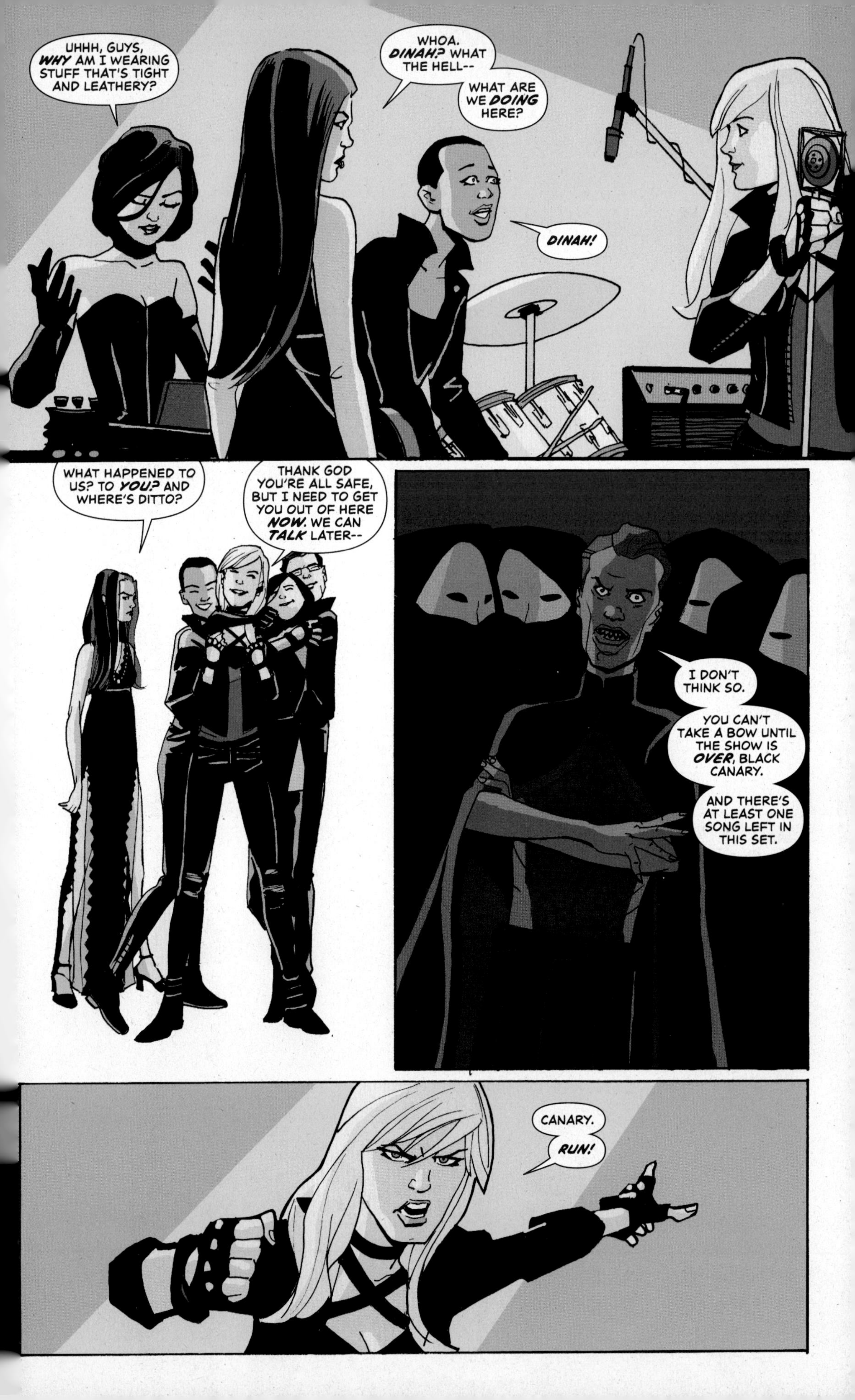
UHHH, GUYS, WHY AM I WEARING STUFF THAT'S TIGHT AND LEATHERY?
WHOA. DINAH? WHAT THE HELL--
WHAT ARE WE DOING HERE?
DINAH!
WHAT HAPPENED TO US? TO YOU? AND WHERE'S DITTO?
THANK GOD YOU'RE ALL SAFE, BUT I NEED TO GET YOU OUT OF HERE NOW. WE CAN TALK LATER--
I DON'T THINK SO.
YOU CAN'T TAKE A BOW UNTIL THE SHOW IS OVER, BLACK CANARY.
AND THERE'S AT LEAST ONE SONG LEFT IN THIS SET.
CANARY.
RUN!

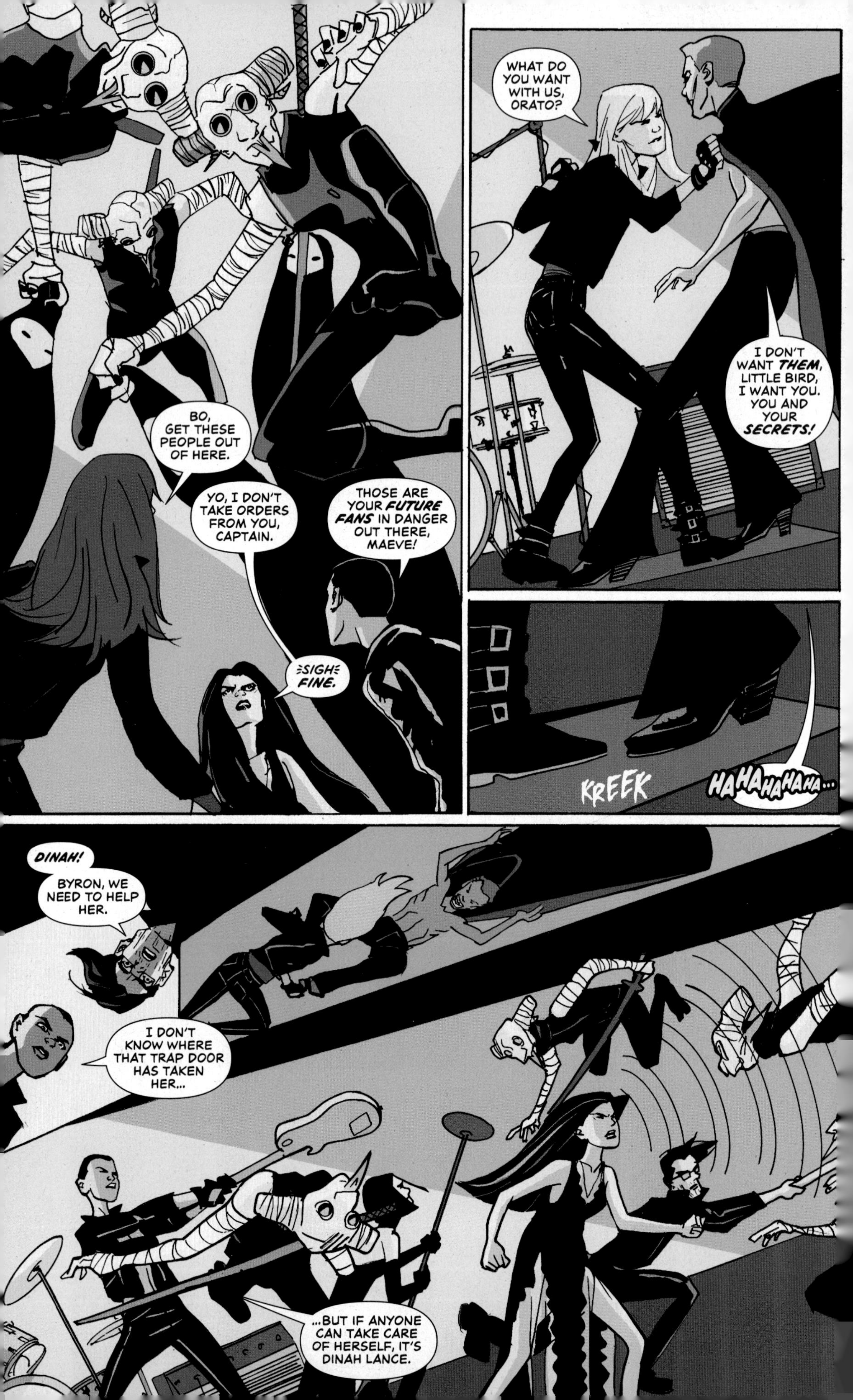
BO, GET THESE PEOPLE OUT OF HERE.
YO, I DON'T TAKE ORDERS FROM YOU, CAPTAIN.
THOSE ARE YOUR FUTURE FANS IN DANGER OUT THERE, MAEVE!
SIGH FINE.
WHAT DO YOU WANT WITH US, ORATO?
I DON'T WANT THEM, LITTLE BIRD, I WANT YOU. YOU AND YOUR SECRETS!
KREEK
HAHAHAHAHA...
DINAH!
BYRON, WE NEED TO HELP HER.
I DON'T KNOW WHERE THAT TRAP DOOR HAS TAKEN HER...
...BUT IF ANYONE CAN TAKE CARE OF HERSELF, IT'S DINAH LANCE.

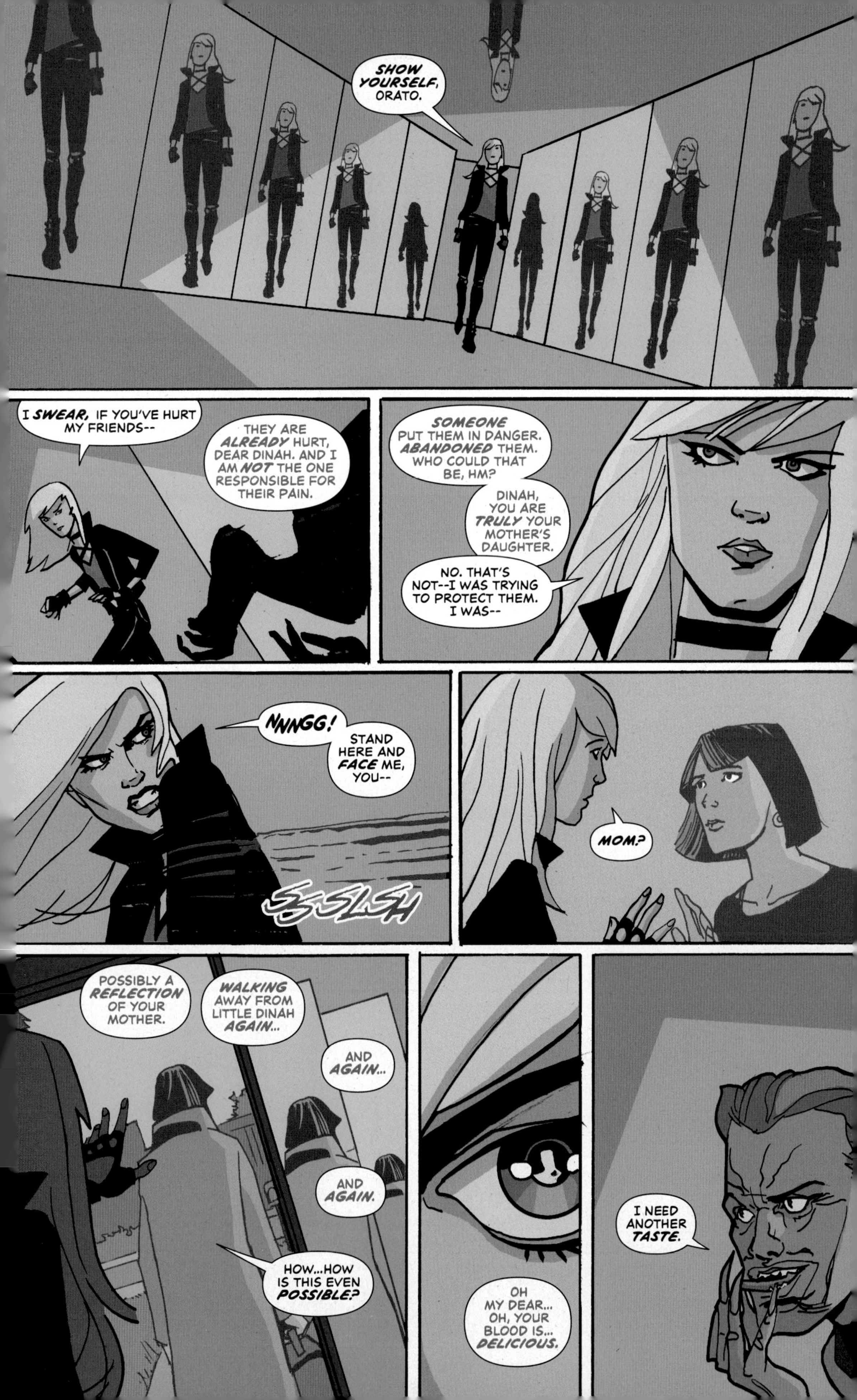
SHOW YOURSELF, ORATO.
I SWEAR, IF YOU'VE HURT MY FRIENDS--
THEY ARE ALREADY HURT, DEAR DINAH. AND I AM NOT THE ONE RESPONSIBLE FOR THEIR PAIN.
SOMEONE PUT THEM IN DANGER. ABANDONED THEM. WHO COULD THAT BE, HM?
DINAH, YOU ARE TRULY YOUR MOTHER'S DAUGHTER.
NO. THAT'S NOT--I WAS TRYING TO PROTECT THEM. I WAS--
NNNGG!
STAND HERE AND FACE ME, YOU--
SSSLSH
MOM?
POSSIBLY A REFLECTION OF YOUR MOTHER.
WALKING AWAY FROM LITTLE DINAH AGAIN...
AND AGAIN...
AND AGAIN.
HOW...HOW IS THIS EVEN POSSIBLE?
OH MY DEAR... OH, YOUR BLOOD IS... DELICIOUS.
I NEED ANOTHER TASTE.

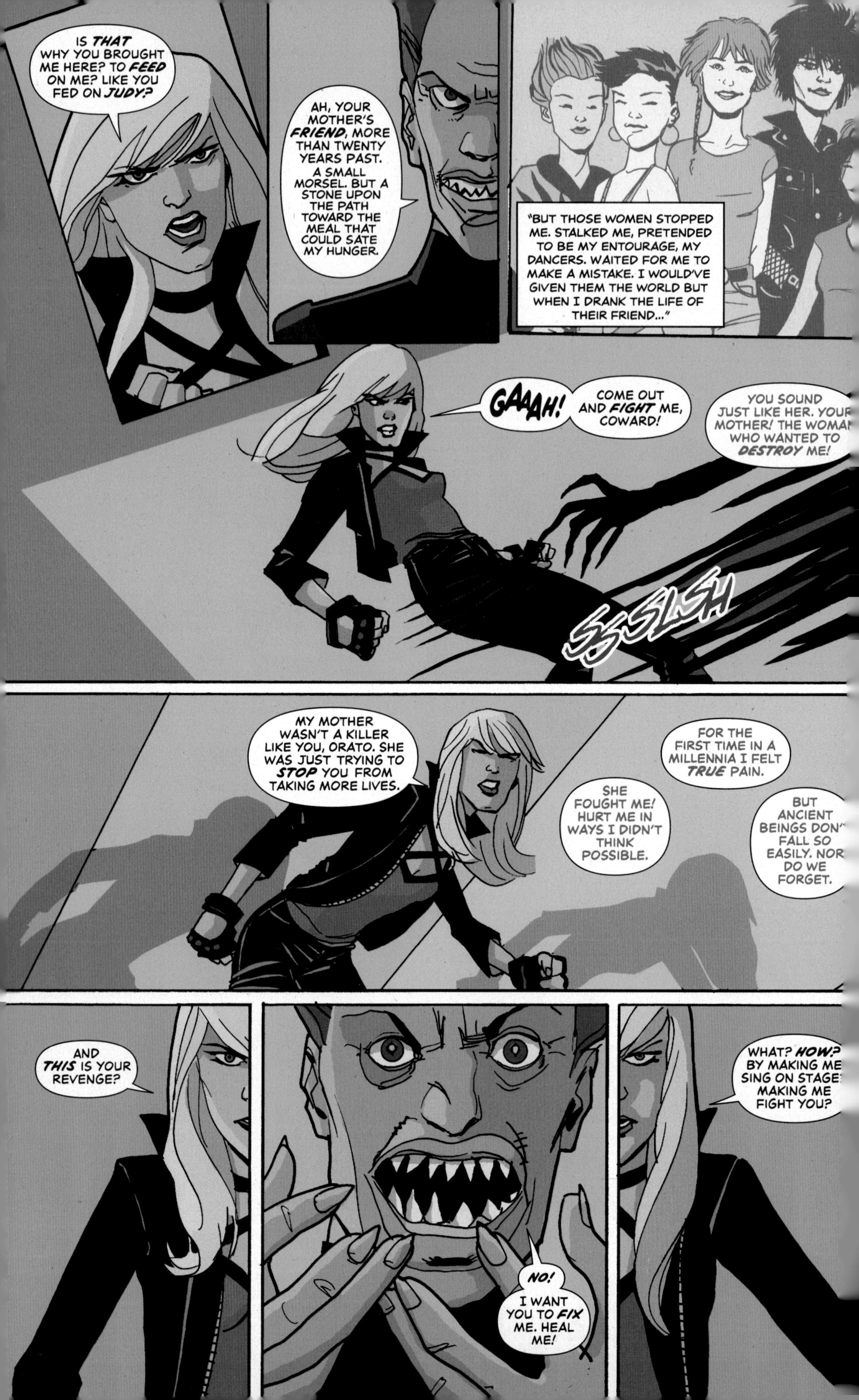
IS THAT WHY YOU BROUGHT ME HERE? TO FEED ON ME? LIKE YOU FED ON JUDY?
AH, YOUR MOTHER'S FRIEND, MORE THAN TWENTY YEARS PAST.
A SMALL MORSEL. BUT A STONE UPON THE PATH TOWARD THE MEAL THAT COULD SATE MY HUNGER.
"BUT THOSE WOMEN STOPPED ME. STALKED ME, PRETENDED TO BE MY ENTOURAGE, MY DANCERS. WAITED FOR ME TO MAKE A MISTAKE. I WOULD'VE GIVEN THEM THE WORLD BUT WHEN I DRANK THE LIFE OF THEIR FRIEND..."
GAAAH!
COME OUT AND FIGHT ME, COWARD!
YOU SOUND JUST LIKE HER. YOUR MOTHER! THE WOMAN WHO WANTED TO DESTROY ME!
SSSLISH
MY MOTHER WASN'T A KILLER LIKE YOU, ORATO. SHE WAS JUST TRYING TO STOP YOU FROM TAKING MORE LIVES.
FOR THE FIRST TIME IN A MILLENNIA I FELT TRUE PAIN.
SHE FOUGHT ME! HURT ME IN WAYS I DIDN'T THINK POSSIBLE.
BUT ANCIENT BEINGS DON'T FALL SO EASILY. NOR DO WE FORGET.
AND THIS IS YOUR REVENGE?
NO!
I WANT YOU TO FIX ME. HEAL ME!
WHAT? HOW? BY MAKING ME SING ON STAGE? MAKING ME FIGHT YOU?

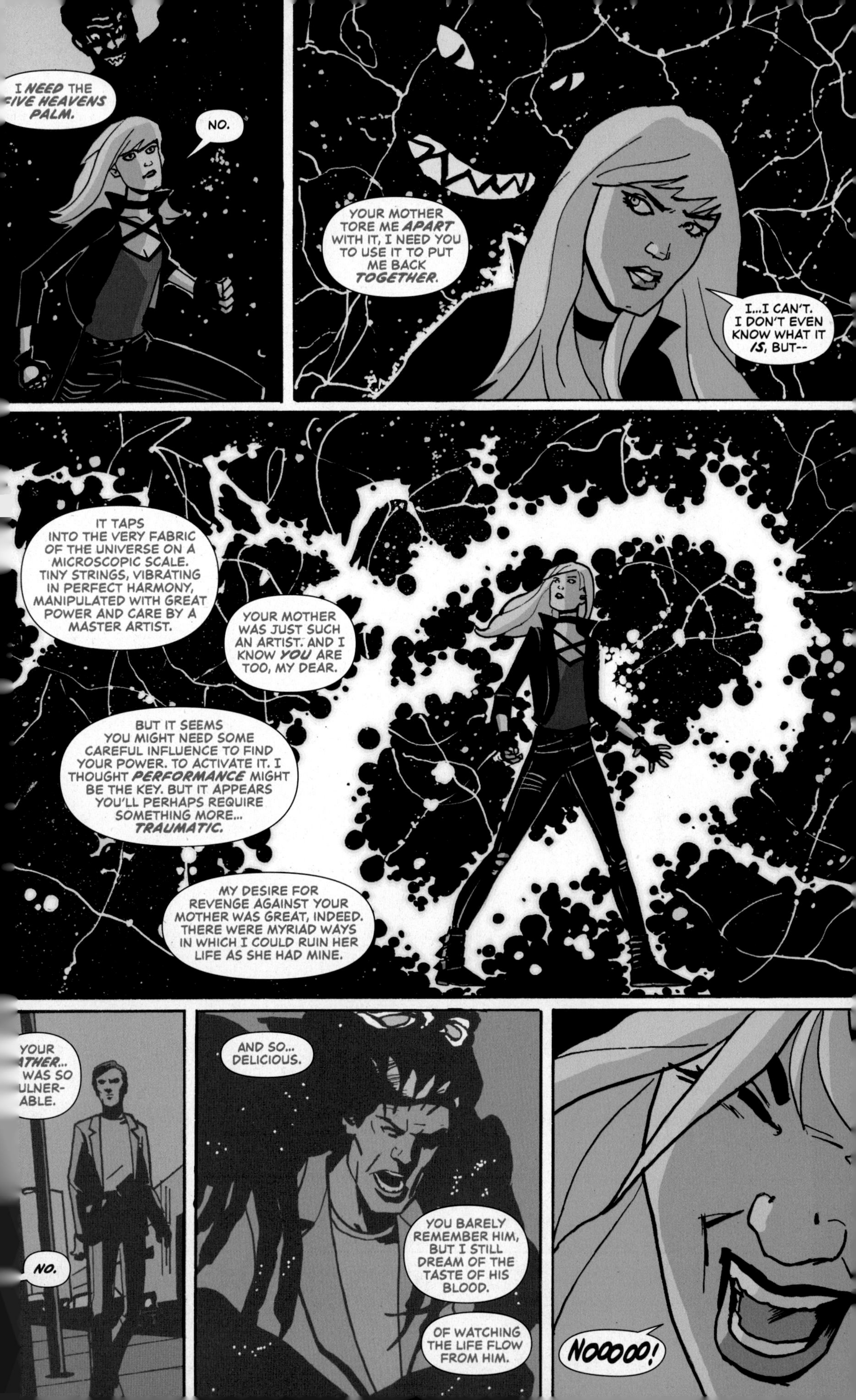
I NEED THE
FIVE HEAVENS
PALM.
NO.
YOUR MOTHER TORE ME APART WITH IT. I NEED YOU TO USE IT TO PUT ME BACK TOGETHER.
I...I CAN'T. I DON'T EVEN KNOW WHAT IT IS, BUT--
IT TAPS INTO THE VERY FABRIC OF THE UNIVERSE ON A MICROSCOPIC SCALE. TINY STRINGS, VIBRATING IN PERFECT HARMONY, MANIPULATED WITH GREAT POWER AND CARE BY A MASTER ARTIST.
YOUR MOTHER WAS JUST SUCH AN ARTIST. AND I KNOW YOU ARE TOO, MY DEAR.
BUT IT SEEMS YOU MIGHT NEED SOME CAREFUL INFLUENCE TO FIND YOUR POWER. TO ACTIVATE IT. I THOUGHT PERFORMANCE MIGHT BE THE KEY. BUT IT APPEARS YOU'LL PERHAPS REQUIRE SOMETHING MORE... TRAUMATIC.
MY DESIRE FOR REVENGE AGAINST YOUR MOTHER WAS GREAT, INDEED. THERE WERE MYRIAD WAYS IN WHICH I COULD RUIN HER LIFE AS SHE HAD MINE.
NO.
AND SO... DELICIOUS.
YOU BARELY REMEMBER HIM, BUT I STILL DREAM OF THE TASTE OF HIS BLOOD.
OF WATCHING THE LIFE FLOW FROM HIM.
NOOOOO!

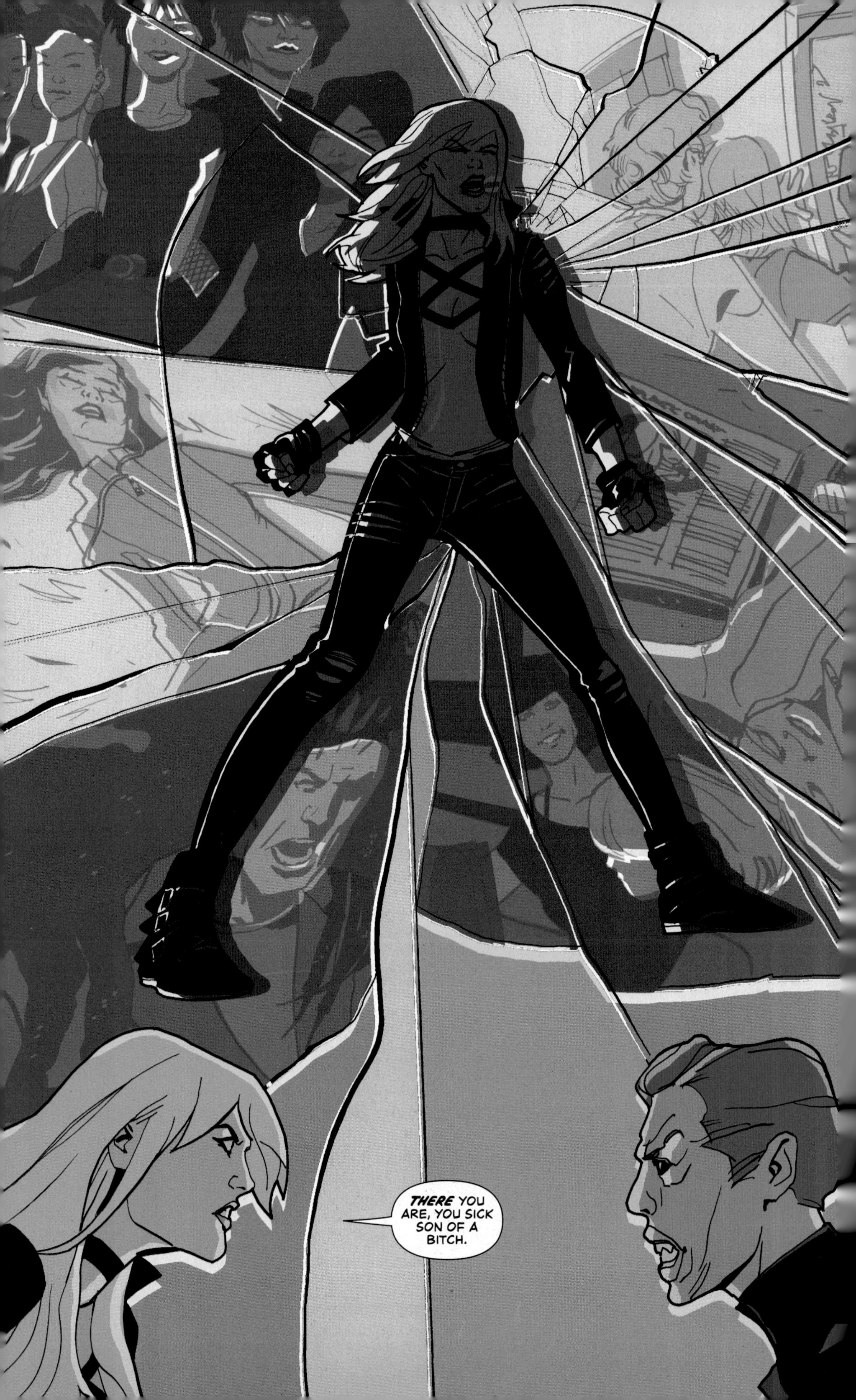
THERE YOU ARE, YOU SICK SON OF A BITCH.

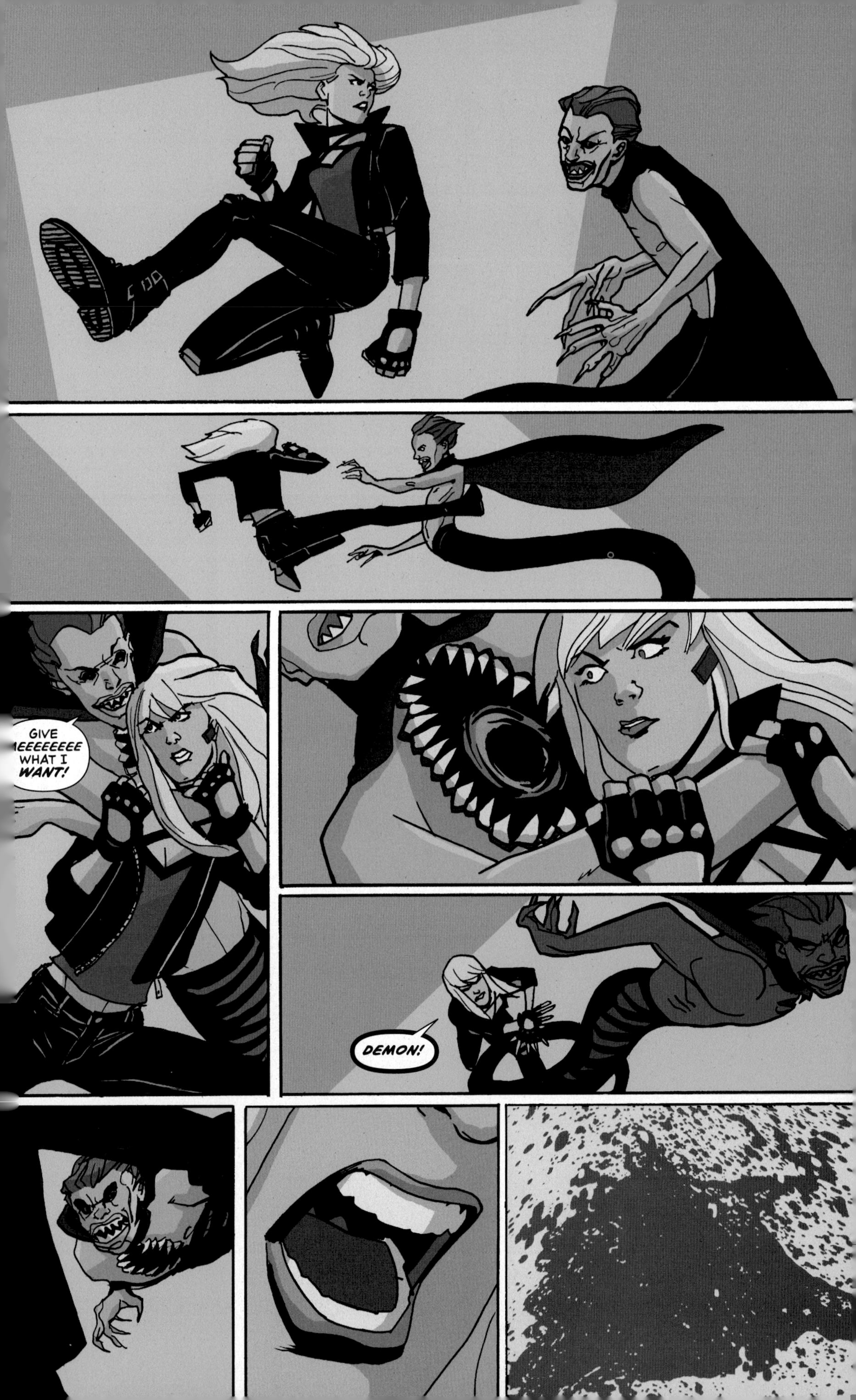
GIVE
MEEEEEEEE
WHAT I
WANT!
DEMON!

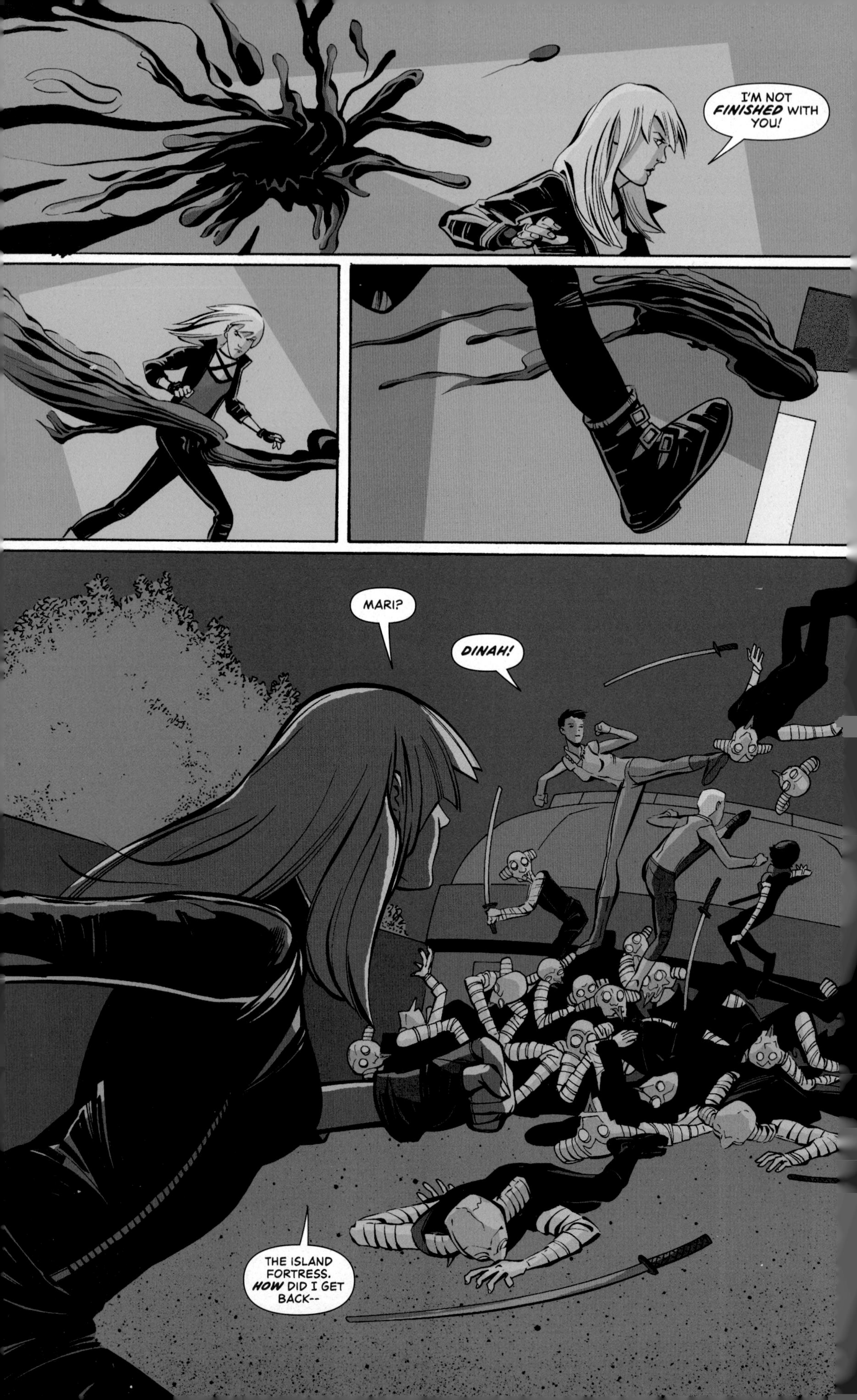
I'M NOT FINISHED WITH YOU!
MARI?
DINAH!
THE ISLAND FORTRESS. HOW DID I GET BACK--

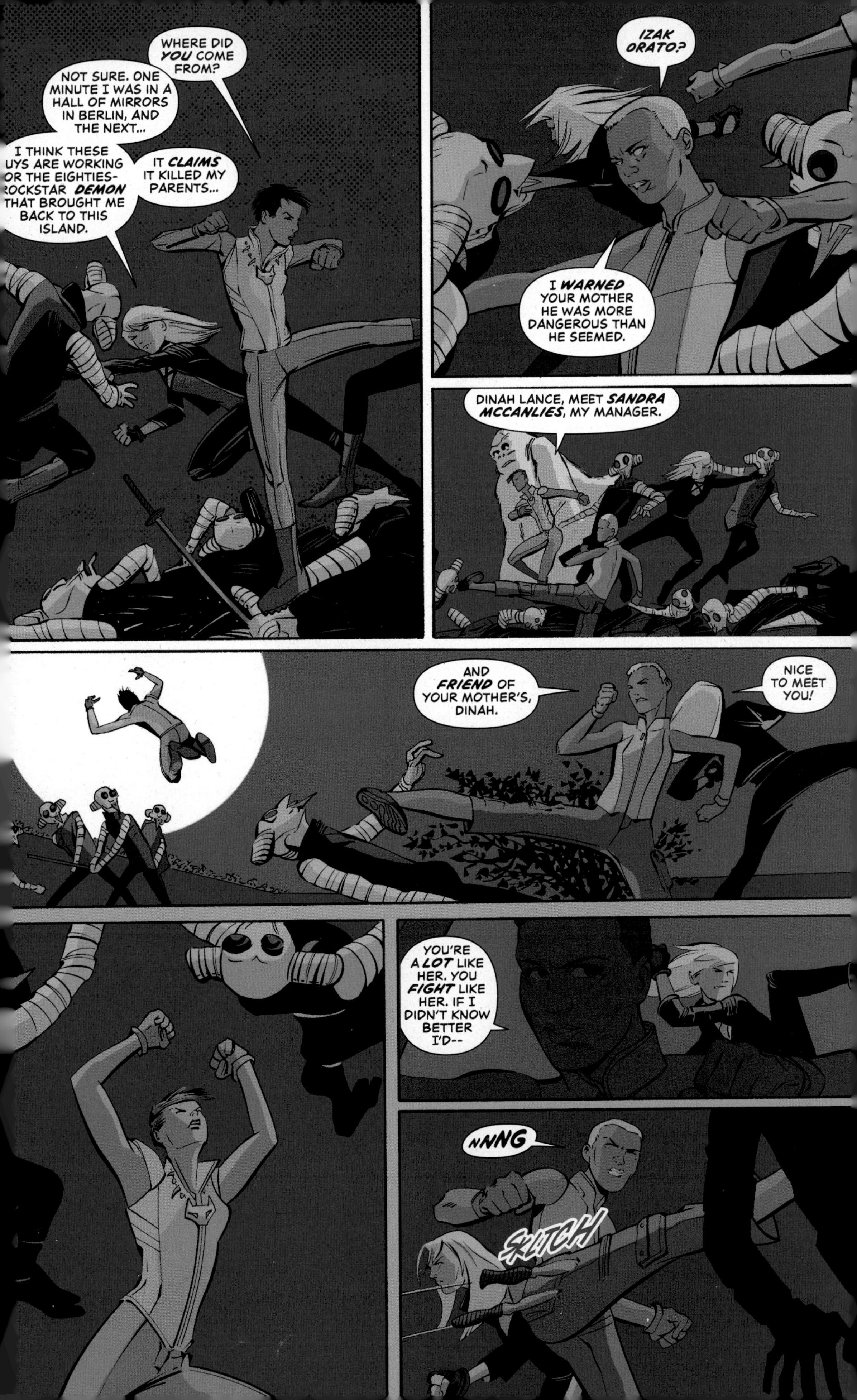
NOT SURE. ONE MINUTE I WAS IN A HALL OF MIRRORS IN BERLIN, AND THE NEXT...
WHERE DID YOU COME FROM?
I THINK THESE GUYS ARE WORKING FOR THE EIGHTIES-ROCKSTAR DEMON THAT BROUGHT ME BACK TO THIS ISLAND.
IT CLAIMS IT KILLED MY PARENTS...
IZAK ORATO?
I WARNED YOUR MOTHER HE WAS MORE DANGEROUS THAN HE SEEMED.
DINAH LANCE, MEET SANDRA MCCANLIES, MY MANAGER.
AND FRIEND OF YOUR MOTHER'S, DINAH.
NICE TO MEET YOU!
YOU'RE A LOT LIKE HER. YOU FIGHT LIKE HER. IF I DIDN'T KNOW BETTER I'D--
NNNG
SKLTCH

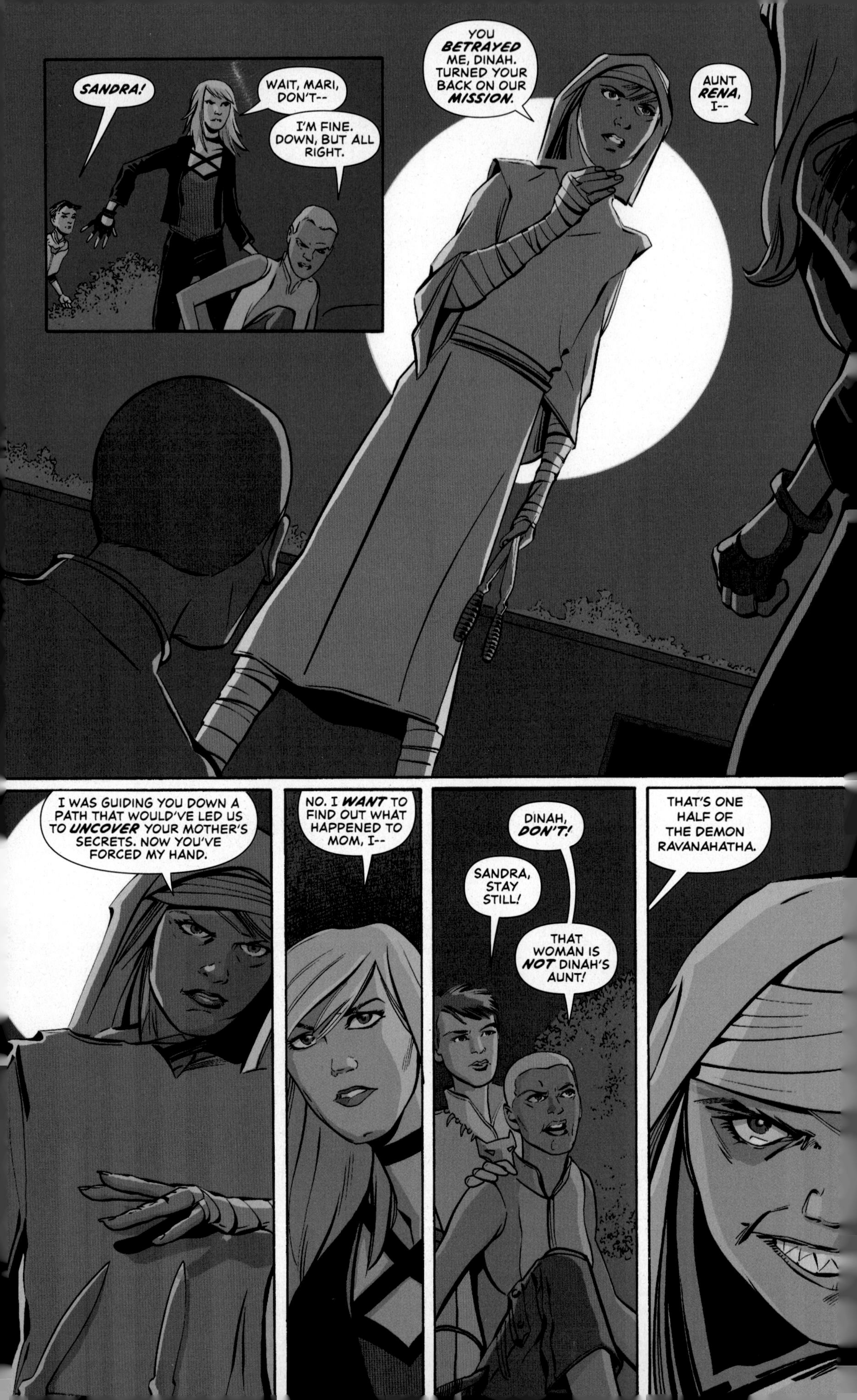
SANDRA!
WAIT, MARI, DON'T--
I'M FINE. DOWN, BUT ALL RIGHT.
YOU **BETRAYED** ME, DINAH. TURNED YOUR BACK ON OUR **MISSION**.
AUNT **RENA**, I--
I WAS GUIDING YOU DOWN A PATH THAT WOULD'VE LED US TO **UNCOVER** YOUR MOTHER'S SECRETS. NOW YOU'VE FORCED MY HAND.
NO. I **WANT** TO FIND OUT WHAT HAPPENED TO MOM, I--
DINAH, **DON'T!**
SANDRA, STAY STILL!
THAT WOMAN IS **NOT** DINAH'S AUNT!
THAT'S ONE HALF OF THE DEMON RAVANAHATHA.

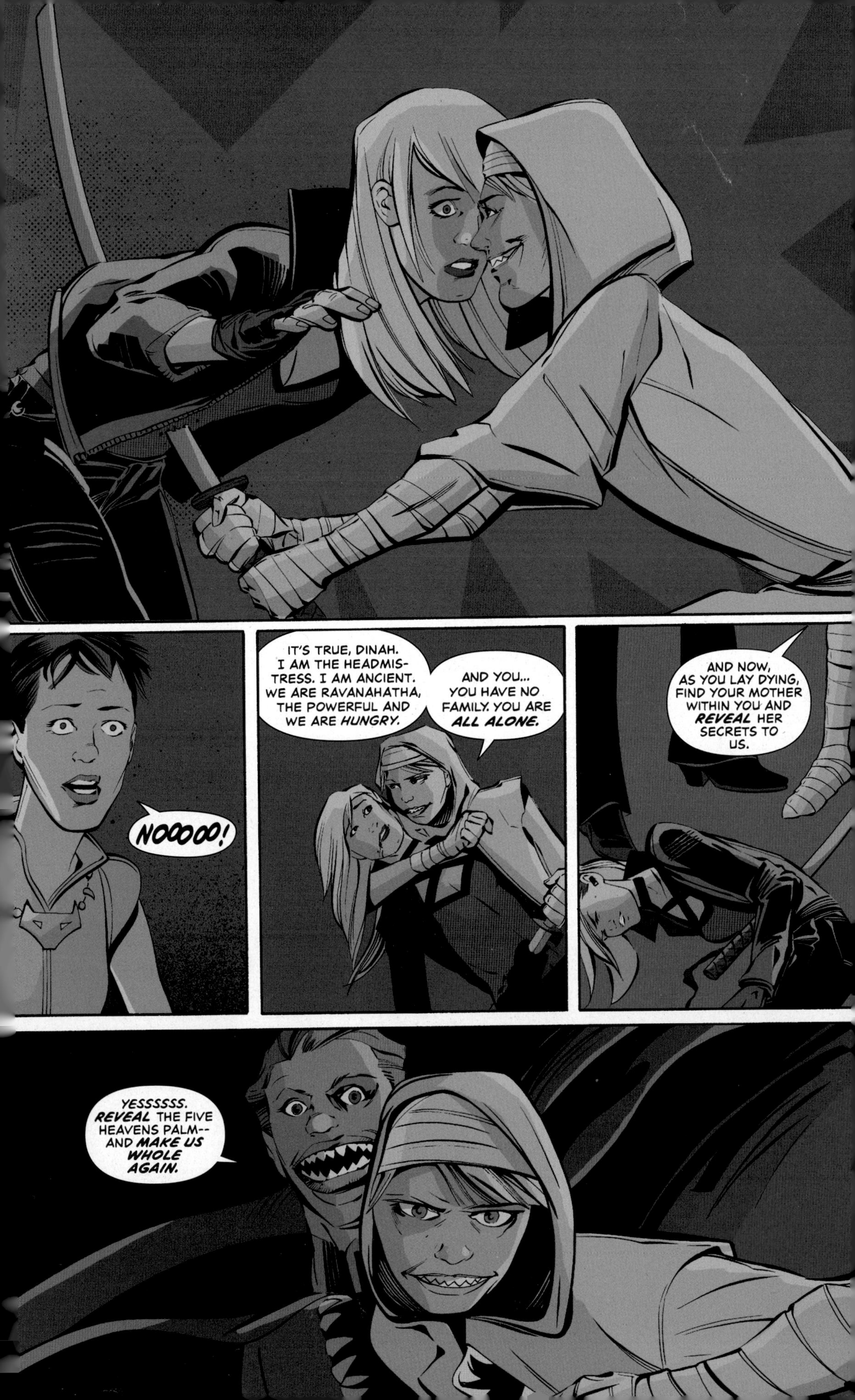
NOOOOO!
IT'S TRUE, DINAH. I AM THE HEADMIS-TRESS. I AM ANCIENT. WE ARE RAVANAHATHA, THE POWERFUL AND WE ARE HUNGRY.
AND YOU... YOU HAVE NO FAMILY. YOU ARE ALL ALONE.
AND NOW, AS YOU LAY DYING, FIND YOUR MOTHER WITHIN YOU AND REVEAL HER SECRETS TO US.
YESSSSSS. REVEAL THE FIVE HEAVENS PALM-- AND MAKE US WHOLE AGAIN.

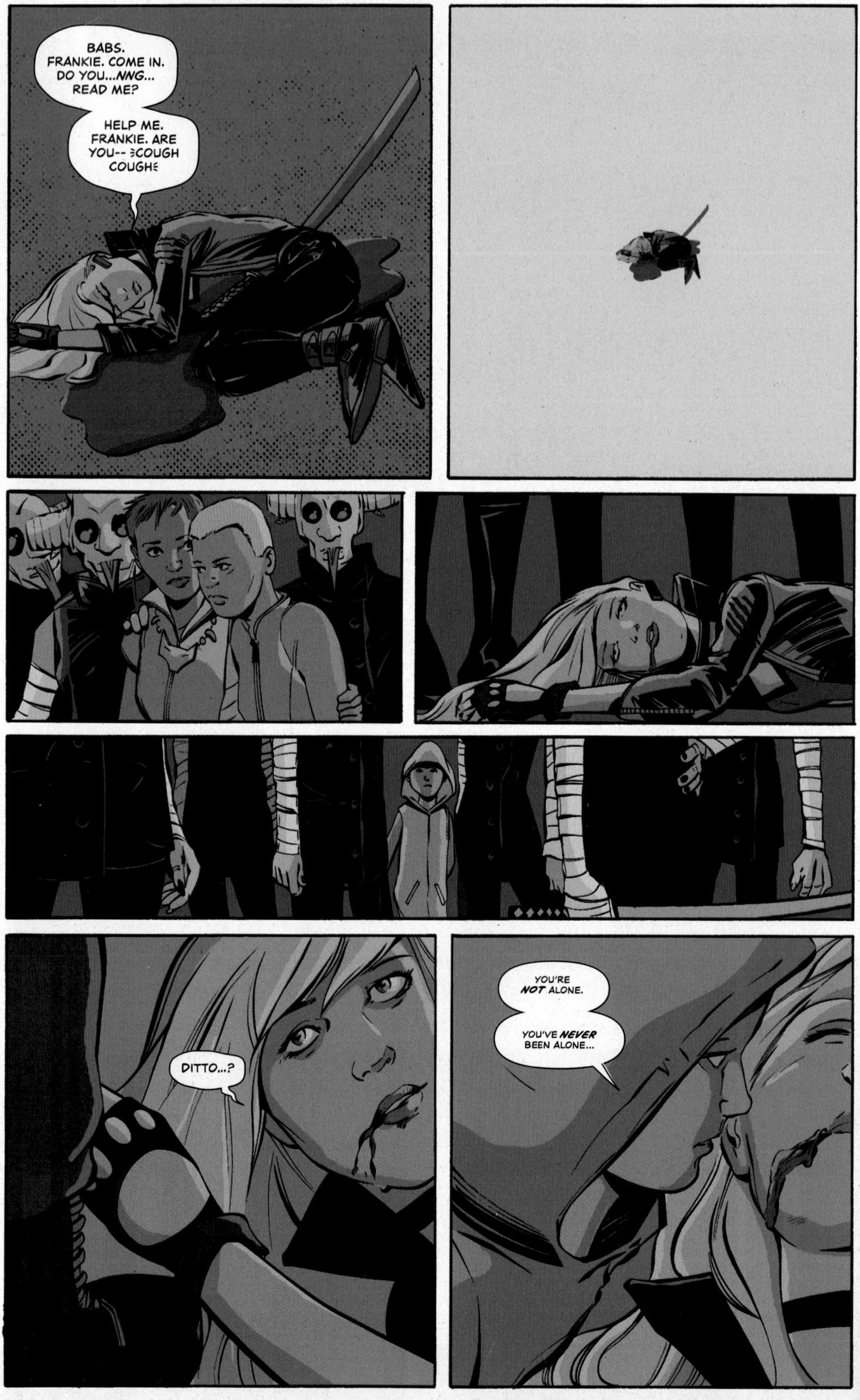
BABS. FRANKIE. COME IN. DO YOU...NNG... READ ME?
HELP ME. FRANKIE. ARE YOU-- ≡COUGH COUGH≡
DITTO...?
YOU'RE NOT ALONE.
YOU'VE NEVER BEEN ALONE...

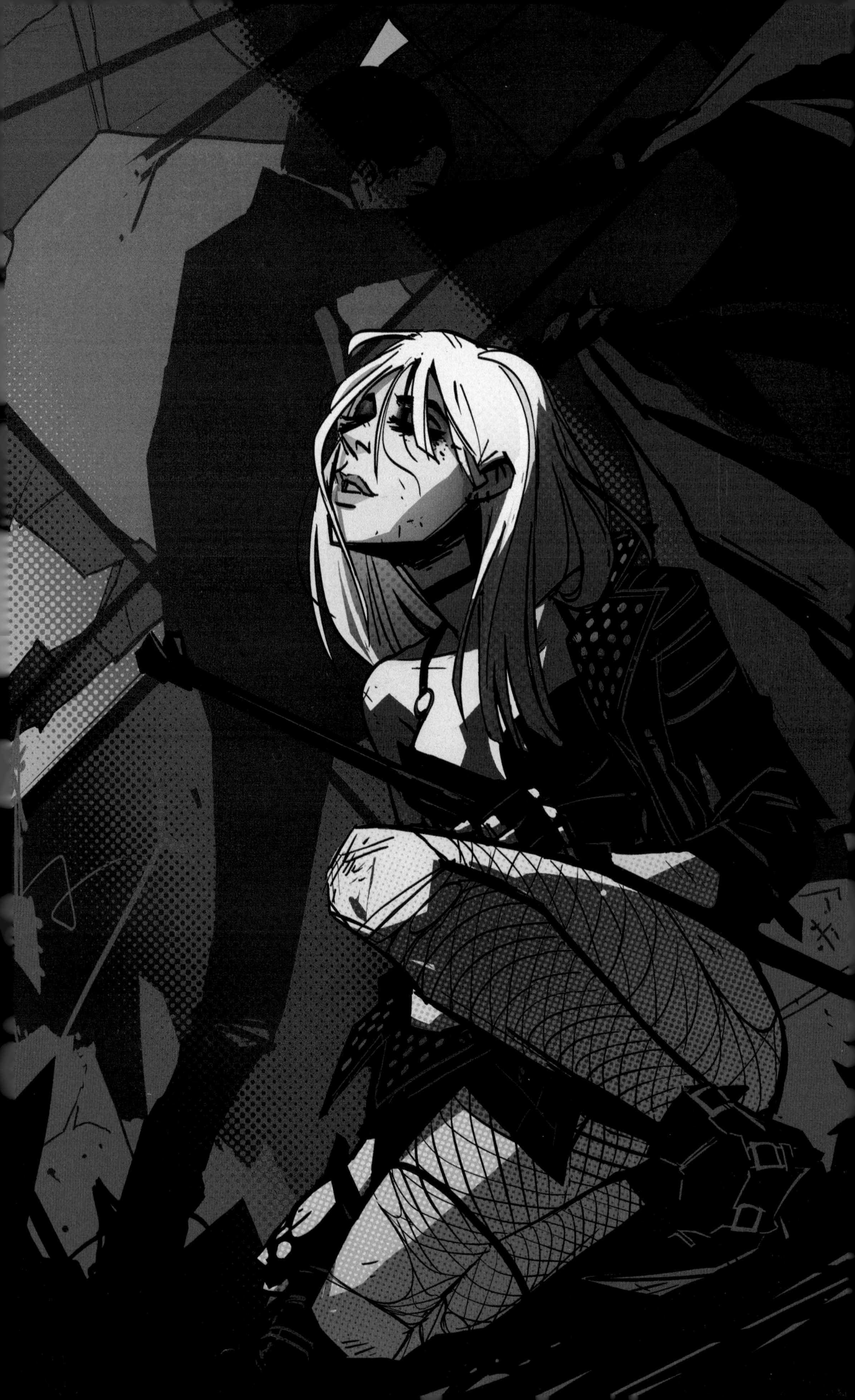

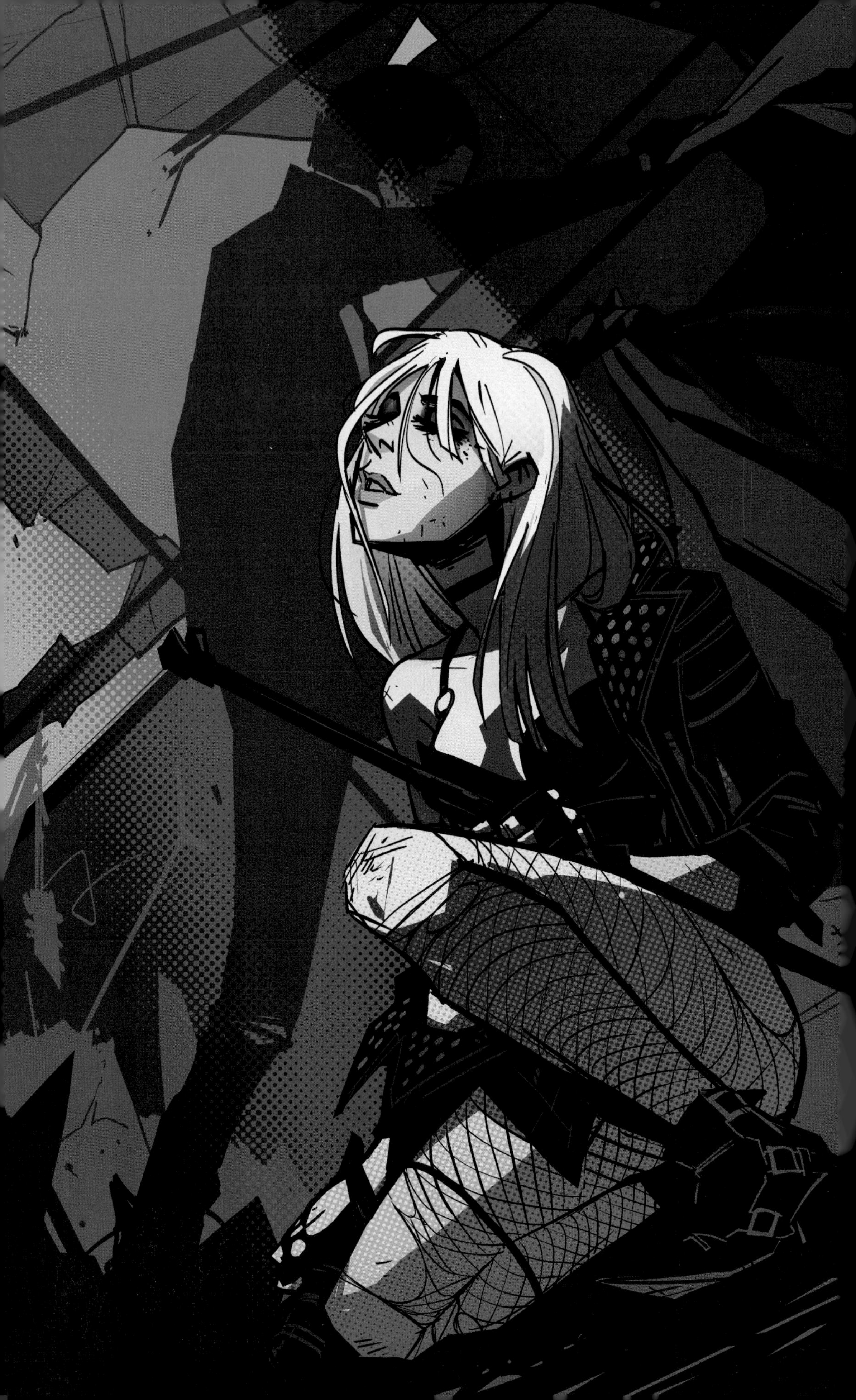

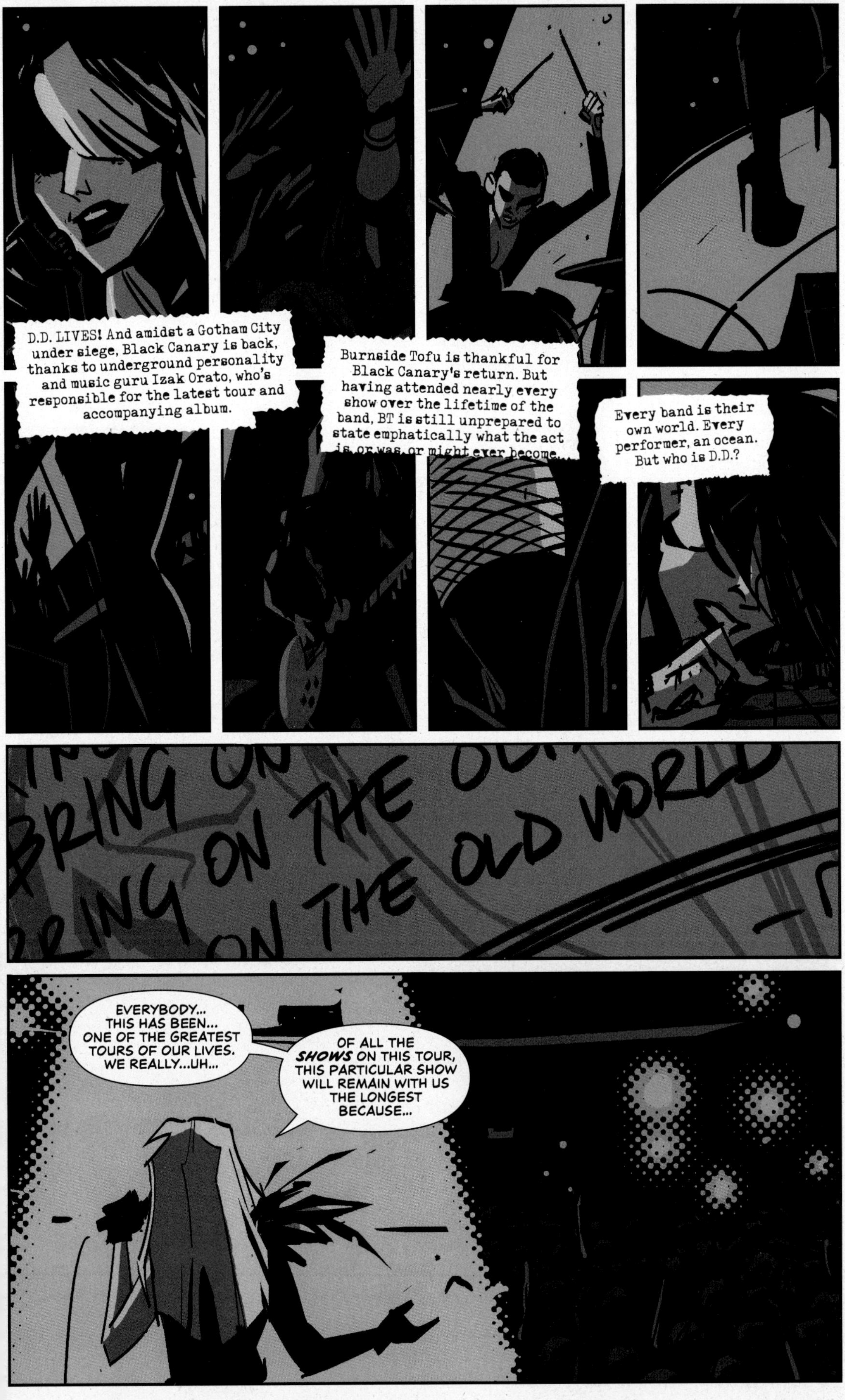
D.D. LIVES! And amidst a Gotham City under siege, Black Canary is back, thanks to underground personality and music guru Izak Orato, who's responsible for the latest tour and accompanying album.
Burnside Tofu is thankful for Black Canary's return. But having attended nearly every show over the lifetime of the band, BT is still unprepared to state emphatically what the act is, or was, or might ever become.
Every band is their own world. Every performer, an ocean. But who is D.D.?
BRING ON THE
BRING ON THE OLD WORLD
BRING ON THE
EVERYBODY... THIS HAS BEEN... ONE OF THE GREATEST TOURS OF OUR LIVES. WE REALLY...UH...
OF ALL THE SHOWS ON THIS TOUR, THIS PARTICULAR SHOW WILL REMAIN WITH US THE LONGEST BECAUSE...

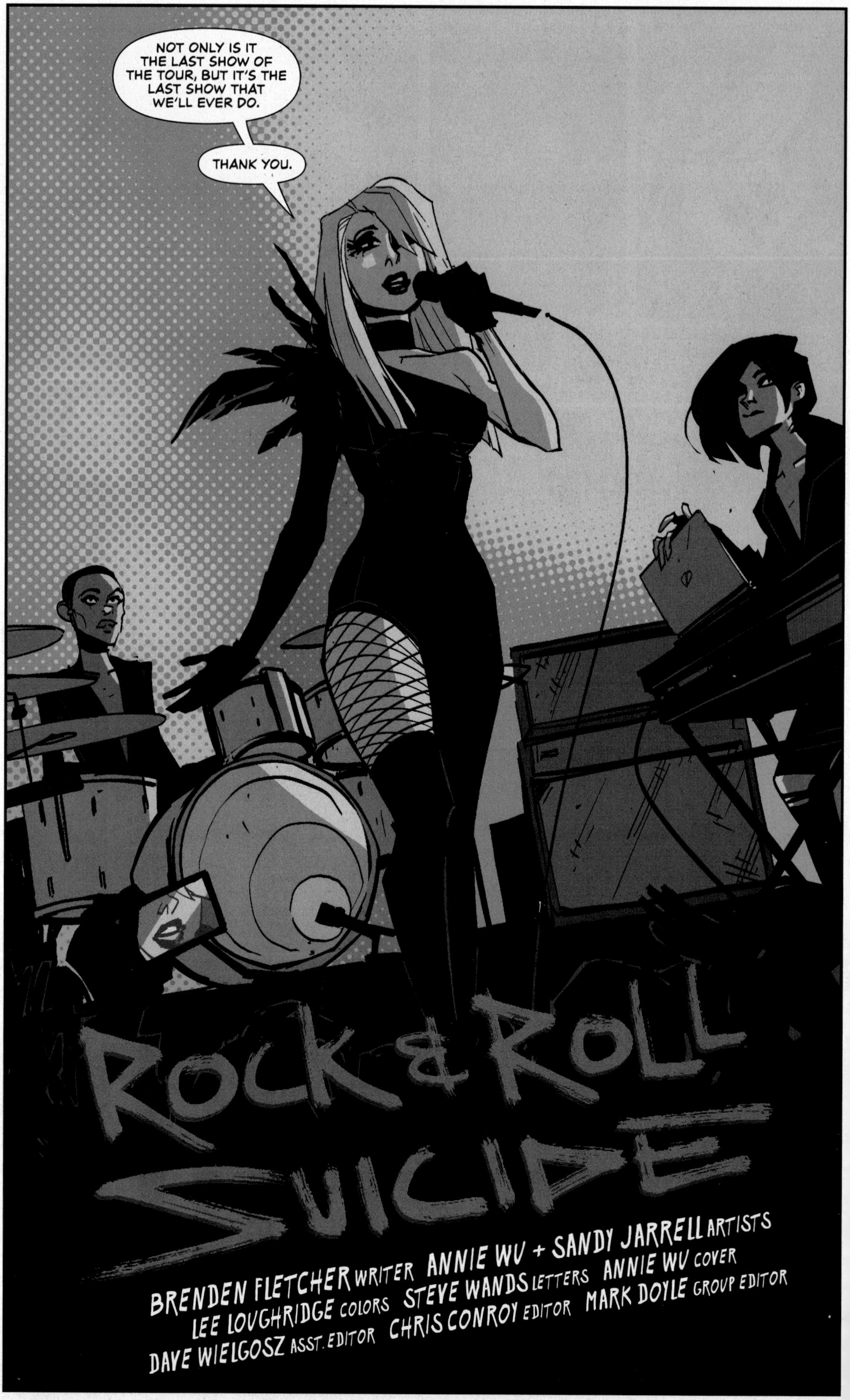
NOT ONLY IS IT THE LAST SHOW OF THE TOUR, BUT IT'S THE LAST SHOW THAT WE'LL EVER DO.
THANK YOU.
ROCK & ROLL SUICIDE
BRENDEN FLETCHER WRITER ANNIE WU + SANDY JARRELL ARTISTS
LEE LOUGHRIDGE COLORS STEVE WANDS LETTERS ANNIE WU COVER
DAVE WIELGOSZ ASST. EDITOR CHRIS CONROY EDITOR MARK DOYLE GROUP EDITOR

NE YEAR LATER.

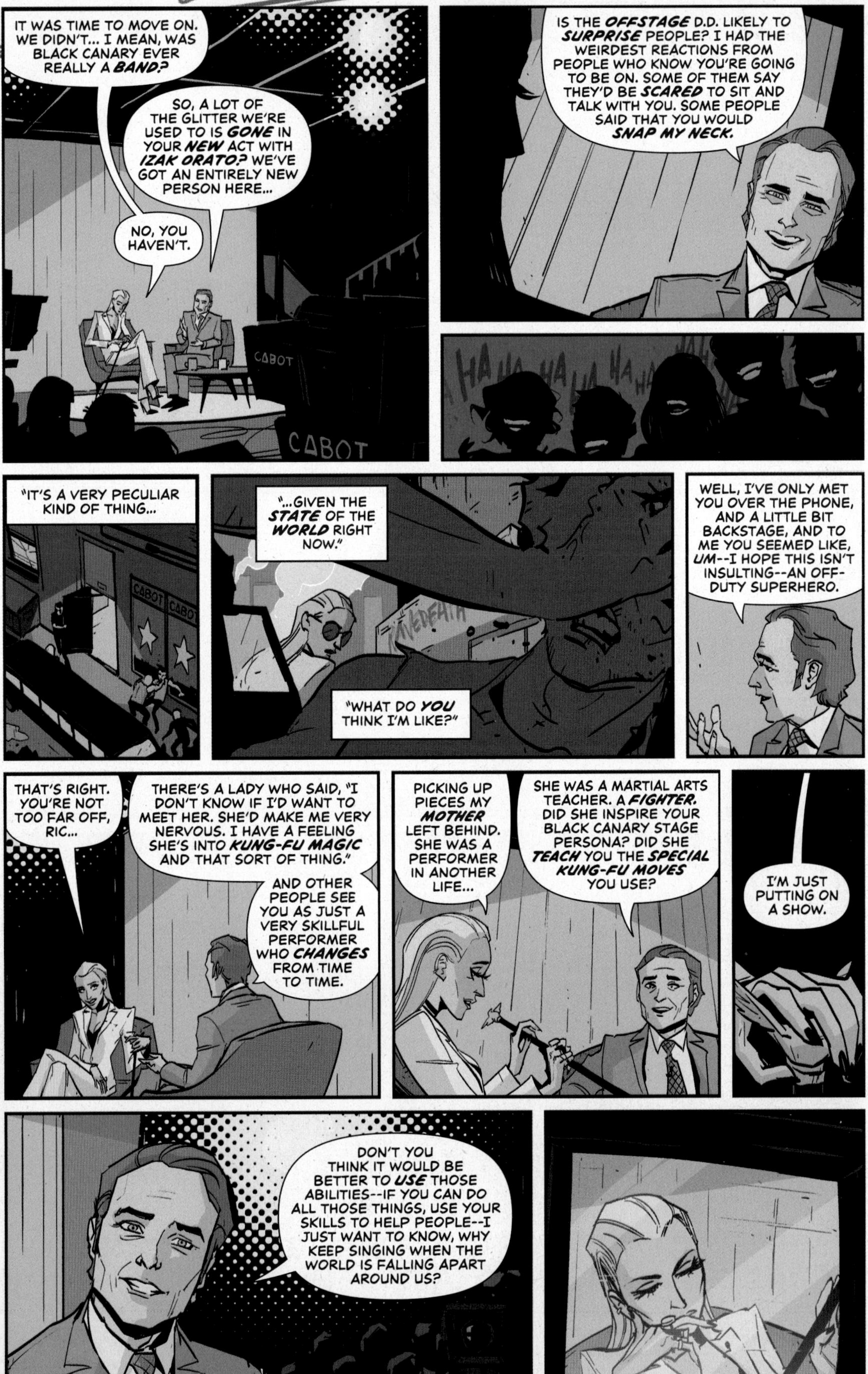
IT WAS TIME TO MOVE ON. WE DIDN'T... I MEAN, WAS BLACK CANARY EVER REALLY A BAND?
SO, A LOT OF THE GLITTER WE'RE USED TO IS GONE IN YOUR NEW ACT WITH IZAK ORATO? WE'VE GOT AN ENTIRELY NEW PERSON HERE...
NO, YOU HAVEN'T.
CABOT
CABOT
IS THE OFFSTAGE D.D. LIKELY TO SURPRISE PEOPLE? I HAD THE WEIRDEST REACTIONS FROM PEOPLE WHO KNOW YOU'RE GOING TO BE ON. SOME OF THEM SAY THEY'D BE SCARED TO SIT AND TALK WITH YOU. SOME PEOPLE SAID THAT YOU WOULD SNAP MY NECK.
"IT'S A VERY PECULIAR KIND OF THING...
CABOT CABOT
"...GIVEN THE STATE OF THE WORLD RIGHT NOW."
"WHAT DO YOU THINK I'M LIKE?"
WELL, I'VE ONLY MET YOU OVER THE PHONE, AND A LITTLE BIT BACKSTAGE, AND TO ME YOU SEEMED LIKE, UM--I HOPE THIS ISN'T INSULTING--AN OFF-DUTY SUPERHERO.
THAT'S RIGHT. YOU'RE NOT TOO FAR OFF, RIC...
THERE'S A LADY WHO SAID, "I DON'T KNOW IF I'D WANT TO MEET HER. SHE'D MAKE ME VERY NERVOUS. I HAVE A FEELING SHE'S INTO KUNG-FU MAGIC AND THAT SORT OF THING."
AND OTHER PEOPLE SEE YOU AS JUST A VERY SKILLFUL PERFORMER WHO CHANGES FROM TIME TO TIME.
PICKING UP PIECES MY MOTHER LEFT BEHIND. SHE WAS A PERFORMER IN ANOTHER LIFE...
SHE WAS A MARTIAL ARTS TEACHER. A FIGHTER. DID SHE INSPIRE YOUR BLACK CANARY STAGE PERSONA? DID SHE TEACH YOU THE SPECIAL KUNG-FU MOVES YOU USE?
I'M JUST PUTTING ON A SHOW.
DON'T YOU THINK IT WOULD BE BETTER TO USE THOSE ABILITIES--IF YOU CAN DO ALL THOSE THINGS, USE YOUR SKILLS TO HELP PEOPLE--I JUST WANT TO KNOW, WHY KEEP SINGING WHEN THE WORLD IS FALLING APART AROUND US?

ONE YEAR LATER

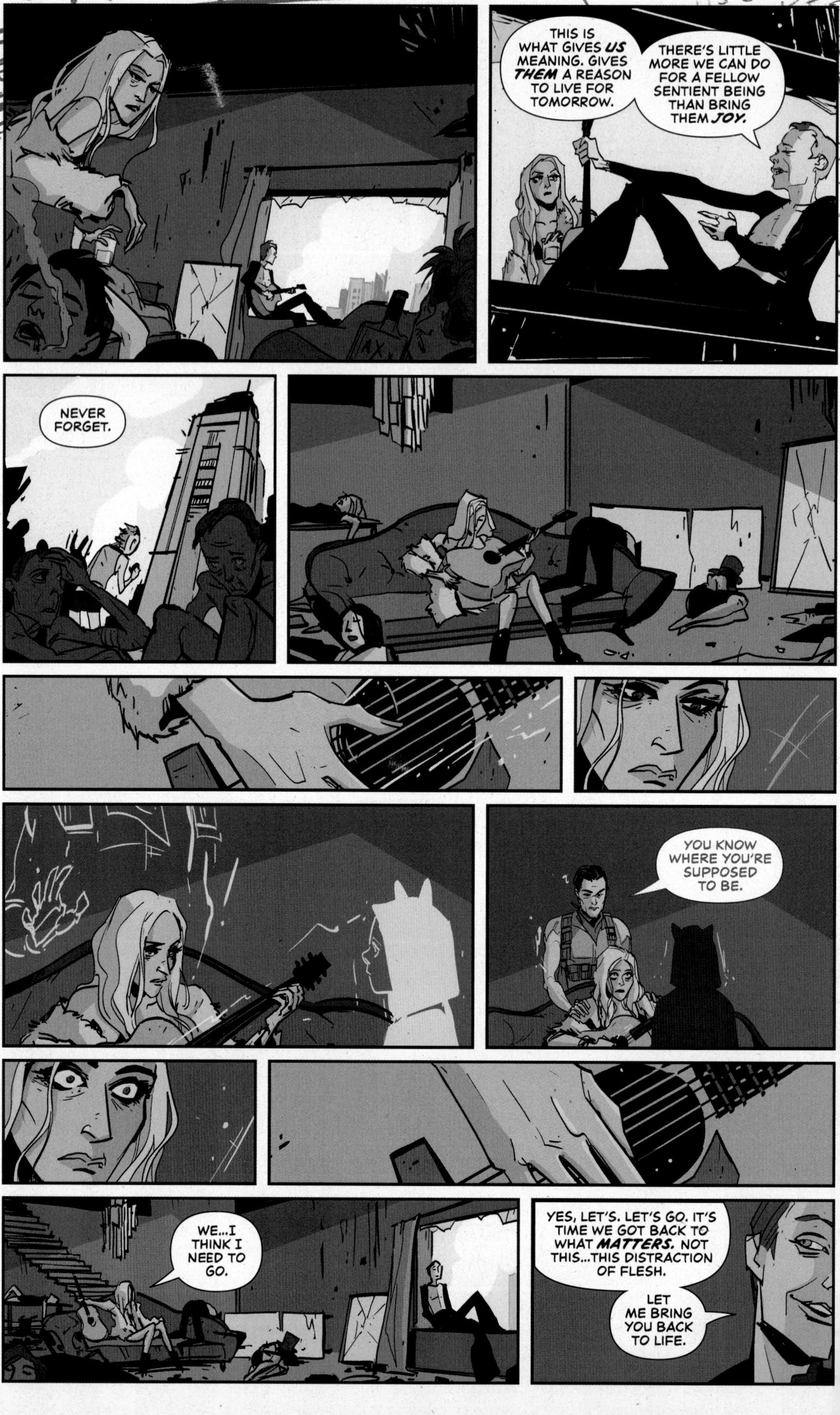
THIS IS WHAT GIVES US MEANING. GIVES THEM A REASON TO LIVE FOR TOMORROW.
THERE'S LITTLE MORE WE CAN DO FOR A FELLOW SENTIENT BEING THAN BRING THEM JOY.
NEVER FORGET.
YOU KNOW WHERE YOU'RE SUPPOSED TO BE.
WE...I THINK I NEED TO GO.
YES, LET'S. LET'S GO. IT'S TIME WE GOT BACK TO WHAT MATTERS. NOT THIS...THIS DISTRACTION OF FLESH.
LET ME BRING YOU BACK TO LIFE.

TWO YEARS LATER

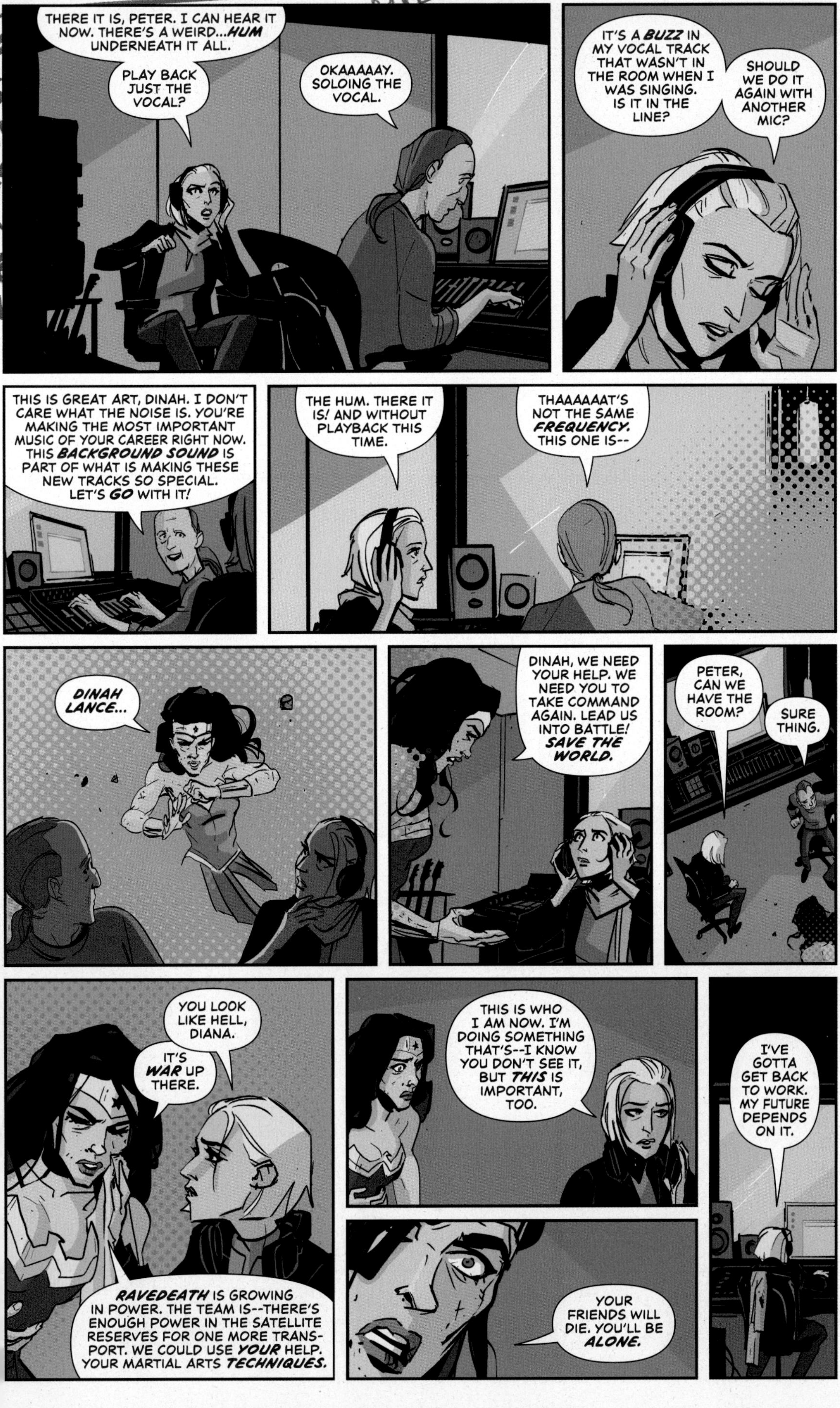
THERE IT IS, PETER. I CAN HEAR IT NOW. THERE'S A WEIRD...HUM UNDERNEATH IT ALL.
PLAY BACK JUST THE VOCAL?
OKAAAAAY. SOLOING THE VOCAL.
IT'S A BUZZ IN MY VOCAL TRACK THAT WASN'T IN THE ROOM WHEN I WAS SINGING. IS IT IN THE LINE?
SHOULD WE DO IT AGAIN WITH ANOTHER MIC?
THIS IS GREAT ART, DINAH. I DON'T CARE WHAT THE NOISE IS. YOU'RE MAKING THE MOST IMPORTANT MUSIC OF YOUR CAREER RIGHT NOW. THIS BACKGROUND SOUND IS PART OF WHAT IS MAKING THESE NEW TRACKS SO SPECIAL. LET'S GO WITH IT!
THE HUM. THERE IT IS! AND WITHOUT PLAYBACK THIS TIME.
THAAAAAAT'S NOT THE SAME FREQUENCY. THIS ONE IS--
DINAH LANCE...
DINAH, WE NEED YOUR HELP. WE NEED YOU TO TAKE COMMAND AGAIN. LEAD US INTO BATTLE! SAVE THE WORLD.
PETER, CAN WE HAVE THE ROOM?
SURE THING.
YOU LOOK LIKE HELL, DIANA.
IT'S WAR UP THERE.
RAVEDEATH IS GROWING IN POWER. THE TEAM IS--THERE'S ENOUGH POWER IN THE SATELLITE RESERVES FOR ONE MORE TRANSPORT. WE COULD USE YOUR HELP. YOUR MARTIAL ARTS TECHNIQUES.
THIS IS WHO I AM NOW. I'M DOING SOMETHING THAT'S--I KNOW YOU DON'T SEE IT, BUT THIS IS IMPORTANT, TOO.
YOUR FRIENDS WILL DIE. YOU'LL BE ALONE.
I'VE GOTTA GET BACK TO WORK. MY FUTURE DEPENDS ON IT.

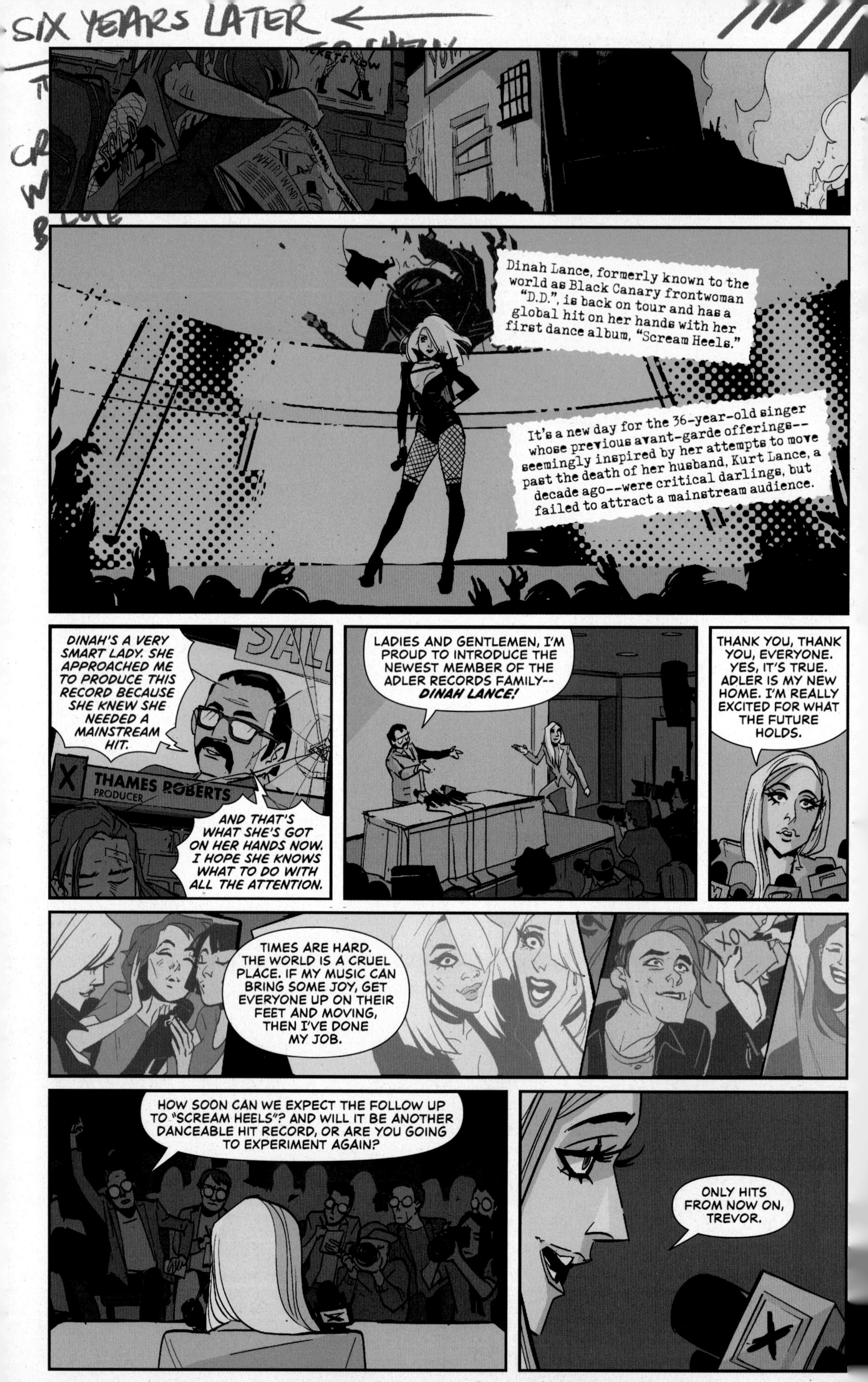

SIX YEARS LATER
SOLD OUT
Dinah Lance, formerly known to the world as Black Canary frontwoman "D.D.", is back on tour and has a global hit on her hands with her first dance album, "Scream Heels."
It's a new day for the 36-year-old singer--whose previous avant-garde offerings--seemingly inspired by her attempts to move past the death of her husband, Kurt Lance, a decade ago--were critical darlings, but failed to attract a mainstream audience.
DINAH'S A VERY SMART LADY. SHE APPROACHED ME TO PRODUCE THIS RECORD BECAUSE SHE KNEW SHE NEEDED A MAINSTREAM HIT.
THAMES ROBERTS
PRODUCER
AND THAT'S WHAT SHE'S GOT ON HER HANDS NOW. I HOPE SHE KNOWS WHAT TO DO WITH ALL THE ATTENTION.
LADIES AND GENTLEMEN, I'M PROUD TO INTRODUCE THE NEWEST MEMBER OF THE ADLER RECORDS FAMILY--*DINAH LANCE!*
THANK YOU, THANK YOU, EVERYONE. YES, IT'S TRUE. ADLER IS MY NEW HOME. I'M REALLY EXCITED FOR WHAT THE FUTURE HOLDS.
TIMES ARE HARD. THE WORLD IS A CRUEL PLACE. IF MY MUSIC CAN BRING SOME JOY, GET EVERYONE UP ON THEIR FEET AND MOVING, THEN I'VE DONE MY JOB.
HOW SOON CAN WE EXPECT THE FOLLOW UP TO "SCREAM HEELS"? AND WILL IT BE ANOTHER DANCEABLE HIT RECORD, OR ARE YOU GOING TO EXPERIMENT AGAIN?
ONLY HITS FROM NOW ON, TREVOR.

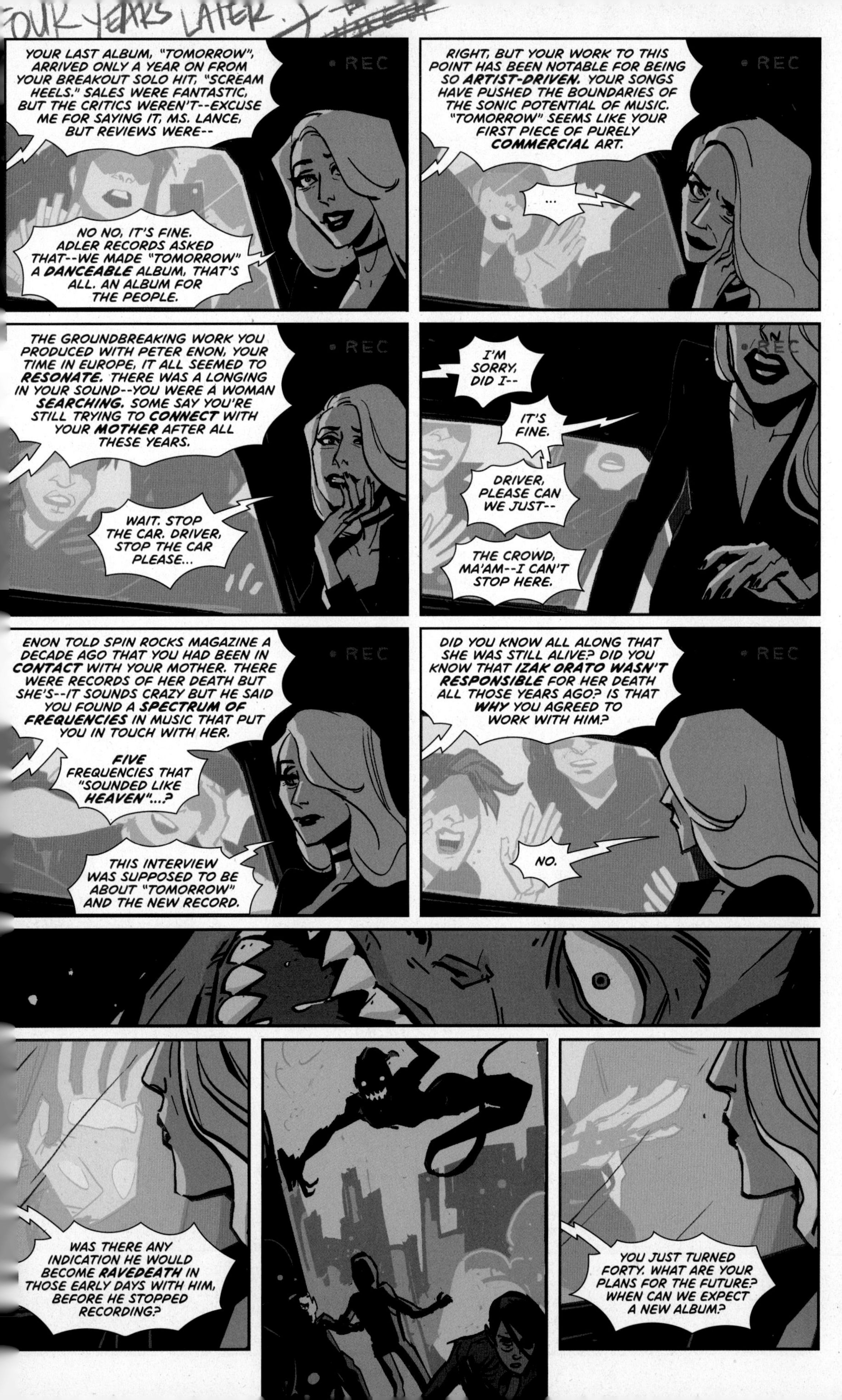
FOUR YEARS LATER.
REC
YOUR LAST ALBUM, "TOMORROW", ARRIVED ONLY A YEAR ON FROM YOUR BREAKOUT SOLO HIT, "SCREAM HEELS." SALES WERE FANTASTIC, BUT THE CRITICS WEREN'T--EXCUSE ME FOR SAYING IT, MS. LANCE, BUT REVIEWS WERE--
NO NO, IT'S FINE. ADLER RECORDS ASKED THAT--WE MADE "TOMORROW" A DANCEABLE ALBUM, THAT'S ALL. AN ALBUM FOR THE PEOPLE.
REC
RIGHT, BUT YOUR WORK TO THIS POINT HAS BEEN NOTABLE FOR BEING SO ARTIST-DRIVEN. YOUR SONGS HAVE PUSHED THE BOUNDARIES OF THE SONIC POTENTIAL OF MUSIC. "TOMORROW" SEEMS LIKE YOUR FIRST PIECE OF PURELY COMMERCIAL ART.
...
REC
THE GROUNDBREAKING WORK YOU PRODUCED WITH PETER ENON, YOUR TIME IN EUROPE, IT ALL SEEMED TO RESONATE. THERE WAS A LONGING IN YOUR SOUND--YOU WERE A WOMAN SEARCHING. SOME SAY YOU'RE STILL TRYING TO CONNECT WITH YOUR MOTHER AFTER ALL THESE YEARS.
WAIT. STOP THE CAR. DRIVER, STOP THE CAR PLEASE...
REC
I'M SORRY, DID I--
IT'S FINE.
DRIVER, PLEASE CAN WE JUST--
THE CROWD, MA'AM--I CAN'T STOP HERE.
REC
ENON TOLD SPIN ROCKS MAGAZINE A DECADE AGO THAT YOU HAD BEEN IN CONTACT WITH YOUR MOTHER. THERE WERE RECORDS OF HER DEATH BUT SHE'S--IT SOUNDS CRAZY BUT HE SAID YOU FOUND A SPECTRUM OF FREQUENCIES IN MUSIC THAT PUT YOU IN TOUCH WITH HER.
FIVE FREQUENCIES THAT "SOUNDED LIKE HEAVEN"...?
THIS INTERVIEW WAS SUPPOSED TO BE ABOUT "TOMORROW" AND THE NEW RECORD.
REC
DID YOU KNOW ALL ALONG THAT SHE WAS STILL ALIVE? DID YOU KNOW THAT IZAK ORATO WASN'T RESPONSIBLE FOR HER DEATH ALL THOSE YEARS AGO? IS THAT WHY YOU AGREED TO WORK WITH HIM?
NO.
WAS THERE ANY INDICATION HE WOULD BECOME RAVEDEATH IN THOSE EARLY DAYS WITH HIM, BEFORE HE STOPPED RECORDING?
YOU JUST TURNED FORTY. WHAT ARE YOUR PLANS FOR THE FUTURE? WHEN CAN WE EXPECT A NEW ALBUM?

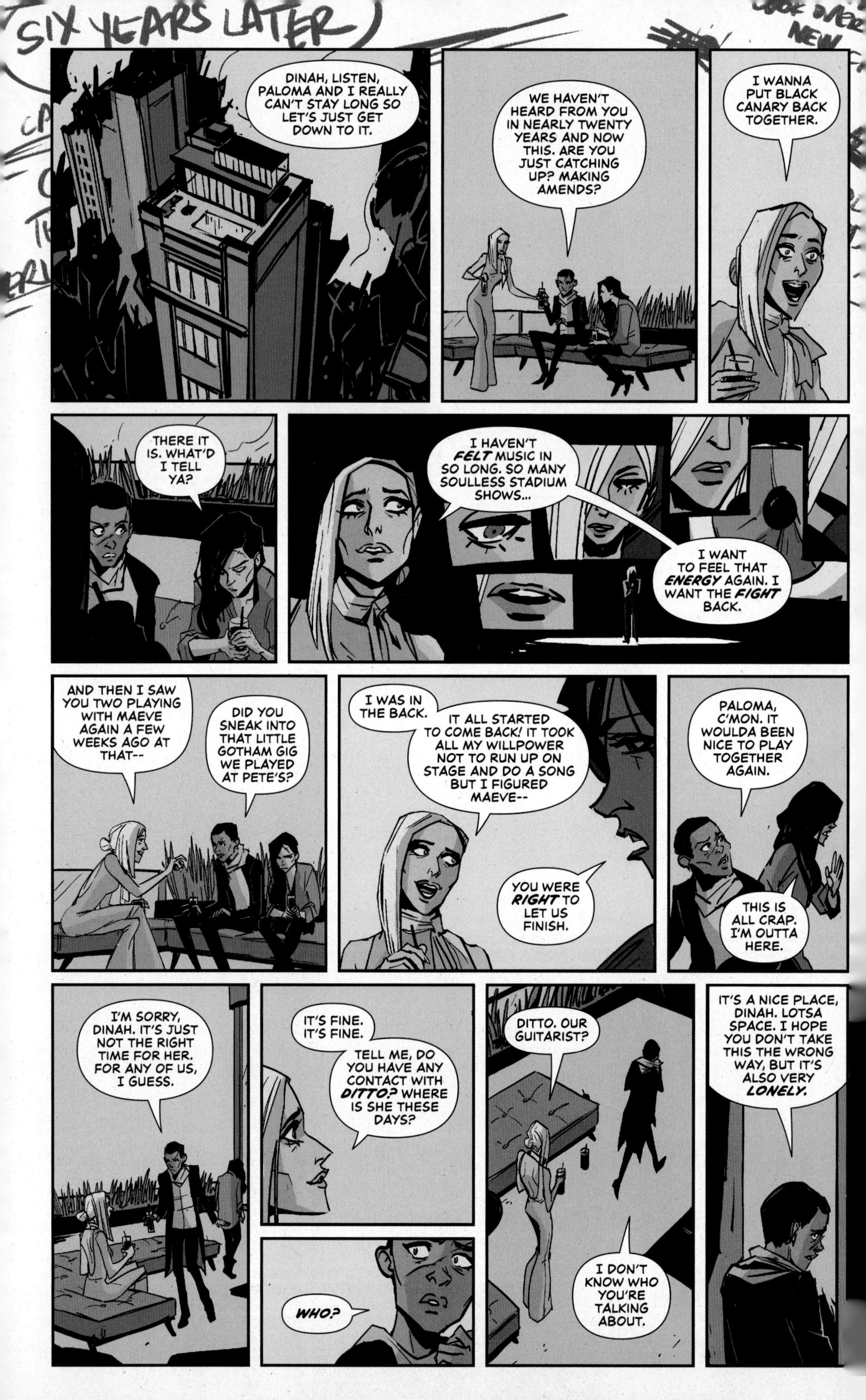
SIX YEARS LATER
DINAH, LISTEN, PALOMA AND I REALLY CAN'T STAY LONG SO LET'S JUST GET DOWN TO IT.
WE HAVEN'T HEARD FROM YOU IN NEARLY TWENTY YEARS AND NOW THIS. ARE YOU JUST CATCHING UP? MAKING AMENDS?
I WANNA PUT BLACK CANARY BACK TOGETHER.
THERE IT IS. WHAT'D I TELL YA?
I HAVEN'T FELT MUSIC IN SO LONG. SO MANY SOULLESS STADIUM SHOWS...
I WANT TO FEEL THAT ENERGY AGAIN. I WANT THE FIGHT BACK.
AND THEN I SAW YOU TWO PLAYING WITH MAEVE AGAIN A FEW WEEKS AGO AT THAT--
DID YOU SNEAK INTO THAT LITTLE GOTHAM GIG WE PLAYED AT PETE'S?
I WAS IN THE BACK.
IT ALL STARTED TO COME BACK! IT TOOK ALL MY WILLPOWER NOT TO RUN UP ON STAGE AND DO A SONG BUT I FIGURED MAEVE--
YOU WERE RIGHT TO LET US FINISH.
PALOMA, C'MON. IT WOULDA BEEN NICE TO PLAY TOGETHER AGAIN.
THIS IS ALL CRAP. I'M OUTTA HERE.
I'M SORRY, DINAH. IT'S JUST NOT THE RIGHT TIME FOR HER. FOR ANY OF US, I GUESS.
IT'S FINE. IT'S FINE.
TELL ME, DO YOU HAVE ANY CONTACT WITH DITTO? WHERE IS SHE THESE DAYS?
WHO?
DITTO. OUR GUITARIST?
I DON'T KNOW WHO YOU'RE TALKING ABOUT.
IT'S A NICE PLACE, DINAH. LOTSA SPACE. I HOPE YOU DON'T TAKE THIS THE WRONG WAY, BUT IT'S ALSO VERY LONELY.

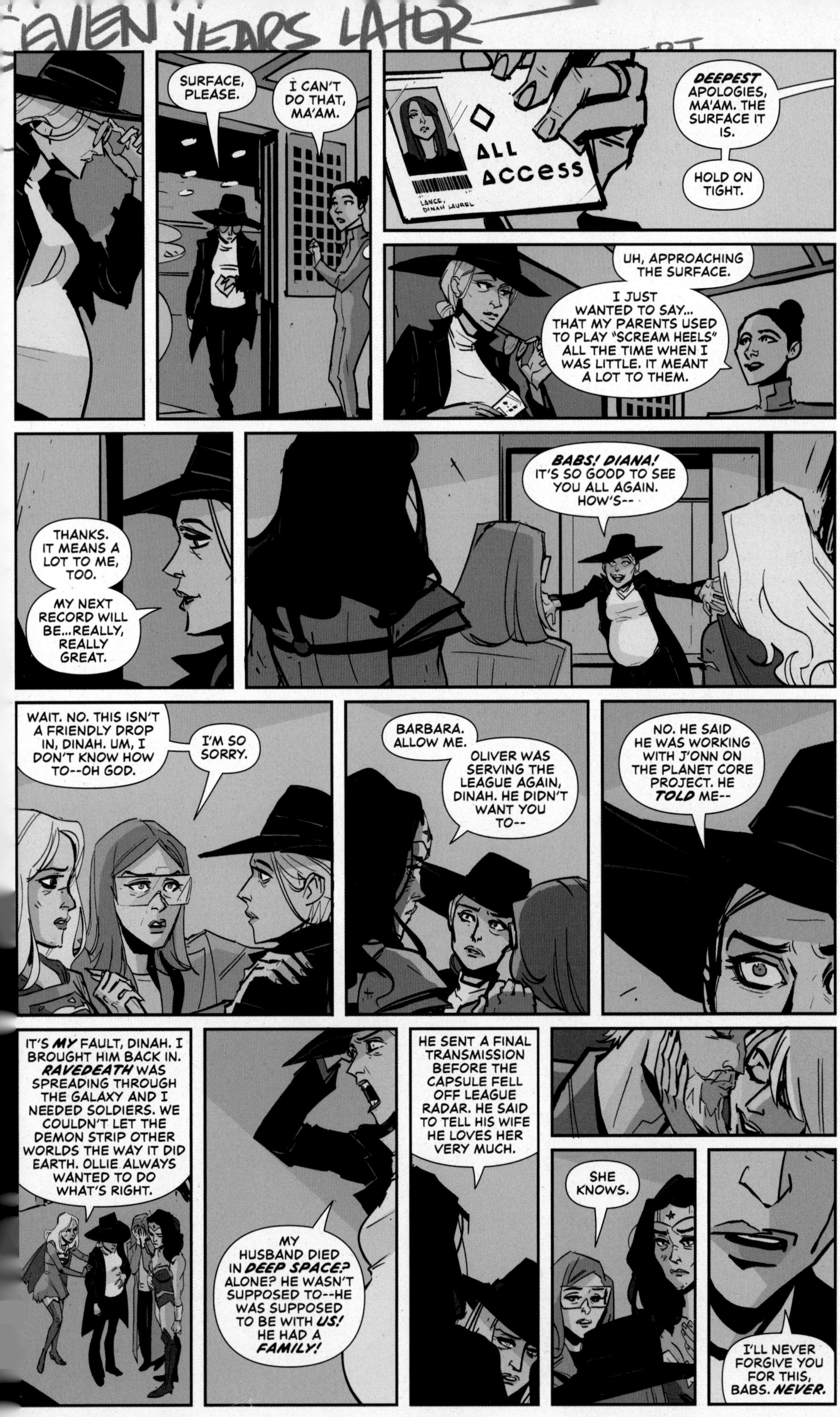
SEVEN YEARS LATER
SURFACE, PLEASE.
I CAN'T DO THAT, MA'AM.
ALL ACCESS
LANCE, DINAH LAUREL
DEEPEST APOLOGIES, MA'AM. THE SURFACE IT IS.
HOLD ON TIGHT.
UH, APPROACHING THE SURFACE.
I JUST WANTED TO SAY... THAT MY PARENTS USED TO PLAY "SCREAM HEELS" ALL THE TIME WHEN I WAS LITTLE. IT MEANT A LOT TO THEM.
THANKS. IT MEANS A LOT TO ME, TOO.
MY NEXT RECORD WILL BE...REALLY, REALLY GREAT.
BABS! DIANA! IT'S SO GOOD TO SEE YOU ALL AGAIN. HOW'S--
WAIT. NO. THIS ISN'T A FRIENDLY DROP IN, DINAH. UM, I DON'T KNOW HOW TO--OH GOD.
I'M SO SORRY.
BARBARA. ALLOW ME.
OLIVER WAS SERVING THE LEAGUE AGAIN, DINAH. HE DIDN'T WANT YOU TO--
NO. HE SAID HE WAS WORKING WITH J'ONN ON THE PLANET CORE PROJECT. HE TOLD ME--
IT'S MY FAULT, DINAH. I BROUGHT HIM BACK IN. RAVEDEATH WAS SPREADING THROUGH THE GALAXY AND I NEEDED SOLDIERS. WE COULDN'T LET THE DEMON STRIP OTHER WORLDS THE WAY IT DID EARTH. OLLIE ALWAYS WANTED TO DO WHAT'S RIGHT.
MY HUSBAND DIED IN DEEP SPACE? ALONE? HE WASN'T SUPPOSED TO--HE WAS SUPPOSED TO BE WITH US! HE HAD A FAMILY!
HE SENT A FINAL TRANSMISSION BEFORE THE CAPSULE FELL OFF LEAGUE RADAR. HE SAID TO TELL HIS WIFE HE LOVES HER VERY MUCH.
SHE KNOWS.
I'LL NEVER FORGIVE YOU FOR THIS, BABS. NEVER.

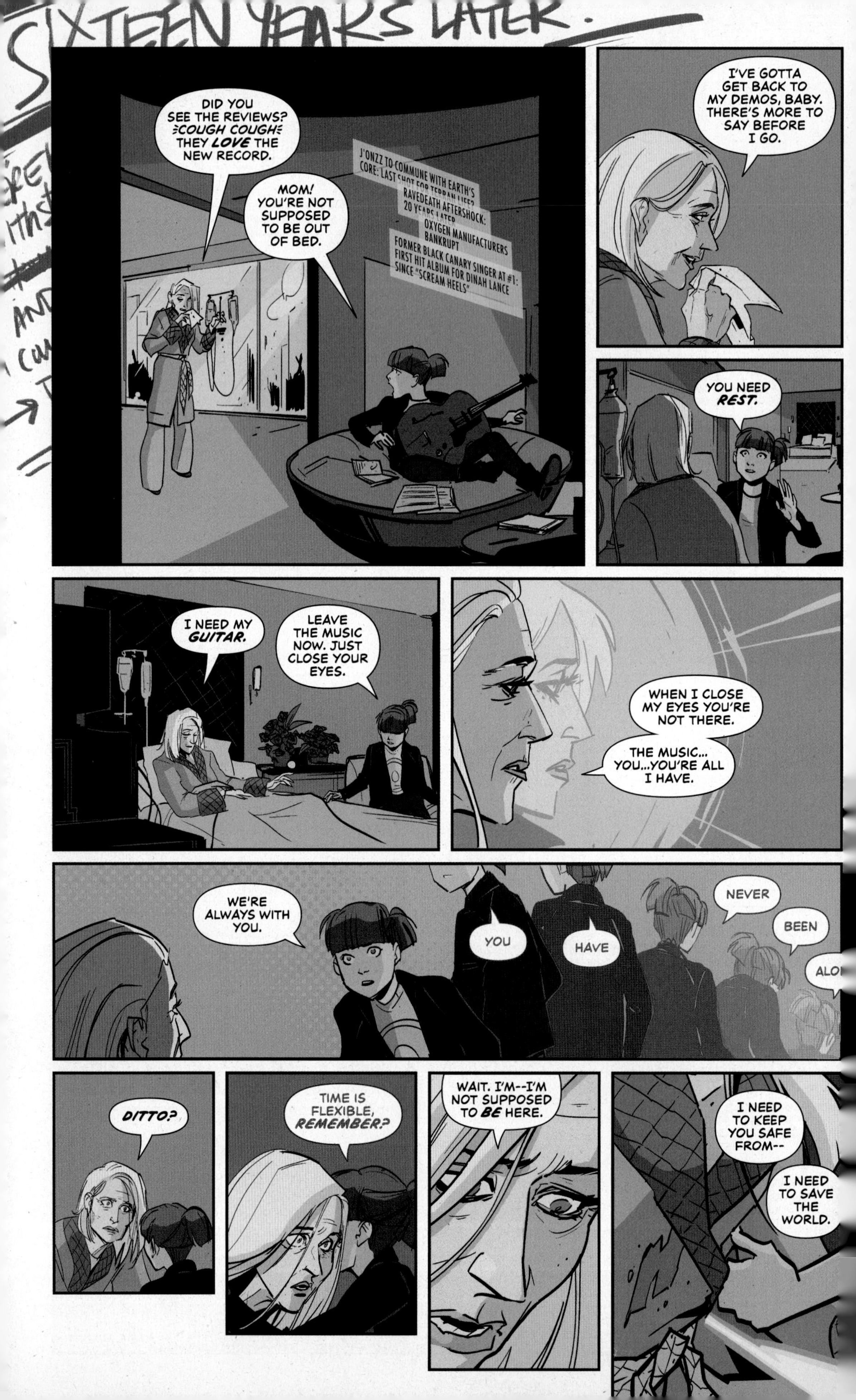
SIXTEEN YEARS LATER.
DID YOU SEE THE REVIEWS? COUGH COUGH THEY LOVE THE NEW RECORD.
MOM! YOU'RE NOT SUPPOSED TO BE OUT OF BED.
J'ONZZ TO COMMUNE WITH EARTH'S CORE: LAST
RAVEDEATH AFTERSHOCK:
20 Y
OXYGEN MANUFACTURERS BANKRUPT
FORMER BLACK CANARY SINGER AT #1: FIRST HIT ALBUM FOR DINAH LANCE SINCE "SCREAM HEELS"
I'VE GOTTA GET BACK TO MY DEMOS, BABY. THERE'S MORE TO SAY BEFORE I GO.
YOU NEED REST.
I NEED MY GUITAR.
LEAVE THE MUSIC NOW. JUST CLOSE YOUR EYES.
WHEN I CLOSE MY EYES YOU'RE NOT THERE.
THE MUSIC... YOU...YOU'RE ALL I HAVE.
WE'RE ALWAYS WITH YOU.
YOU
HAVE
NEVER
BEEN
ALO
DITTO?
TIME IS FLEXIBLE, REMEMBER?
WAIT. I'M--I'M NOT SUPPOSED TO BE HERE.
I NEED TO KEEP YOU SAFE FROM--
I NEED TO SAVE THE WORLD.

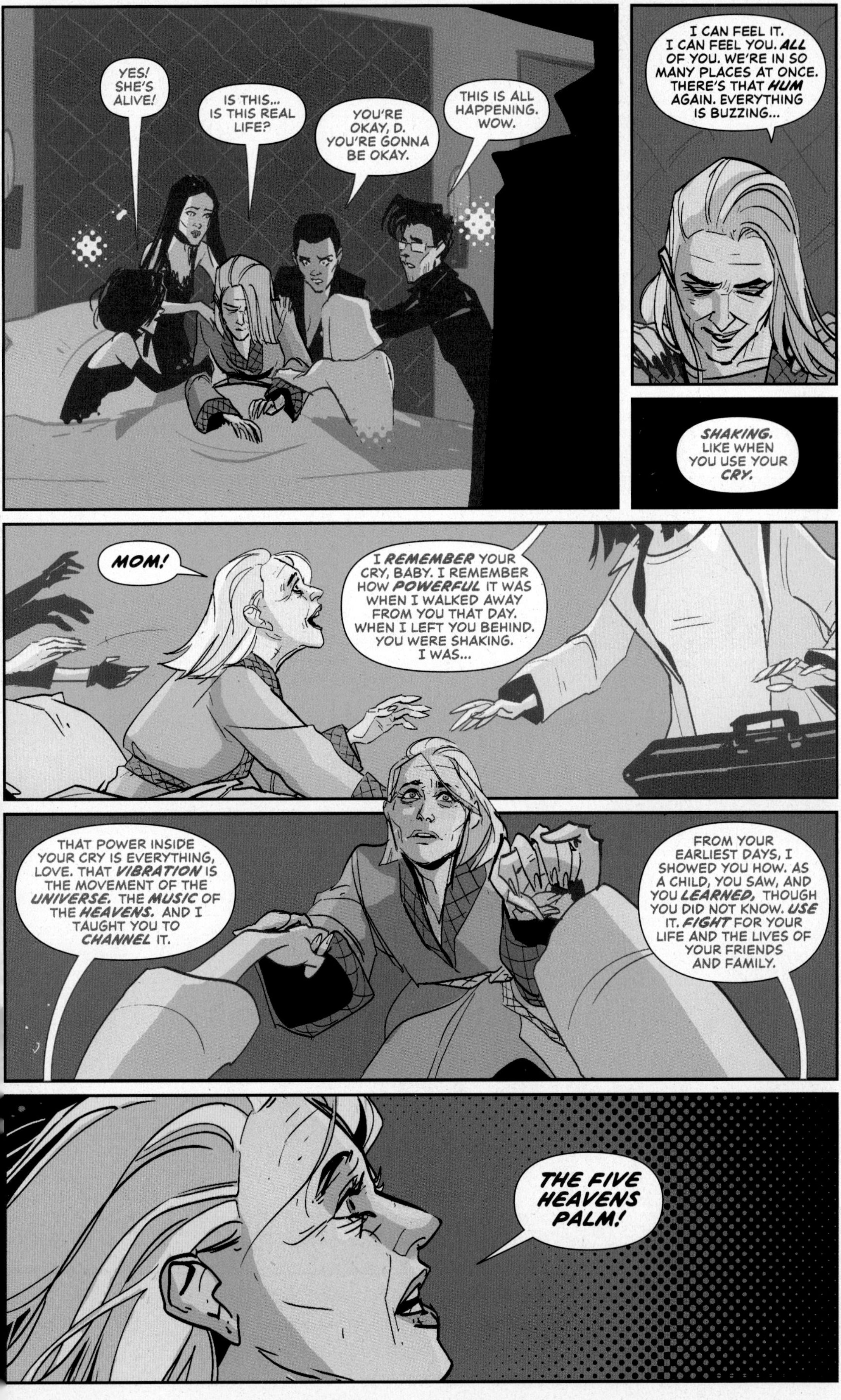
YES! SHE'S ALIVE!
IS THIS... IS THIS REAL LIFE?
YOU'RE OKAY, D. YOU'RE GONNA BE OKAY.
THIS IS ALL HAPPENING. WOW.
I CAN FEEL IT. I CAN FEEL YOU. ALL OF YOU. WE'RE IN SO MANY PLACES AT ONCE. THERE'S THAT HUM AGAIN. EVERYTHING IS BUZZING...
SHAKING. LIKE WHEN YOU USE YOUR CRY.
MOM!
I REMEMBER YOUR CRY, BABY. I REMEMBER HOW POWERFUL IT WAS WHEN I WALKED AWAY FROM YOU THAT DAY. WHEN I LEFT YOU BEHIND. YOU WERE SHAKING. I WAS...
THAT POWER INSIDE YOUR CRY IS EVERYTHING, LOVE. THAT VIBRATION IS THE MOVEMENT OF THE UNIVERSE. THE MUSIC OF THE HEAVENS. AND I TAUGHT YOU TO CHANNEL IT.
FROM YOUR EARLIEST DAYS, I SHOWED YOU HOW. AS A CHILD, YOU SAW, AND YOU LEARNED, THOUGH YOU DID NOT KNOW. USE IT. FIGHT FOR YOUR LIFE AND THE LIVES OF YOUR FRIENDS AND FAMILY.
THE FIVE HEAVENS PALM!

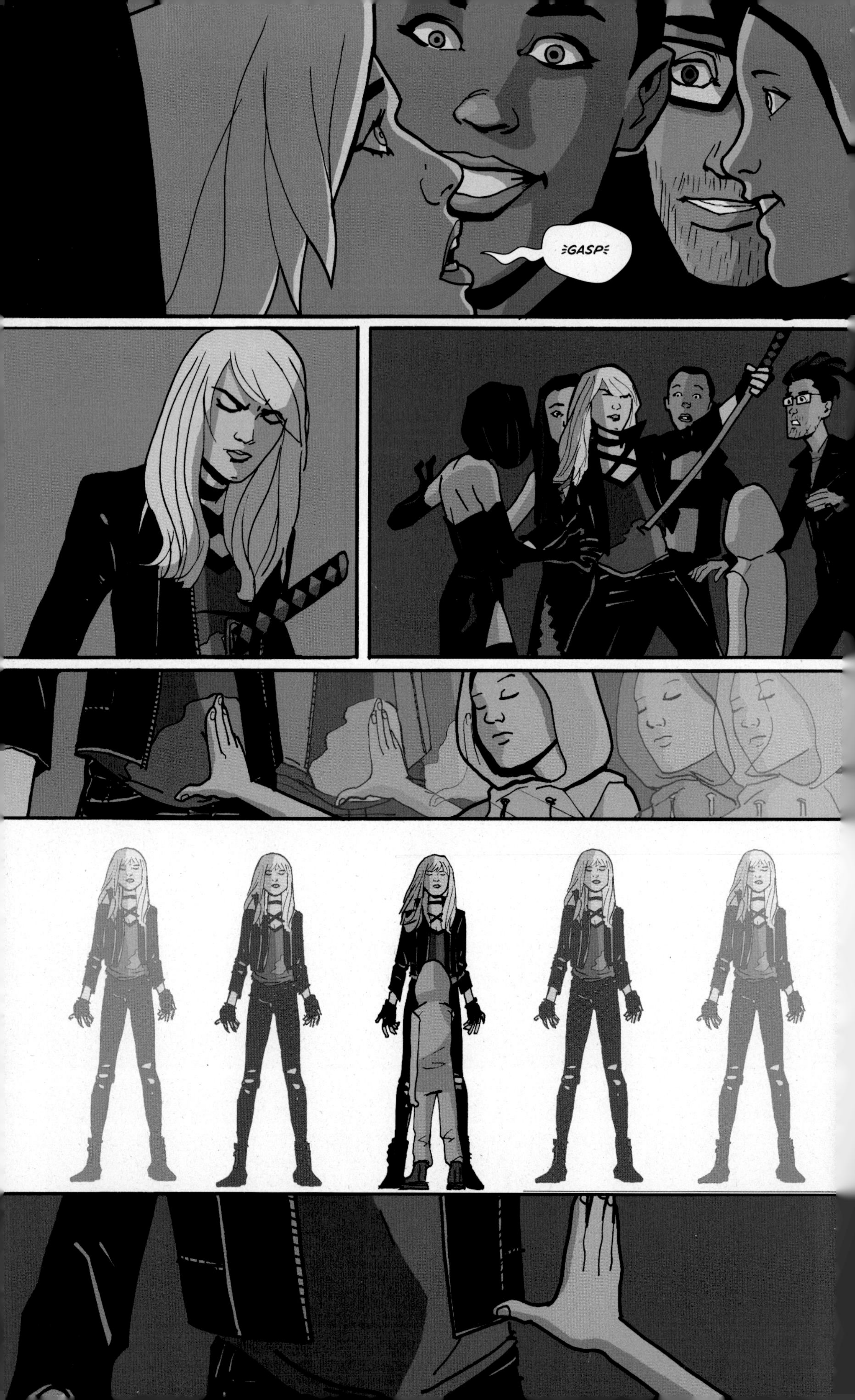
GASP

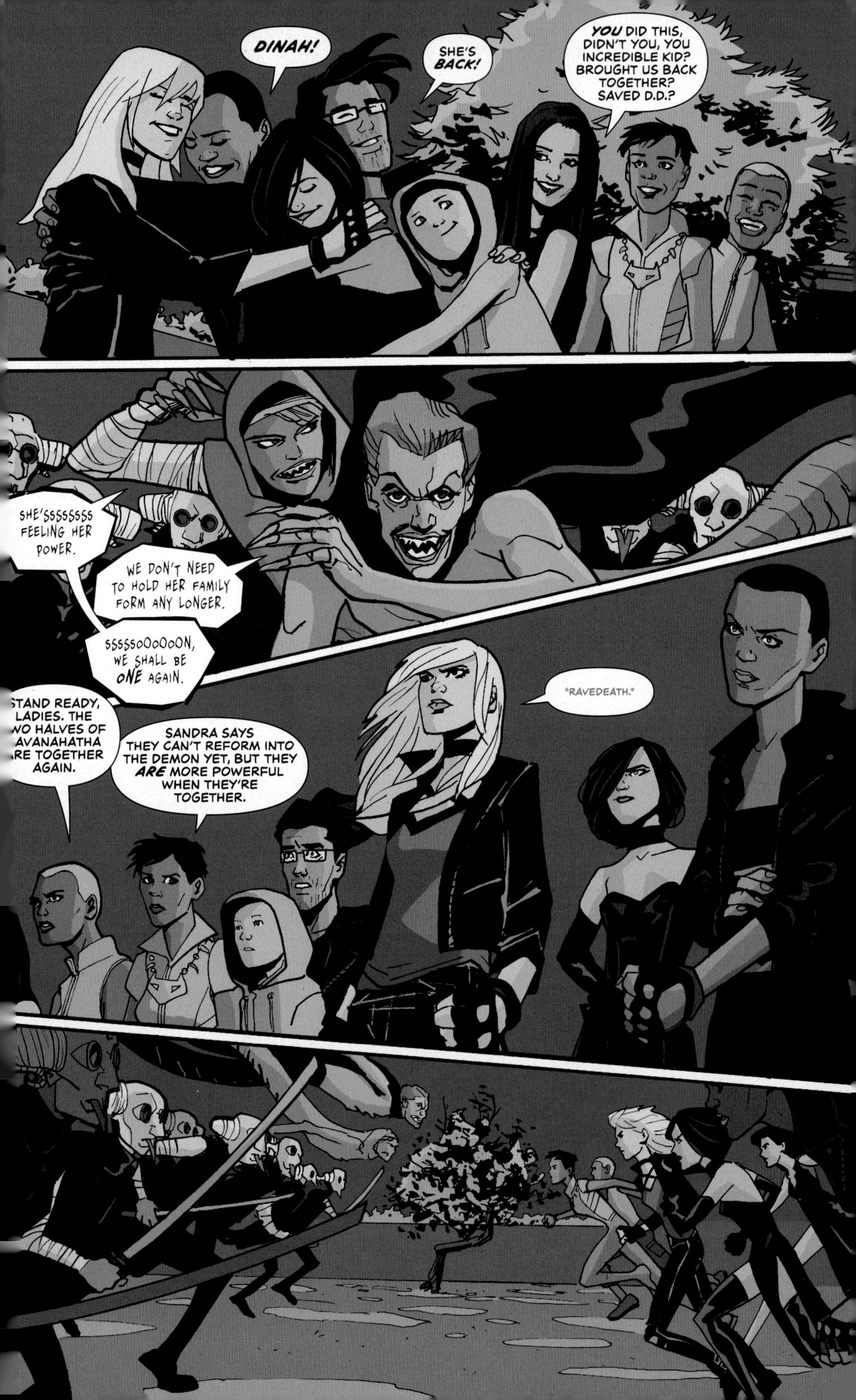
DINAH!
SHE'S BACK!
YOU DID THIS, DIDN'T YOU, YOU INCREDIBLE KID? BROUGHT US BACK TOGETHER? SAVED D.D.?
SHE'SSSSSSSS FEELING HER POWER.
WE DON'T NEED TO HOLD HER FAMILY FORM ANY LONGER.
SSSSSOOOOOON, WE SHALL BE ONE AGAIN.
"RAVEDEATH."
STAND READY, LADIES. THE TWO HALVES OF AVANAHATHA ARE TOGETHER AGAIN.
SANDRA SAYS THEY CAN'T REFORM INTO THE DEMON YET, BUT THEY ARE MORE POWERFUL WHEN THEY'RE TOGETHER.

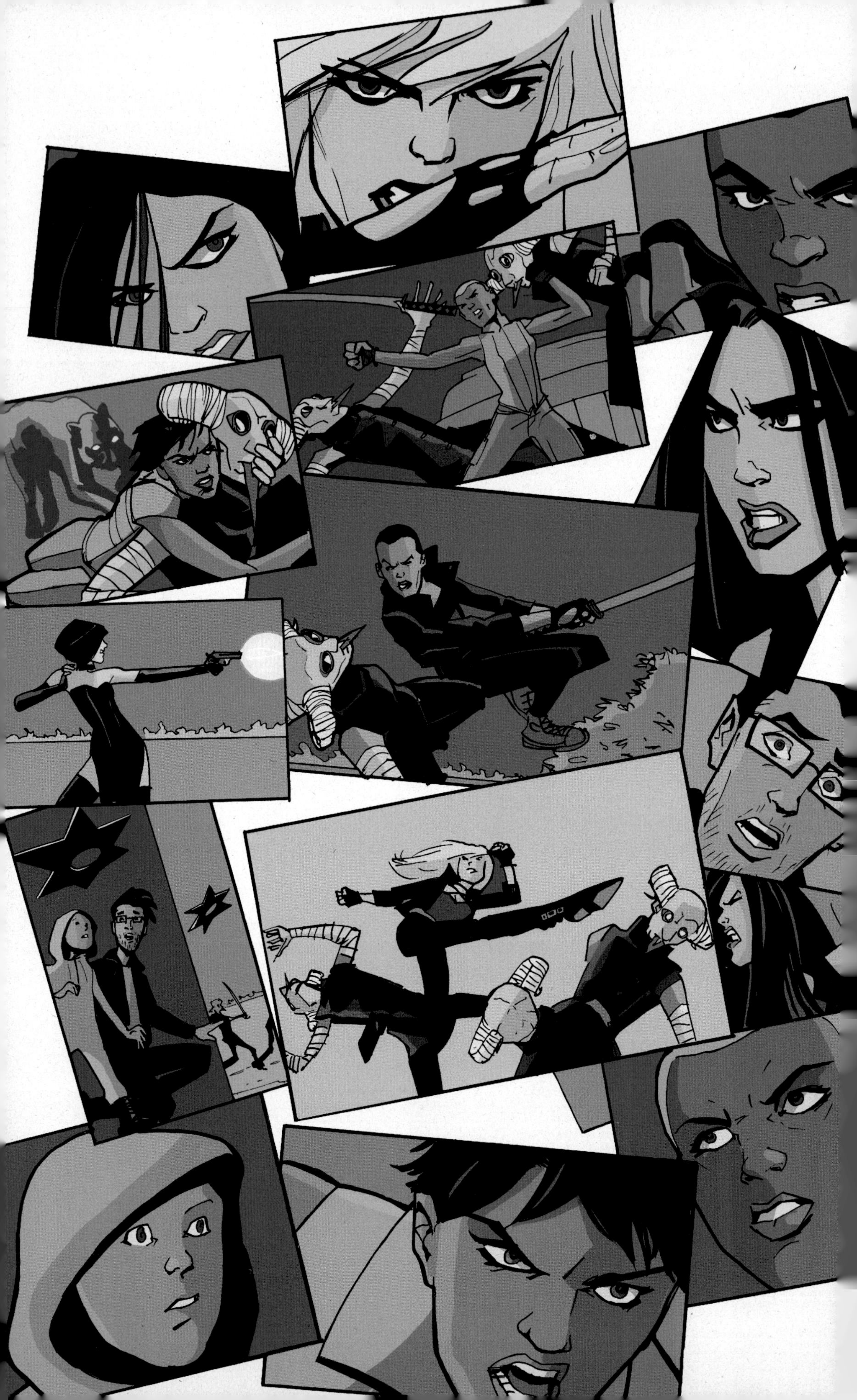

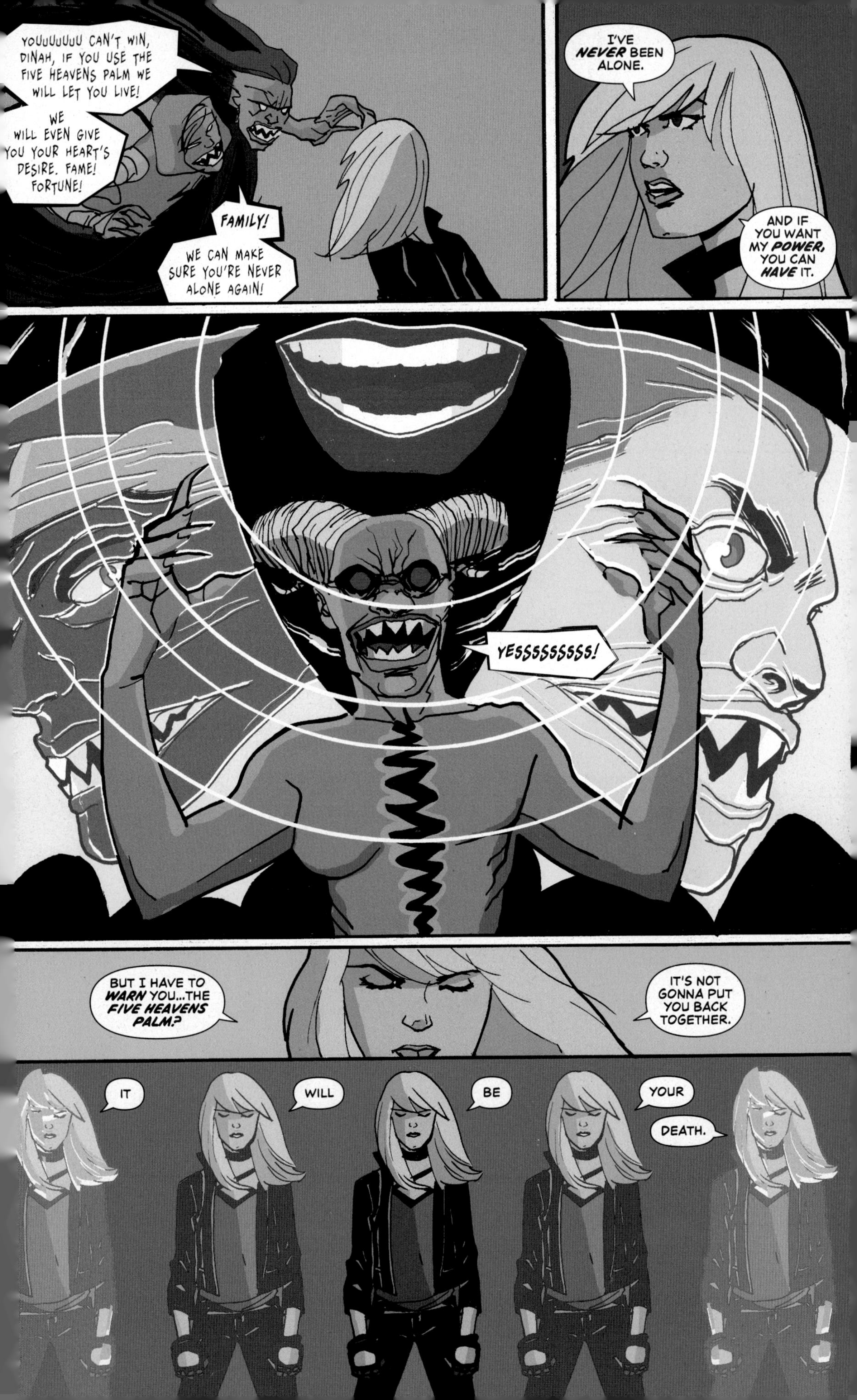
YOUUUUUUU CAN'T WIN, DINAH, IF YOU USE THE FIVE HEAVENS PALM WE WILL LET YOU LIVE!
WE WILL EVEN GIVE YOU YOUR HEART'S DESIRE. FAME! FORTUNE!
FAMILY!
WE CAN MAKE SURE YOU'RE NEVER ALONE AGAIN!
I'VE NEVER BEEN ALONE.
AND IF YOU WANT MY POWER, YOU CAN HAVE IT.
YESSSSSSSSS!
BUT I HAVE TO WARN YOU...THE FIVE HEAVENS PALM?
IT'S NOT GONNA PUT YOU BACK TOGETHER.
IT
WILL
BE
YOUR
DEATH.

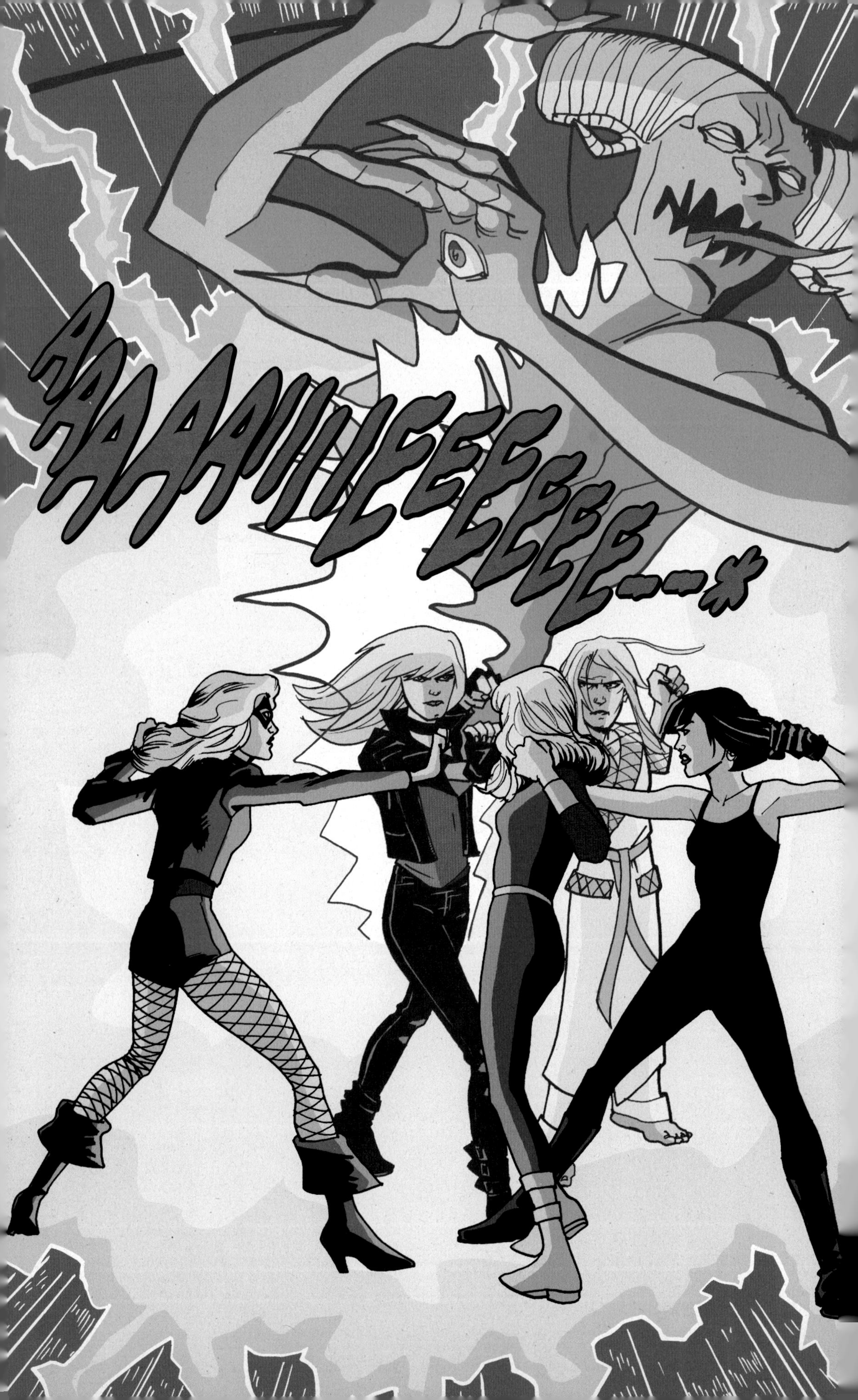
AAAAIIIIEEEEEEE--*

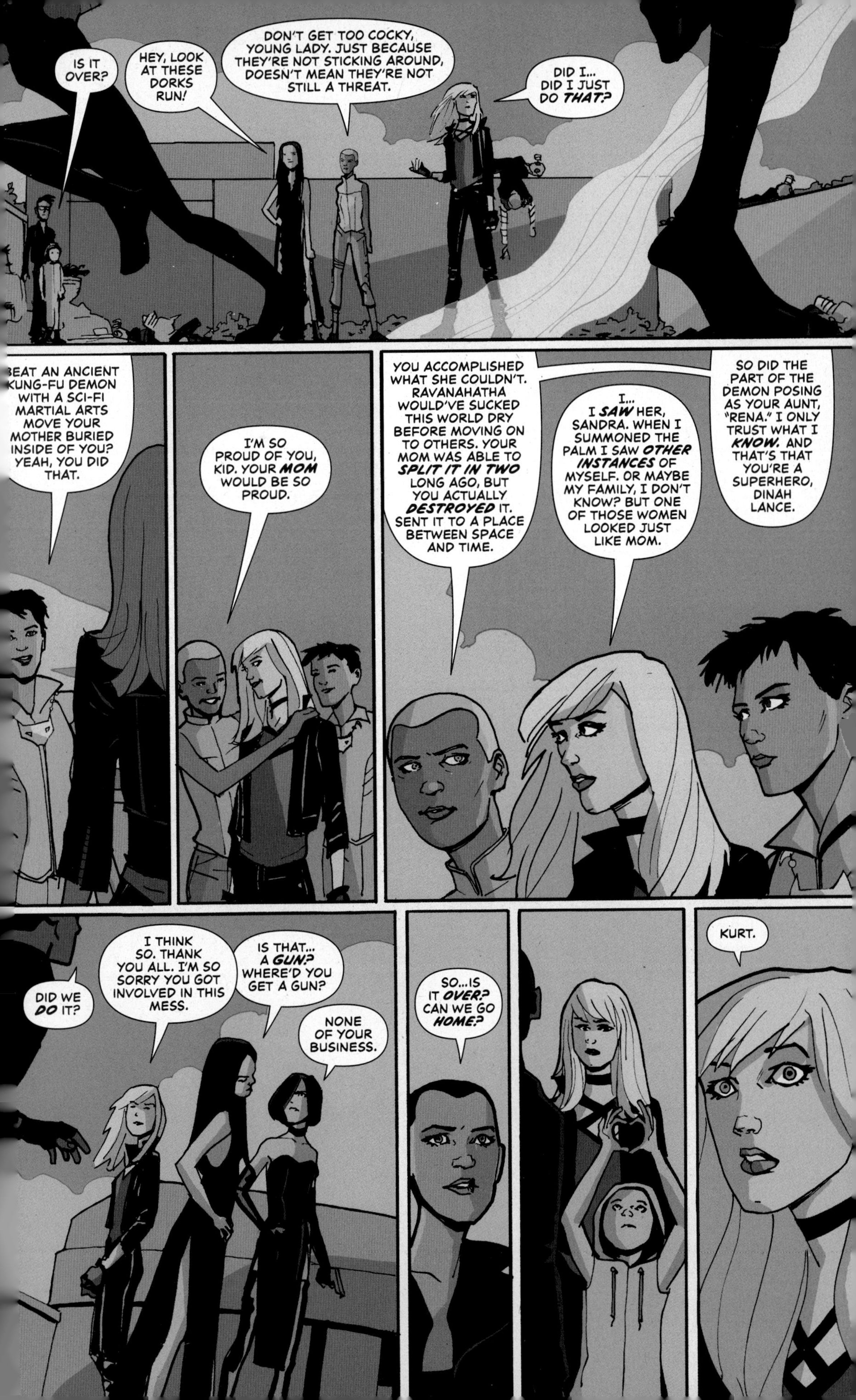
IS IT OVER?
HEY, LOOK AT THESE DORKS RUN!
DON'T GET TOO COCKY, YOUNG LADY. JUST BECAUSE THEY'RE NOT STICKING AROUND, DOESN'T MEAN THEY'RE NOT STILL A THREAT.
DID I... DID I JUST DO THAT?
BEAT AN ANCIENT KUNG-FU DEMON WITH A SCI-FI MARTIAL ARTS MOVE YOUR MOTHER BURIED INSIDE OF YOU? YEAH, YOU DID THAT.
I'M SO PROUD OF YOU, KID. YOUR MOM WOULD BE SO PROUD.
YOU ACCOMPLISHED WHAT SHE COULDN'T. RAVANAHATHA WOULD'VE SUCKED THIS WORLD DRY BEFORE MOVING ON TO OTHERS. YOUR MOM WAS ABLE TO SPLIT IT IN TWO LONG AGO, BUT YOU ACTUALLY DESTROYED IT. SENT IT TO A PLACE BETWEEN SPACE AND TIME.
SO DID THE PART OF THE DEMON POSING AS YOUR AUNT, "RENA." I ONLY TRUST WHAT I KNOW. AND THAT'S THAT YOU'RE A SUPERHERO, DINAH LANCE.
I... I SAW HER, SANDRA. WHEN I SUMMONED THE PALM I SAW OTHER INSTANCES OF MYSELF. OR MAYBE MY FAMILY, I DON'T KNOW? BUT ONE OF THOSE WOMEN LOOKED JUST LIKE MOM.
DID WE DO IT?
I THINK SO. THANK YOU ALL. I'M SO SORRY YOU GOT INVOLVED IN THIS MESS.
IS THAT... A GUN? WHERE'D YOU GET A GUN?
NONE OF YOUR BUSINESS.
SO...IS IT OVER? CAN WE GO HOME?
KURT.

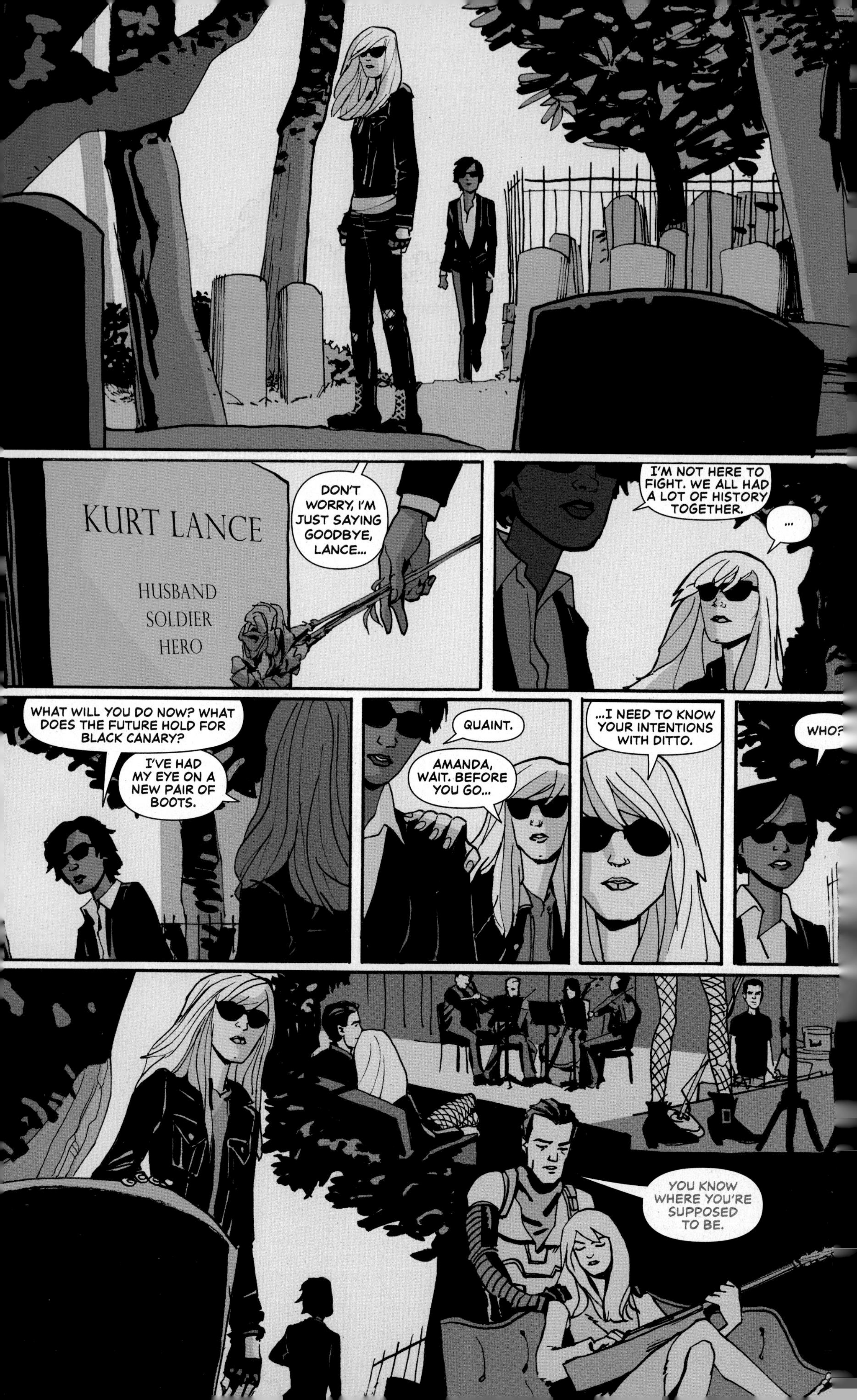
KURT LANCE
HUSBAND
SOLDIER
HERO
DON'T WORRY, I'M JUST SAYING GOODBYE, LANCE...
I'M NOT HERE TO FIGHT. WE ALL HAD A LOT OF HISTORY TOGETHER.
...
WHAT WILL YOU DO NOW? WHAT DOES THE FUTURE HOLD FOR BLACK CANARY?
I'VE HAD MY EYE ON A NEW PAIR OF BOOTS.
QUAINT.
AMANDA, WAIT. BEFORE YOU GO...
...I NEED TO KNOW YOUR INTENTIONS WITH DITTO.
WHO?
YOU KNOW WHERE YOU'RE SUPPOSED TO BE.

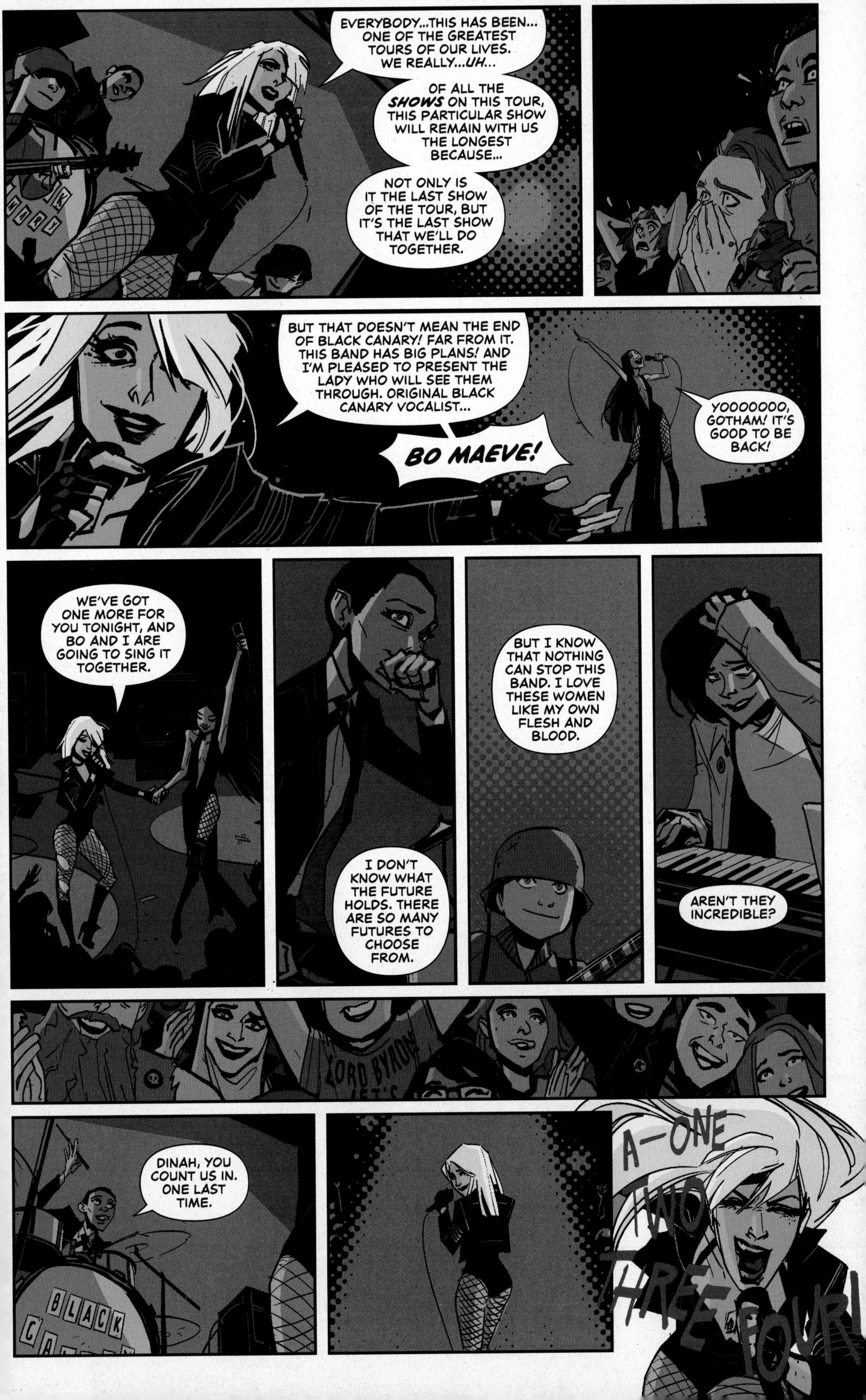
EVERYBODY...THIS HAS BEEN... ONE OF THE GREATEST TOURS OF OUR LIVES. WE REALLY...UH...
OF ALL THE SHOWS ON THIS TOUR, THIS PARTICULAR SHOW WILL REMAIN WITH US THE LONGEST BECAUSE...
NOT ONLY IS IT THE LAST SHOW OF THE TOUR, BUT IT'S THE LAST SHOW THAT WE'LL DO TOGETHER.
BUT THAT DOESN'T MEAN THE END OF BLACK CANARY! FAR FROM IT. THIS BAND HAS BIG PLANS! AND I'M PLEASED TO PRESENT THE LADY WHO WILL SEE THEM THROUGH. ORIGINAL BLACK CANARY VOCALIST...
BO MAEVE!
YOOOOOOO, GOTHAM! IT'S GOOD TO BE BACK!
WE'VE GOT ONE MORE FOR YOU TONIGHT, AND BO AND I ARE GOING TO SING IT TOGETHER.
I DON'T KNOW WHAT THE FUTURE HOLDS. THERE ARE SO MANY FUTURES TO CHOOSE FROM.
BUT I KNOW THAT NOTHING CAN STOP THIS BAND. I LOVE THESE WOMEN LIKE MY OWN FLESH AND BLOOD.
AREN'T THEY INCREDIBLE?
LORD BYRON
DINAH, YOU COUNT US IN. ONE LAST TIME.
BLACK
A-ONE TWO THREE FOUR!

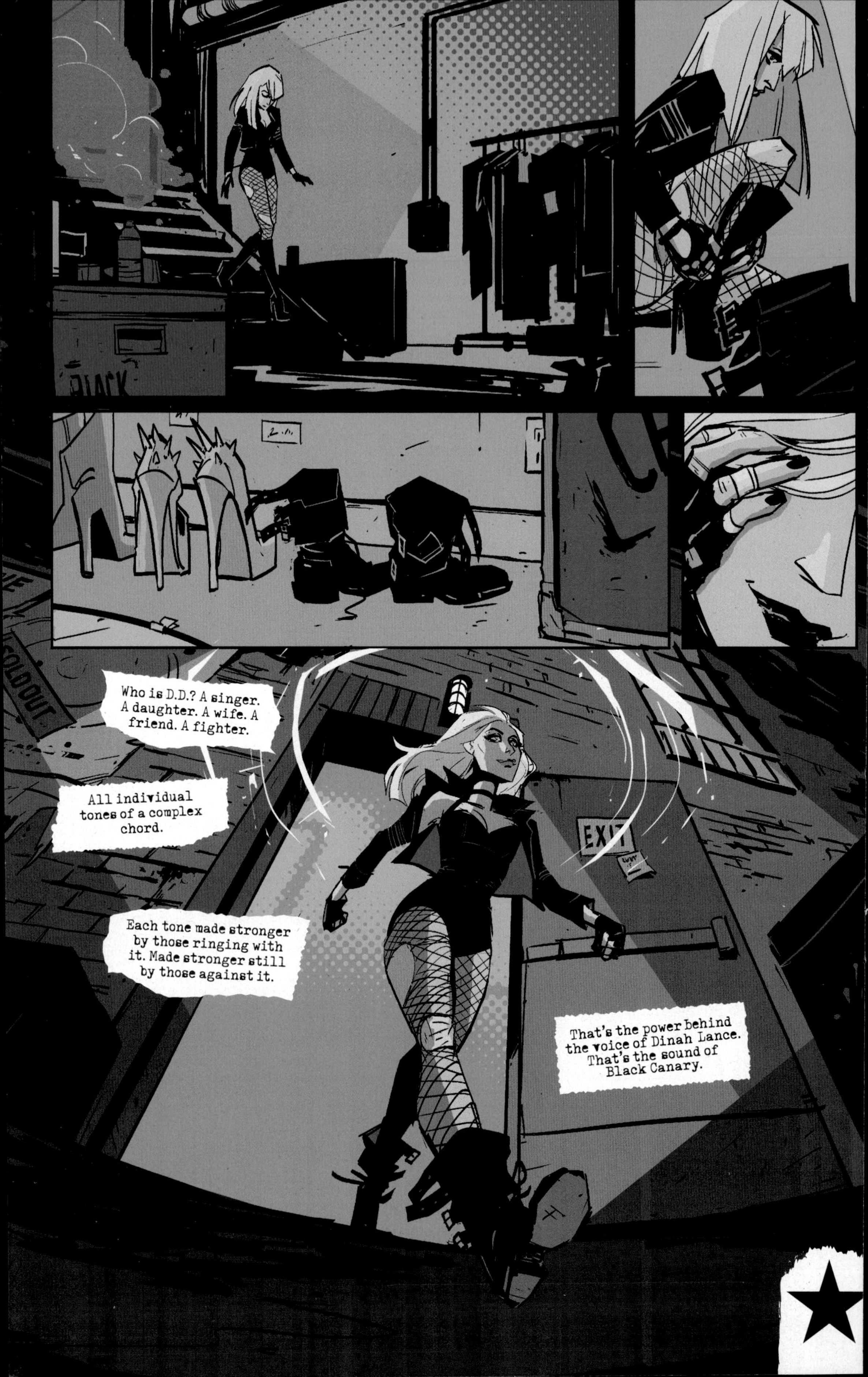
SOLDOUT
Who is D.D.? A singer. A daughter. A wife. A friend. A fighter.
All individual tones of a complex chord.
EXIT
Each tone made stronger by those ringing with it. Made stronger still by those against it.
That's the power behind the voice of Dinah Lance. That's the sound of Black Canary.

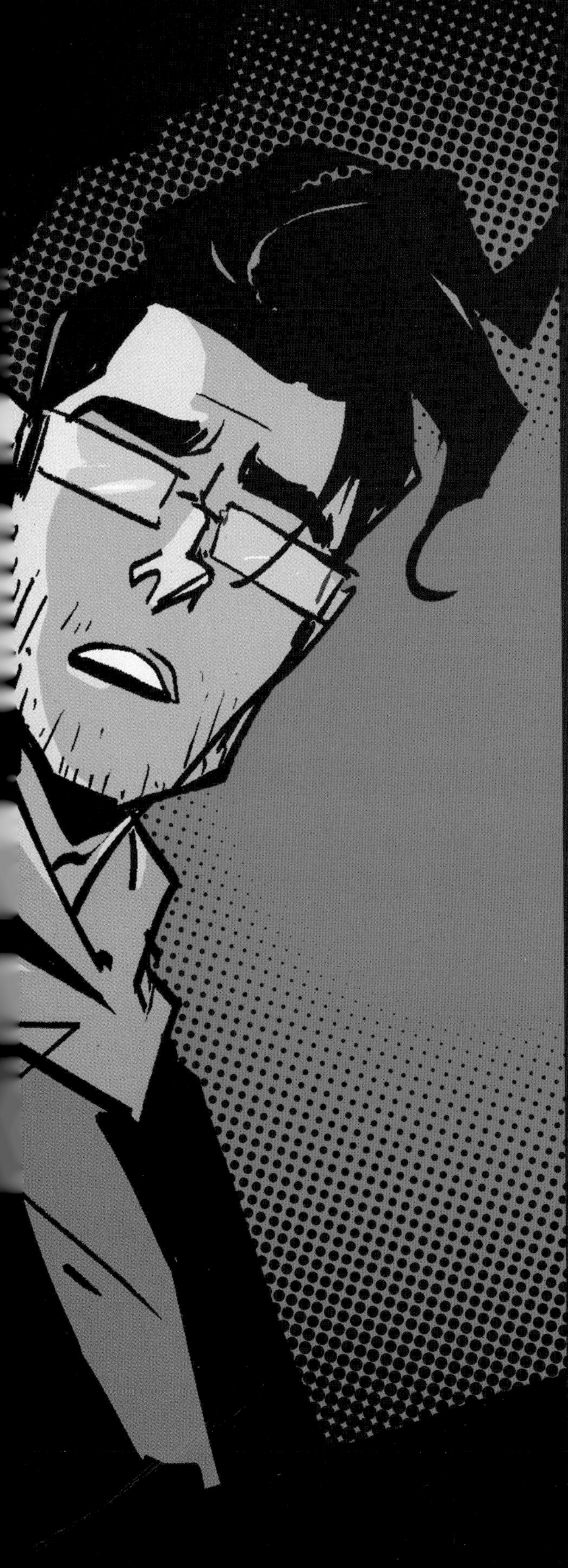

Believe it or not, before Heathcliff hit the road as Black Canary's tour manager, he was a student at Gotham City's most prestigious boarding school: Gotham Academy!

While the plaid skirts and embroidered blazers may fool you, Gotham Academy has its fair share of bizarre and creepy mysteries. Heathcliff's former classmates and friends spend their days avoiding both detention and werewolves, and occasionally save their school from supernatural calamity.

This story, recounting Heathcliff's return to the Academy, was originally published in the **GOTHAM ACADEMY: YEARBOOK** anthology arc, featuring short stories from a host of talented writers and artists exploring the previously unseen nooks and crannies of Bruce Wayne's alma mater. Catch up on Heathcliff's other school adventures in the first three volumes of **GOTHAM ACADEMY**.

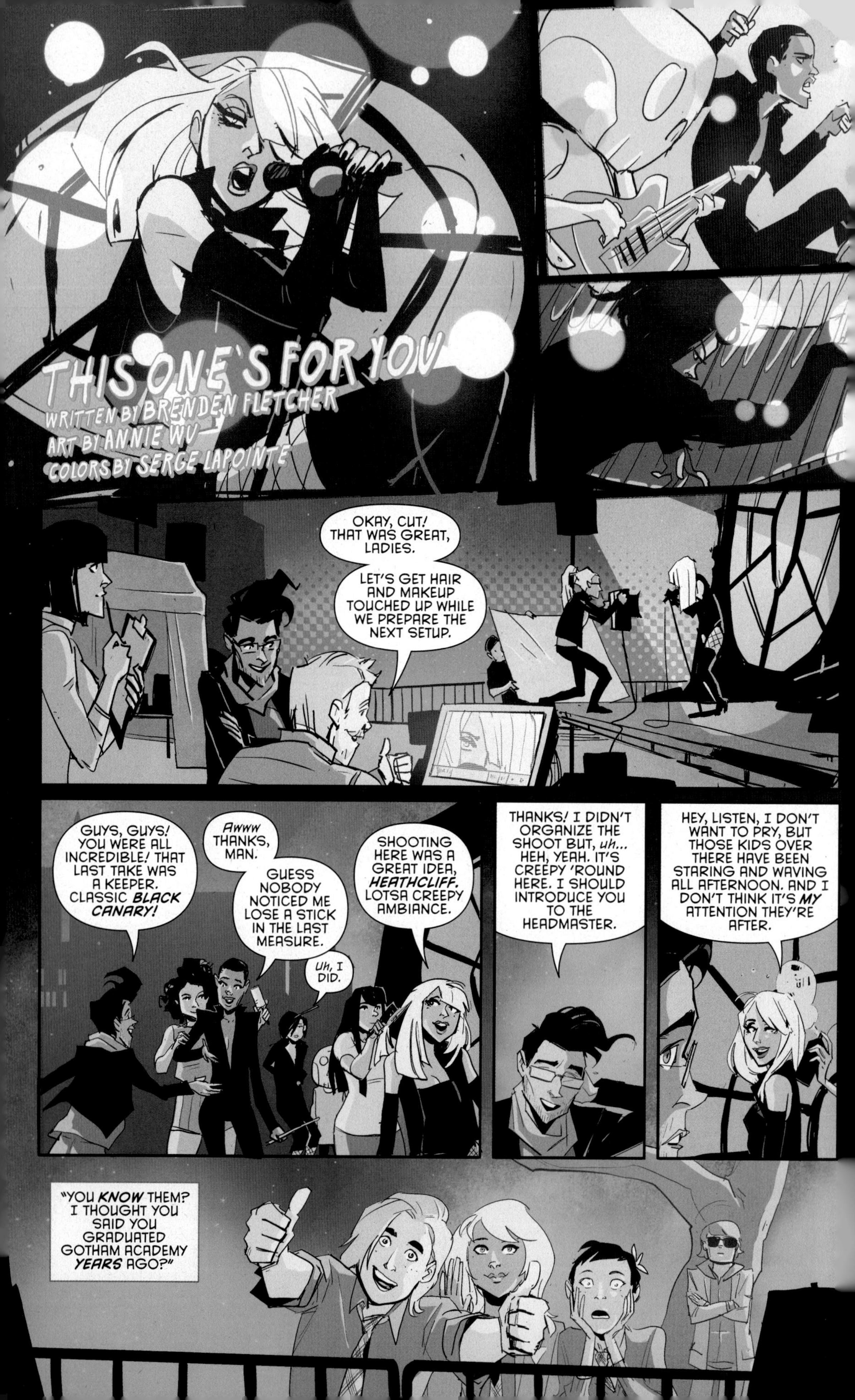
THIS ONE'S FOR YOU
WRITTEN BY BRENDEN FLETCHER
ART BY ANNIE WU
COLORS BY SERGE LAPOINTE
OKAY, CUT! THAT WAS GREAT, LADIES.
LET'S GET HAIR AND MAKEUP TOUCHED UP WHILE WE PREPARE THE NEXT SETUP.
GUYS, GUYS! YOU WERE ALL INCREDIBLE! THAT LAST TAKE WAS A KEEPER. CLASSIC BLACK CANARY!
Awww THANKS, MAN.
GUESS NOBODY NOTICED ME LOSE A STICK IN THE LAST MEASURE.
Uh, I DID.
SHOOTING HERE WAS A GREAT IDEA, HEATHCLIFF. LOTSA CREEPY AMBIANCE.
THANKS! I DIDN'T ORGANIZE THE SHOOT BUT, uh... HEH, YEAH. IT'S CREEPY 'ROUND HERE. I SHOULD INTRODUCE YOU TO THE HEADMASTER.
HEY, LISTEN, I DON'T WANT TO PRY, BUT THOSE KIDS OVER THERE HAVE BEEN STARING AND WAVING ALL AFTERNOON. AND I DON'T THINK IT'S MY ATTENTION THEY'RE AFTER.
"YOU KNOW THEM? I THOUGHT YOU SAID YOU GRADUATED GOTHAM ACADEMY YEARS AGO?"

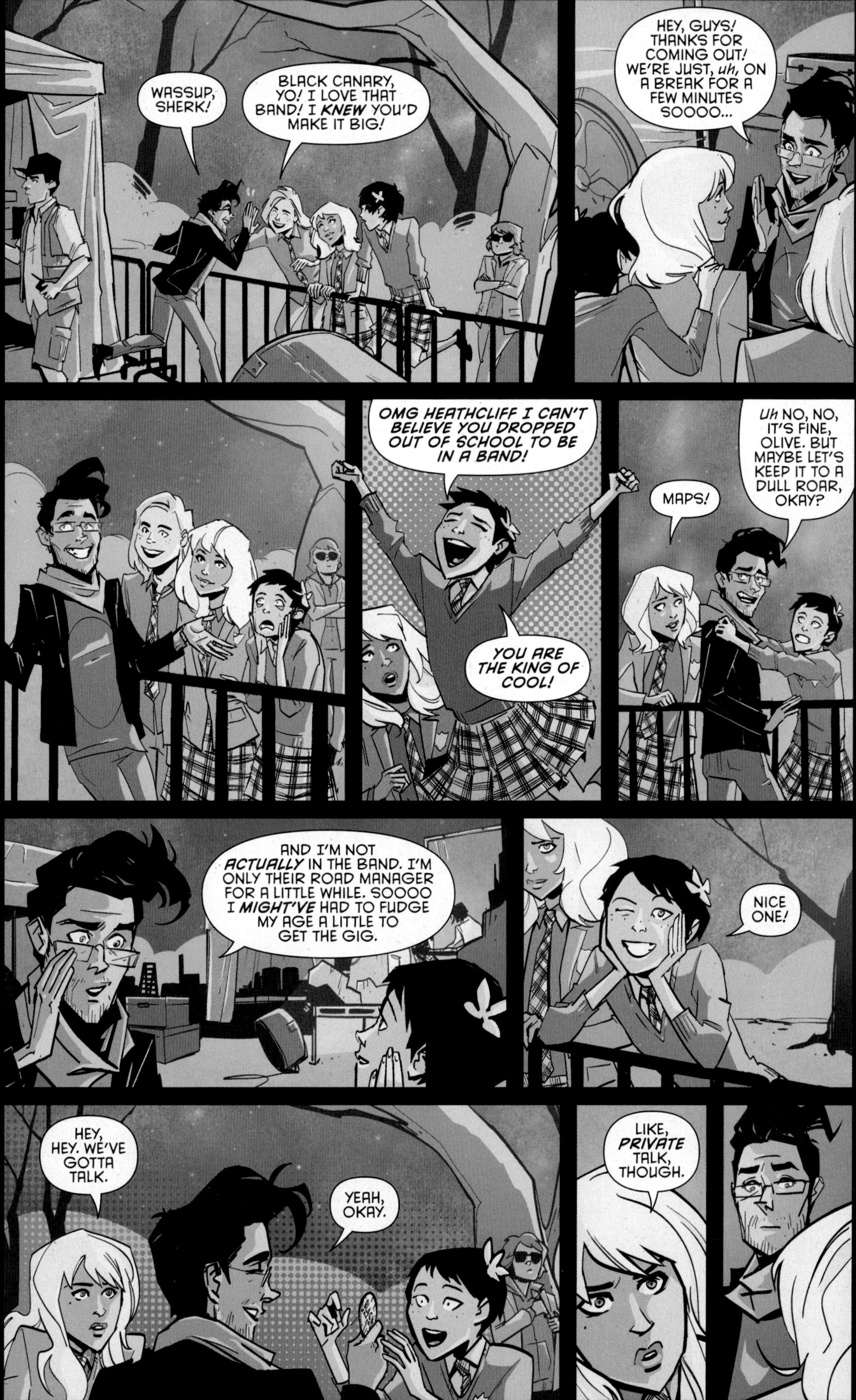
WASSUP, SHERK!
BLACK CANARY, YO! I LOVE THAT BAND! I *KNEW* YOU'D MAKE IT BIG!
HEY, GUYS! THANKS FOR COMING OUT! WE'RE JUST, *uh*, ON A BREAK FOR A FEW MINUTES SOOOO...
OMG HEATHCLIFF I CAN'T BELIEVE YOU DROPPED OUT OF SCHOOL TO BE IN A BAND!
YOU ARE THE KING OF COOL!
MAPS!
Uh NO, NO, IT'S FINE, OLIVE. BUT MAYBE LET'S KEEP IT TO A DULL ROAR, OKAY?
AND I'M NOT *ACTUALLY* IN THE BAND. I'M ONLY THEIR ROAD MANAGER FOR A LITTLE WHILE. SOOOO I *MIGHT'VE* HAD TO FUDGE MY AGE A LITTLE TO GET THE GIG.
NICE ONE!
HEY, HEY. WE'VE GOTTA TALK.
YEAH, OKAY.
LIKE, *PRIVATE* TALK, THOUGH.

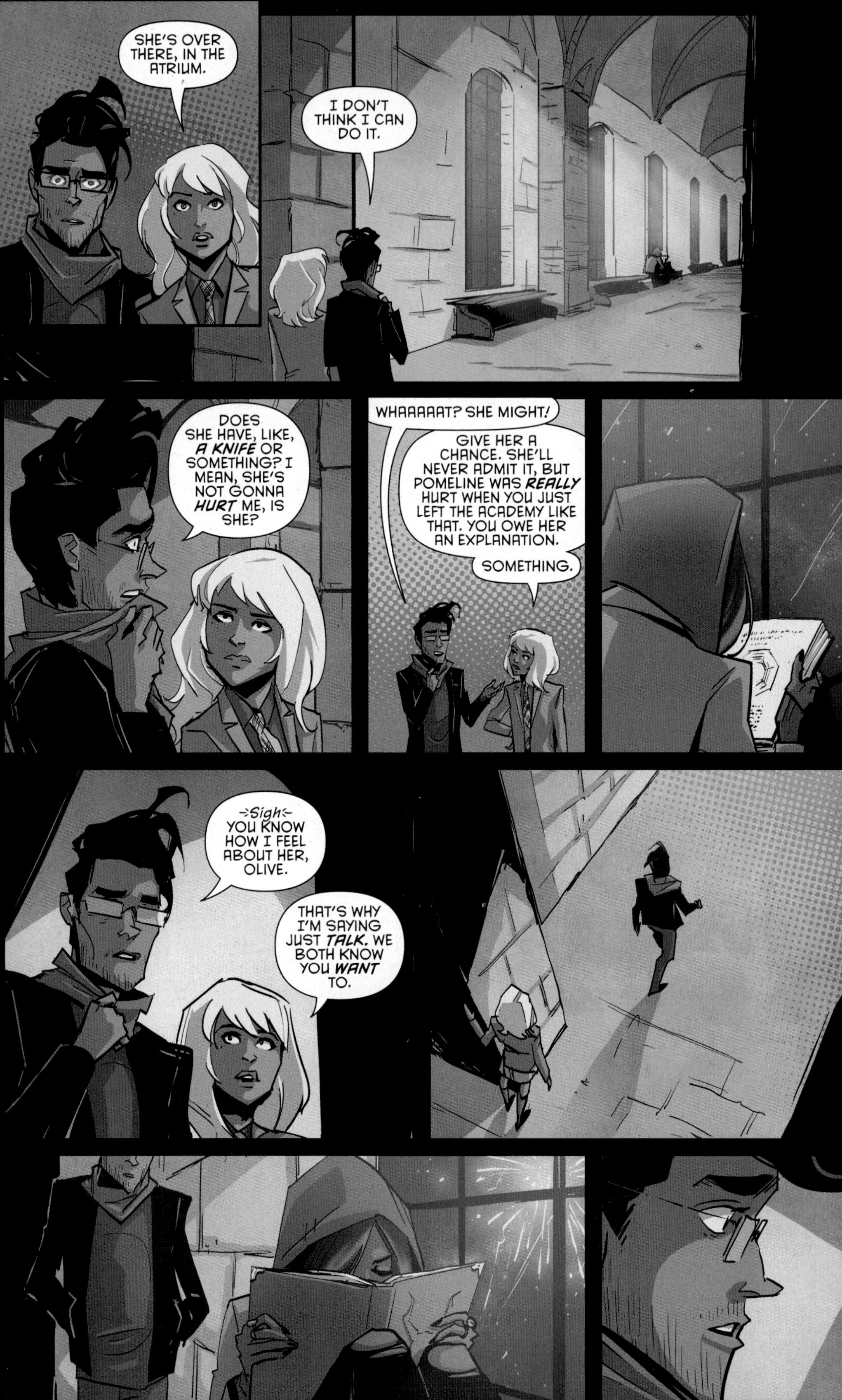
SHE'S OVER THERE, IN THE ATRIUM.
I DON'T THINK I CAN DO IT.
DOES SHE HAVE, LIKE, A KNIFE OR SOMETHING? I MEAN, SHE'S NOT GONNA HURT ME, IS SHE?
WHAAAAAT? SHE MIGHT!
GIVE HER A CHANCE. SHE'LL NEVER ADMIT IT, BUT POMELINE WAS REALLY HURT WHEN YOU JUST LEFT THE ACADEMY LIKE THAT. YOU OWE HER AN EXPLANATION.
SOMETHING.
Sigh
YOU KNOW HOW I FEEL ABOUT HER, OLIVE.
THAT'S WHY I'M SAYING JUST TALK. WE BOTH KNOW YOU WANT TO.

GUESS WHO'S BACK?

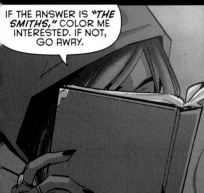

IF THE ANSWER IS *"THE SMITHS,"* COLOR ME INTERESTED. IF NOT, GO AWAY.

I'M... I'M SORRY, POM. SORRY I BOTHERED YOU. AND FOR ALL THE OTHER STUFF.

I WATCHED THAT CLIP WHERE BLACK CANARY GOT IN A FIGHT AND YOU HAD TO TAKE OVER A *PRESS CONFERENCE.*

THAT WAS PRETTY WILD.

YEAH. IT *WAS.* I NEARLY TOOK A MICROPHONE TO THE FACE.

WHAT'S THE BOOK?

OH.

CULTS. SECRET SOCIETIES. NO BIG DEAL.

HEY...

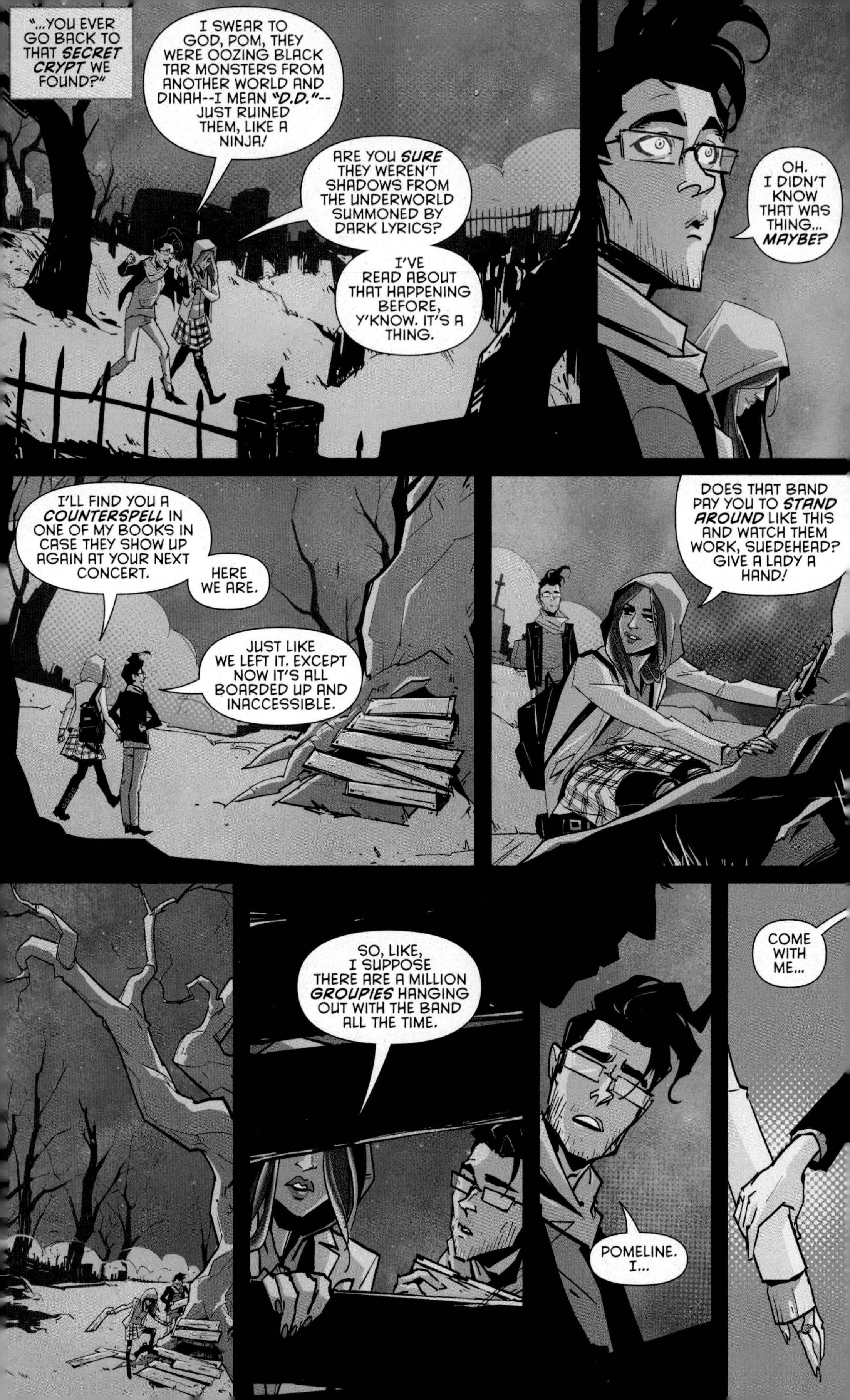
"...YOU EVER GO BACK TO THAT SECRET CRYPT WE FOUND?"
I SWEAR TO GOD, POM, THEY WERE OOZING BLACK TAR MONSTERS FROM ANOTHER WORLD AND DINAH--I MEAN "D.D."--JUST RUINED THEM, LIKE A NINJA!
ARE YOU SURE THEY WEREN'T SHADOWS FROM THE UNDERWORLD SUMMONED BY DARK LYRICS?
I'VE READ ABOUT THAT HAPPENING BEFORE, Y'KNOW. IT'S A THING.
OH. I DIDN'T KNOW THAT WAS THING... MAYBE?
I'LL FIND YOU A COUNTERSPELL IN ONE OF MY BOOKS IN CASE THEY SHOW UP AGAIN AT YOUR NEXT CONCERT.
HERE WE ARE.
JUST LIKE WE LEFT IT. EXCEPT NOW IT'S ALL BOARDED UP AND INACCESSIBLE.
DOES THAT BAND PAY YOU TO STAND AROUND LIKE THIS AND WATCH THEM WORK, SUEDEHEAD? GIVE A LADY A HAND!
SO, LIKE, I SUPPOSE THERE ARE A MILLION GROUPIES HANGING OUT WITH THE BAND ALL THE TIME.
POMELINE. I...
COME WITH ME...

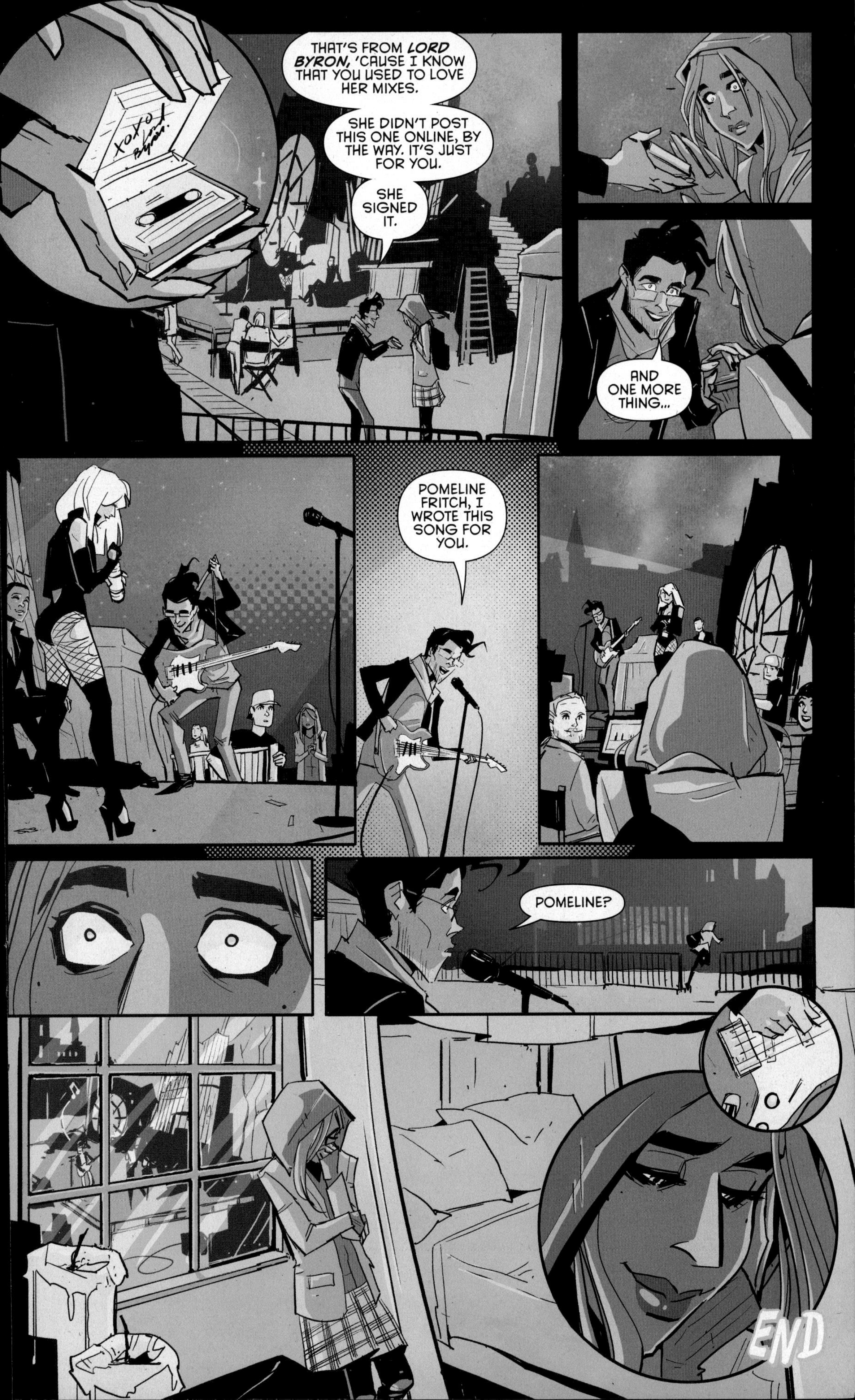
XOXO Lord Byron.
THAT'S FROM LORD BYRON, 'CAUSE I KNOW THAT YOU USED TO LOVE HER MIXES.
SHE DIDN'T POST THIS ONE ONLINE, BY THE WAY. IT'S JUST FOR YOU.
SHE SIGNED IT.
AND ONE MORE THING...
POMELINE FRITCH, I WROTE THIS SONG FOR YOU.
POMELINE?
END

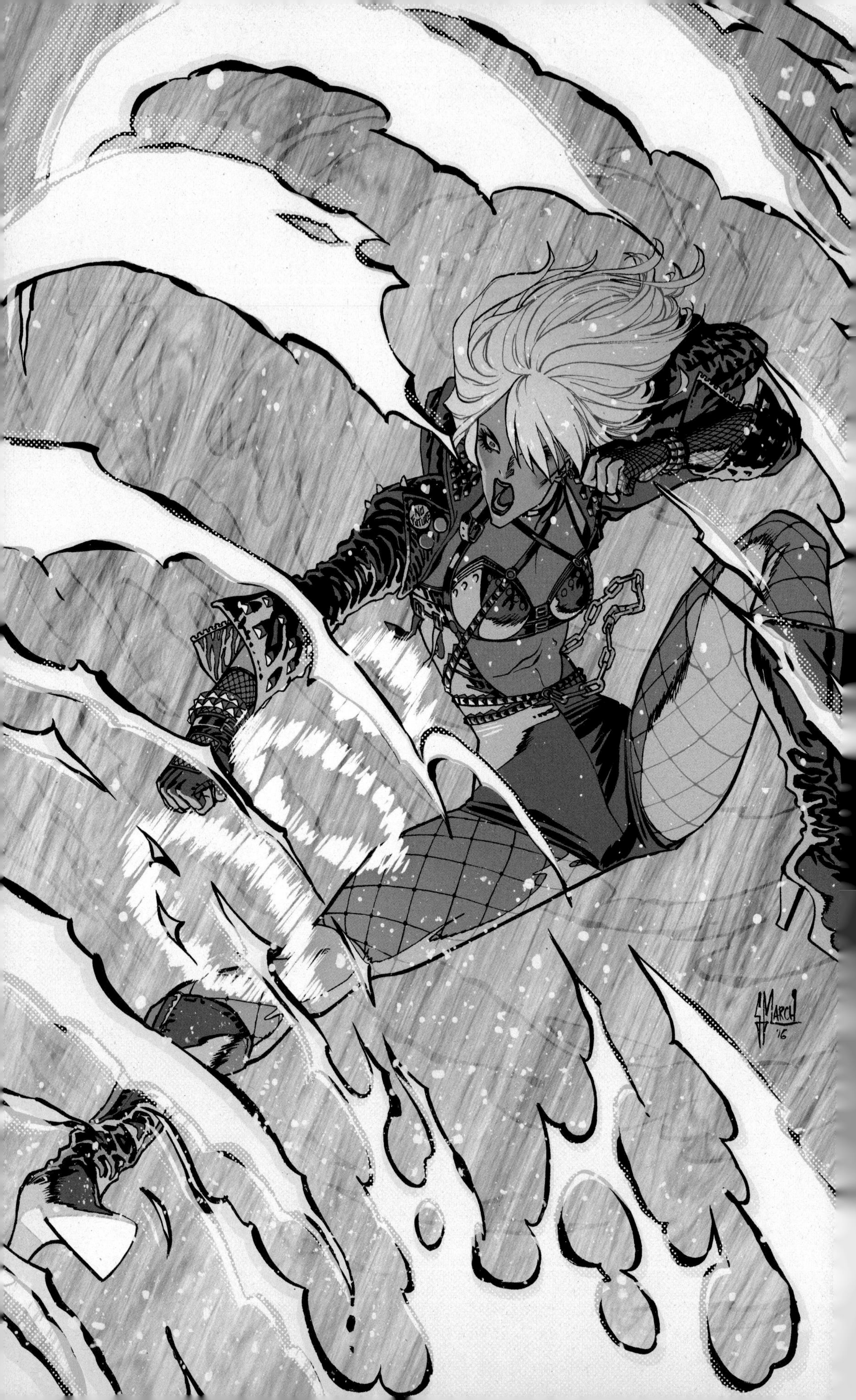
NO FUTURE
MARCH '16

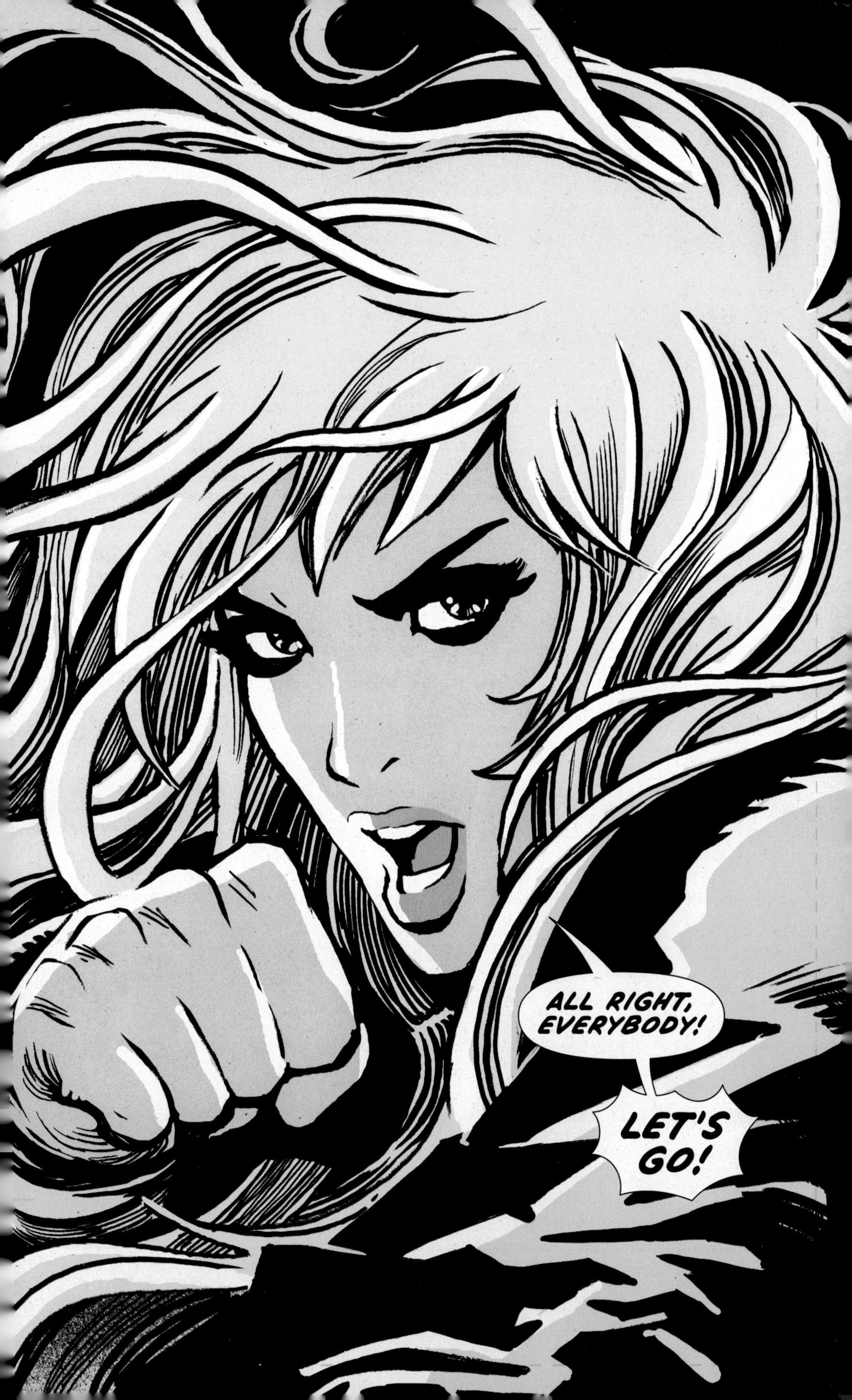
ALL RIGHT, EVERYBODY!
LET'S GO!

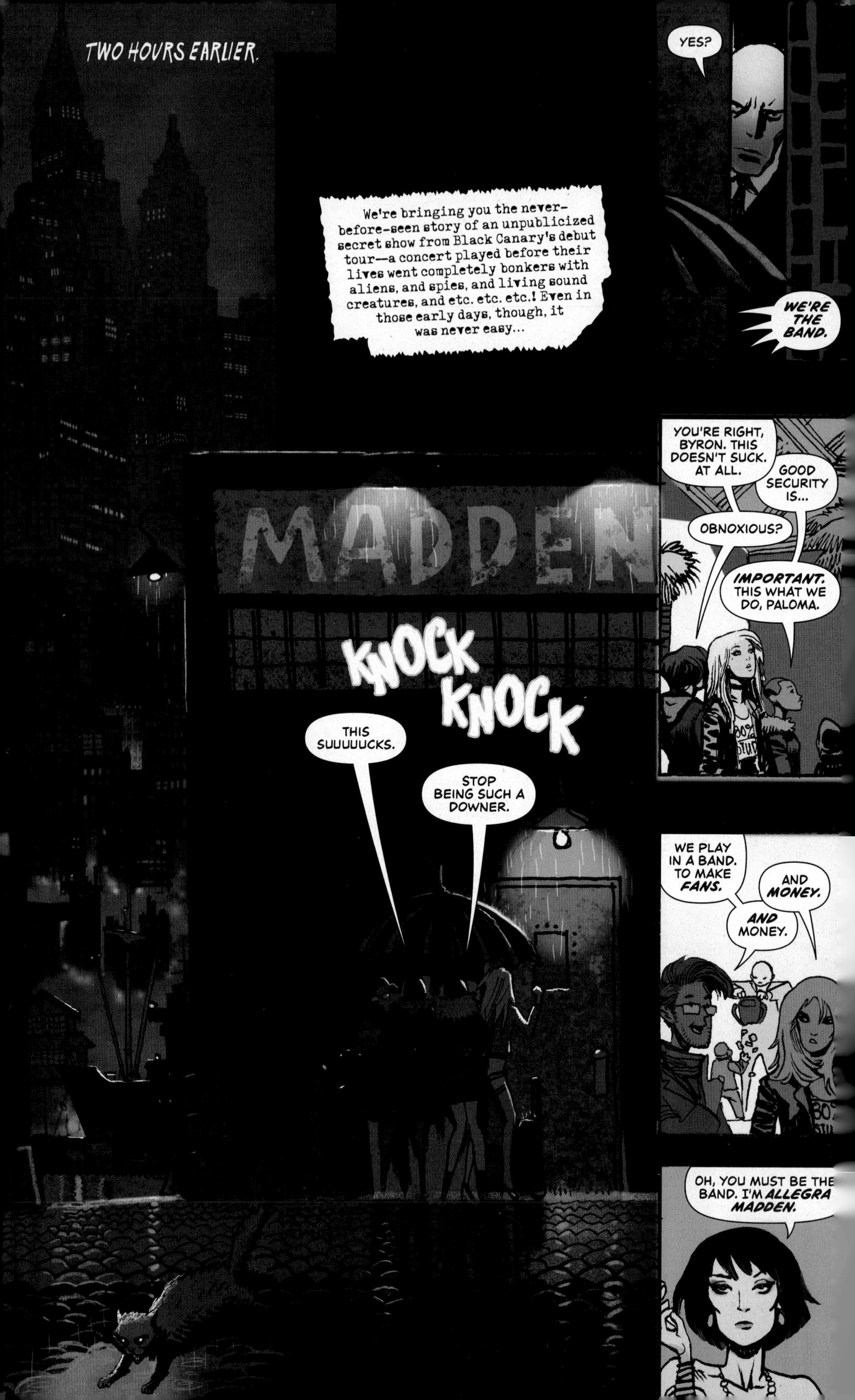
TWO HOURS EARLIER.
We're bringing you the never-before-seen story of an unpublicized secret show from Black Canary's debut tour—a concert played before their lives went completely bonkers with aliens, and spies, and living sound creatures, and etc. etc. etc.! Even in those early days, though, it was never easy...
MADDEN
KNOCK KNOCK
THIS SUUUUUCKS.
STOP BEING SUCH A DOWNER.
YES?
WE'RE THE BAND.
YOU'RE RIGHT, BYRON. THIS DOESN'T SUCK. AT ALL.
GOOD SECURITY IS...
OBNOXIOUS?
IMPORTANT. THIS WHAT WE DO, PALOMA.
WE PLAY IN A BAND. TO MAKE FANS.
AND MONEY.
AND MONEY.
OH, YOU MUST BE THE BAND. I'M ALLEGRA MADDEN.

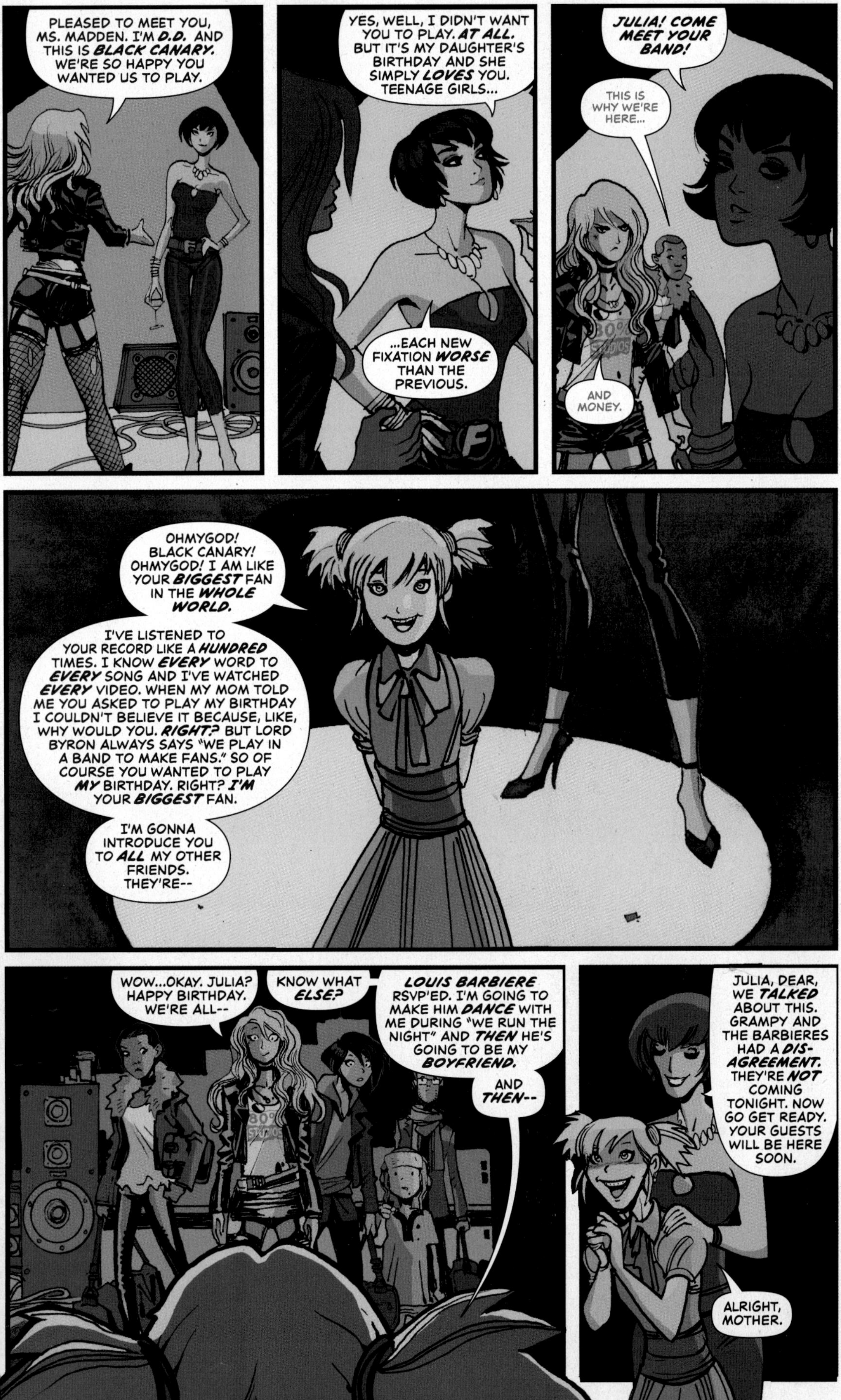
PLEASED TO MEET YOU, MS. MADDEN. I'M D.D. AND THIS IS BLACK CANARY. WE'RE SO HAPPY YOU WANTED US TO PLAY.
YES, WELL, I DIDN'T WANT YOU TO PLAY. AT ALL. BUT IT'S MY DAUGHTER'S BIRTHDAY AND SHE SIMPLY LOVES YOU. TEENAGE GIRLS...
...EACH NEW FIXATION WORSE THAN THE PREVIOUS.
JULIA! COME MEET YOUR BAND!
THIS IS WHY WE'RE HERE...
AND MONEY.
OHMYGOD! BLACK CANARY! OHMYGOD! I AM LIKE YOUR BIGGEST FAN IN THE WHOLE WORLD.
I'VE LISTENED TO YOUR RECORD LIKE A HUNDRED TIMES. I KNOW EVERY WORD TO EVERY SONG AND I'VE WATCHED EVERY VIDEO. WHEN MY MOM TOLD ME YOU ASKED TO PLAY MY BIRTHDAY I COULDN'T BELIEVE IT BECAUSE, LIKE, WHY WOULD YOU. RIGHT?! BUT LORD BYRON ALWAYS SAYS "WE PLAY IN A BAND TO MAKE FANS." SO OF COURSE YOU WANTED TO PLAY MY BIRTHDAY. RIGHT? I'M YOUR BIGGEST FAN.
I'M GONNA INTRODUCE YOU TO ALL MY OTHER FRIENDS. THEY'RE--
WOW...OKAY. JULIA? HAPPY BIRTHDAY. WE'RE ALL--
KNOW WHAT ELSE?
LOUIS BARBIERE RSVP'ED. I'M GOING TO MAKE HIM DANCE WITH ME DURING "WE RUN THE NIGHT" AND THEN HE'S GOING TO BE MY BOYFRIEND.
AND THEN--
JULIA, DEAR, WE TALKED ABOUT THIS. GRAMPY AND THE BARBIERES HAD A DIS-AGREEMENT. THEY'RE NOT COMING TONIGHT. NOW GO GET READY. YOUR GUESTS WILL BE HERE SOON.
ALRIGHT, MOTHER.

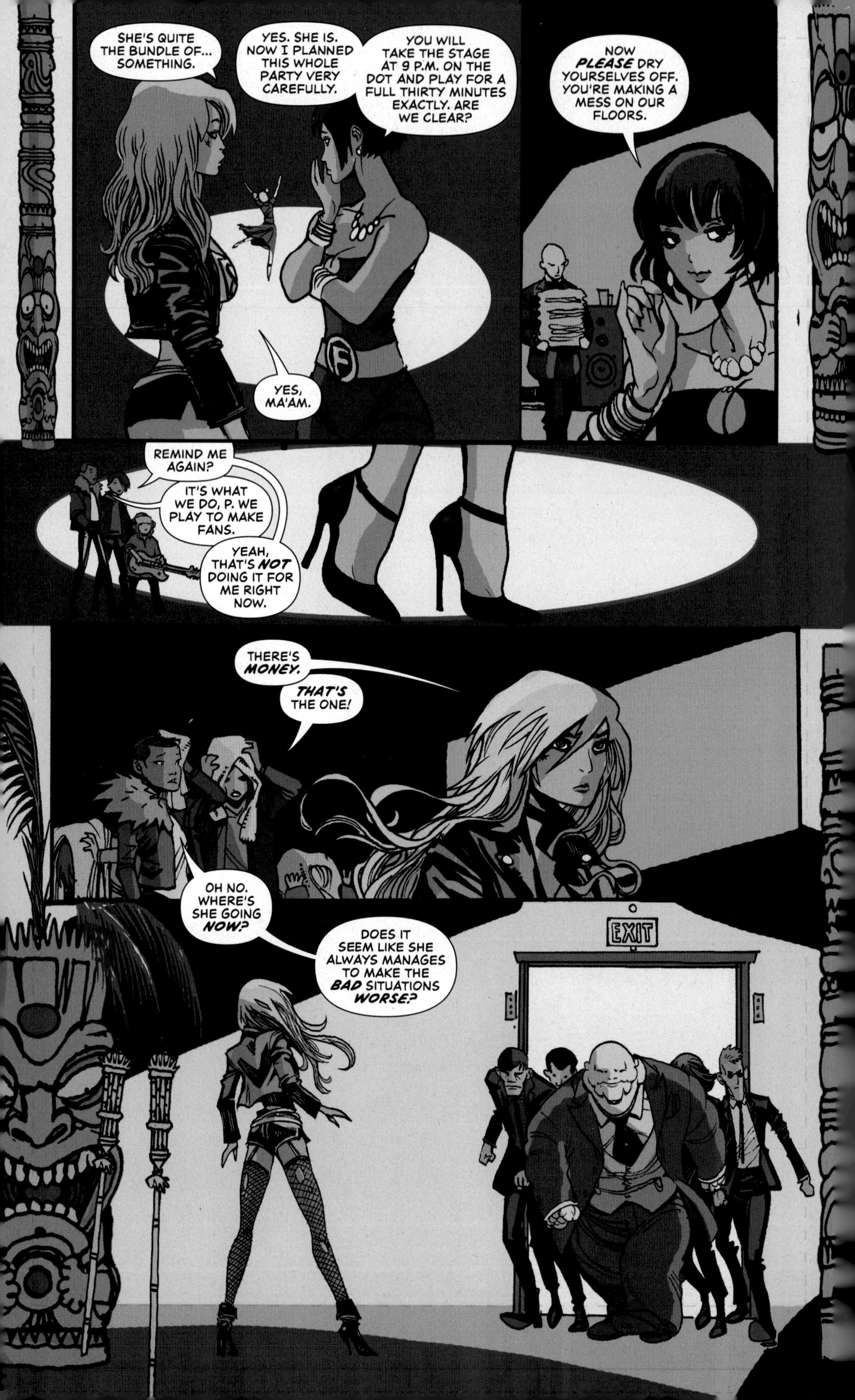
SHE'S QUITE THE BUNDLE OF... SOMETHING.
YES. SHE IS. NOW I PLANNED THIS WHOLE PARTY VERY CAREFULLY.
YOU WILL TAKE THE STAGE AT 9 P.M. ON THE DOT AND PLAY FOR A FULL THIRTY MINUTES EXACTLY. ARE WE CLEAR?
YES, MA'AM.
NOW PLEASE DRY YOURSELVES OFF. YOU'RE MAKING A MESS ON OUR FLOORS.
REMIND ME AGAIN?
IT'S WHAT WE DO, P. WE PLAY TO MAKE FANS.
YEAH, THAT'S NOT DOING IT FOR ME RIGHT NOW.
THERE'S MONEY.
THAT'S THE ONE!
OH NO. WHERE'S SHE GOING NOW?
DOES IT SEEM LIKE SHE ALWAYS MANAGES TO MAKE THE BAD SITUATIONS WORSE?
EXIT

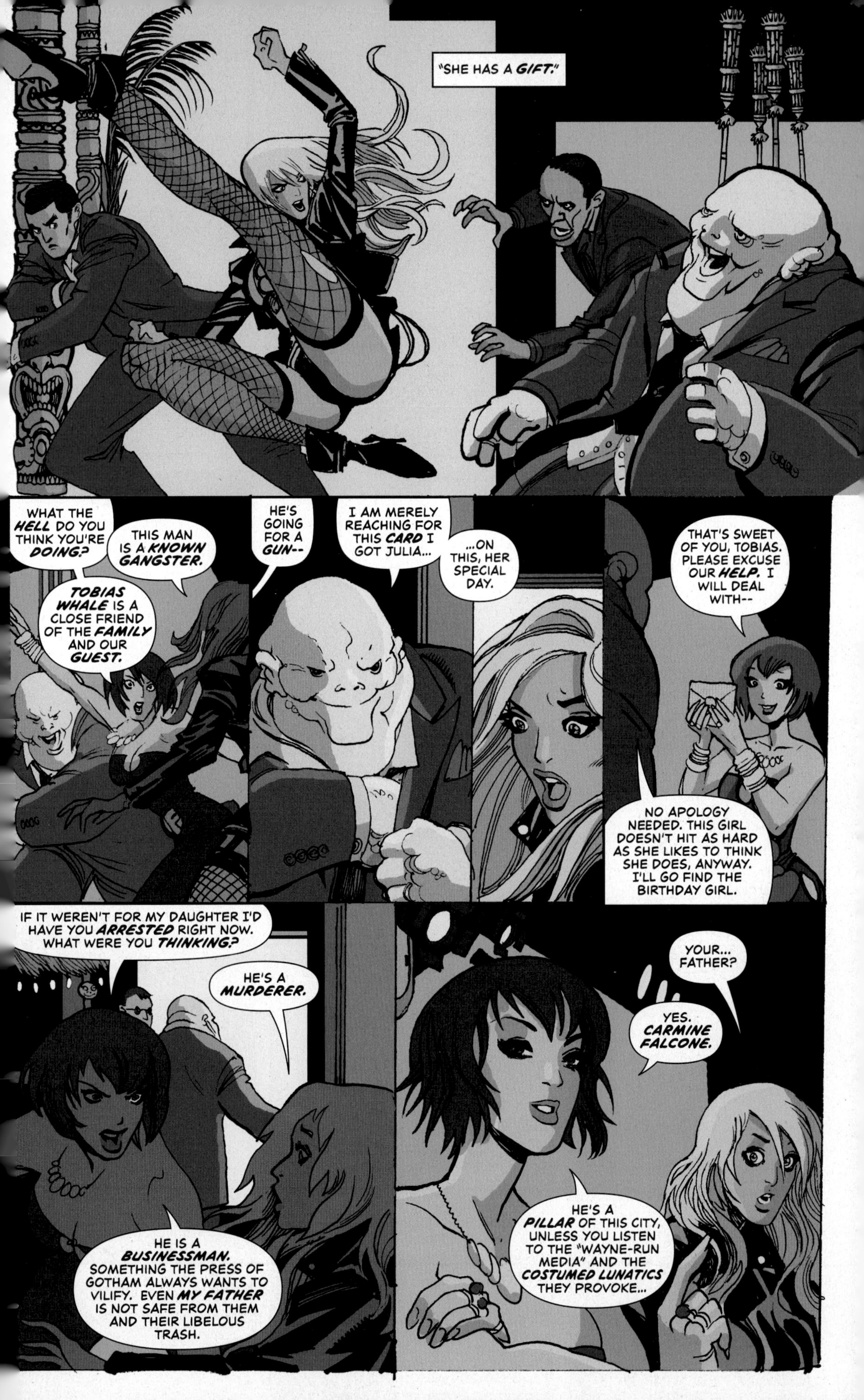
"SHE HAS A GIFT."
WHAT THE HELL DO YOU THINK YOU'RE DOING?
THIS MAN IS A KNOWN GANGSTER.
TOBIAS WHALE IS A CLOSE FRIEND OF THE FAMILY AND OUR GUEST.
HE'S GOING FOR A GUN--
I AM MERELY REACHING FOR THIS CARD I GOT JULIA...
...ON THIS, HER SPECIAL DAY.
THAT'S SWEET OF YOU, TOBIAS. PLEASE EXCUSE OUR HELP. I WILL DEAL WITH--
NO APOLOGY NEEDED. THIS GIRL DOESN'T HIT AS HARD AS SHE LIKES TO THINK SHE DOES, ANYWAY. I'LL GO FIND THE BIRTHDAY GIRL.
IF IT WEREN'T FOR MY DAUGHTER I'D HAVE YOU ARRESTED RIGHT NOW. WHAT WERE YOU THINKING?
HE'S A MURDERER.
HE IS A BUSINESSMAN. SOMETHING THE PRESS OF GOTHAM ALWAYS WANTS TO VILIFY. EVEN MY FATHER IS NOT SAFE FROM THEM AND THEIR LIBELOUS TRASH.
YOUR... FATHER?
YES. CARMINE FALCONE.
HE'S A PILLAR OF THIS CITY, UNLESS YOU LISTEN TO THE "WAYNE-RUN MEDIA" AND THE COSTUMED LUNATICS THEY PROVOKE...

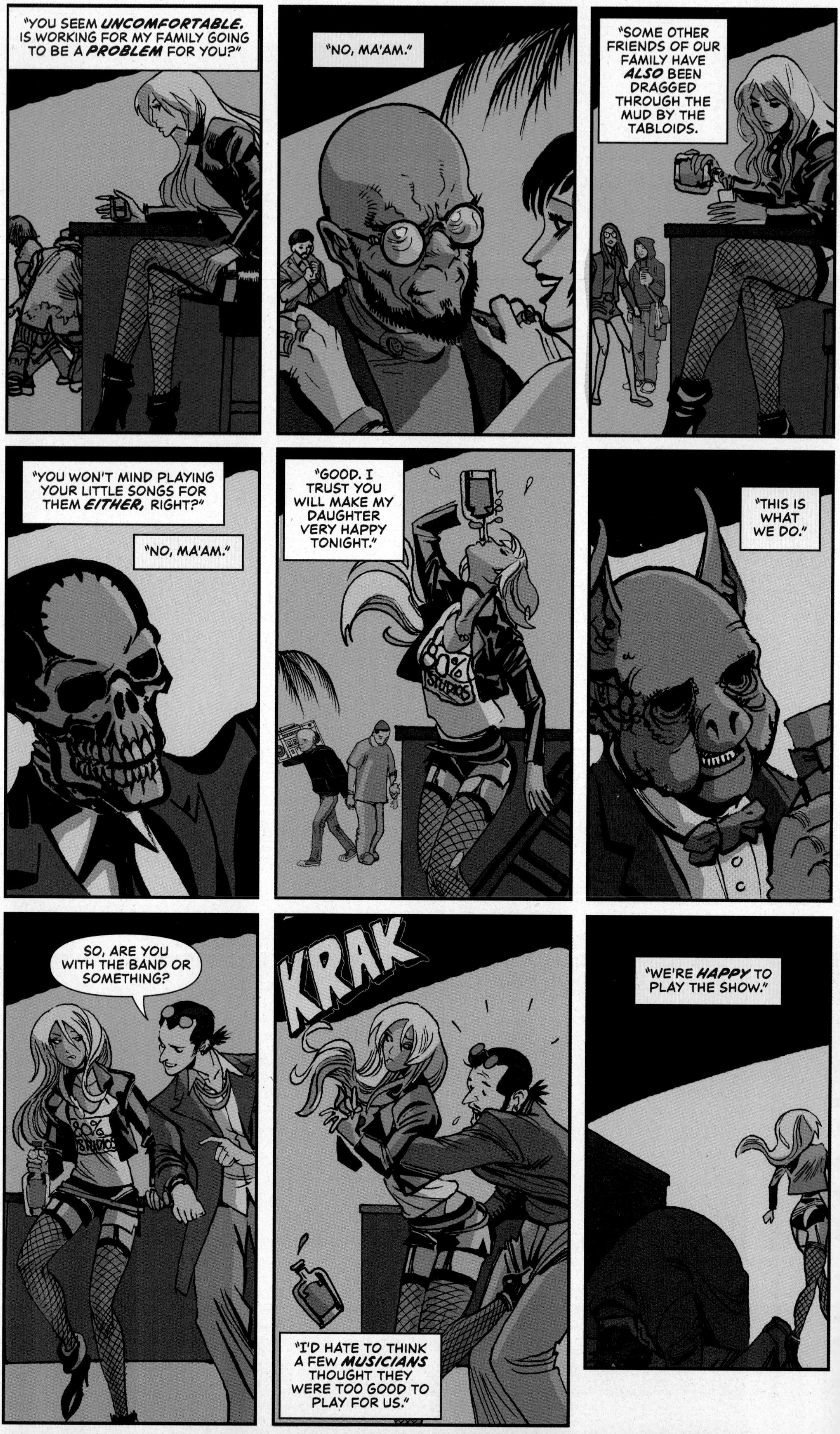
"YOU SEEM UNCOMFORTABLE. IS WORKING FOR MY FAMILY GOING TO BE A PROBLEM FOR YOU?"
"NO, MA'AM."
"SOME OTHER FRIENDS OF OUR FAMILY HAVE ALSO BEEN DRAGGED THROUGH THE MUD BY THE TABLOIDS.
"YOU WON'T MIND PLAYING YOUR LITTLE SONGS FOR THEM EITHER, RIGHT?"
"NO, MA'AM."
"GOOD. I TRUST YOU WILL MAKE MY DAUGHTER VERY HAPPY TONIGHT."
80% STUDIOS
"THIS IS WHAT WE DO."
SO, ARE YOU WITH THE BAND OR SOMETHING?
80% STUDIOS
KRAK
"I'D HATE TO THINK A FEW MUSICIANS THOUGHT THEY WERE TOO GOOD TO PLAY FOR US."
"WE'RE HAPPY TO PLAY THE SHOW."

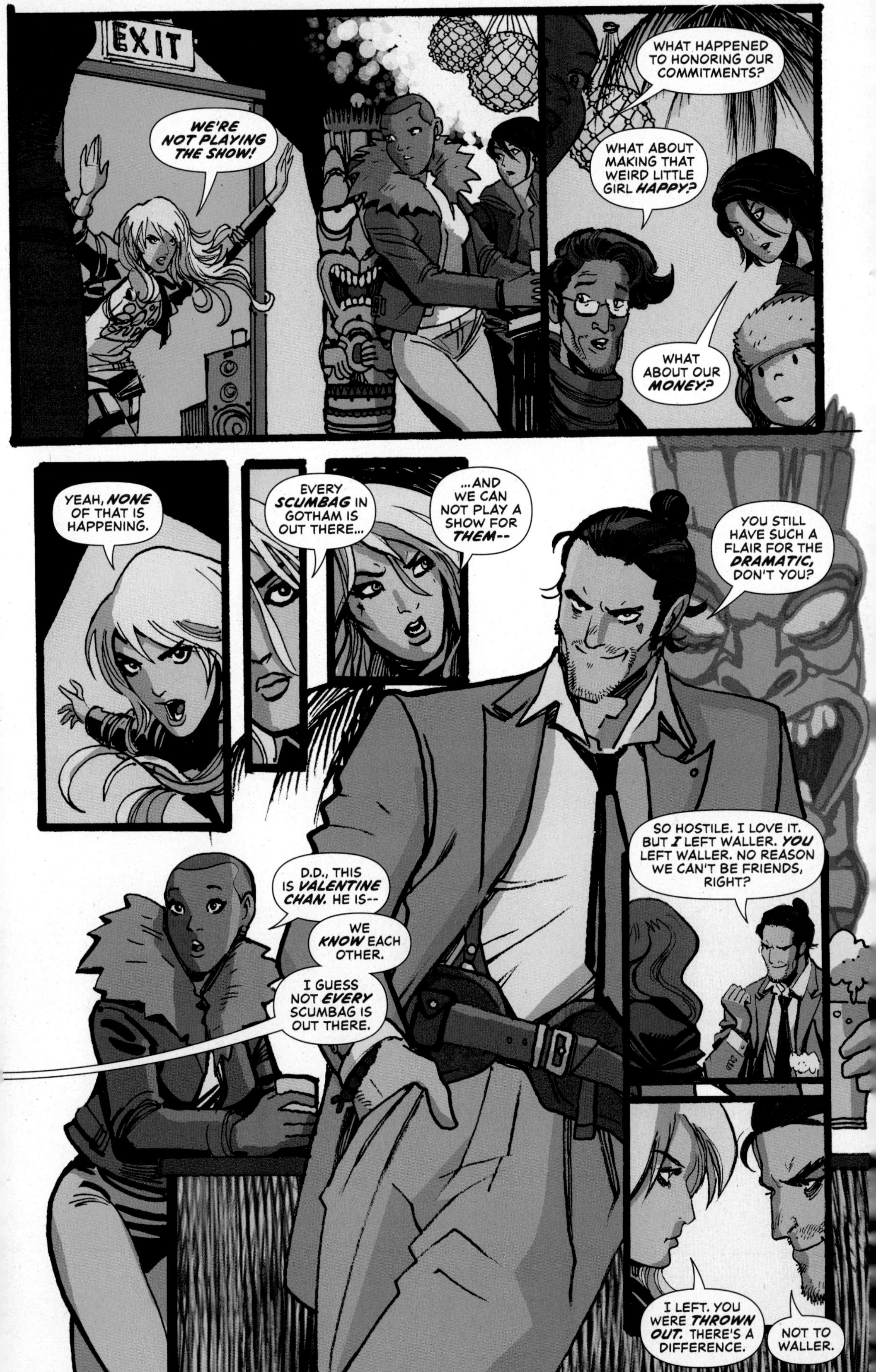
EXIT
WE'RE NOT PLAYING THE SHOW!
WHAT HAPPENED TO HONORING OUR COMMITMENTS?
WHAT ABOUT MAKING THAT WEIRD LITTLE GIRL HAPPY?
WHAT ABOUT OUR MONEY?
YEAH, NONE OF THAT IS HAPPENING.
EVERY SCUMBAG IN GOTHAM IS OUT THERE...
...AND WE CAN NOT PLAY A SHOW FOR THEM--
YOU STILL HAVE SUCH A FLAIR FOR THE DRAMATIC, DON'T YOU?
D.D., THIS IS VALENTINE CHAN. HE IS--
WE KNOW EACH OTHER.
I GUESS NOT EVERY SCUMBAG IS OUT THERE.
SO HOSTILE. I LOVE IT. BUT I LEFT WALLER. YOU LEFT WALLER. NO REASON WE CAN'T BE FRIENDS, RIGHT?
I LEFT. YOU WERE THROWN OUT. THERE'S A DIFFERENCE.
NOT TO WALLER.

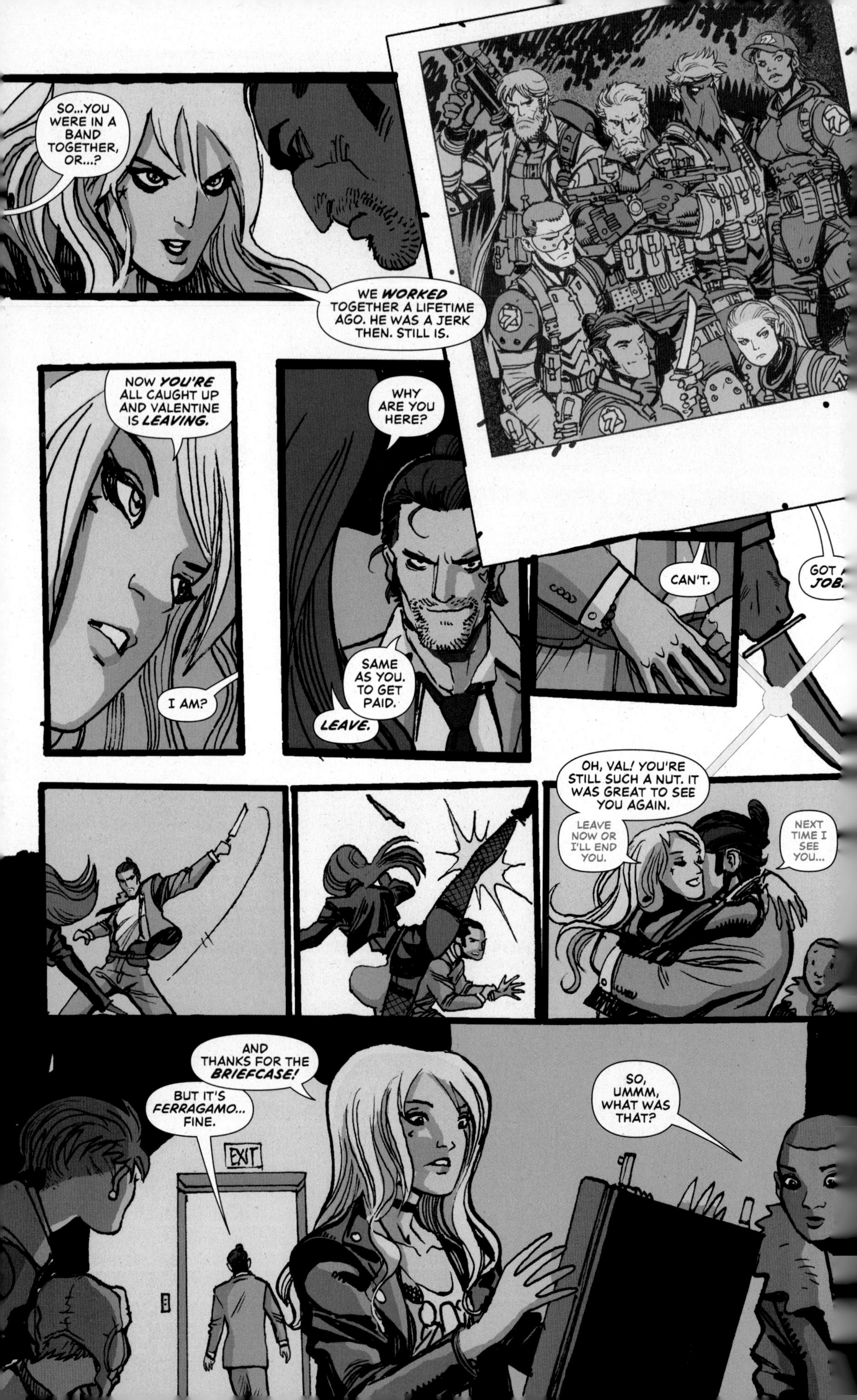
SO...YOU WERE IN A BAND TOGETHER, OR...?
WE WORKED TOGETHER A LIFETIME AGO. HE WAS A JERK THEN. STILL IS.
NOW YOU'RE ALL CAUGHT UP AND VALENTINE IS LEAVING.
I AM?
WHY ARE YOU HERE?
SAME AS YOU. TO GET PAID.
LEAVE.
CAN'T.
OH, VAL! YOU'RE STILL SUCH A NUT. IT WAS GREAT TO SEE YOU AGAIN.
LEAVE NOW OR I'LL END YOU.
NEXT TIME I SEE YOU...
AND THANKS FOR THE BRIEFCASE!
BUT IT'S FERRAGAMO... FINE.
EXIT
SO, UMMM, WHAT WAS THAT?

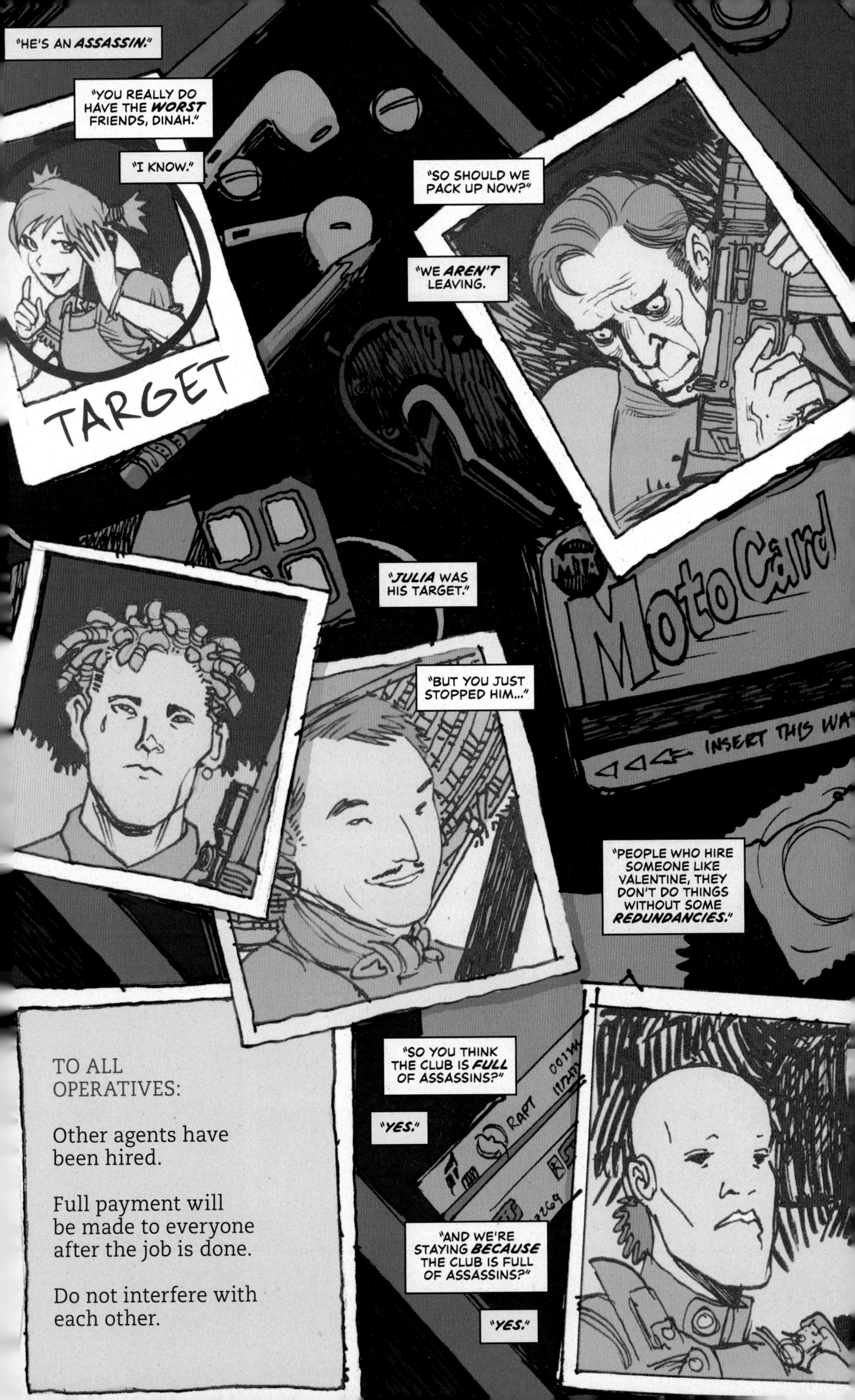
"HE'S AN ASSASSIN."
"YOU REALLY DO HAVE THE WORST FRIENDS, DINAH."
"I KNOW."
TARGET
"SO SHOULD WE PACK UP NOW?"
"WE AREN'T LEAVING.
"JULIA WAS HIS TARGET."
MotoCard
INSERT THIS WA
"BUT YOU JUST STOPPED HIM..."
"PEOPLE WHO HIRE SOMEONE LIKE VALENTINE, THEY DON'T DO THINGS WITHOUT SOME REDUNDANCIES."
TO ALL OPERATIVES:
Other agents have been hired.
Full payment will be made to everyone after the job is done.
Do not interfere with each other.
"SO YOU THINK THE CLUB IS FULL OF ASSASSINS?"
"YES."
RAPT
"AND WE'RE STAYING BECAUSE THE CLUB IS FULL OF ASSASSINS?"
"YES."

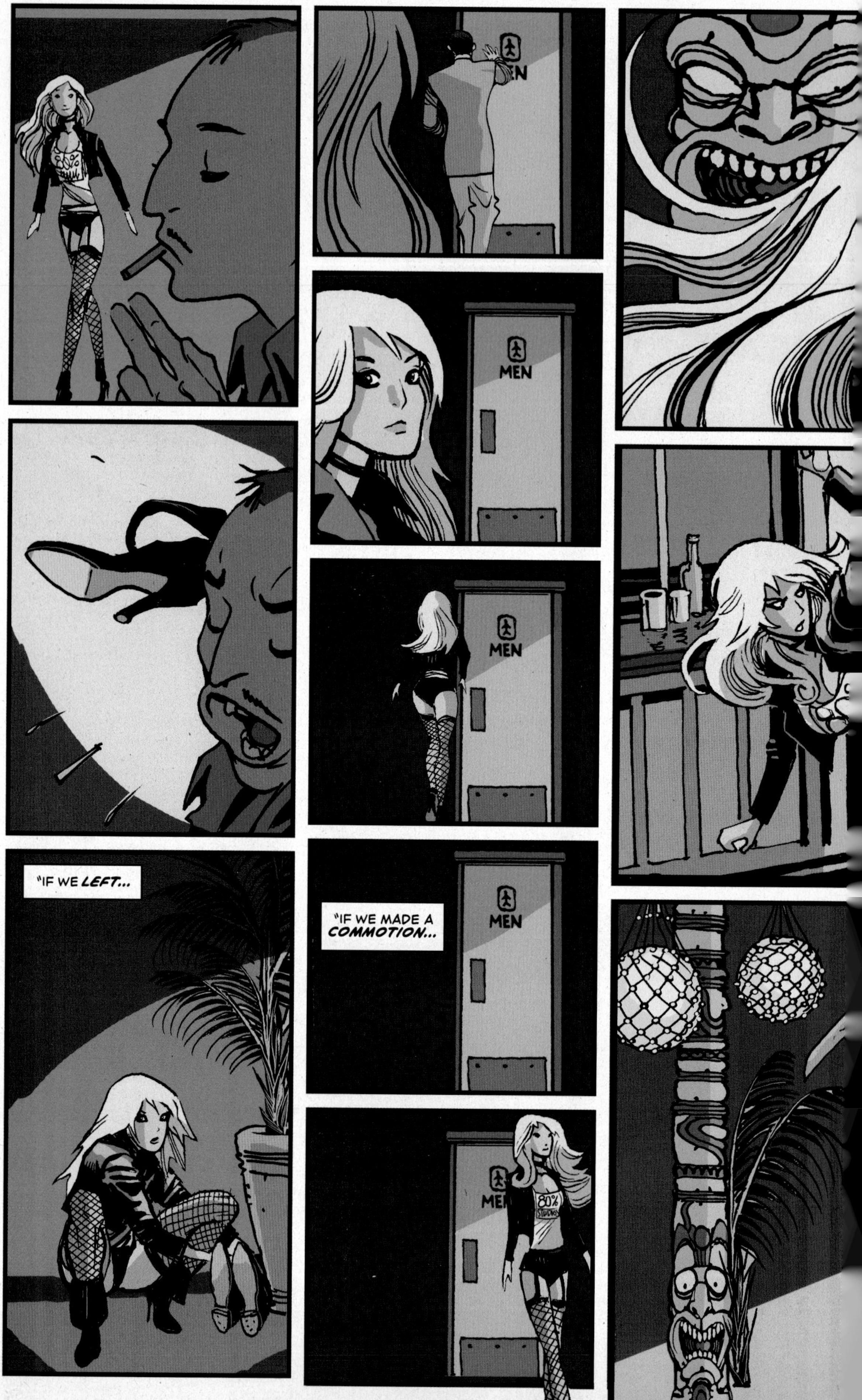
MEN
"IF WE *LEFT*...
"IF WE MADE A *COMMOTION*...
80% STUDENTS

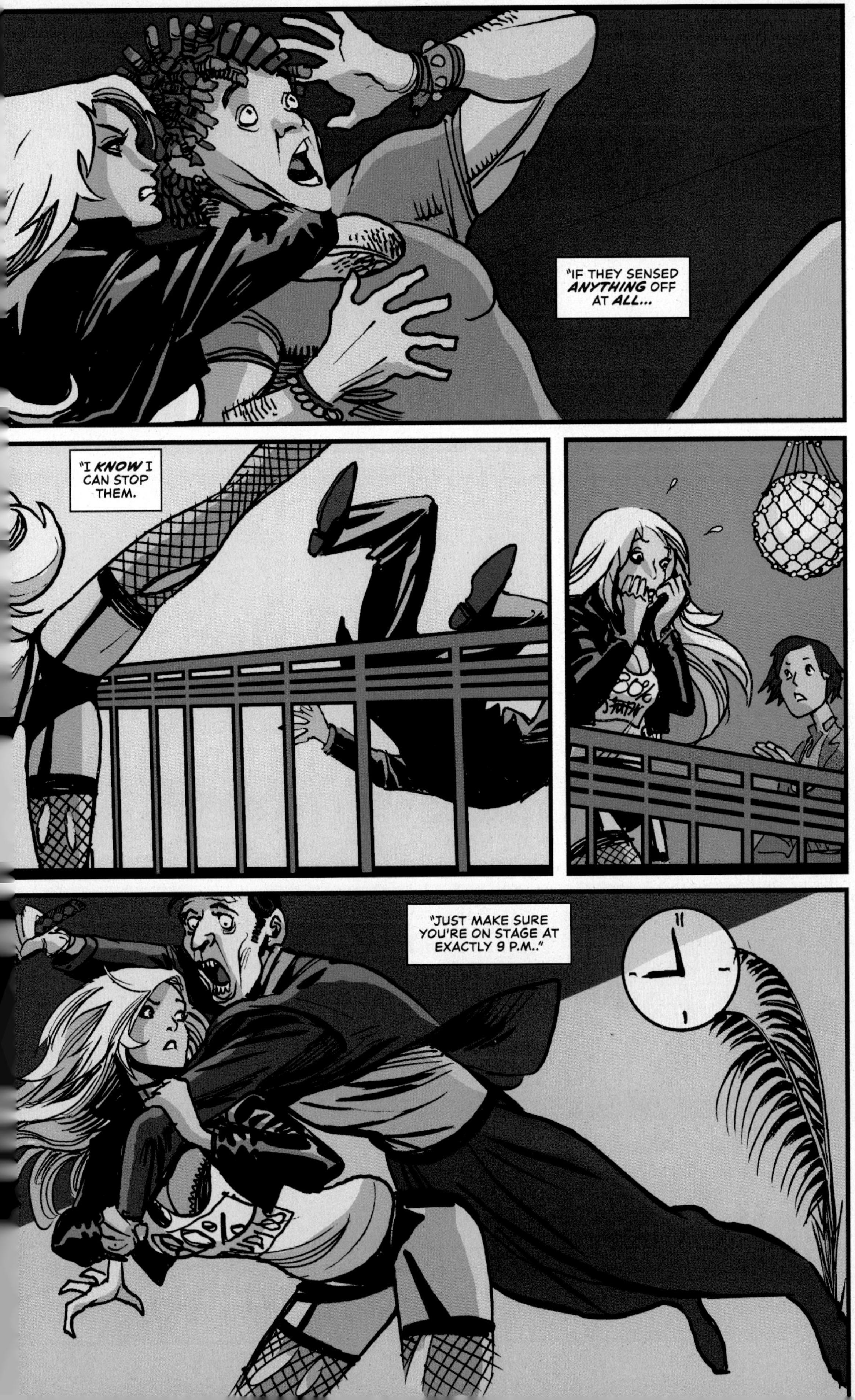
"IF THEY SENSED ANYTHING OFF AT ALL...
"I KNOW I CAN STOP THEM.
"JUST MAKE SURE YOU'RE ON STAGE AT EXACTLY 9 P.M.."

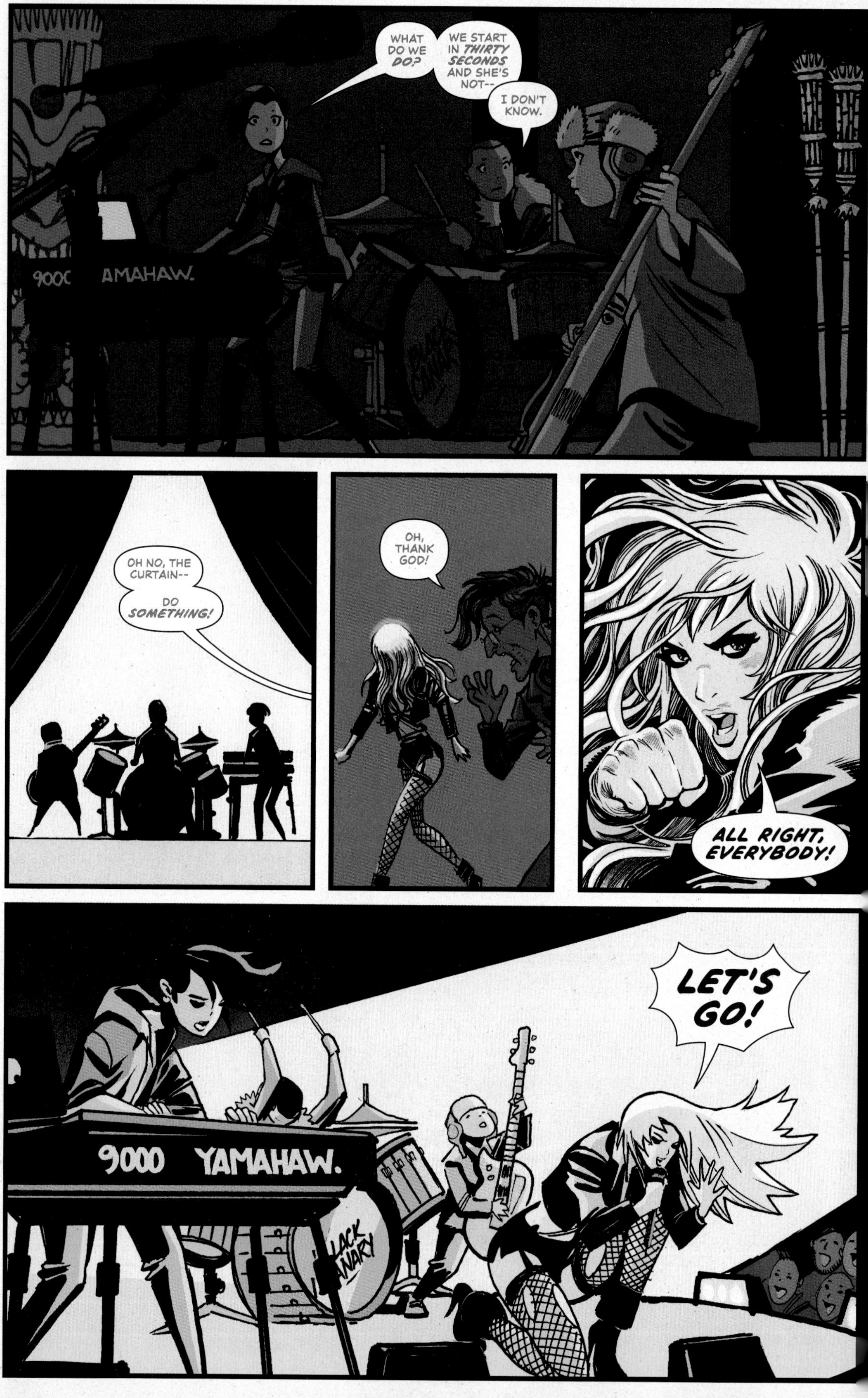
WHAT DO WE DO?
WE START IN THIRTY SECONDS AND SHE'S NOT--
I DON'T KNOW.
9000 YAMAHAW.
OH NO, THE CURTAIN--
DO SOMETHING!
OH, THANK GOD!
ALL RIGHT, EVERYBODY!
LET'S GO!
9000 YAMAHAW.
LACK ANARY

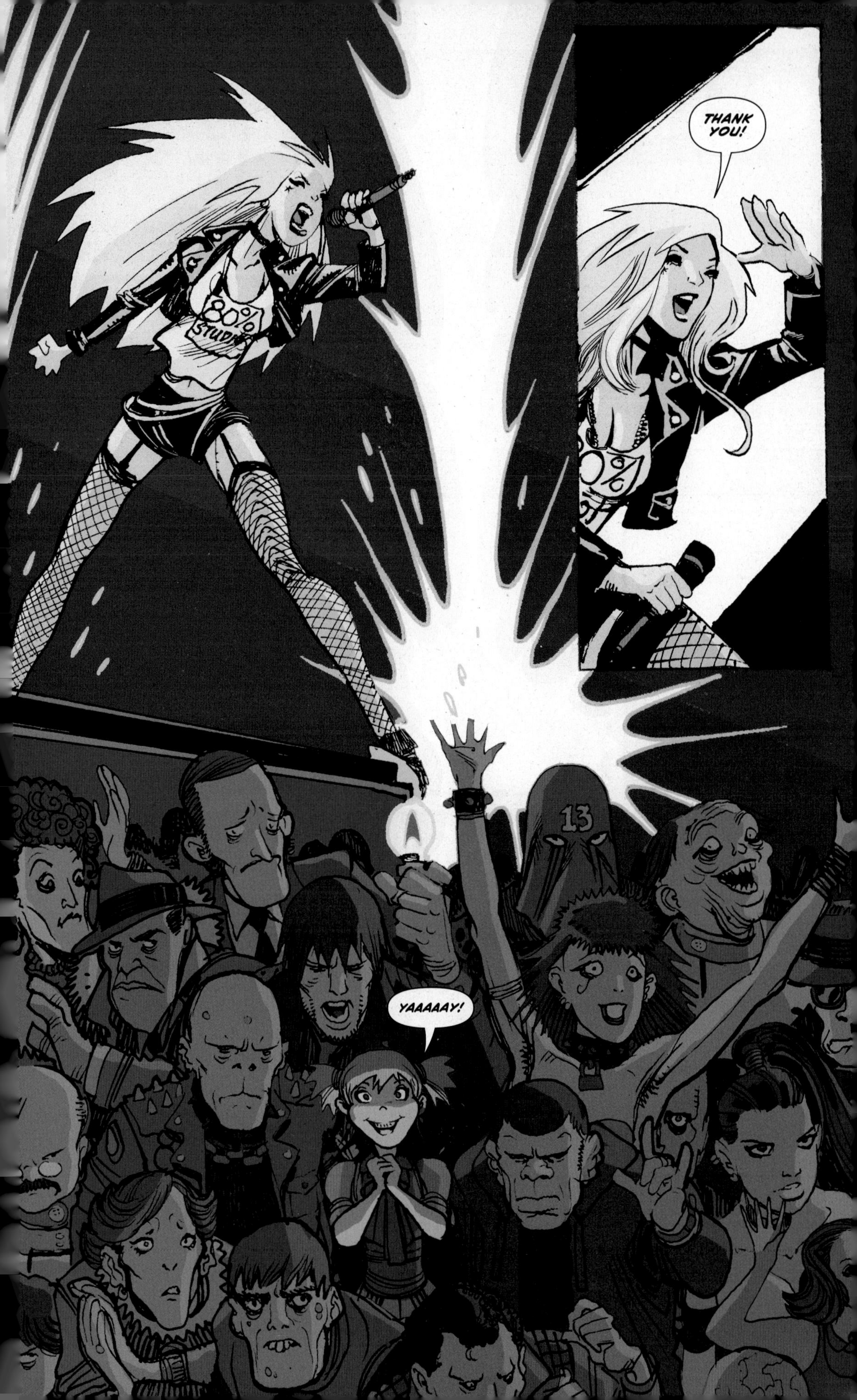
THANK YOU!
YAAAAAY!

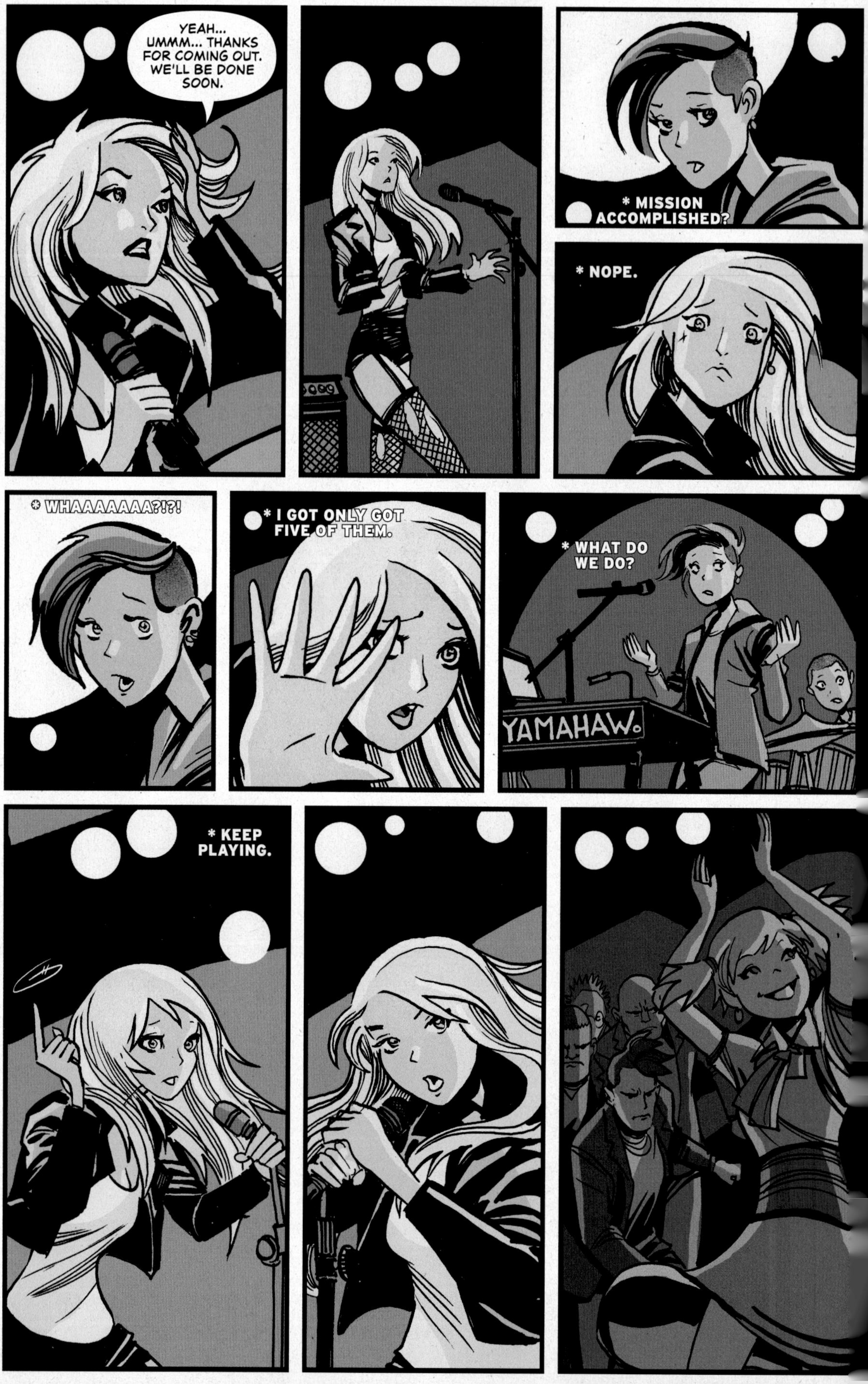
YEAH... UMMM... THANKS FOR COMING OUT. WE'LL BE DONE SOON.
* MISSION ACCOMPLISHED?
* NOPE.
* WHAAAAAAA?!?!
* I GOT ONLY GOT FIVE OF THEM.
* WHAT DO WE DO?
YAMAHAW
* KEEP PLAYING.

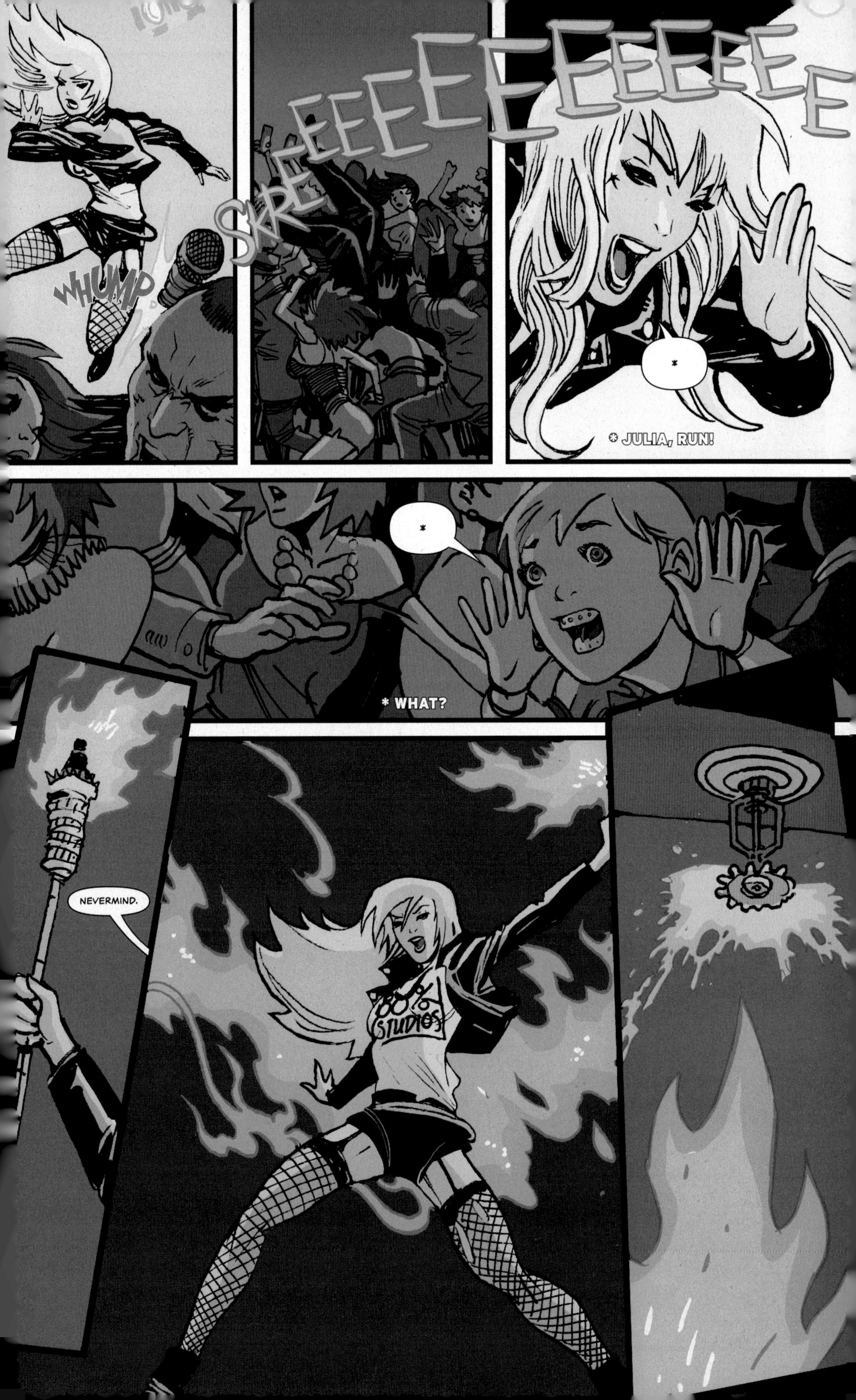
WHUMP
SKREEEEEEEEEEEEEE
*
* JULIA, RUN!
*
* WHAT?
NEVERMIND.

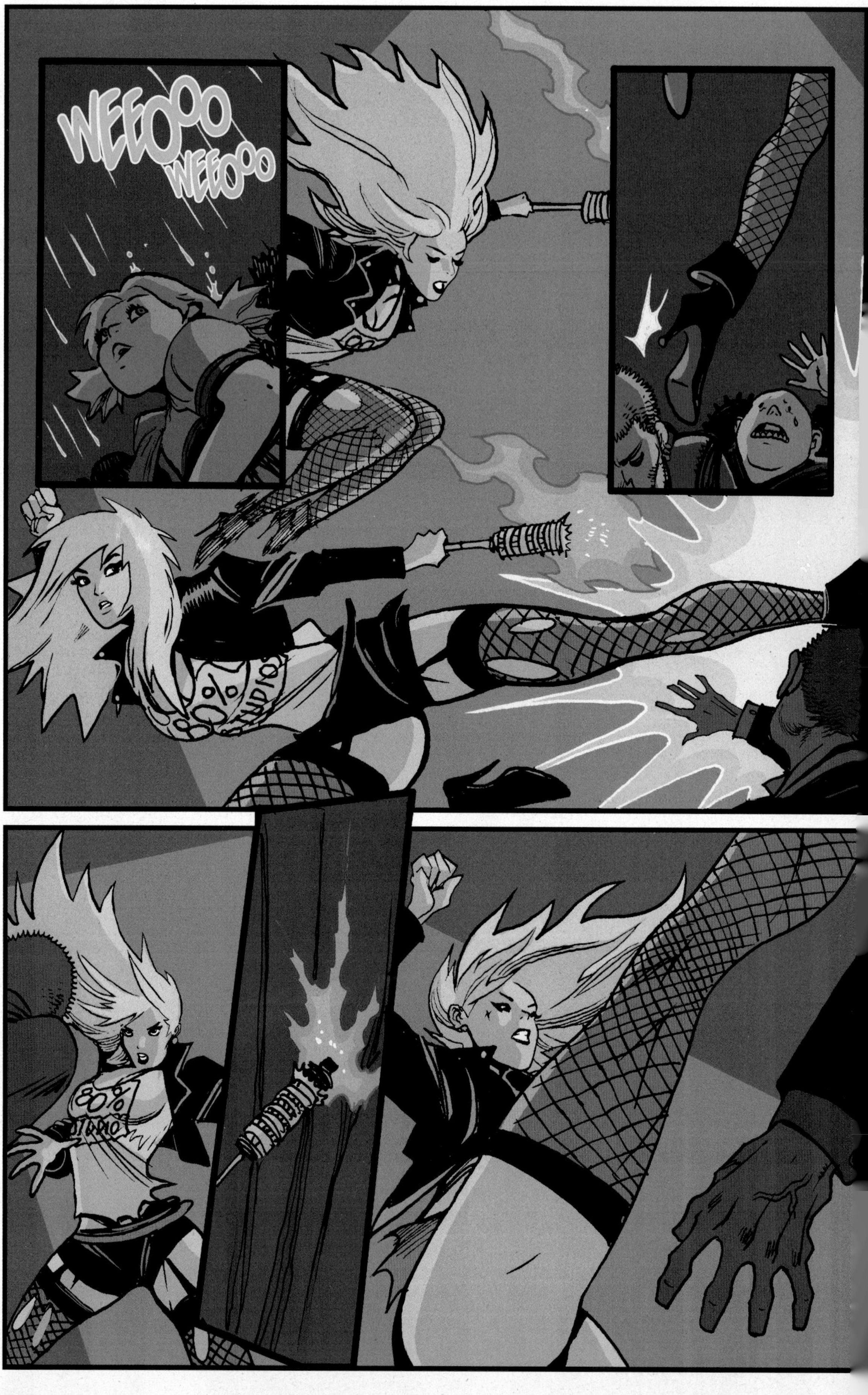
WEEOOO
WEEOOO

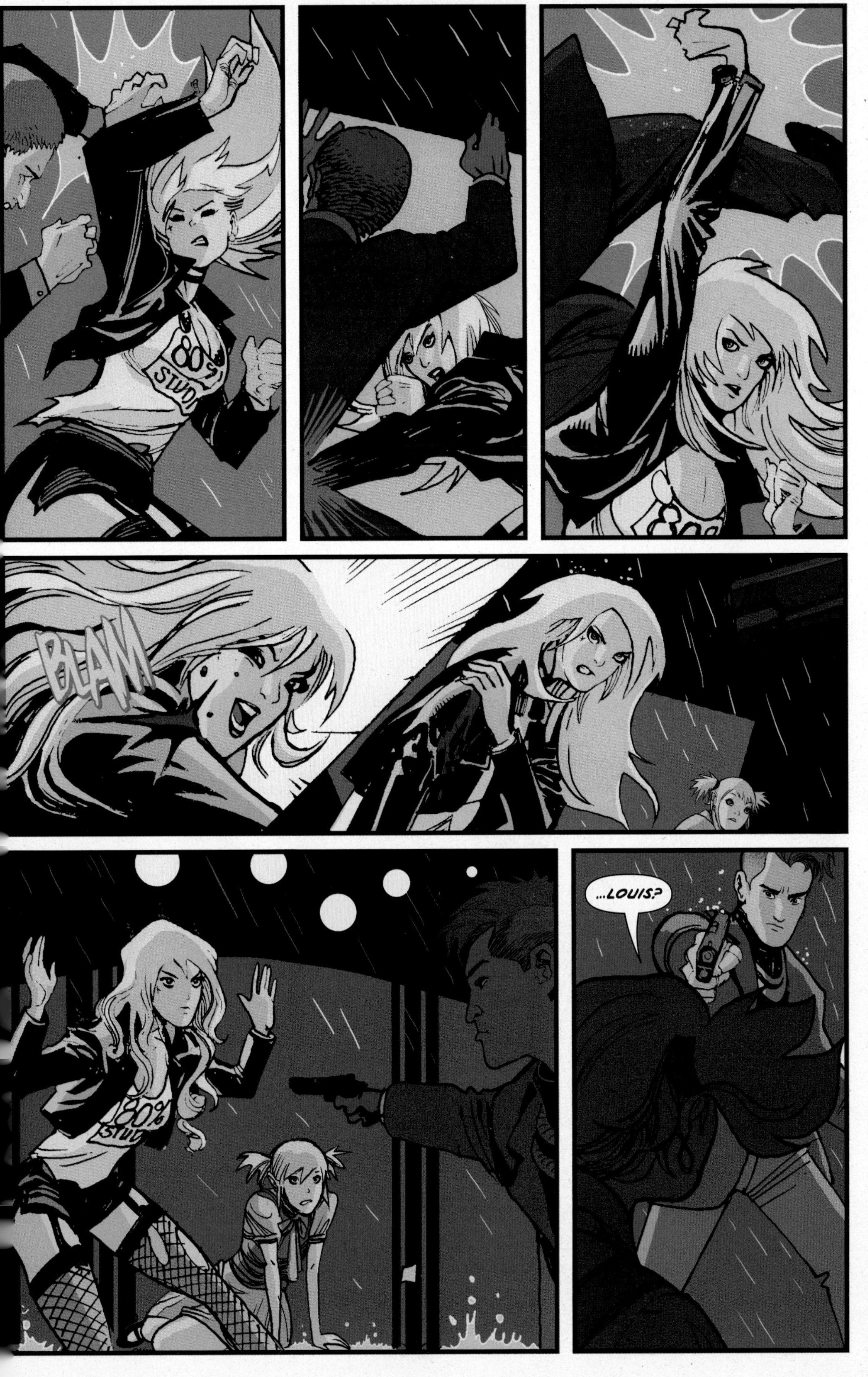
BLAM
...LOUIS?

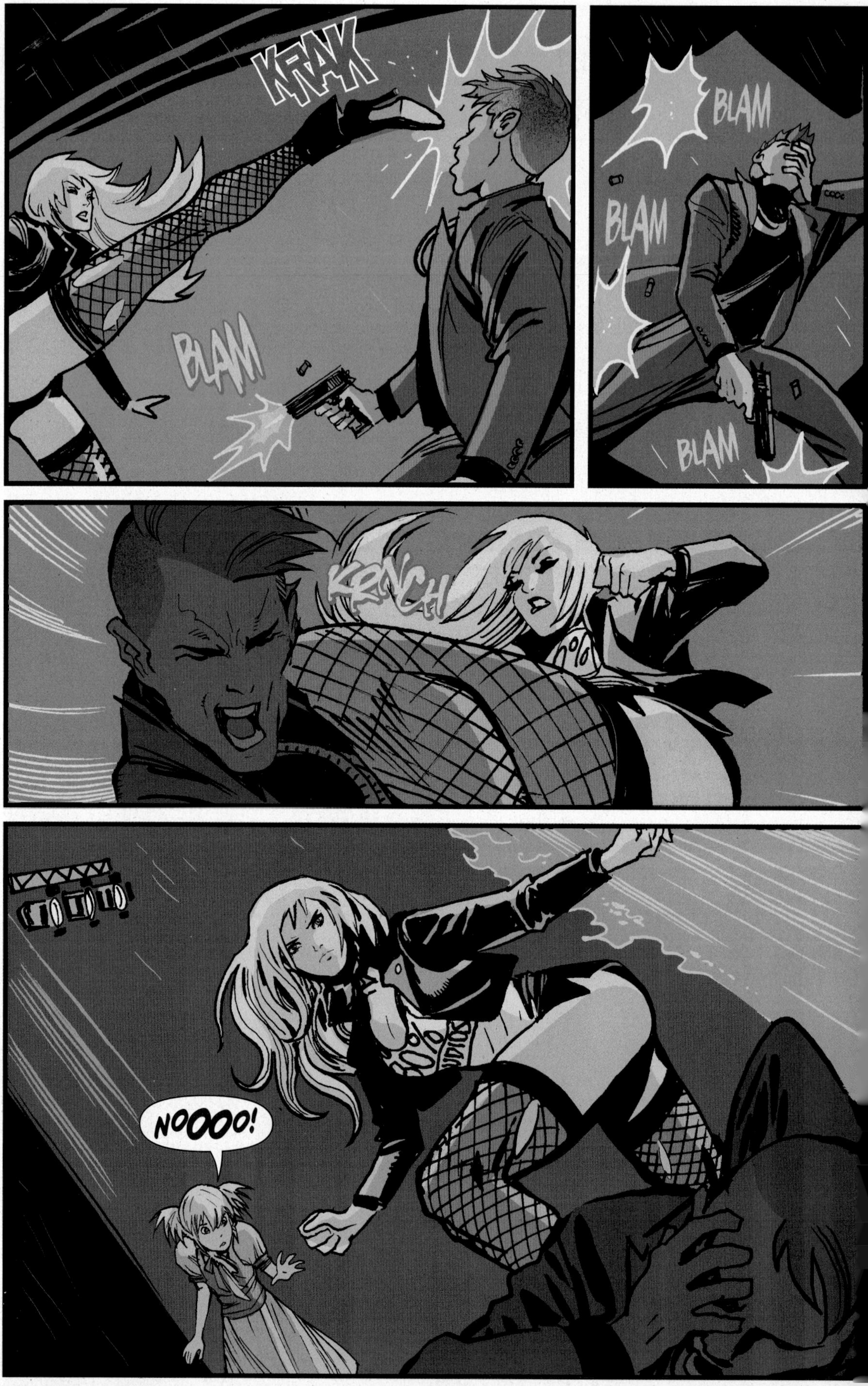
KRAK
BLAM
BLAM
BLAM
BLAM
KRNCH!
NoOOO!

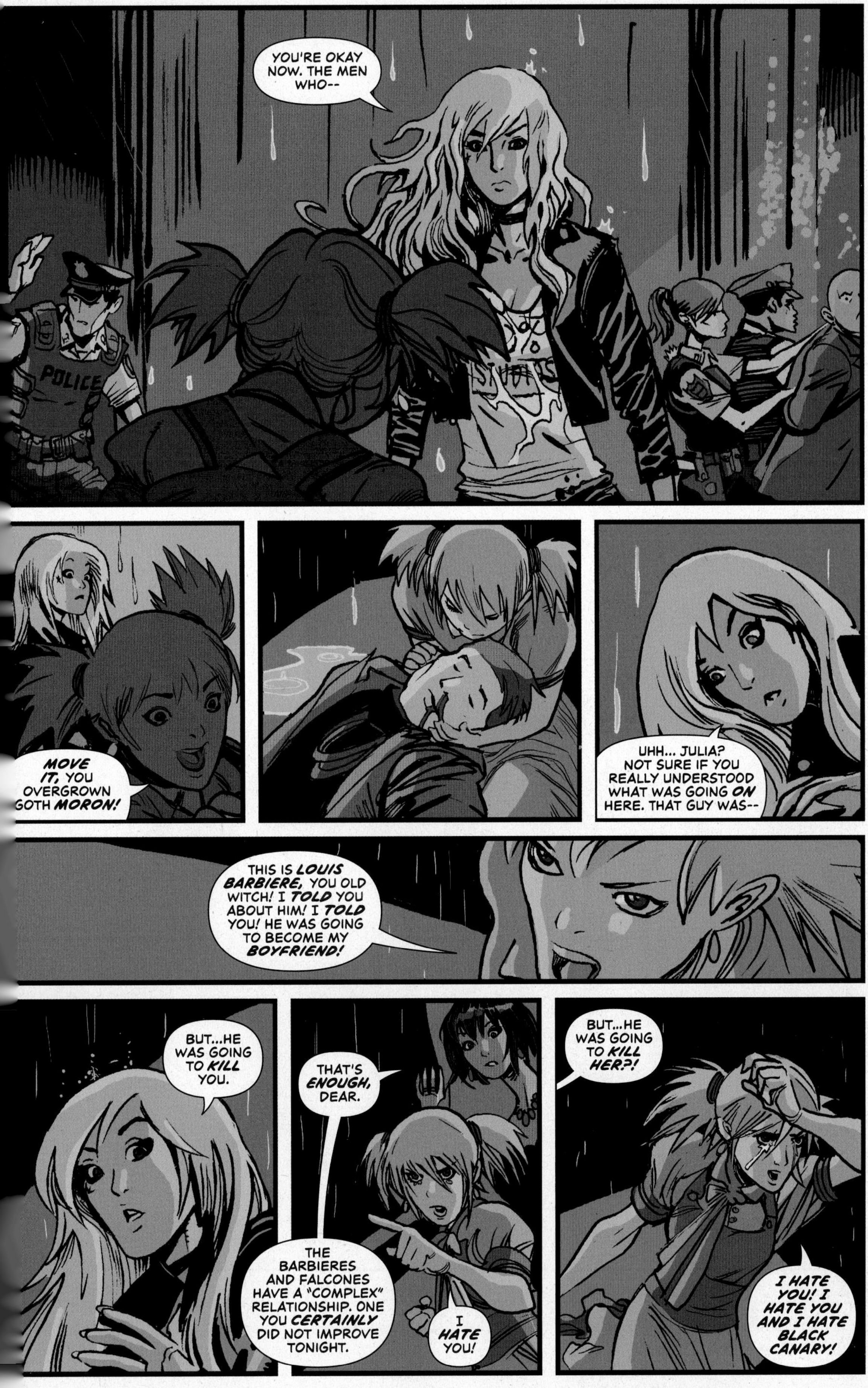
YOU'RE OKAY NOW. THE MEN WHO--
MOVE IT, YOU OVERGROWN GOTH MORON!
UHH... JULIA? NOT SURE IF YOU REALLY UNDERSTOOD WHAT WAS GOING ON HERE. THAT GUY WAS--
THIS IS LOUIS BARBIERE, YOU OLD WITCH! I TOLD YOU ABOUT HIM! I TOLD YOU! HE WAS GOING TO BECOME MY BOYFRIEND!
BUT...HE WAS GOING TO KILL YOU.
THAT'S ENOUGH, DEAR.
THE BARBIERES AND FALCONES HAVE A "COMPLEX" RELATIONSHIP. ONE YOU CERTAINLY DID NOT IMPROVE TONIGHT.
I HATE YOU!
BUT...HE WAS GOING TO KILL HER?!
I HATE YOU! I HATE YOU AND I HATE BLACK CANARY!

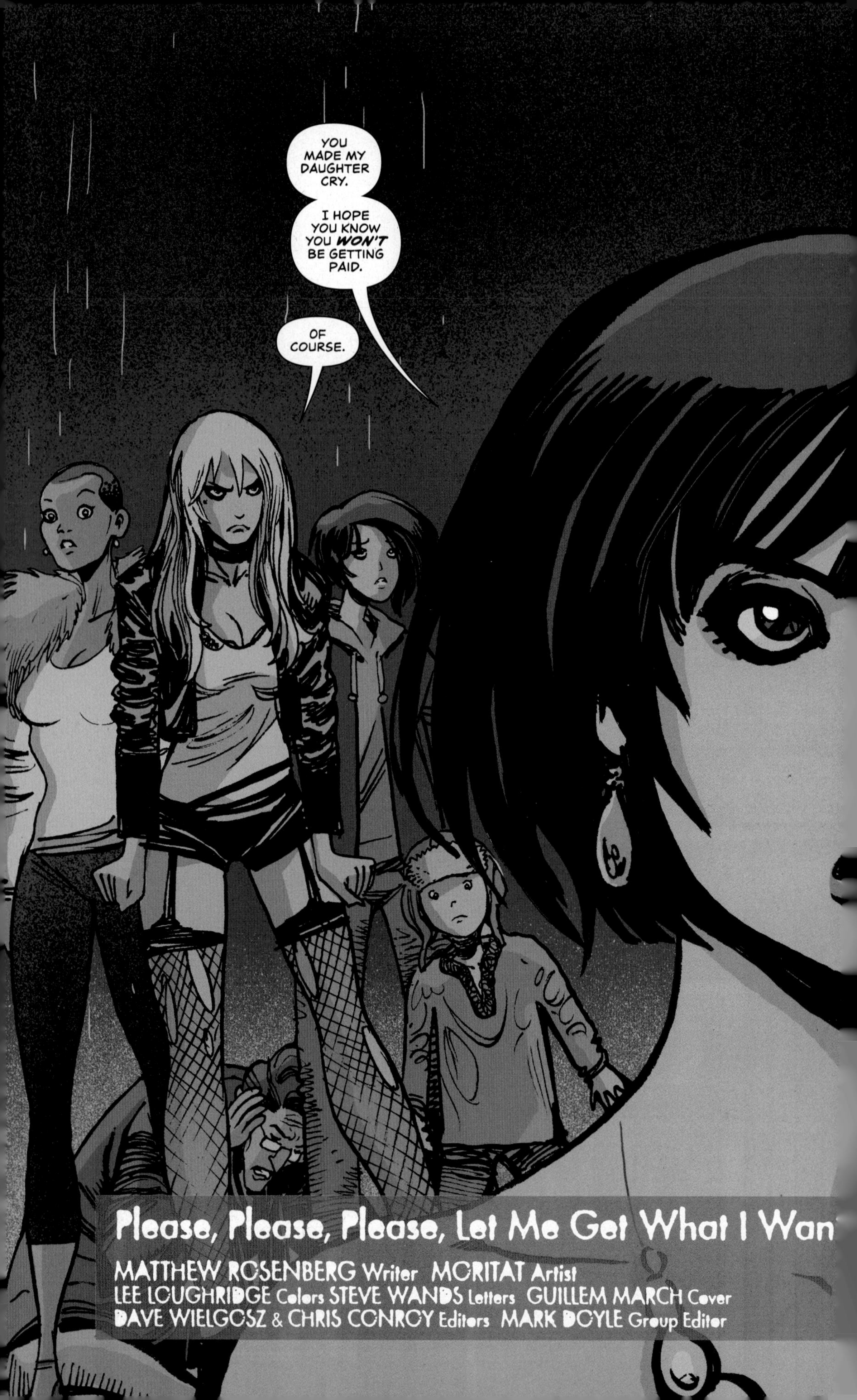
YOU MADE MY DAUGHTER CRY.
I HOPE YOU KNOW YOU *WON'T* BE GETTING PAID.
OF COURSE.
Please, Please, Please, Let Me Get What I Wan
MATTHEW ROSENBERG Writer MORITAT Artist
LEE LOUGHRIDGE Colors STEVE WANDS Letters GUILLEM MARCH Cover
DAVE WIELGOSZ & CHRIS CONROY Editors MARK DOYLE Group Editor

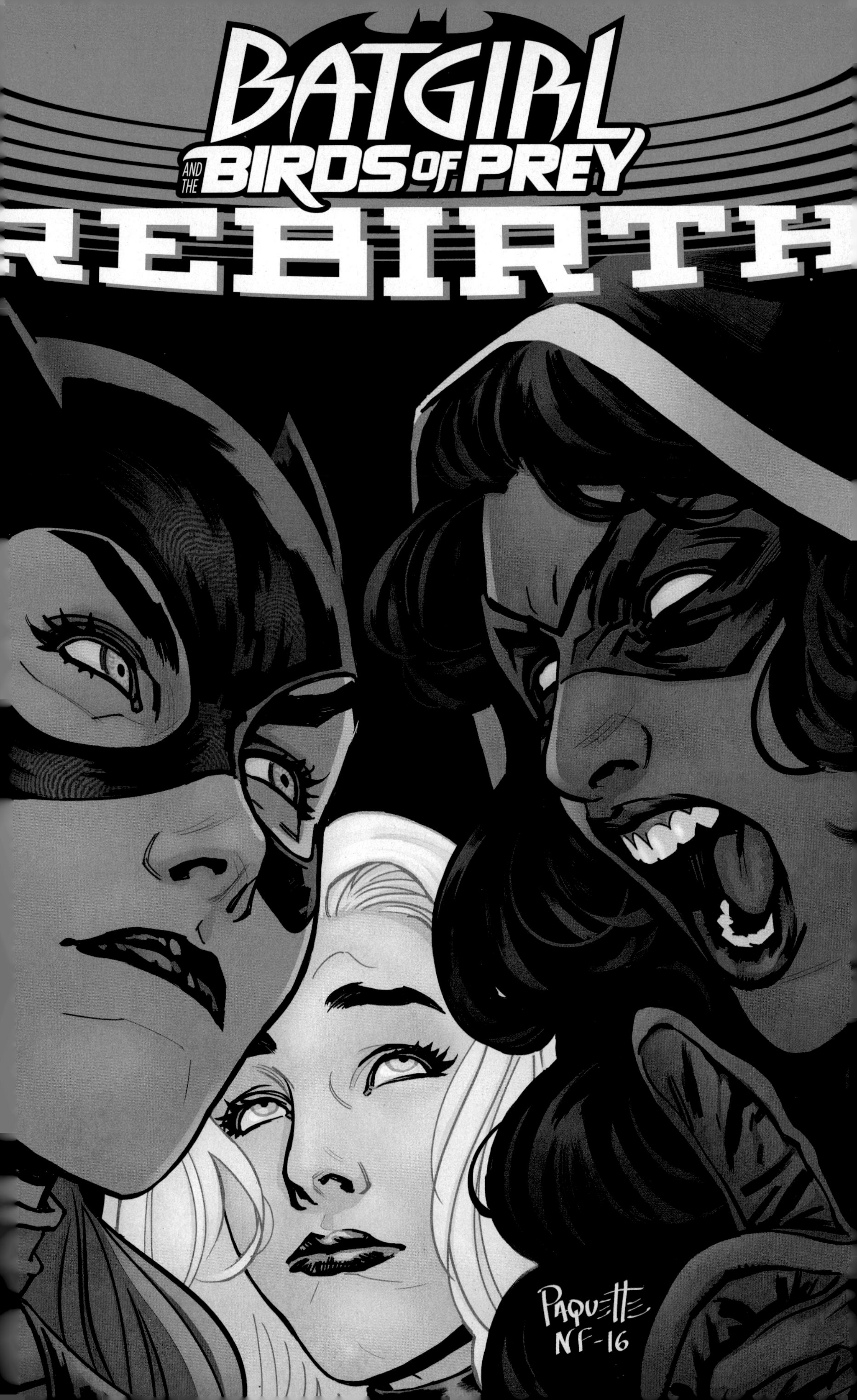
BATGIRL
AND THE BIRDS OF PREY
REBIRTH
PAQUETTE
NF-16

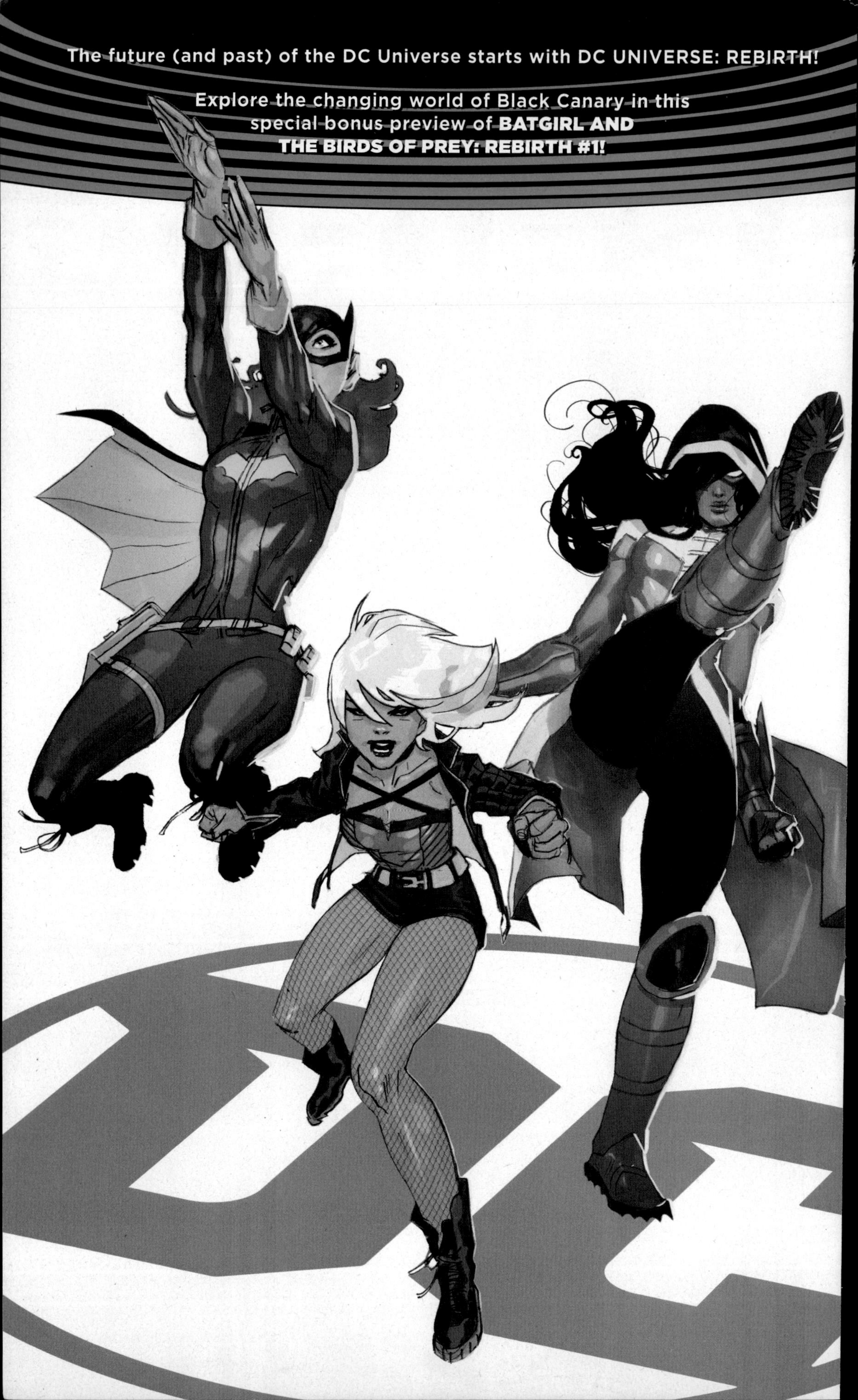

The future (and past) of the DC Universe starts with DC UNIVERSE: REBIRTH!
Explore the changing world of Black Canary in this special bonus preview of **BATGIRL AND THE BIRDS OF PREY: REBIRTH #1!**

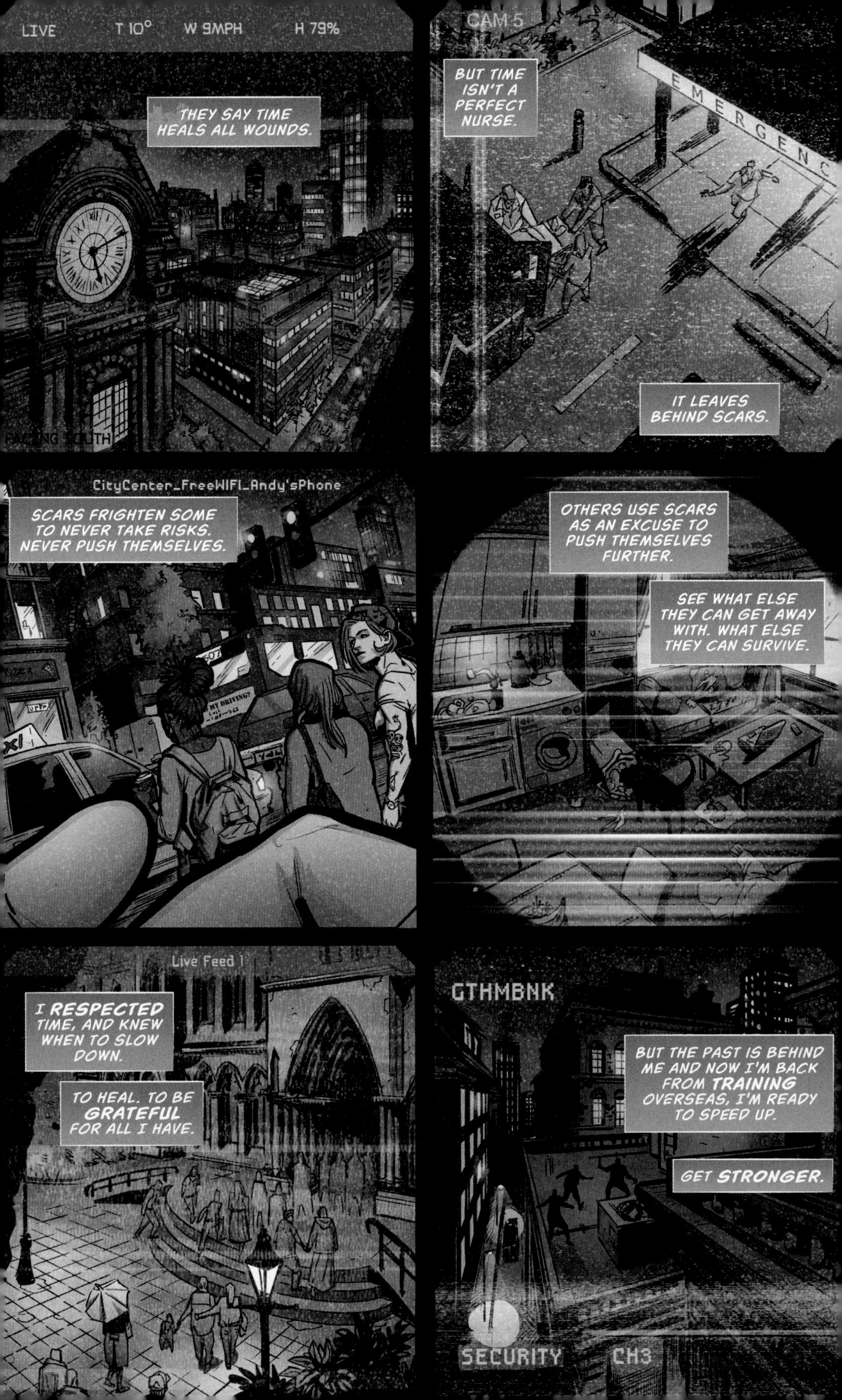
LIVE
T 10°
W 9MPH
H 79%
THEY SAY TIME HEALS ALL WOUNDS.
CAM 5
BUT TIME ISN'T A PERFECT NURSE.
EMERGENC
IT LEAVES BEHIND SCARS.
CityCenter_FreeWIFI_Andy'sPhone
SCARS FRIGHTEN SOME TO NEVER TAKE RISKS. NEVER PUSH THEMSELVES.
OTHERS USE SCARS AS AN EXCUSE TO PUSH THEMSELVES FURTHER.
SEE WHAT ELSE THEY CAN GET AWAY WITH. WHAT ELSE THEY CAN SURVIVE.
Live Feed 1
I **RESPECTED** TIME, AND KNEW WHEN TO SLOW DOWN.
TO HEAL. TO BE **GRATEFUL** FOR ALL I HAVE.
GTHMBNK
BUT THE PAST IS BEHIND ME AND NOW I'M BACK FROM **TRAINING** OVERSEAS, I'M READY TO SPEED UP.
GET **STRONGER**.
SECURITY
CH3

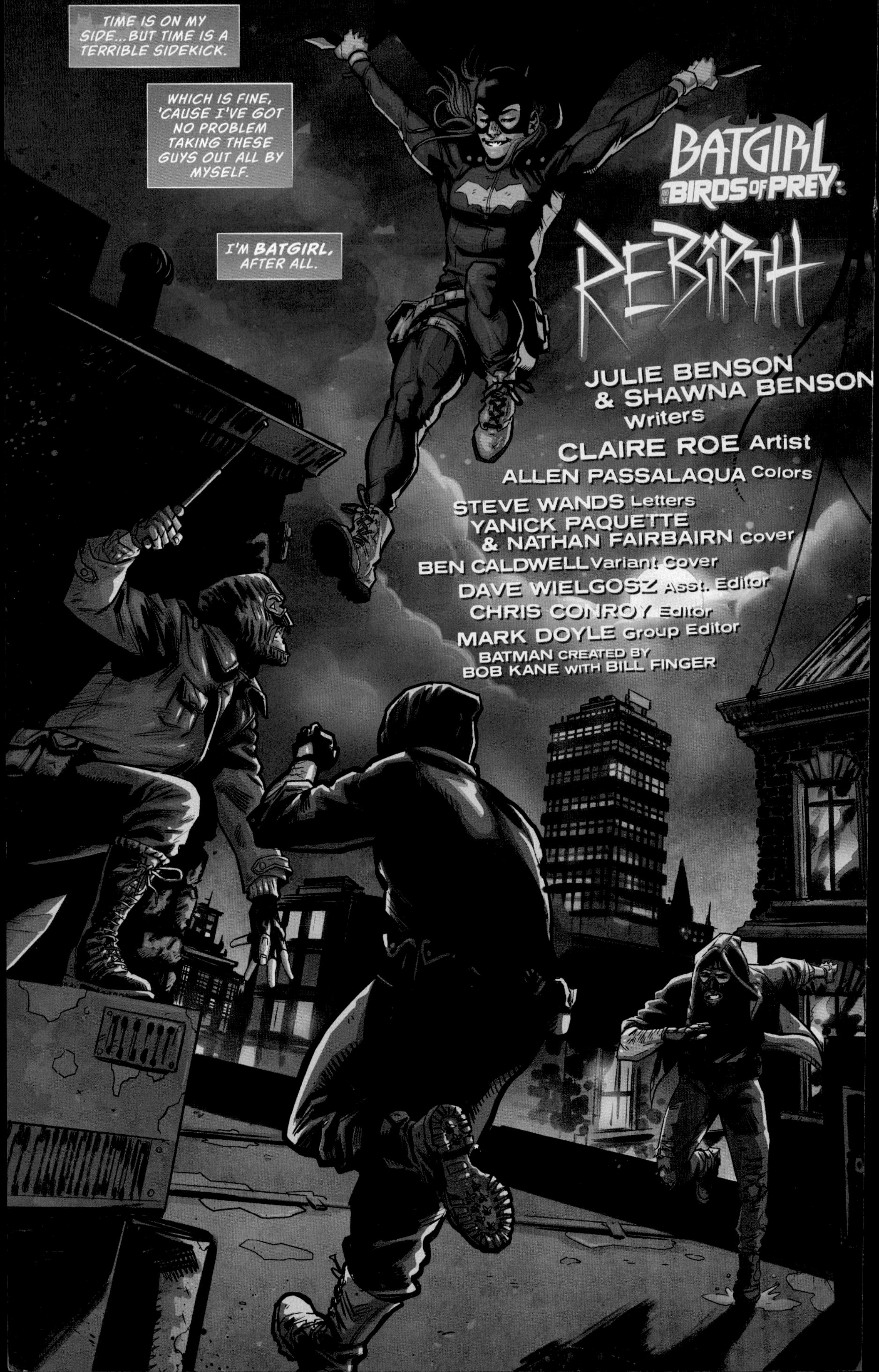
TIME IS ON MY SIDE...BUT TIME IS A TERRIBLE SIDEKICK.
WHICH IS FINE, 'CAUSE I'VE GOT NO PROBLEM TAKING THESE GUYS OUT ALL BY MYSELF.
I'M BATGIRL, AFTER ALL.
BATGIRL AND THE BIRDS OF PREY: REBIRTH
JULIE BENSON & SHAWNA BENSON Writers
CLAIRE ROE Artist
ALLEN PASSALAQUA Colors
STEVE WANDS Letters
YANICK PAQUETTE & NATHAN FAIRBAIRN Cover
BEN CALDWELL Variant Cover
DAVE WIELGOSZ Asst. Editor
CHRIS CONROY Editor
MARK DOYLE Group Editor
BATMAN CREATED BY BOB KANE WITH BILL FINGER

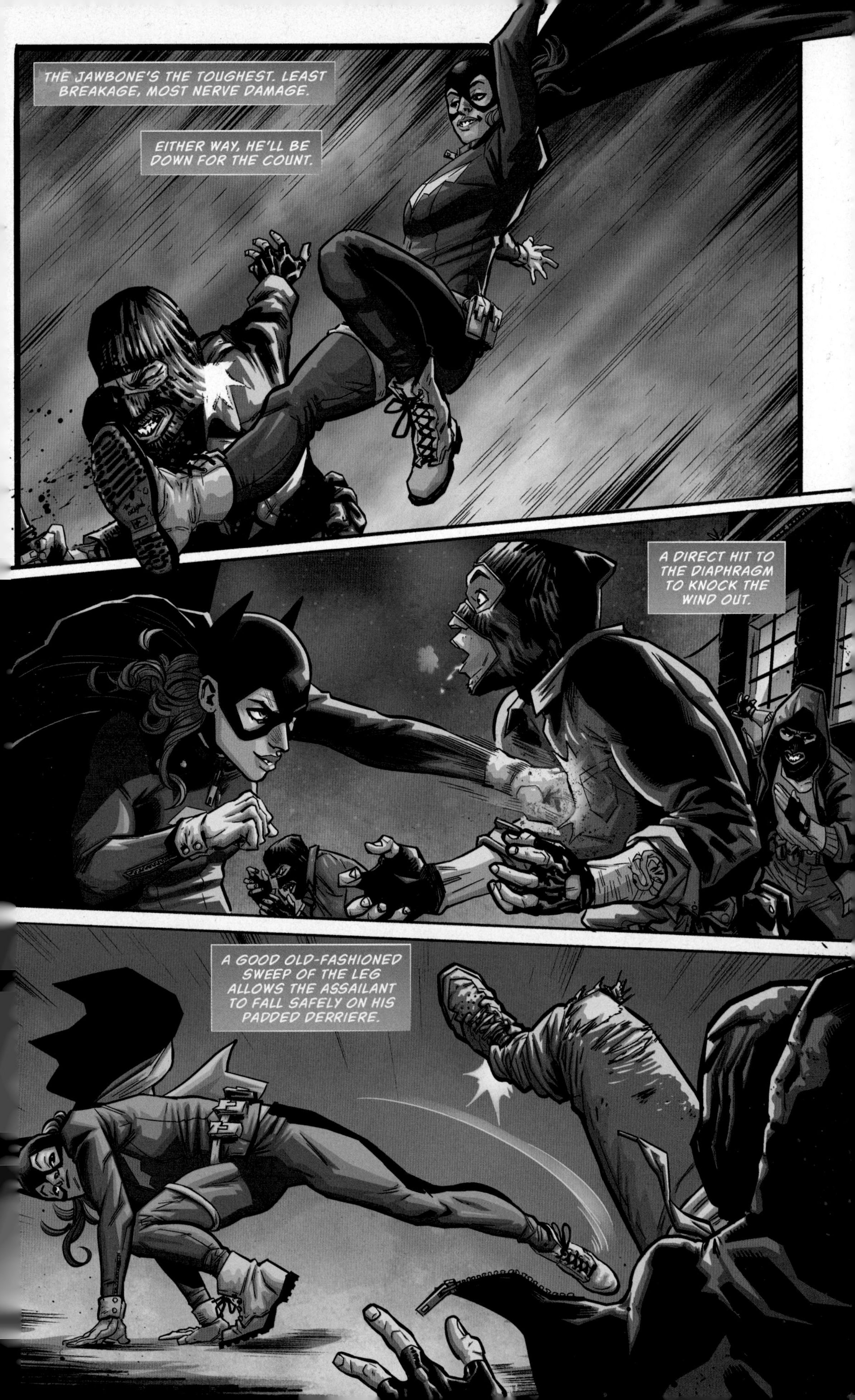
THE JAWBONE'S THE TOUGHEST. LEAST BREAKAGE, MOST NERVE DAMAGE.
EITHER WAY, HE'LL BE DOWN FOR THE COUNT.
A DIRECT HIT TO THE DIAPHRAGM TO KNOCK THE WIND OUT.
A GOOD OLD-FASHIONED SWEEP OF THE LEG ALLOWS THE ASSAILANT TO FALL SAFELY ON HIS PADDED DERRIERE.

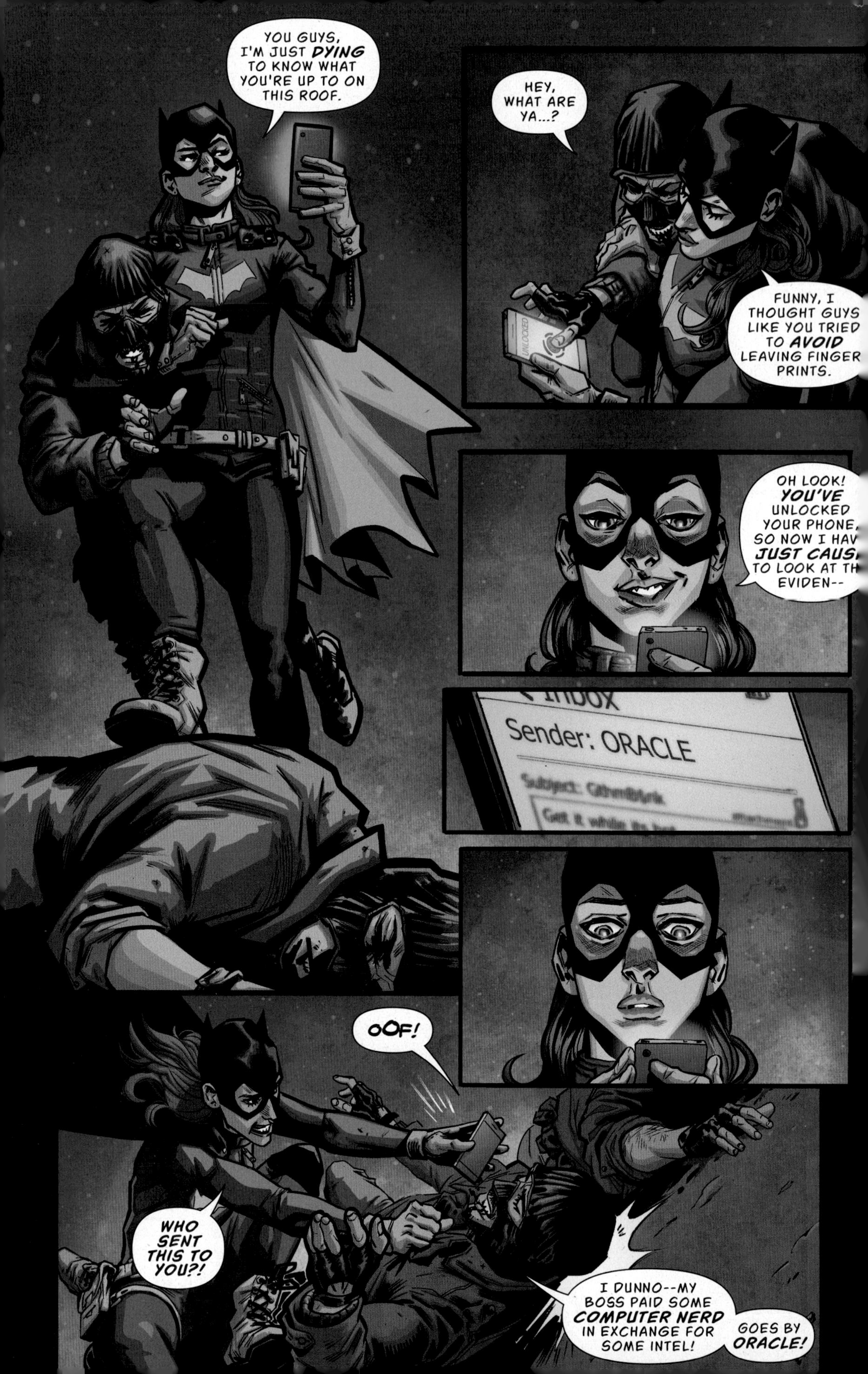

YOU GUYS, I'M JUST **DYING** TO KNOW WHAT YOU'RE UP TO ON THIS ROOF.
HEY, WHAT ARE YA...?
FUNNY, I THOUGHT GUYS LIKE YOU TRIED TO **AVOID** LEAVING FINGER PRINTS.
UNLOCKED
OH LOOK! **YOU'VE** UNLOCKED YOUR PHONE, SO NOW I HAV **JUST CAUS** TO LOOK AT TH EVIDEN--
Sender: ORACLE
OOF!
WHO SENT THIS TO YOU?!
I DUNNO--MY BOSS PAID SOME **COMPUTER NERD** IN EXCHANGE FOR SOME INTEL!
GOES BY **ORACLE!**

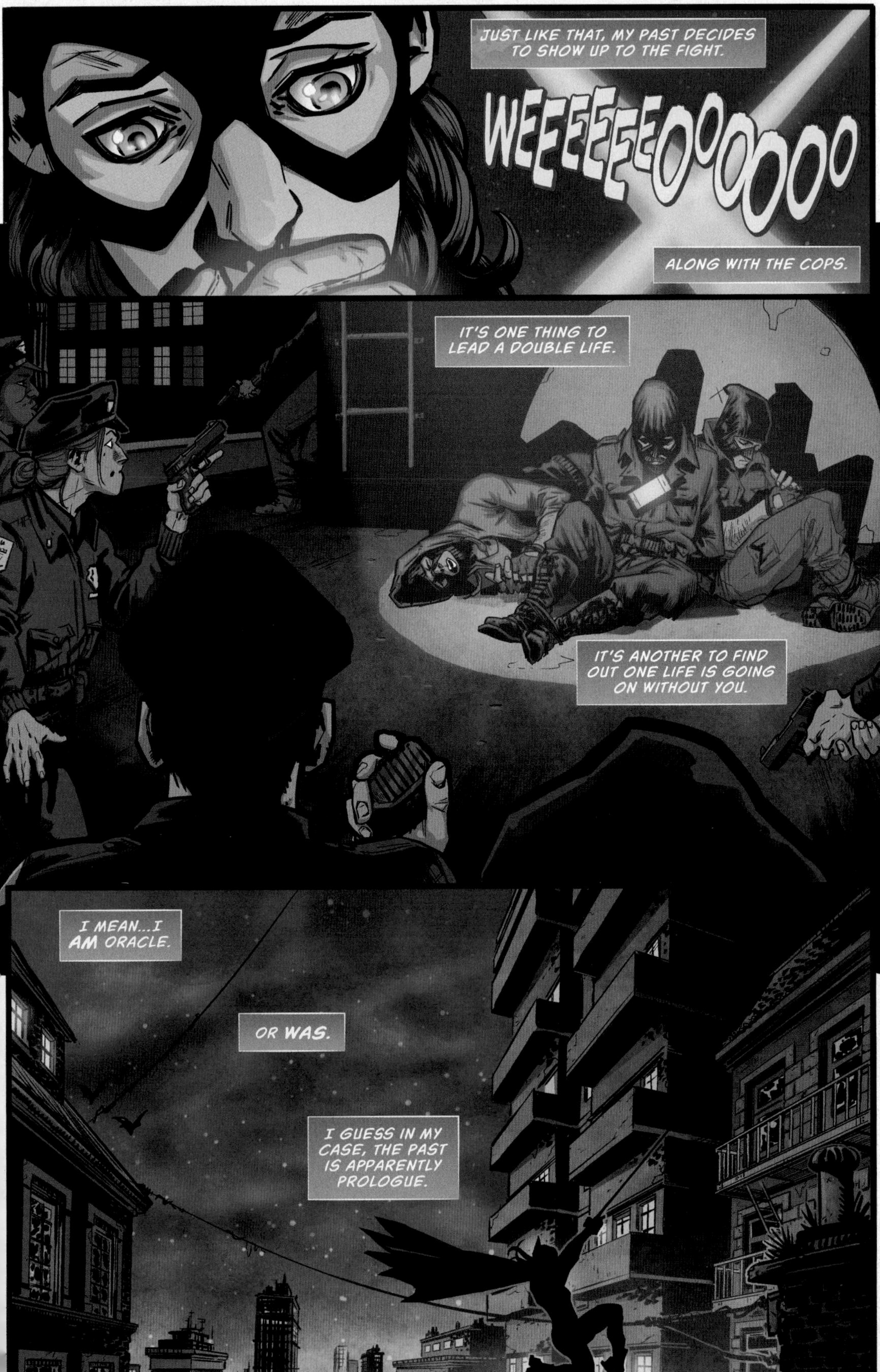
JUST LIKE THAT, MY PAST DECIDES TO SHOW UP TO THE FIGHT.
WEEEEEEOOOOOO
ALONG WITH THE COPS.
IT'S ONE THING TO LEAD A DOUBLE LIFE.
IT'S ANOTHER TO FIND OUT ONE LIFE IS GOING ON WITHOUT YOU.
I MEAN...I AM ORACLE.
OR WAS.
I GUESS IN MY CASE, THE PAST IS APPARENTLY PROLOGUE.

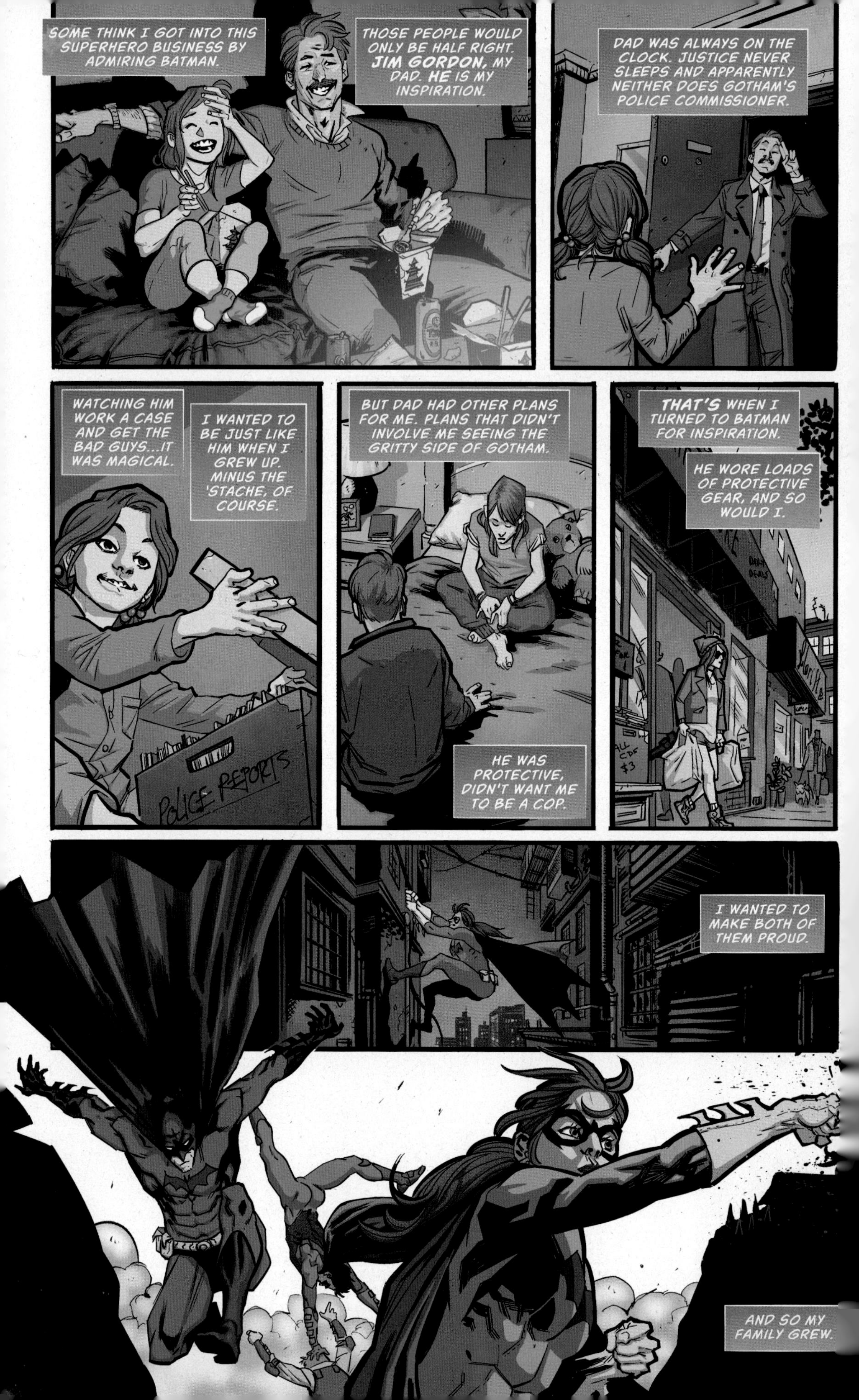
SOME THINK I GOT INTO THIS SUPERHERO BUSINESS BY ADMIRING BATMAN.
THOSE PEOPLE WOULD ONLY BE HALF RIGHT. JIM GORDON, MY DAD. HE IS MY INSPIRATION.
DAD WAS ALWAYS ON THE CLOCK. JUSTICE NEVER SLEEPS AND APPARENTLY NEITHER DOES GOTHAM'S POLICE COMMISSIONER.
WATCHING HIM WORK A CASE AND GET THE BAD GUYS...IT WAS MAGICAL.
I WANTED TO BE JUST LIKE HIM WHEN I GREW UP. MINUS THE 'STACHE, OF COURSE.
POLICE REPORTS
BUT DAD HAD OTHER PLANS FOR ME. PLANS THAT DIDN'T INVOLVE ME SEEING THE GRITTY SIDE OF GOTHAM.
HE WAS PROTECTIVE, DIDN'T WANT ME TO BE A COP.
THAT'S WHEN I TURNED TO BATMAN FOR INSPIRATION.
HE WORE LOADS OF PROTECTIVE GEAR, AND SO WOULD I.
I WANTED TO MAKE BOTH OF THEM PROUD.
AND SO MY FAMILY GREW.

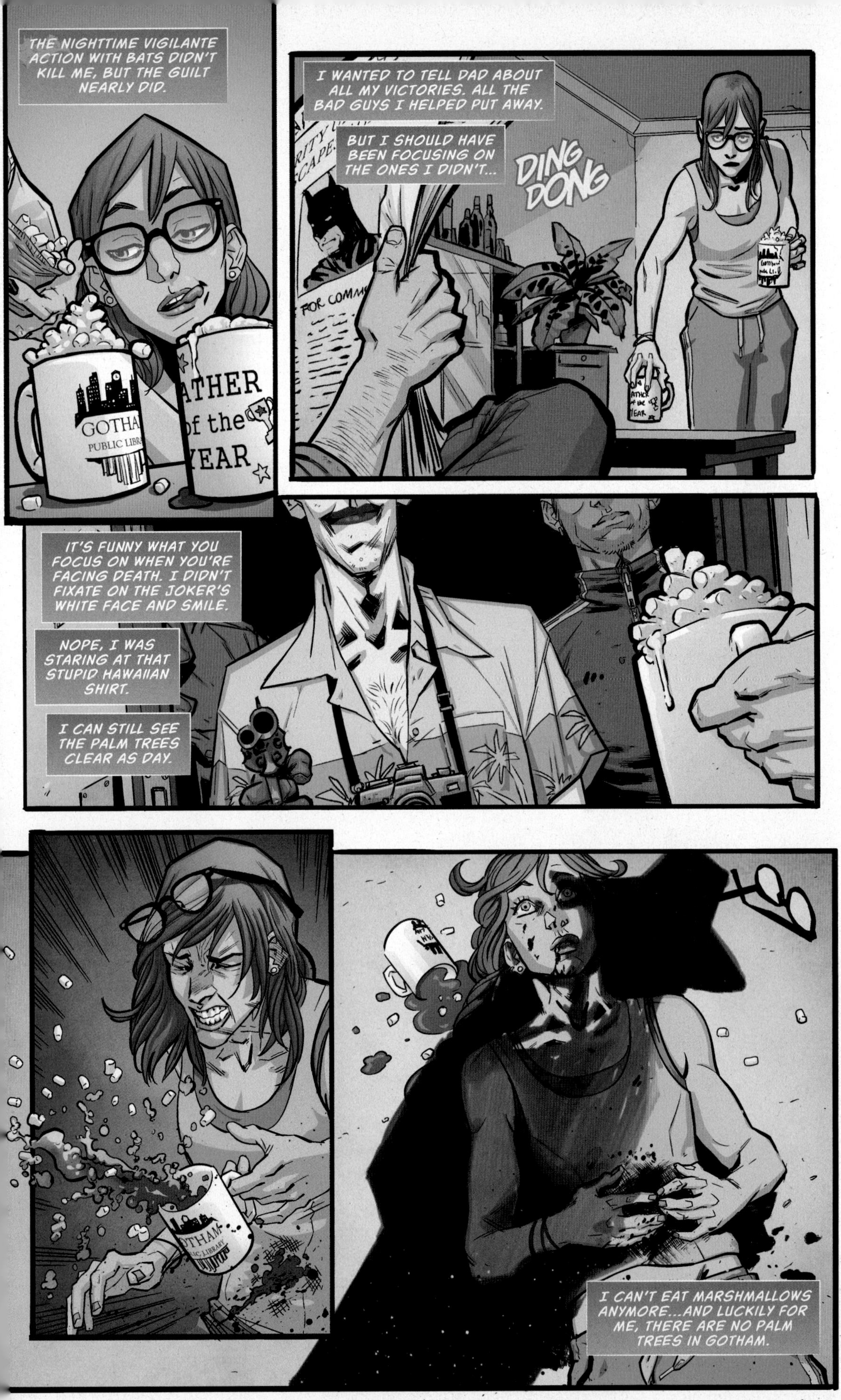
THE NIGHTTIME VIGILANTE ACTION WITH BATS DIDN'T KILL ME, BUT THE GUILT NEARLY DID.
GOTHAM PUBLIC LIBRARY
FATHER of the YEAR
I WANTED TO TELL DAD ABOUT ALL MY VICTORIES. ALL THE BAD GUYS I HELPED PUT AWAY.
BUT I SHOULD HAVE BEEN FOCUSING ON THE ONES I DIDN'T...
DING DONG
IT'S FUNNY WHAT YOU FOCUS ON WHEN YOU'RE FACING DEATH. I DIDN'T FIXATE ON THE JOKER'S WHITE FACE AND SMILE.
NOPE, I WAS STARING AT THAT STUPID HAWAIIAN SHIRT.
I CAN STILL SEE THE PALM TREES CLEAR AS DAY.
I CAN'T EAT MARSHMALLOWS ANYMORE...AND LUCKILY FOR ME, THERE ARE NO PALM TREES IN GOTHAM.

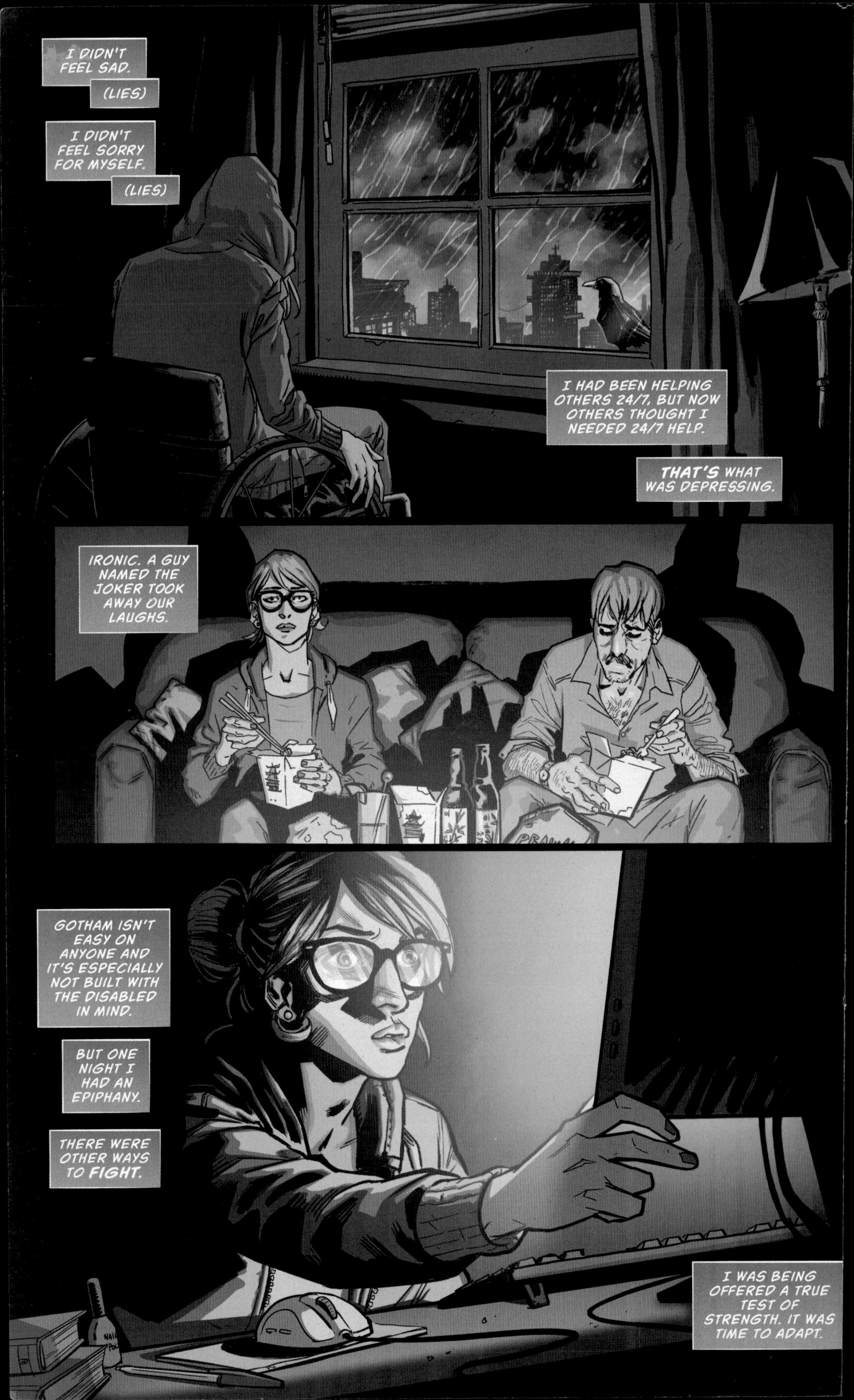
I DIDN'T FEEL SAD.
(LIES)
I DIDN'T FEEL SORRY FOR MYSELF.
(LIES)
I HAD BEEN HELPING OTHERS 24/7, BUT NOW OTHERS THOUGHT I NEEDED 24/7 HELP.
THAT'S WHAT WAS DEPRESSING.
IRONIC. A GUY NAMED THE JOKER TOOK AWAY OUR LAUGHS.
GOTHAM ISN'T EASY ON ANYONE AND IT'S ESPECIALLY NOT BUILT WITH THE DISABLED IN MIND.
BUT ONE NIGHT I HAD AN EPIPHANY.
THERE WERE OTHER WAYS TO FIGHT.
I WAS BEING OFFERED A TRUE TEST OF STRENGTH. IT WAS TIME TO ADAPT.

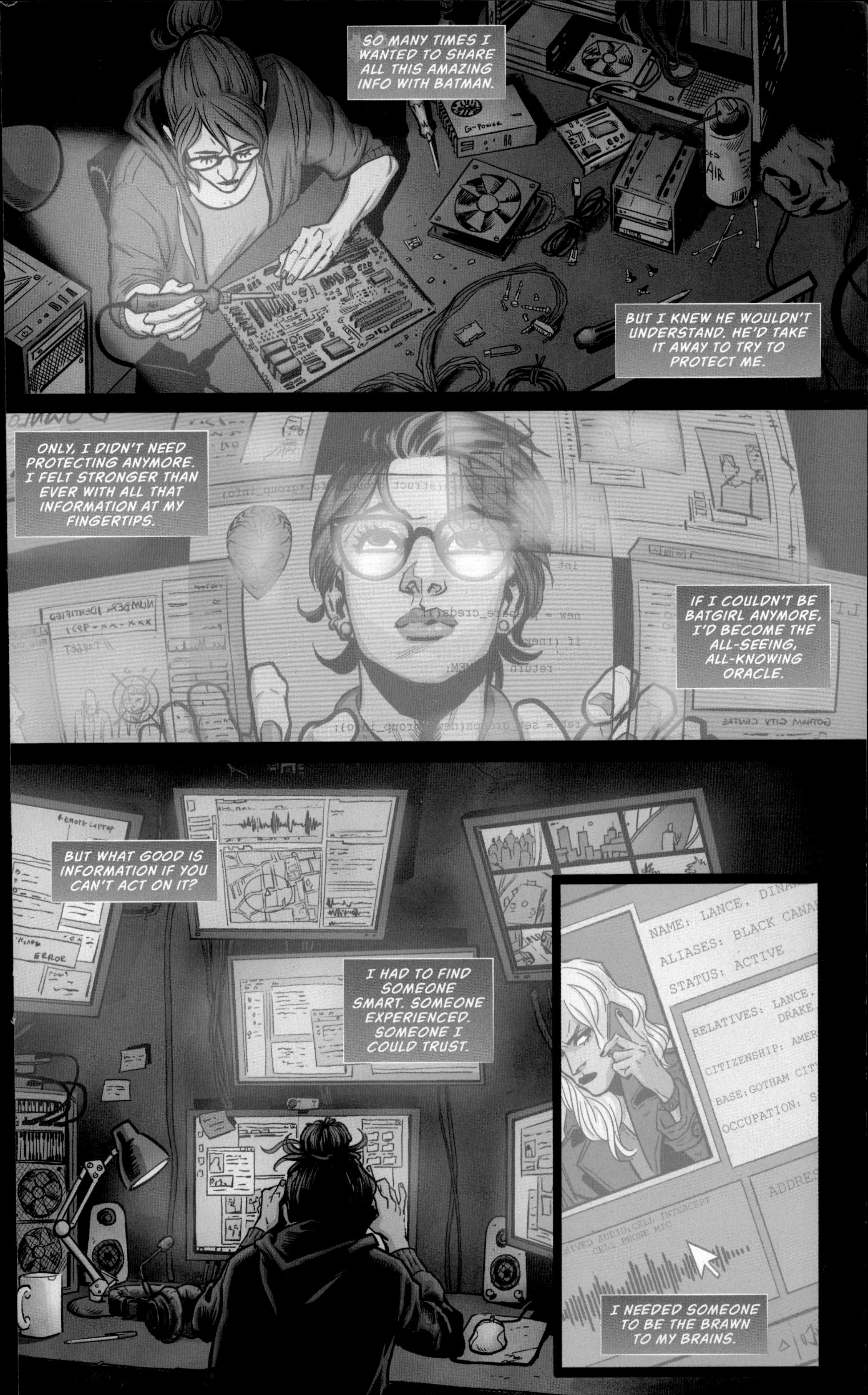
SO MANY TIMES I WANTED TO SHARE ALL THIS AMAZING INFO WITH BATMAN.
BUT I KNEW HE WOULDN'T UNDERSTAND. HE'D TAKE IT AWAY TO TRY TO PROTECT ME.
ONLY, I DIDN'T NEED PROTECTING ANYMORE. I FELT STRONGER THAN EVER WITH ALL THAT INFORMATION AT MY FINGERTIPS.
IF I COULDN'T BE BATGIRL ANYMORE, I'D BECOME THE ALL-SEEING, ALL-KNOWING ORACLE.
BUT WHAT GOOD IS INFORMATION IF YOU CAN'T ACT ON IT?
I HAD TO FIND SOMEONE SMART. SOMEONE EXPERIENCED. SOMEONE I COULD TRUST.
STATUS: ACTIVE
I NEEDED SOMEONE TO BE THE BRAWN TO MY BRAINS.

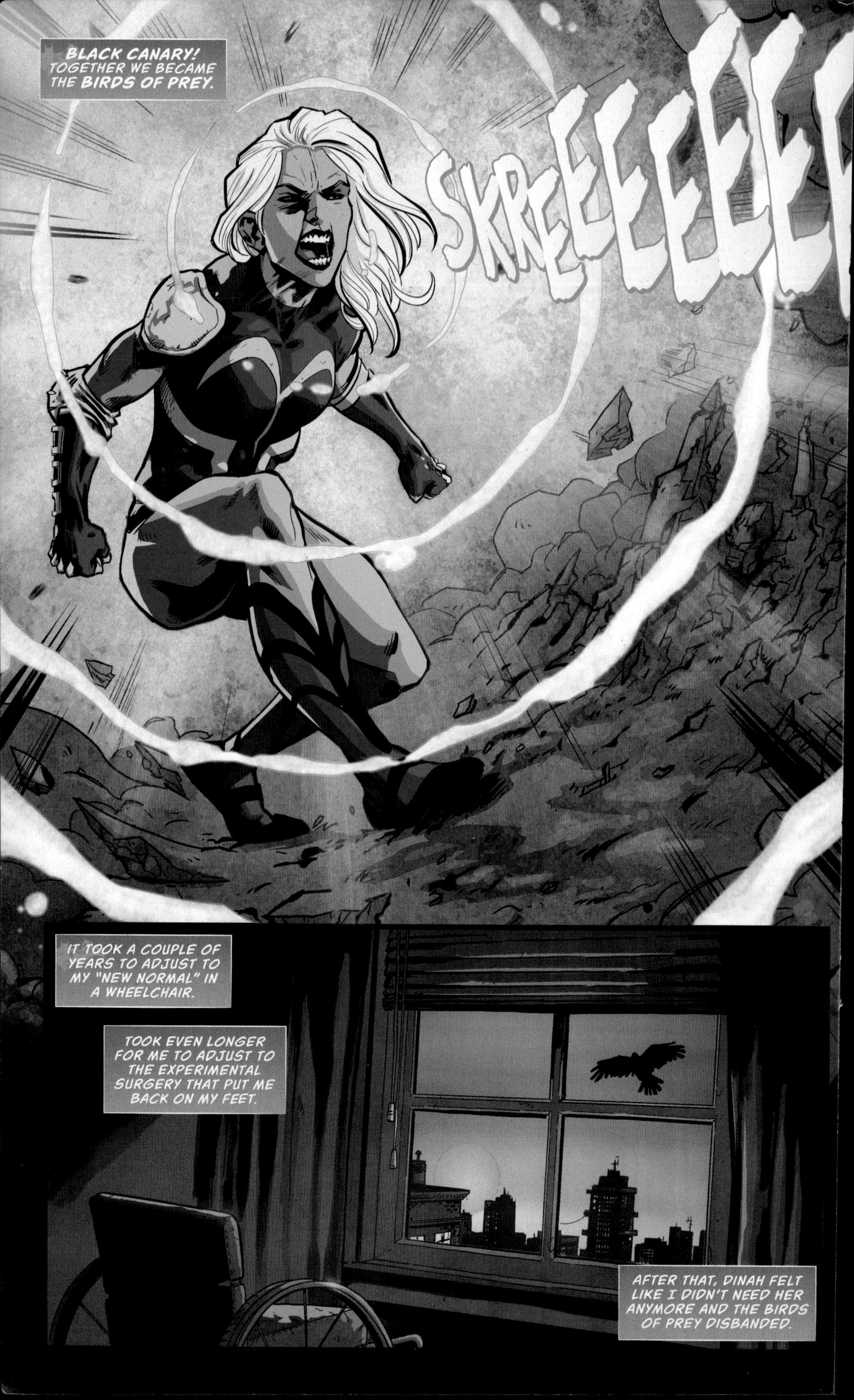
BLACK CANARY! TOGETHER WE BECAME THE BIRDS OF PREY.
SKREEEEEE
IT TOOK A COUPLE OF YEARS TO ADJUST TO MY "NEW NORMAL" IN A WHEELCHAIR.
TOOK EVEN LONGER FOR ME TO ADJUST TO THE EXPERIMENTAL SURGERY THAT PUT ME BACK ON MY FEET.
AFTER THAT, DINAH FELT LIKE I DIDN'T NEED HER ANYMORE AND THE BIRDS OF PREY DISBANDED.

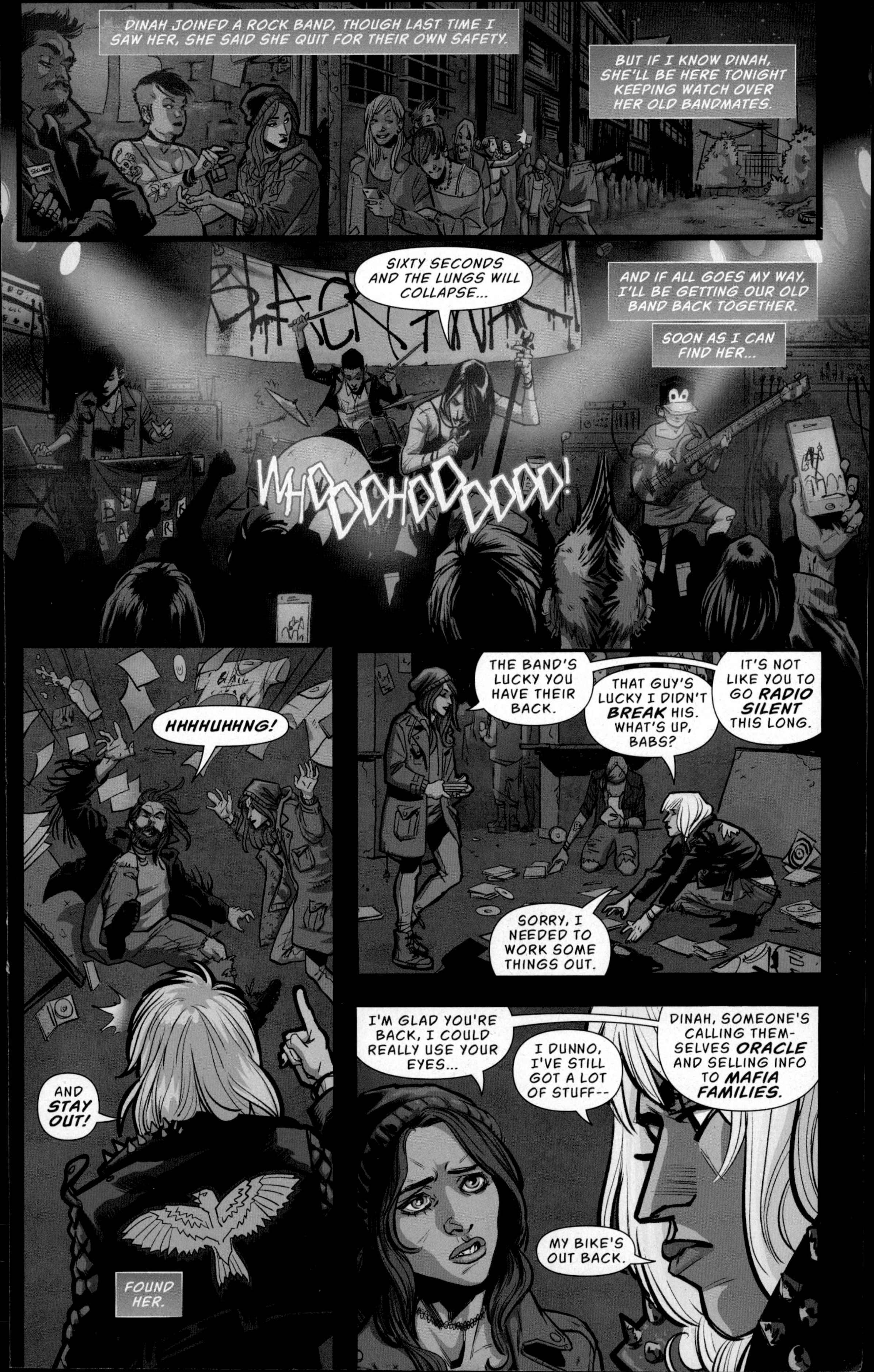

DINAH JOINED A ROCK BAND, THOUGH LAST TIME I SAW HER, SHE SAID SHE QUIT FOR THEIR OWN SAFETY.
BUT IF I KNOW DINAH, SHE'LL BE HERE TONIGHT KEEPING WATCH OVER HER OLD BANDMATES.
SIXTY SECONDS AND THE LUNGS WILL COLLAPSE...
AND IF ALL GOES MY WAY, I'LL BE GETTING OUR OLD BAND BACK TOGETHER.
SOON AS I CAN FIND HER...
WHOOOHOOOOOOO!
HHHHUHHNG!
AND STAY OUT!
FOUND HER.
THE BAND'S LUCKY YOU HAVE THEIR BACK.
THAT GUY'S LUCKY I DIDN'T BREAK HIS. WHAT'S UP, BABS?
IT'S NOT LIKE YOU TO GO RADIO SILENT THIS LONG.
SORRY, I NEEDED TO WORK SOME THINGS OUT.
I'M GLAD YOU'RE BACK, I COULD REALLY USE YOUR EYES...
I DUNNO, I'VE STILL GOT A LOT OF STUFF--
DINAH, SOMEONE'S CALLING THEMSELVES ORACLE AND SELLING INFO TO MAFIA FAMILIES.
MY BIKE'S OUT BACK.

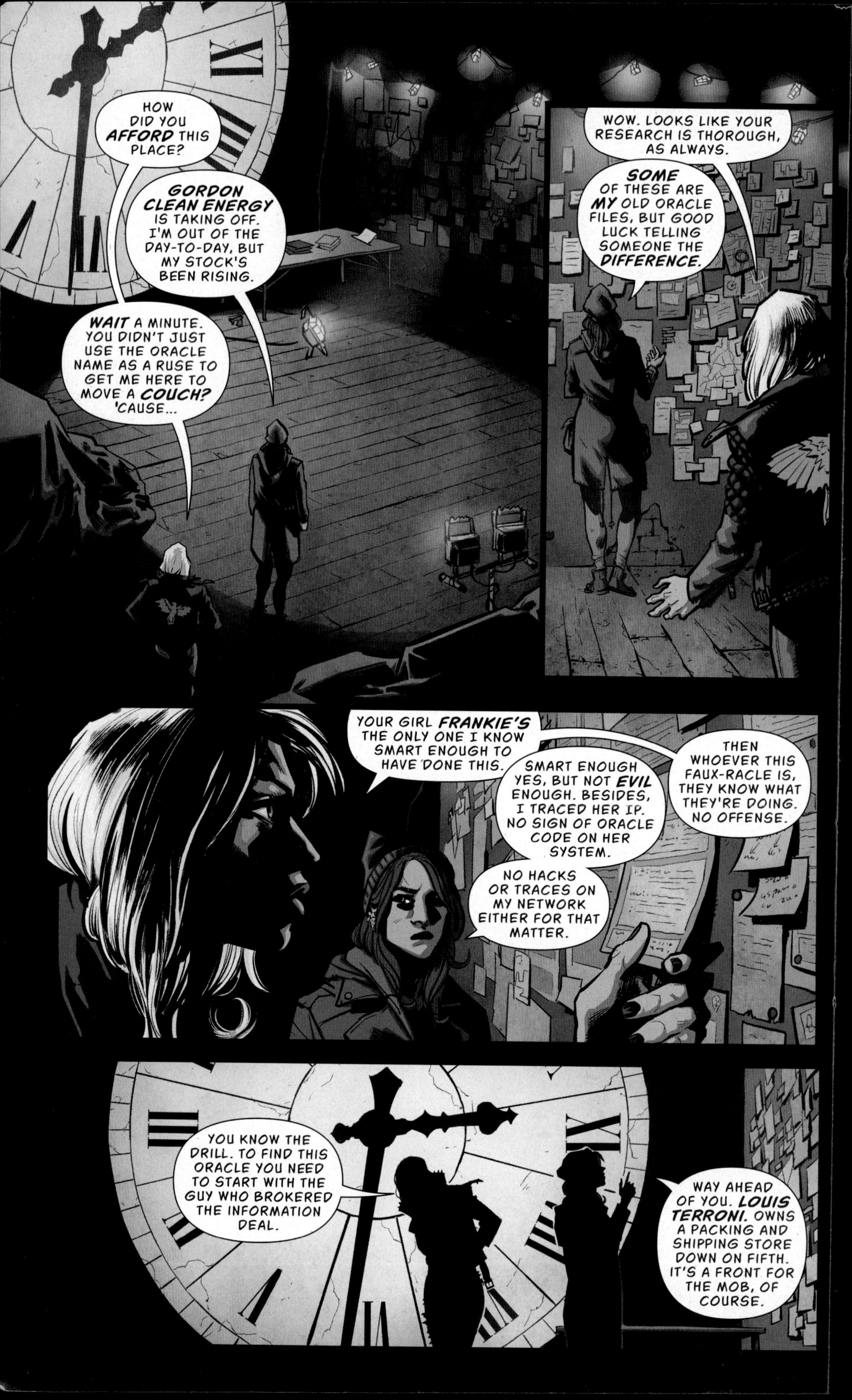
HOW DID YOU AFFORD THIS PLACE?
GORDON CLEAN ENERGY IS TAKING OFF. I'M OUT OF THE DAY-TO-DAY, BUT MY STOCK'S BEEN RISING.
WAIT A MINUTE. YOU DIDN'T JUST USE THE ORACLE NAME AS A RUSE TO GET ME HERE TO MOVE A COUCH? 'CAUSE...
WOW. LOOKS LIKE YOUR RESEARCH IS THOROUGH, AS ALWAYS.
SOME OF THESE ARE MY OLD ORACLE FILES, BUT GOOD LUCK TELLING SOMEONE THE DIFFERENCE.
YOUR GIRL FRANKIE'S THE ONLY ONE I KNOW SMART ENOUGH TO HAVE DONE THIS.
SMART ENOUGH YES, BUT NOT EVIL ENOUGH. BESIDES, I TRACED HER IP. NO SIGN OF ORACLE CODE ON HER SYSTEM.
NO HACKS OR TRACES ON MY NETWORK EITHER FOR THAT MATTER.
THEN WHOEVER THIS FAUX-RACLE IS, THEY KNOW WHAT THEY'RE DOING. NO OFFENSE.
YOU KNOW THE DRILL. TO FIND THIS ORACLE YOU NEED TO START WITH THE GUY WHO BROKERED THE INFORMATION DEAL.
WAY AHEAD OF YOU. LOUIS TERRONI. OWNS A PACKING AND SHIPPING STORE DOWN ON FIFTH. IT'S A FRONT FOR THE MOB, OF COURSE.

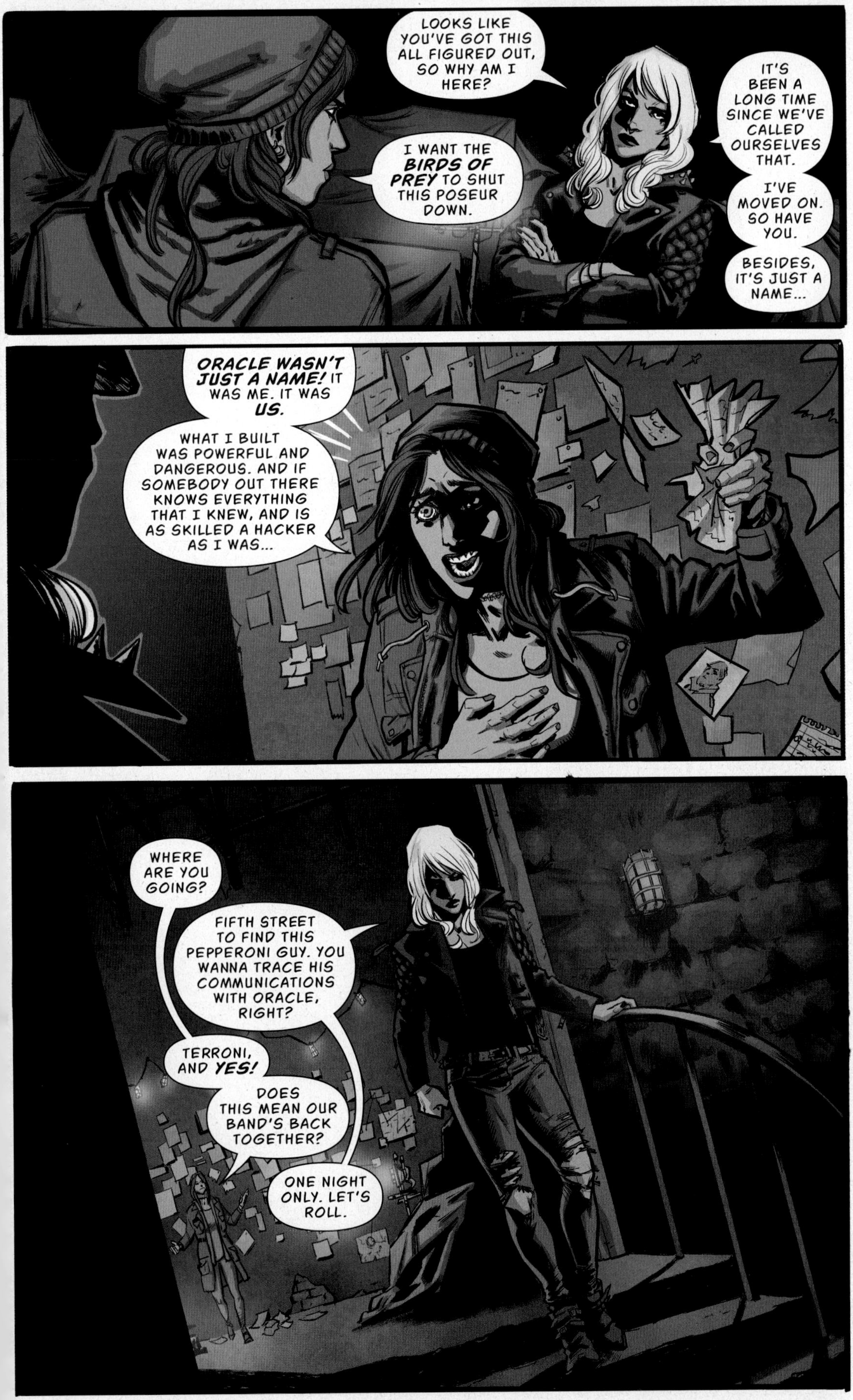
LOOKS LIKE YOU'VE GOT THIS ALL FIGURED OUT, SO WHY AM I HERE?
I WANT THE BIRDS OF PREY TO SHUT THIS POSEUR DOWN.
IT'S BEEN A LONG TIME SINCE WE'VE CALLED OURSELVES THAT.
I'VE MOVED ON. SO HAVE YOU.
BESIDES, IT'S JUST A NAME...
ORACLE WASN'T JUST A NAME! IT WAS ME. IT WAS US.
WHAT I BUILT WAS POWERFUL AND DANGEROUS. AND IF SOMEBODY OUT THERE KNOWS EVERYTHING THAT I KNEW, AND IS AS SKILLED A HACKER AS I WAS...
WHERE ARE YOU GOING?
FIFTH STREET TO FIND THIS PEPPERONI GUY. YOU WANNA TRACE HIS COMMUNICATIONS WITH ORACLE, RIGHT?
TERRONI, AND YES!
DOES THIS MEAN OUR BAND'S BACK TOGETHER?
ONE NIGHT ONLY. LET'S ROLL.

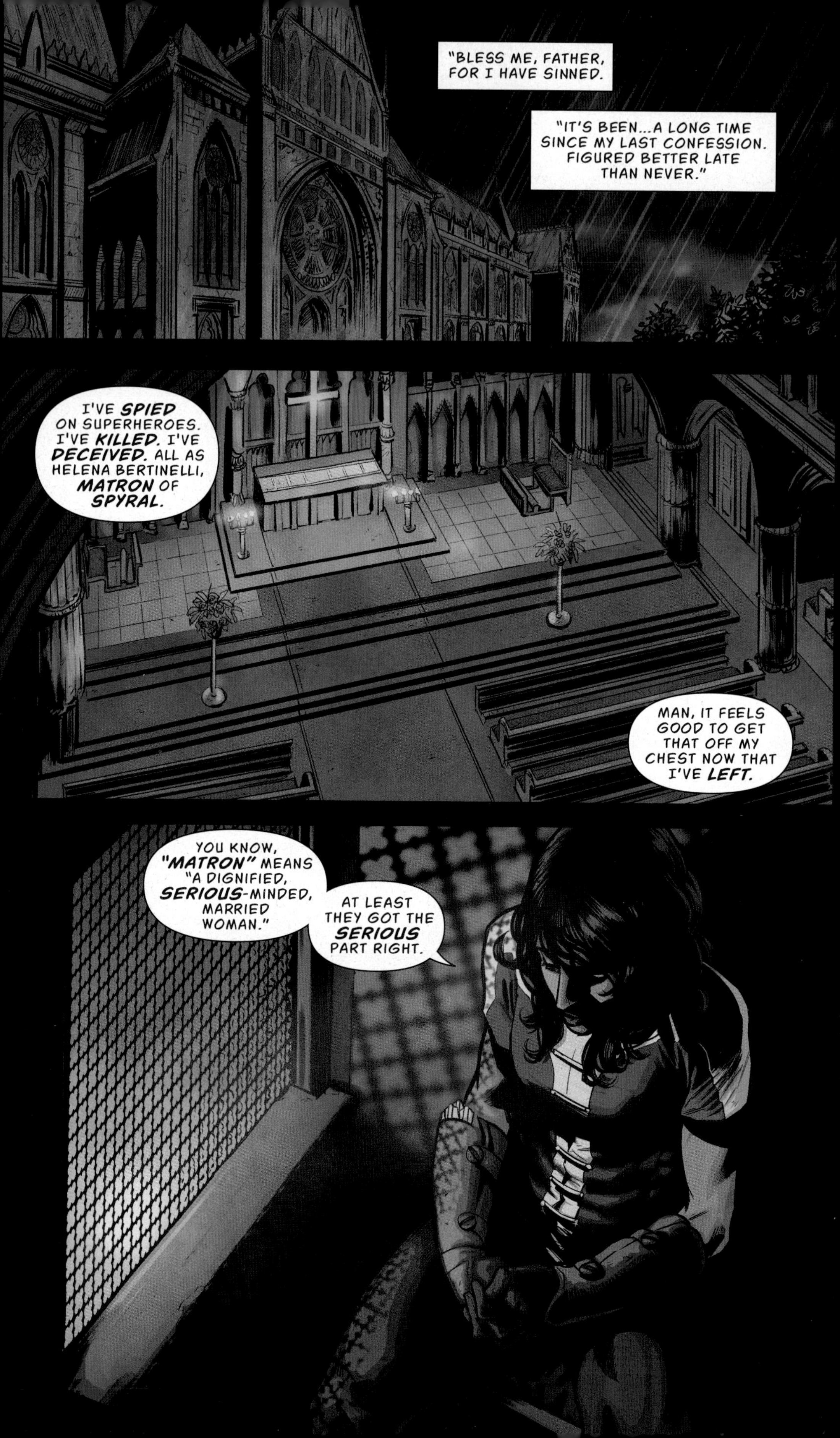
"BLESS ME, FATHER, FOR I HAVE SINNED.
"IT'S BEEN...A LONG TIME SINCE MY LAST CONFESSION. FIGURED BETTER LATE THAN NEVER."
I'VE SPIED ON SUPERHEROES. I'VE KILLED. I'VE DECEIVED. ALL AS HELENA BERTINELLI, MATRON OF SPYRAL.
MAN, IT FEELS GOOD TO GET THAT OFF MY CHEST NOW THAT I'VE LEFT.
YOU KNOW, "MATRON" MEANS "A DIGNIFIED, SERIOUS-MINDED, MARRIED WOMAN."
AT LEAST THEY GOT THE SERIOUS PART RIGHT.

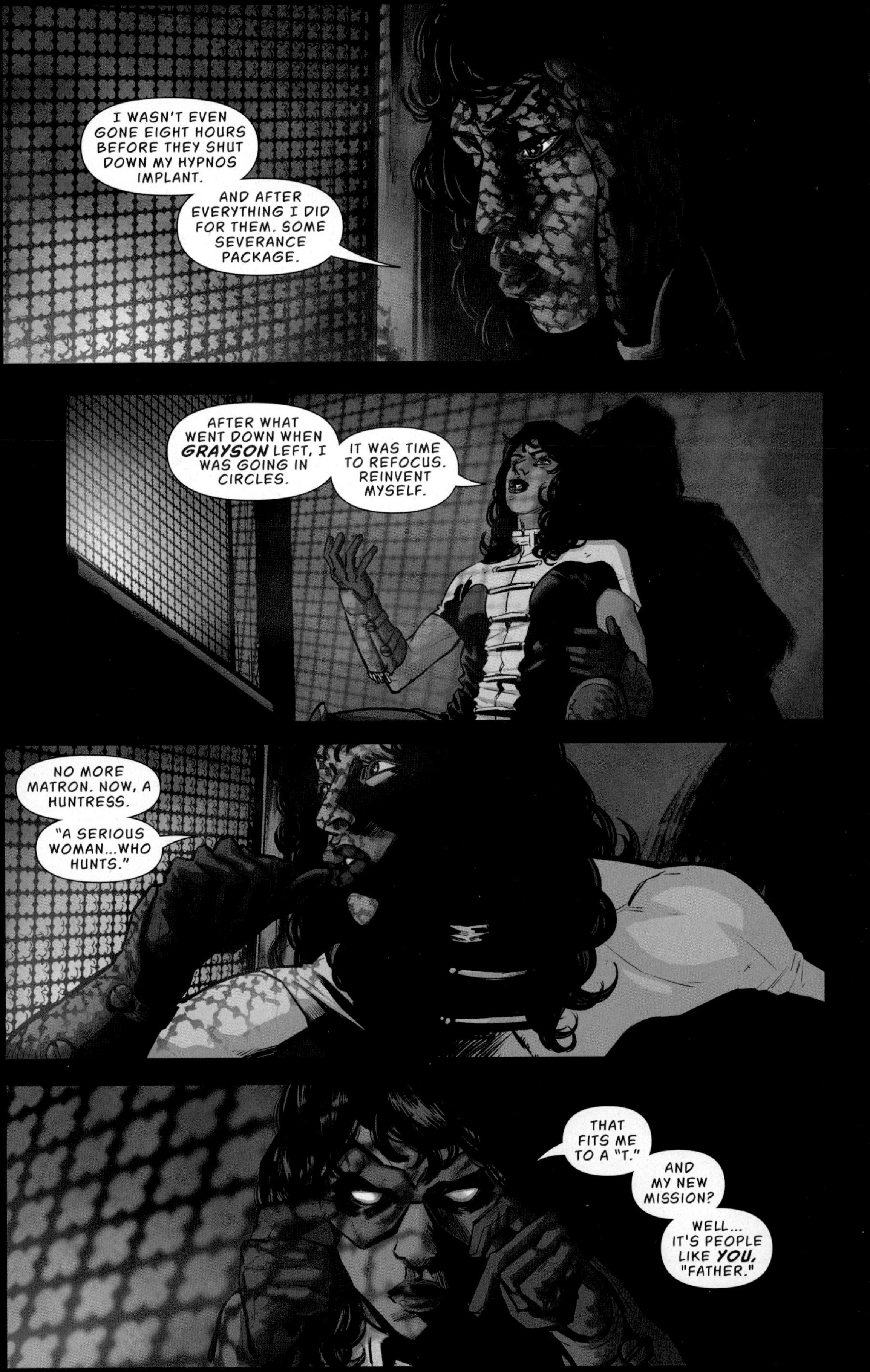
I WASN'T EVEN GONE EIGHT HOURS BEFORE THEY SHUT DOWN MY HYPNOS IMPLANT.
AND AFTER EVERYTHING I DID FOR THEM. SOME SEVERANCE PACKAGE.
AFTER WHAT WENT DOWN WHEN GRAYSON LEFT, I WAS GOING IN CIRCLES.
IT WAS TIME TO REFOCUS. REINVENT MYSELF.
NO MORE MATRON. NOW, A HUNTRESS.
"A SERIOUS WOMAN...WHO HUNTS."
THAT FITS ME TO A "T."
AND MY NEW MISSION?
WELL... IT'S PEOPLE LIKE YOU, "FATHER."

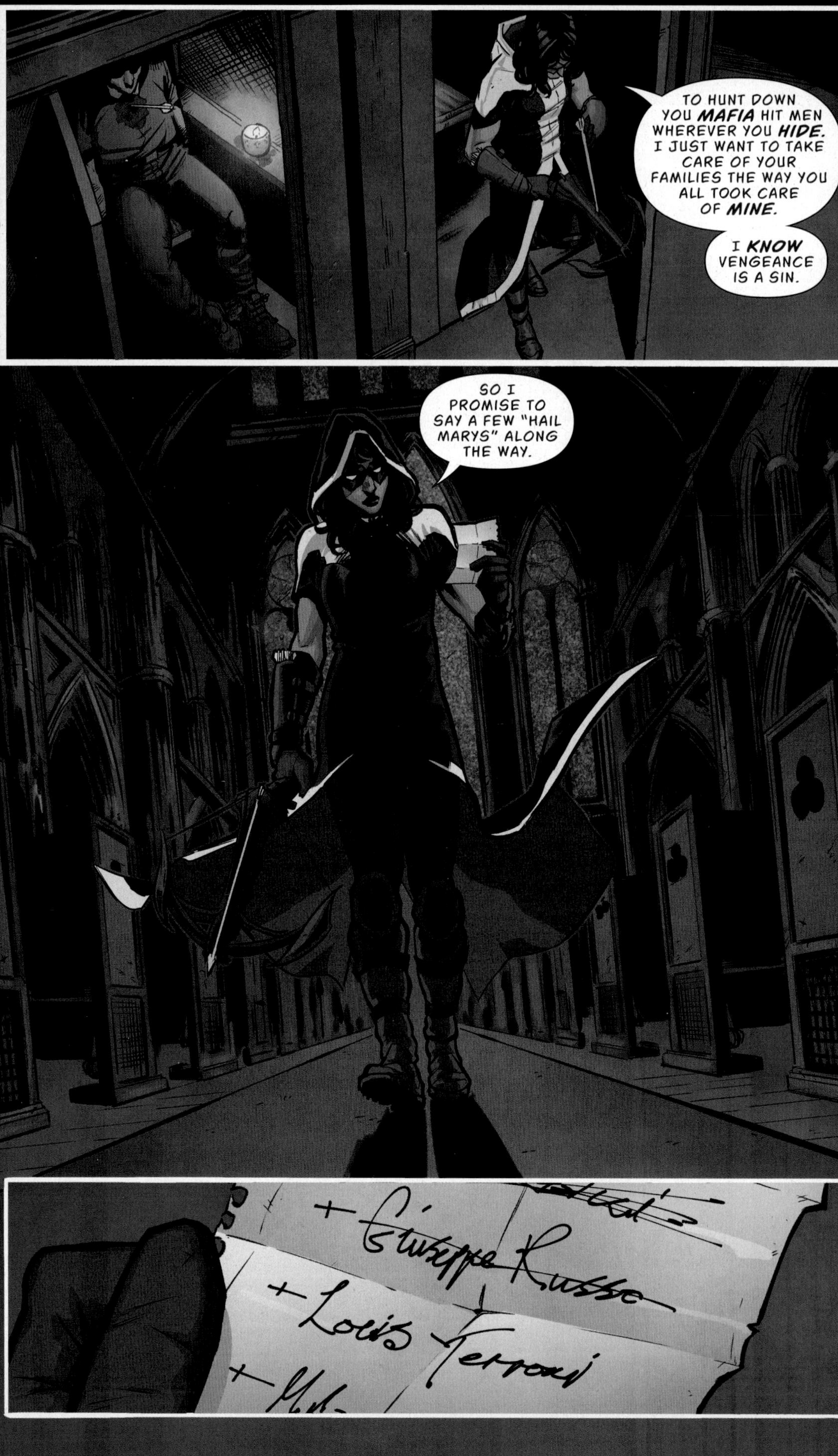
TO HUNT DOWN YOU MAFIA HIT MEN WHEREVER YOU HIDE. I JUST WANT TO TAKE CARE OF YOUR FAMILIES THE WAY YOU ALL TOOK CARE OF MINE.
I KNOW VENGEANCE IS A SIN.
SO I PROMISE TO SAY A FEW "HAIL MARYS" ALONG THE WAY.
Giuseppe Russo

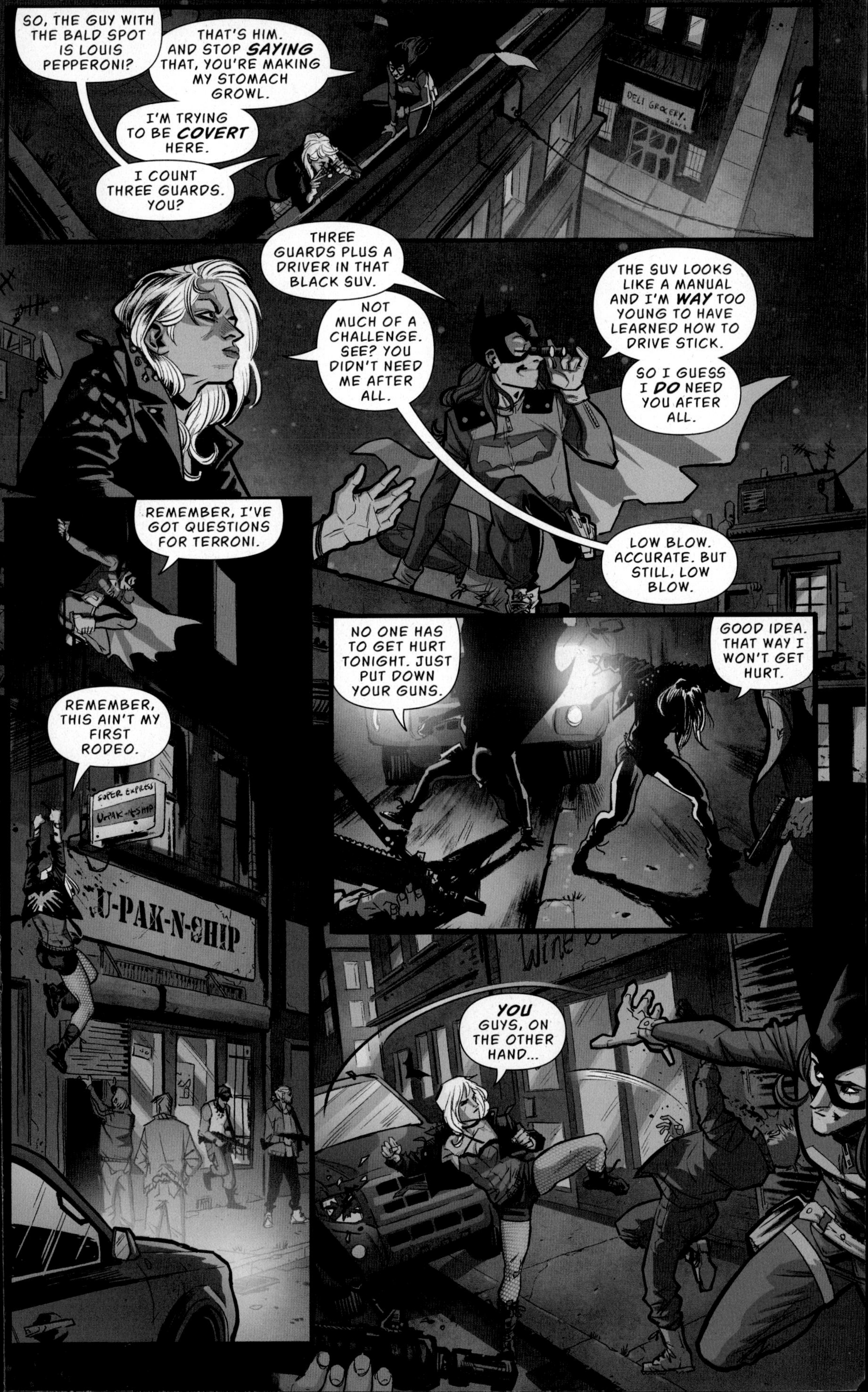
SO, THE GUY WITH THE BALD SPOT IS LOUIS PEPPERONI?
THAT'S HIM. AND STOP SAYING THAT, YOU'RE MAKING MY STOMACH GROWL.
I'M TRYING TO BE COVERT HERE.
I COUNT THREE GUARDS. YOU?
DELI GROCERY
THREE GUARDS PLUS A DRIVER IN THAT BLACK SUV.
NOT MUCH OF A CHALLENGE. SEE? YOU DIDN'T NEED ME AFTER ALL.
THE SUV LOOKS LIKE A MANUAL AND I'M WAY TOO YOUNG TO HAVE LEARNED HOW TO DRIVE STICK.
SO I GUESS I DO NEED YOU AFTER ALL.
LOW BLOW. ACCURATE. BUT STILL, LOW BLOW.
REMEMBER, I'VE GOT QUESTIONS FOR TERRONI.
REMEMBER, THIS AIN'T MY FIRST RODEO.
SUPER EXPRESS
U-PAK-N-SHIP
U-PAK-N-SHIP
NO ONE HAS TO GET HURT TONIGHT. JUST PUT DOWN YOUR GUNS.
GOOD IDEA. THAT WAY I WON'T GET HURT.
YOU GUYS, ON THE OTHER HAND...

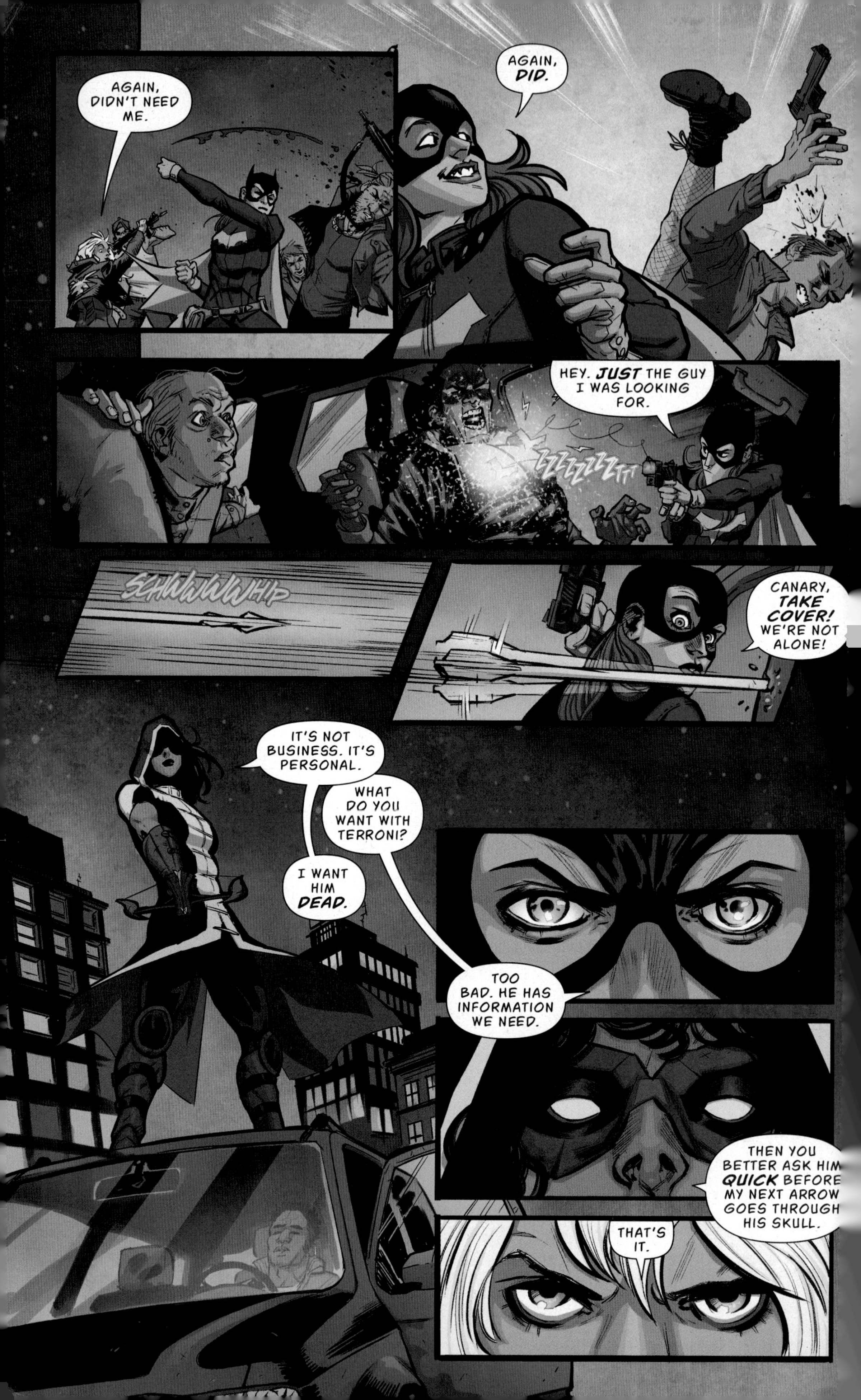
AGAIN, DIDN'T NEED ME.
AGAIN, DID.
HEY. JUST THE GUY I WAS LOOKING FOR.
ZZZZZZZZTTT
SCHWWWWHIP
CANARY, TAKE COVER! WE'RE NOT ALONE!
WHAT DO YOU WANT WITH TERRONI?
IT'S NOT BUSINESS. IT'S PERSONAL.
I WANT HIM DEAD.
TOO BAD. HE HAS INFORMATION WE NEED.
THEN YOU BETTER ASK HIM QUICK BEFORE MY NEXT ARROW GOES THROUGH HIS SKULL.
THAT'S IT.

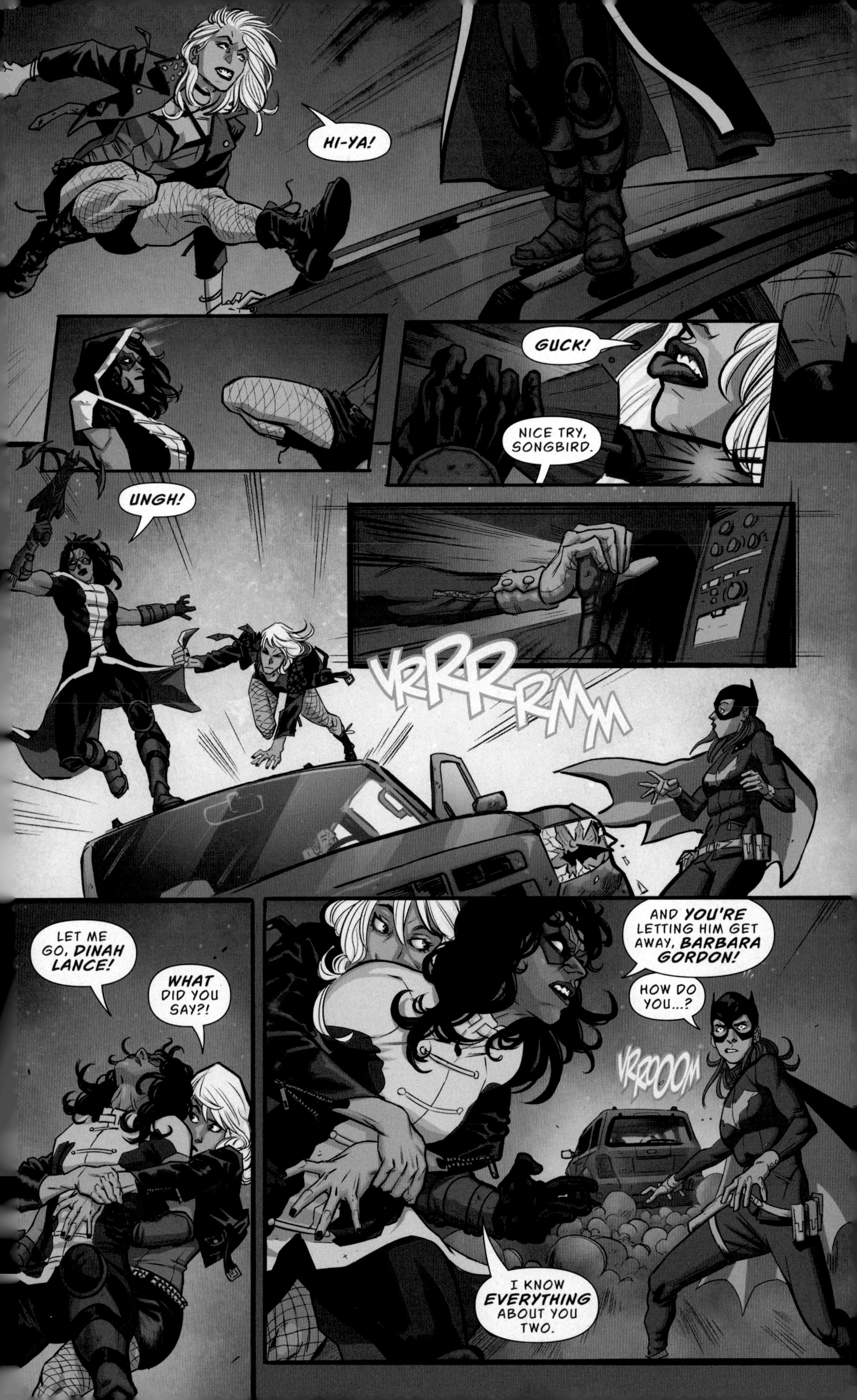
HI-YA!
GUCK!
NICE TRY, SONGBIRD.
UNGH!
VRRRRMM
LET ME GO, DINAH LANCE!
WHAT DID YOU SAY?!
AND YOU'RE LETTING HIM GET AWAY, BARBARA GORDON!
HOW DO YOU...?
VRROOOM
I KNOW EVERYTHING ABOUT YOU TWO.

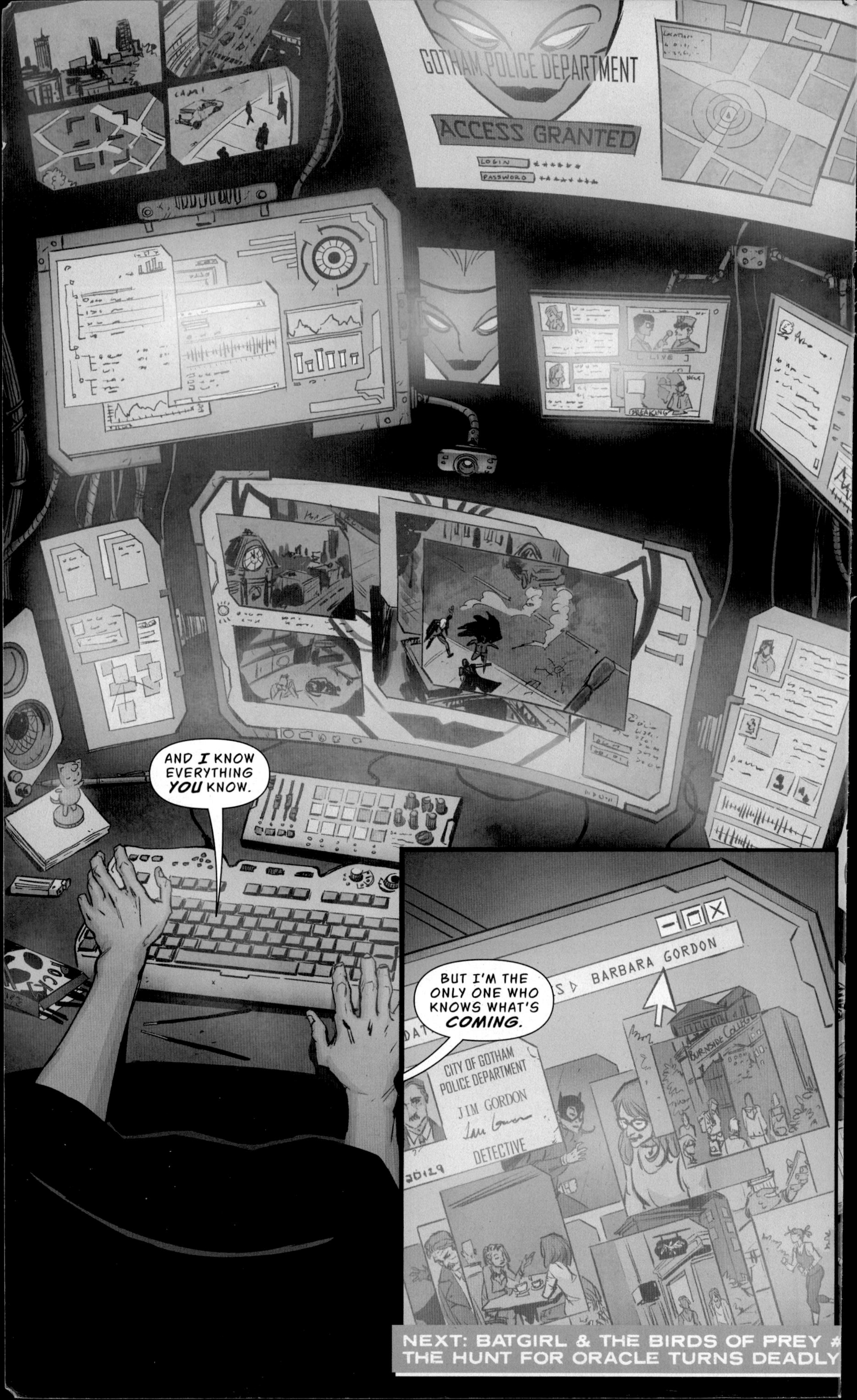
GOTHAM POLICE DEPARTMENT
ACCESS GRANTED
LOGIN
PASSWORD
LIVE
BREAKING
AND I KNOW EVERYTHING YOU KNOW.
BARBARA GORDON
BUT I'M THE ONLY ONE WHO KNOWS WHAT'S COMING.
CITY OF GOTHAM POLICE DEPARTMENT
JIM GORDON
DETECTIVE
BURNSIDE COLLEGE
NEXT: BATGIRL & THE BIRDS OF PREY #
THE HUNT FOR ORACLE TURNS DEADLY

DC COMICS™

"Simone and artist Ardian Syaf not only do justice to Babs' legacy, but build in a new complexity that is the starting point for a future full of new storytelling possibilities. A hell of a ride."
—IGN

START AT THE BEGINNING!

BATGIRL VOLUME 1: THE DARKEST REFLECTION

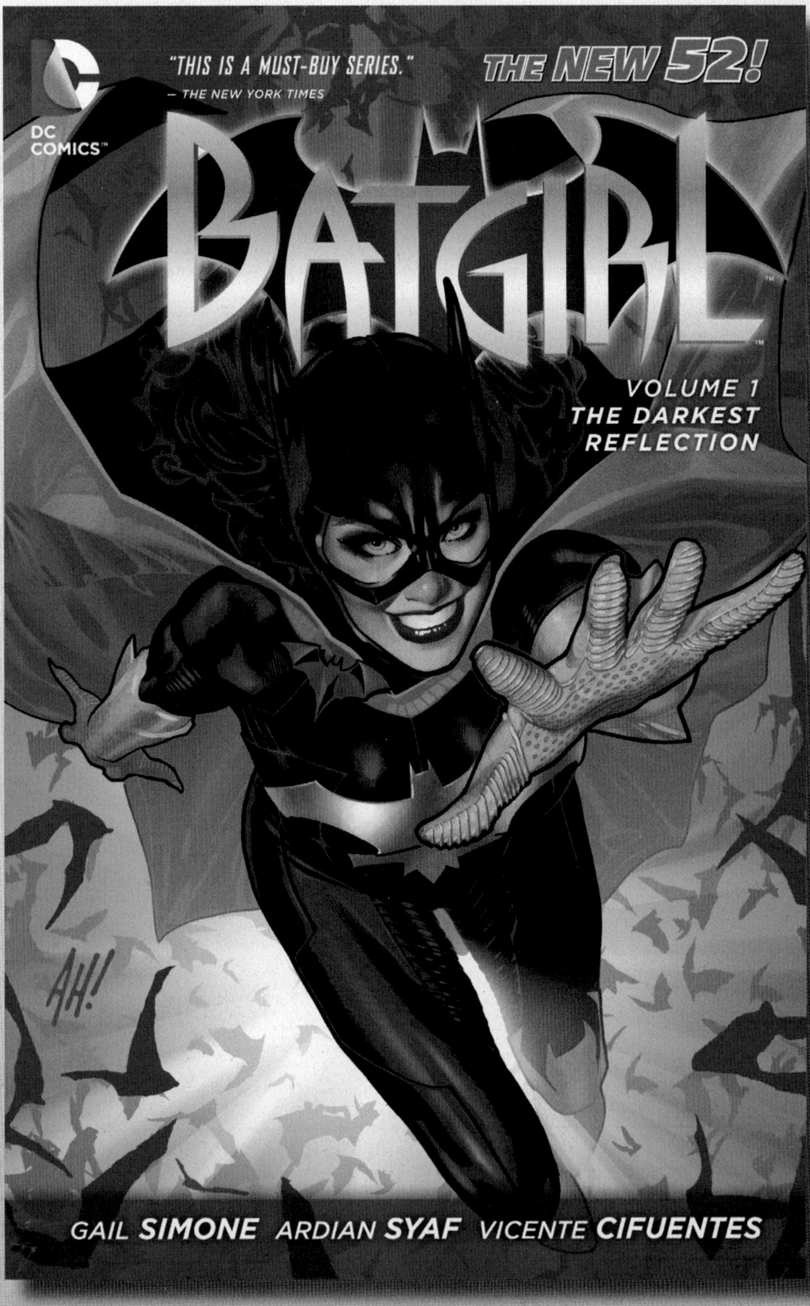

DC COMICS™
"THIS IS A MUST-BUY SERIES."
– THE NEW YORK TIMES
THE NEW 52!
BATGIRL
VOLUME 1
THE DARKEST REFLECTION
AH!
GAIL SIMONE ARDIAN SYAF VICENTE CIFUENTES

BATWOMAN VOLUME 1: HYDROLOGY

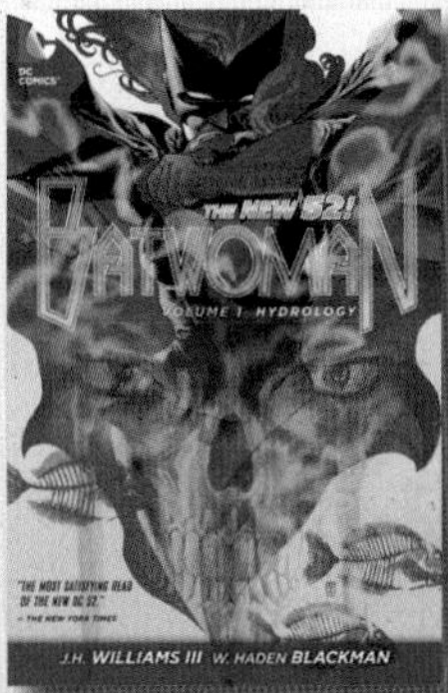

THE NEW 52!
BATWOMAN
VOLUME 1 HYDROLOGY
J.H. WILLIAMS III W. HADEN BLACKMAN

RED HOOD AND THE OUTLAWS VOLUME 1: REDEMPTION

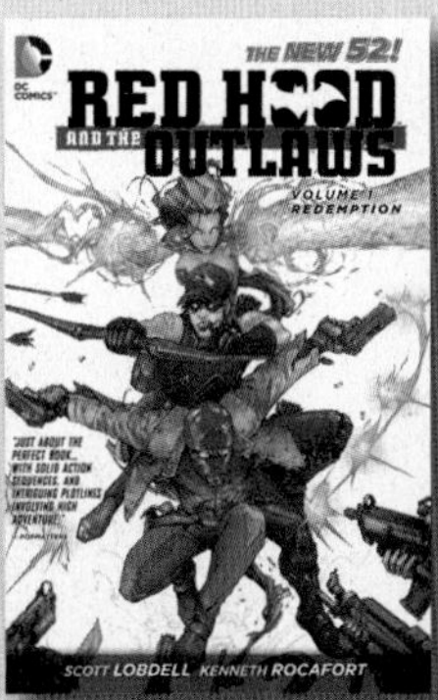

THE NEW 52!
RED HOOD AND THE OUTLAWS
VOLUME 1 REDEMPTION
SCOTT LOBDELL KENNETH ROCAFORT

BATWING VOLUME 1: THE LOST KINGDOM

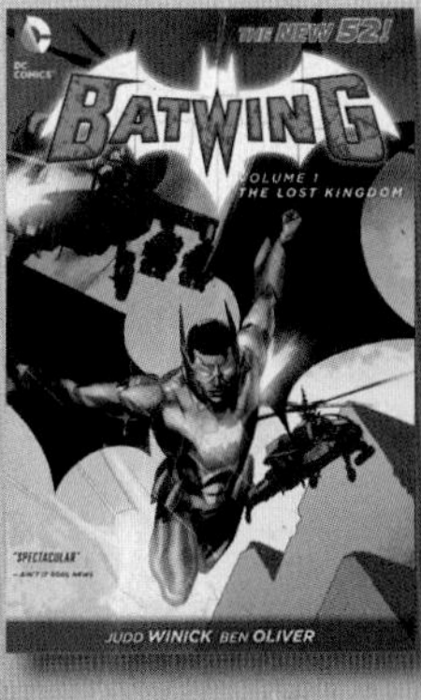

THE NEW 52!
BATWING
VOLUME 1 THE LOST KINGDOM
JUDD WINICK BEN OLIVER

DC COMICS™

"So, great writing, awesome artwork, fun premise and looks of cool action? Yep, Green Arrow's got it all."—IGN

"Sharply written and featuring beautiful artwork, this is another hidden gem in the New 52 crown."—CRAVE ONLINE

FROM THE WRITER OF *JUSTICE LEAGUE UNITED* AND *ANIMAL MAN*

GREEN ARROW

VOLUME 4: THE KILL MACHINE

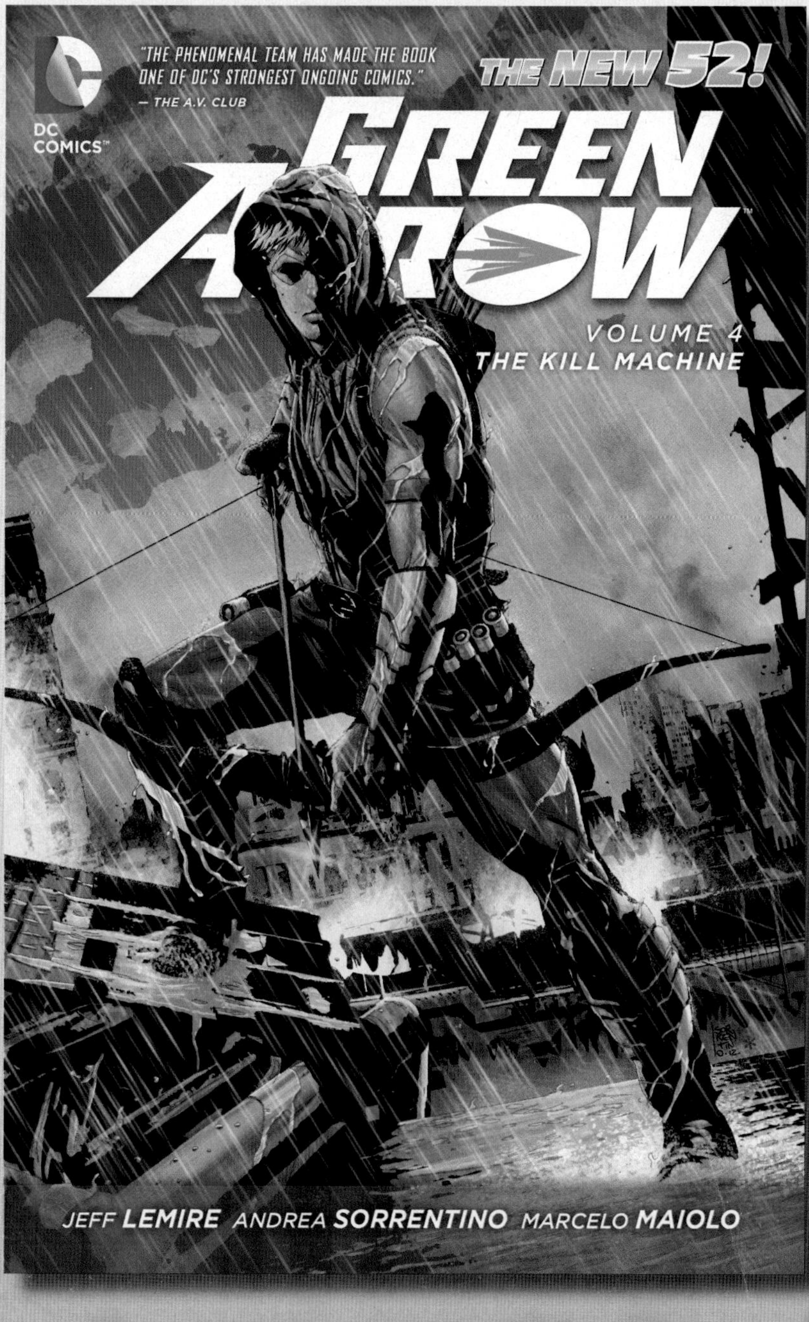
"THE PHENOMENAL TEAM HAS MADE THE BOOK ONE OF DC'S STRONGEST ONGOING COMICS."
— THE A.V. CLUB
DC COMICS™
THE NEW 52!
GREEN ARROW™
VOLUME 4
THE KILL MACHINE
JEFF LEMIRE ANDREA SORRENTINO MARCELO MAIOLO

GREEN ARROW VOL. 1: THE MIDAS TOUCH

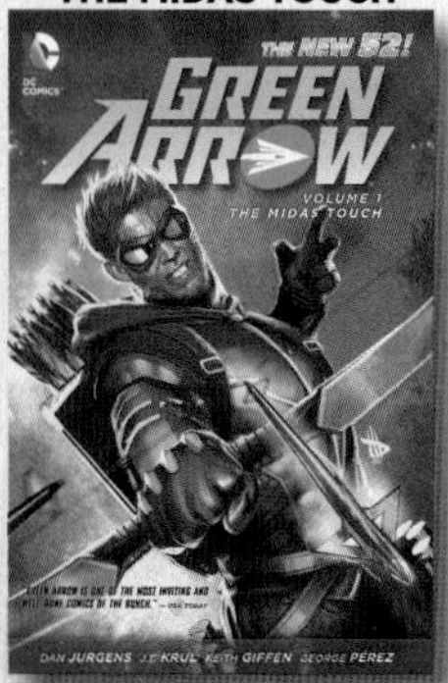
THE NEW 52!
GREEN ARROW
VOLUME 1
THE MIDAS TOUCH
DAN JURGENS J.T. KRUL KEITH GIFFEN GEORGE PÉREZ

with KEITH GIFFEN, DAN JURGENS, J.T. KRUL, and GEORGE PÉREZ

GREEN ARROW VOL. 2: TRIPLE THREAT

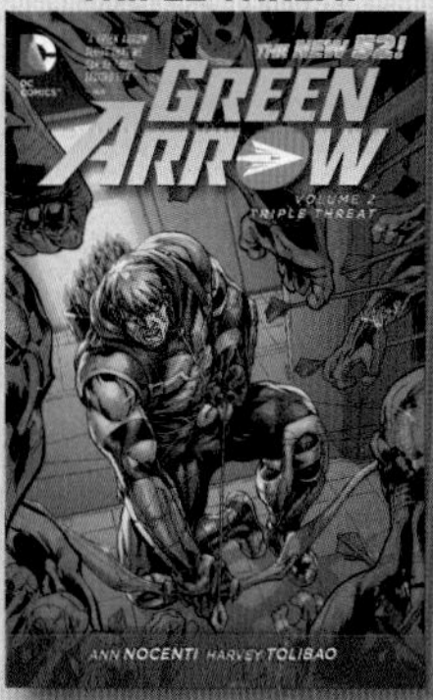
THE NEW 52!
GREEN ARROW
VOLUME 2
TRIPLE THREAT
ANN NOCENTI HARVEY TOLIBAO

with ANN NOCENTI and HARVEY TOLIBAO

GREEN ARROW VOL. 3: HARROW

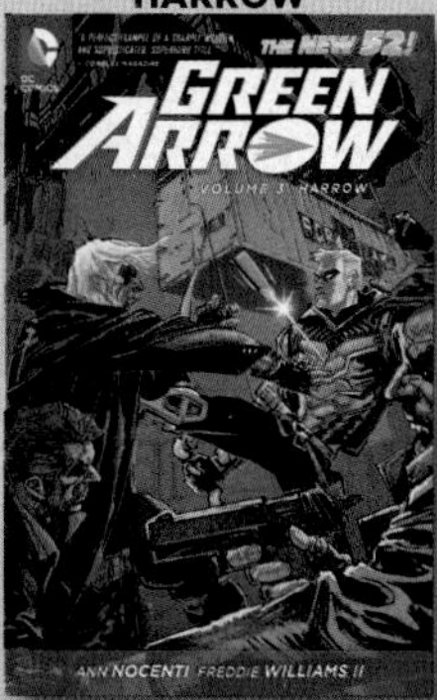
THE NEW 52!
GREEN ARROW
VOLUME 3 HARROW
ANN NOCENTI FREDDIE WILLIAMS II

with ANN NOCENTI and FREDDIE WILLIAMS III